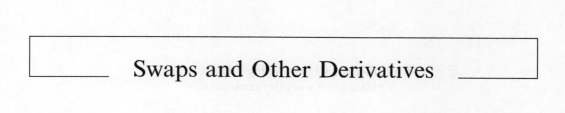

Swaps and Other Derivatives

Swaps and Other Derivatives

Second Edition

Richard Flavell

A John Wiley and Sons, Ltd, Publication

Contents

Preface

EXTRACT FROM THE PREFACE TO THE FIRST EDITION

This book is designed for financial professionals to understand how the vast bulk of OTC derivatives are used, structured, priced and hedged, and ultimately how to use such derivatives themselves. A wide range of books already exist that describe in conceptual terms how and why such derivatives are used, and it is not the ambition of this book to supplant them. There are also a number of books which describe the pricing and hedging of derivatives, especially exotic ones, primarily in mathematical terms. Whilst exotics are an important and growing segment of the market, by far the majority of derivatives are still very much first generation, and as such relatively straightforward.

For example, interest rate swaps constitute over half of the $100 trillion OTC derivative market, and yet there have been few books published in the last decade that describe how they are created and valued in practical detail. So how do many of the professionals gain their knowledge? One popular way is "learning on the job", reinforced by the odd training course. But swap structures can be quite complex, requiring more than just superficial knowledge, and probably every professional uses a computer-based system, certainly for the booking and regular valuation of trades, and most likely for their initial pricing and risk management. These systems are complex, having to deal with real-world situations, and their practical inner details bear little resemblance to the idealised world of most books. So often, practitioners tend to treat the systems as black boxes, relying on some initial and frequently inadequate range of tests, and hoping their intuition will guide them. The greatest sources of comfort are often the existing customer list of the system (they can't all be wrong!) and, if the system is replacing an old one, comparative valuations.

The objective of this book is to describe how the pricing, valuation and risk management of generic OTC derivatives may be performed, in sufficient detail and with various alternatives, so that the approaches may be applied in practice. It is based upon some 15 years of varying experience as a financial engineer for ANZ Merchant Bank in London, as a trainer and consultant to banks worldwide, and as Director of Financial Engineering at Lombard Risk Systems responsible for all the mathematics in the various pricing and risk management systems.

The audience for the book is, first, traders, sales people and front-line risk managers. But increasingly such knowledge needs to be more widely spread within financial institutions, such as internal audit, risk control, and IT. Then there are the counterparties such as organisations using derivatives for risk management, who have frequently identified the need for transparent pricing. This need has been exacerbated in recent years as many developed countries now require that these organisations demonstrate the effectiveness of risk management, and also perform regular (usually annual) mark-to-market. Similarly, organisations using complex funding structures want to understand how the structures are created and priced. Turning to the other side, many fund managers and in particular hedge funds are also using derivatives to manage their risk profile, and then to report using one of the Value-at-Risk techniques. This has been particularly true since the collapse of Long Term Capital Management, despite the fact that most implementations of VaR would not have recognised the risk. Other potential readers are the auditors, consultants, and regulators of the banks and their client organisations.

PREFACE TO THE SECOND EDITION

Many of the above statements are still true. The swap market has continued to grow six-fold over the intervening years, to a staggering $328 trillion. Yet, there has been little published to provide guidance and assistance to the professionals in the market. Why was it thought useful to write a second edition? There were two main reasons. First, many readers had suggested changes and developments, which I thought appropriate to include. Second, the exponential growth in credit default swaps and structured securities identified areas which were little discussed in the first edition. This edition attempts to redress that omission.

Institutions offer derivatives with a wide range of maturities, ranging from a few hours (used to provide risk management over the announcement of an economic figure) to perpetuals (i.e. no upfront maturity defined). There is however a golden rule when pricing derivatives, namely always price them off the market that will be used to hedge them. This leads to the first separation in the interest rate swap market between:

Chapter 2:   The short end of the curve, which uses cash, futures and occasionally FRAs to hedge swaps. This chapter first discusses the derivation of discount factors from cashrates, and concentrates on the range of alternative approaches that may be used. It then looks at the derivation of forward interest rates, and how FRAs may be priced using cash and futures. The convexity effect is highlighted for future discussion. Finally an approach is introduced that does not require discounting, but permits the introduction of a funding cost.

Chapter 3:   The medium to long end of the curve. The highly liquid interbank market typically trades plain swaps (usually known as "generic" or "vanilla"), very often between market makers and intermediaries. These are hedged in other financial markets, typically futures for the shorter exposures and bonds for the longer ones. This chapter concentrates initially on the relationship between the bond and swap markets, and how generic swap prices may be implied. It concludes by developing various techniques for the estimation of discount factors from a generic swap curve.

Chapter 4:   The end-user market provides customers with tailored (i.e. non-generic) swaps designed to meet their specific requirements. Such swaps are not traded as such, but created as one-off structures. This chapter describes a range of simple non-generic swaps, and discusses various techniques for pricing them, including one that requires no discounting. Finally two approaches to the ongoing valuation of an existing (seasoned) swap are demonstrated.

Chapter 5: Swaps are often used to restructure new or existing securities. This chapter describes some initial structures, par asset packaging and par maturity asset packaging, that are commonly used.

Chapter 6: Credit derivatives effectively evolved from the asset packaging or securitisation markets. The chapter first discusses total return swaps as being the earliest form of credit derivative, but then moves rapidly on to its successor, single-name credit default swaps. The chapter is in three parts. First, a broad description of the mechanics of the market, especially following the Big and Small Bangs in 2009. Second, an analysis of the relationship between asset packaging and the hedging of CDSs, leading to a discussion around the credit basis. Third, a derivation of implied forward default probabilities from CDS prices using a couple of slightly different approaches. This in turn allows the pricing of non-generic CDSs such as forward starts, amortising and floating rate.

Chapter 7: This discusses a range of more complex swaps known generally as mismatch swaps. This includes structures such as yield curve (also known as CMSs), in arrears, average rate, and compound. The chapter and its appendix re-introduce the concept of convexity-adjusted pricing more formally.

Chapter 8: This introduces a range of what are often called cross-market swaps. These involve the normal interbank floating rate (or indeed a fixed rate) on one side, and another reference rate drawn from another market on the other side, such as an overnight rate, or a base rate, or a mortgage rate, or an inflation rate, or an equity return, and so on. The main purpose of these swaps is to permit people with exposures in the other market to gain access to the range of risk management instruments that exists in the interbank market.

Chapter 9: The earliest swap structures were cross-currency swaps, although this market has been long overtaken by interest rate swaps. Nevertheless they possess some unique characteristics and structures. This chapter starts with the fundamental CCS building block, the cross-currency basis swap, and explores its characteristics, uses, pricing and hedging. This employs a novel approach: worst case simulation. The role of CCBSs in the derivation of cross-currency discount factors is also explored. The main other types of swaps are then discussed: fixed–floating, floating–floating, diff, and quanto–diff. Fixed–fixed swaps occupy a special place because they are a general case of long-term FX forward contracts, so the pricing and hedging of these is considered in some detail. Finally swap valuation is revisited because, in the CCS market, such swaps are frequently valued annually and the principals reset to the current exchange rate.

Chapter 10: There is an active market in many currencies in medium to long-term options on forward interest rates, usually known as the cap and floor market. Such structures are intimately linked to swaps for two reasons: first, because combinations of options can create swaps and, second, swaps are generally used to hedge them. In many banks, they are actually traded and risk-managed together. This chapter reviews a range of different option structures and touches albeit briefly on option pricing. Volatility plays a crucial role and various techniques for estimation, including transformation from par to forward as well as volatility smiles and volatility spaces, are described in detail. These options are also frequently embedded in many swap structures, and the breakdown and pricing of a range of structures is discussed. There is also an active market in options on forward swaps (aka swaptions or swoptions) which, not unnaturally, is closely related to the swap market. The pricing and embedding of swaptions is described. The chapter concludes with two sections on FX options. These options are mainly traded OTC, although there is some activity on a few exchanges such as Philadelphia. The first section concentrates on the pricing of these options, and how it may be varied depending on the method of quoting the underlying currencies. The second section shows how traders would dynamically create a delta-neutral hedge for such an option, together with the hedging errors through time.

Chapter 11: This chapter concentrates on more complex swaps arising from the need to swap structured securities. It starts by discussing the swapping of range accruals. It goes on to price structures such as callable bonds, Bermudan swaptions and path-dependent products such as target accrual redemption notes and snowballs using both numerical trees and Libor-based simulation.

Chapter 12: In the early days of the swap market, swap portfolios were risk-managed either using asset–liability methods such as gapping or the more advanced institutions used bond techniques such as duration. By the late 1980s a number of well-publicised losses had forced banks to develop more appropriate techniques such as gridpoint hedging. These (in today's eyes) traditional approaches stood the banks in good stead for the next decade. This chapter describes the main techniques of both gridpoint and curve hedging, taking into account both first and second-order sensitivities. In passing, mapping cashflows to gridpoints is also discussed. The use of swap futures, as a relatively new hedging instrument, is also considered. The chapter then extends risk management to interest rate options. Most texts discuss the "Greeks" using short-dated options; unfortunately the discussion often does not apply to long-term options, and so their different characteristics, especially as a function of time, are examined. The effectiveness of some optimisation techniques to construct robust hedges are examined as an alternative to the more traditional delta–gamma methods. Finally, the chapter shows how the same techniques can be used to create an inflation hedge for a portfolio of inflation swaps.

Chapter 13: Risk management however is not a static subject, but has evolved rapidly during the latter half of the 1990s and beyond. Traditional risk management operates quite successfully, but there is a very sensible desire by senior management to be able to assess the riskiness of the entire trading operation and even wider. The traditional risk measures are not combinable in any fashion and cannot be used. Value-at-Risk was developed as a family of approaches designed very much to address this objective. It is now being developed further to encompass not only market risk but also credit and even operational risks into the same set of measures.[1] This chapter describes the major approaches used to estimate VaR: delta, historic and Monte Carlo simulations, as well as second-order delta–gamma approaches. The advantages and disadvantages of each approach are discussed, along with various extensions such as extreme value theory and sampling strategies. The measurement of spread VaR and equity VaR using either individual stocks or a stock index are also considered. Finally, stress testing or how to make significant moves in the properties of the underlying risk factors (especially correlation) is described.

The book is supported by a full range of detailed spreadsheet models, which underpin all the tables, graphs and figures in the main text. Some of the models have not been described in detail in the text, but hopefully the instructions on the sheets should be adequate. Many of the models are designed so that the reader may implement them in practice without much difficulty.

Many of the ideas, techniques and models described here have been developed over the years with colleagues at both ANZ and Lombard Risk Systems, and through various consulting assignments with a wide range of banks across the world.

BIOGRAPHY

Richard Flavell has spent over twenty years working as a financial engineer, consultant and trainer, specialising in complex derivatives and risk management. He spent seven years as Director of Financial Engineering at Lombard Risk, where he was responsible for the mathematical development and implementation of models in its varied pricing and risk systems. He is currently Chairman of Lucidate, a company which specialises in the provision of consultancy and training to financial institutions.

---

[1] See the proposed Basel Accord (for details see the BIS website: *www.bis.org*) for the regulatory requirements using VaR-style approaches.

Worksheets

(*see* the accompanying CD inside the back cover)

Explanatory note: The vast majority of spreadsheets refer to a base spreadsheet called "Market Data". Under current Excel rules, this needs to be opened should the reader wish to save any model.

In most cases, there is one spreadsheet containing all the models for each chapter. The nomenclature is clear: for example, "Ch 2 Short-term Swaps" contains all the models for Chapter 2. There are however some exceptions, where some models are contained in separate spreadsheets. These usually involve models containing either optimisation or Monte Carlo simulation, when it is recommended that these models should be run with all other spreadsheets closed. This refers in particular to Chapters 8 and 11, running LPI and BGM simulations, respectively. The names of the individual spreadsheets are included in the list below:

Spreadsheet "Ch 10 SABR Model"

Spreadsheet "Ch 11—Summary of Spreadsheets"
(lists the main spreadsheets for this chapter)

Spreadsheet "Ch 11.41 Example of Very Long-step BGM Simulation"

Spreadsheet "Ch 11.49 Modelling a Sticky Floater"

Spreadsheet "Ch 11.56 Modelling a TARN"

Spreadsheet "Ch 11.62 Modelling a Callable Snowball"

Spreadsheet "Ch 11.67 BDT with a Smile"

Abbreviations

ABCDS	Asset-Backed CDS
ALM	Asset Liability Management
ARCH	AutoRegressive Conditional Heteroskedastic
ASW	Asset SWap
ATM	At The Money
B&S	Black and Scholes
BDT	Black–Derman–Toy
BGM	Brace–Gatarek–Musiela
BIS	Bank for International Settlement
c-c	continuously compounded
CADF	Credit-Adjusted Discount Factor
CBOT	Chicago Board of Trade
CCBS	Cross-Currency Basis Swap
CCE	Current Credit Exposure
CCS	Cross-Currency Swap
CCVN	Cross-Currency Variable Notional
CDO	Collateralised Debt Obligation
CEA	Credit Event Auction
CET	Central European Time
CME	Chicago Mercantile Exchange
CMS	Constant Maturity Swap
CP	Commercial Paper
CSA	Credit Support Annex
CTFF	Cash To First Futures
DC	Determination Committee
DF	Discount Factor
DMO	Debt Management Office
DP	Dirty (purchase) Price
DTCC	Depository Trust and Clearing Corporation
EBRD	European Bank for Reconstruction and Development
ECB	European Central Bank
EIB	European Investment Bank
EMEA	Europe, Middle East and Africa
EONIA	Euro OverNight Index Average
EPE	Expected Positive Exposure

EVT	Extreme Value Theory
FDP	Forward Default Probability
FR	Full (or complete) Restructuring
FRA	Forward Rate Agreement
FRN	Floating Rate Note
FSA	Financial Services Authority
FX	Foreign Exchange
G–K	Garman–Kohlhagen
GARCH	Generalised ARCH
GC	General Collateral
GEV	Generalised Extreme Value
GP	Generalised Pareto (Chapter 13);
	Goal Programming (Chapter 12)
HICP	Harmonised Index of Consumer Prices
HICPXT	HICP excluding Tobacco
HJM	Heath–Jarrow–Morton
IBOR	Inter Bank Offer Rate
IF	Implied Forward
IMM	International Monetary Market (based in CME)
IRB	Internal Rating Based
IRS	Interest Rate Swap
ISDA	International Swap and Derivatives Association
ITM	Into The Money
KfW	Kreditanstalt für Wiederaufbau (Reconstitution Credit Institute)
LF	Likelihood Function
Libor	London inter-bank overnight rate
Liffe	London International Financial Futures and Options Exchange
LPI	Limited Price Index
LTFX	Long-Term FX
LV	Local Volatility
MC	Monte Carlo
MG	Metallgesellschaft
MMR	Modified Modified Restructuring
MR	Modified Restructuring
NP	Notional Principal
NPA	Notional Principal Amount
OF	Objective Function
OIS	Overnight Indexed Swap
OTC	Over The Counter
OTM	Out The Money
PCA	Principal Component Analysis
pd	per day
PEL	Peak Exposure Limit
PFE	Potential Future Exposure
POT	Peaks Over Threshold
PRDC	Power Reverse Dual-Currency
PV	Present Value
PV01	Another name for PVBP

PVBP	Present Value of 1 bp
QDS	Quanto Diff Swap
ROD	Rand Overnight Deposit
RP	Robust Programming
SABR	Stochastic–$\alpha\beta\rho$
SONIA	Sterling OverNight Index Average
TARN	Target Accrual Redemption Note
TRS	Total Return Swap
VaR	Value-at-Risk
VBA	Visual BAsic
VCV	Another name for Delta VaR
VM	Variable Maturity
WB	World Bank
YoY	Year On Year
YTM	Yield To Maturity
ZAR	South African Rand
z-c	zero coupon

In memory of Marilyn, 1948 to 2003

1

Swaps and Other Derivatives

This is the second edition. Much has changed since the first was written in 2000. For the first seven years of the new century, the derivative market continued to grow at an exponential pace. From 2008, its growth reversed, albeit not by much, as the global economic recession bit. In terms of notional amount, it reduced by just over 13% in the second half of 2008, to just under USD600 trillion. Between the publication of the first edition and the writing of the second, there have been some major developments. Two in particular stand out: the growth in the credit transfer market, and the massive issuance of complex securities enabling investors to earn potentially higher returns by taking on more risks.[1] Hence the requirement for a second edition, which addresses both of these topics in considerable detail.

1.1 INTRODUCTION

In the 1970s there was an active Parallel Loan market. This arose during a period of exchange controls in Europe. Imagine that there is a UK company that needs to provide its US subsidiary with $100 million. The subsidiary is not of sufficiently good credit standing to borrow the money from a US bank without paying a considerable margin. The parent however cannot borrow the dollars itself and then pass them on to its subsidiary, or provide a parent guarantee, without being subject to the exchange control regulations which may make the transaction impossible or merely extremely expensive.

The Parallel Loan market requires a friendly US company prepared to provide the dollars, and at the same time requiring sterling in the UK, perhaps for its own subsidiary. Two loans with identical maturities are created in the two countries as shown. Usually the two principals would be at the prevailing spot FX rate, and the interest levels at the market rates. Obviously credit is a major concern, which would be alleviated by a set-off clause. This clause allowed each party to off-set unpaid receipts against payments due. As the spot and interest rates moved, one party would find that their loan would be "cheap", i.e. below the current market levels, whilst the other would find their loan "expensive". If the parties marked the loans to market—in other words, valued the loans relative to the current market levels—then the former would have a positive value and the latter a negative one. A "topping-up" clause, similar in today's market to a regular mark-to-market and settlement, would often be used to call for adjustments in the principals if the rates moved by more than a trigger amount.

---

[1] Whether investors actually understood the risks they were taking on is an unanswered question, and very much outside the remit of this book.

Parallel loans

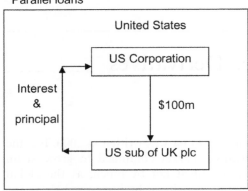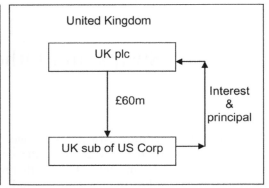

As exchange controls were abolished, the Parallel Loan became replaced with the back-to-back Loan market whereby the two parent organisations would enter into the loans directly with each other. This simplified the transactions, and reduced the operational risks. Because these loans were deemed to be separate transactions, albeit with an off-setting clause, they appeared on both sides of the balance sheet, with a potential adverse effect on the debt/equity ratios.

Back-to-Back Loan

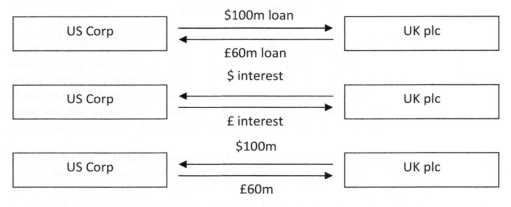

The economic driving force behind back-to-back loans is an extremely important concept called "comparative advantage". Suppose the UK company is little known in the US; it would be expensive to raise USD directly. Therefore borrowing sterling and doing a back-to-back loan with a US company (who may of course be in exactly the reverse position) is likely to be cheaper. In theory, comparative advantage cannot exist in efficient markets; in reality, markets are not efficient but are racked by varieties of distortions. Consider the simple corporate tax system: if a company is profitable, it has to pay tax; if a company is unprofitable, it doesn't. The system is asymmetric; unprofitable companies do not receive "negative" tax (except possibly in the form of off-sets against future profits). Any asymmetry is a distortion, and it is frequently feasible to derive mechanisms to exploit it—such as the leasing industry.

Cross-currency swaps were rapidly developed from back-to-back loans in the late 1970s. In appearance they are very similar, and from an outside observer only able to see the cashflows, identical. But subtly different in that all cashflows are described as contingent sales or purchases, i.e. each sale is contingent upon the counter-sale. These transactions, being forward conditional commitments, are off-balance sheet. We have the beginning of the OTC swap market!

Cross-currency Swap

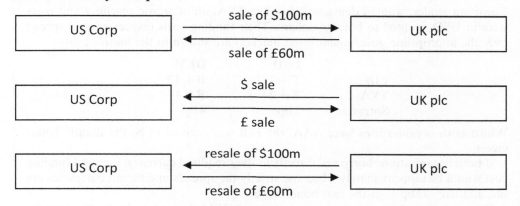

The structure of a generic (or vanilla) cross-currency swap is therefore:

- initial exchange of principal amounts;
- periodic exchanges of interest payments;[2]
- re-exchange of the principal amounts at maturity.

Notice that, if the first exchange is done at the current spot exchange rate, then it possesses no economic value and can be omitted.

Interest rate, or single-currency swaps, followed soon afterwards. Obviously exchange of principals in the same currency makes no economic sense, and hence an interest swap only consists of the single stage:

- periodic exchanges of interest payments;

where interest is calculated on different reference rates. The most common form is with one side using a variable (or floating) rate which is determined at regular intervals, and the other a fixed reference rate throughout the lifetime of the swap.

1.2 APPLICATIONS OF SWAPS

As suggested by its origins, the earliest applications of the swap market were to assist in the raising of cheap funds through the comparative advantage concept. The EIB–TVA transaction in 1996 was a classic example of this, and is described in the box below. The overall

---

[2] Remember: legally these cashflows are not "interest" but contingent sales, but for clarity of exposition they will be called "interest" as they are calculated in exactly the same way.

benefit to the two parties was about $3 million over a 10-year period, and therefore they were both willing to enter into the swap.

Comparative Advantage:
European Investment Bank–Tennessee Valley Authority swap
Date: September 1996

Both counterparties had the same objective: to raise cheap funds. The EIB, being an European lender, wanted deutschmarks. The TVA, all of whose revenues and costs were in USD, wanted to borrow dollars. Their funding costs (expressed as a spread over the appropriate government bond market) are shown in the matrix below:

	USD	DEM
EIB	$T + 17$	$B + 13$
TVA	$T + 24$	$B + 17$
Spread	7 bp	4 bp

Whilst both organisations were AAA, the EIB was deemed to be the slightly better credit.

If both organisations borrowed directly in their required currency, the total funding cost would be (approximately—because strictly the spreads in different currencies are not additive) 37 bp over the two bond curves.

However, the relative spread is much closer in DEM than it is in USD. This was for two reasons:

- the TVA had always borrowed USD, and hence was starting to pay the price of excess supply;
- it had never borrowed DEM, hence there was a considerable demand from European investors at a lower rate.

The total cost if the TVA borrowed DEM and the EIB borrowed USD would be only 34 bp, saving 3 bp pa.
    The end result:

- EIB issued a 10-year $1 billion bond;
- TVA issued a 10-year DM1.5 billion bond; and
- they swapped the proceeds to raise cheaper funding, saving roughly $3 million over the 10 years.

This was a real exercise in Comparative Advantage; neither party wanted the currency of their bond issues, but it was cheaper to issue and then swap.

It was quickly realised that swaps, especially being off-balance sheet instruments, could also be effective in the management of both currency and interest rate medium-term risk. The commonest example is of a company who is currently paying floating interest, and who is concerned about interest rates rising in the future; by entering into an interest rate swap to pay a fixed rate and to receive a floating rate, uncertainty has been removed.

To ensure that the risk management is effective, the floating interest receipts under the swap must exactly match the interest payments under the debt. Therefore the swap must mirror any structural complexities in the debt, such as principal repayment schedules, or options to repay early, and so on. Usually a swap entered into between a bank and a customer is tailored specifically for that situation. This book will provide details of many of the techniques used to structure such swaps.

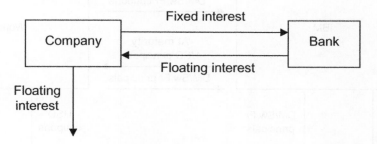

A well-known and very early example of the use of swaps is the one conducted between the World Bank and IBM in August 1981—described in the box below. This swap had the reputation of kick-starting the swap market because it was performed by two extremely prestigious organisations, and received a lot of publicity which attracted many other end-users to come into the market. It was the first long-term swap done by the World Bank, who is now one of the biggest users of the swap market.

World Bank–IBM Swap
Date: August 1981

This is a simplified version of the famous swap. The two counterparties have very different objectives.

IBM had embarked upon a world-wide funding programme some years earlier, raising money inter alia in deutschmarks and Swiss francs. The money was remitted back to the US for general funding. This had created a FX exposure, because IBM had to convert USDs into DEMs and CHFs regularly to make the coupon payments. Over the years the USD had significantly strengthened, creating a gain for IBM. It now wished to lock in the gain and remove any future exposure.

The World Bank had a policy of raising money in hard currency; namely DEM, CHF and yen. It was a prolific borrower, and by 1981 was finding that its cost of funds in these currencies was rising simply through an excess supply of WB paper. Its objective, as always, was to raise cheap funds.

Salomon Brothers suggested the following transactions:

(a) The WB could still raise USD at relatively cheap rates, therefore it should issue two euro-dollar bonds:
   ● one matched the principal and maturity of IBM's DEM liabilities equivalent to $210 million;
   ● the other matched IBM's Swiss franc liabilities equivalent to $80 million.
   Each bond had a short first period to enable the timing of all the future cashflows to match.
(b) There was a 2-week settlement period, so WB entered into a FX forward contract to:
   ● sell the total bond proceeds of $290 million;
   ● buy the equivalent in DEM and CHF;
(c) IBM and WB entered into a two-stage swap whereby:

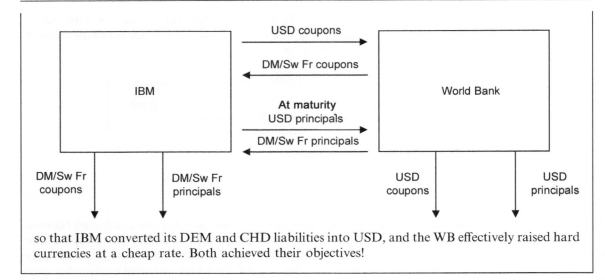

so that IBM converted its DEM and CHD liabilities into USD, and the WB effectively raised hard currencies at a cheap rate. Both achieved their objectives!

1.3   AN OVERVIEW OF THE SWAP MARKET

From these earliest beginnings, the swap market has grown exponentially. As the graph shows, the volume of interest rate swap business now totally dominates cross-currency swaps,[3] suggesting that risk management using swaps is commonplace.

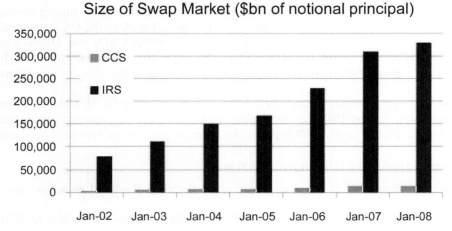

The graph is shown in terms of notional principal outstanding, i.e. the principals of all swaps transacted but not yet matured; for the cross-currency swap described above, this would be recorded as [$100m + £60m * S]/2 where S is the current spot rate. The market has shown a remarkable and consistent growth in activity.

---

[3] The source of these data is the Bank for International Settlement (BIS) which conducts a semi-annual survey of some 48 central banks and monetary authorities. It also does a more extensive triennial survey.

It is arguable whether this is a very appropriate way of describing the current size of the market, although it certainly attracts headlines. Many professionals would use "gross market value" or total replacement cost of all contracts as a more realistic measure. This measure had been in broad decline as banks improve their risk management, and are unwilling to take on greater risks due to the imposition of capital charges. However, as can be seen from the figures below, the gross value increased in the second half of 2008, especially in interest rate and credit derivatives, due to the dramatic movements in these markets.

A brief overview of the OTC derivative market is shown in the table below. Probably the most important statistic is that, despite all the publicity given to more exotic transactions, the overwhelming workhorse of this market is the relatively short-term interest rate swap.

The derivative markets continue to grow at an astounding rate—why? There are two main sources of growth—breadth and depth:

- financial markets around the world have increasingly deregulated over the past 30 years, witness activities in Greece and Portugal, the Far East and Eastern Europe. As they do, cash and bond markets first develop followed rapidly by swap and option markets;
- the original swaps were done in relatively large principal amounts with high-credit counterparties. Banks have however been increasingly pushing derivatives down into the lower credit depths in the search of return. It is feasible to get quite small transactions, and some institutions even specialise in aggregating retail demand into a wholesale transaction.

A brief overview of the current state of the derivative market (in December 2008) (extracted from the semiannual BIS surveys)

The total OTC derivative market was estimated to be just under $600 trillion, measured in terms of outstanding principal amount, broken up as shown below (in US billions):

	Notional principal				Gross values	
	Dec-06	Dec-07	Jun-08	Dec-08	Jun-08	Dec-08
FX	40,271	56,238	62,983	49,753	2,262	3,917
Forwards	19,882	29,144	31,966	24,562	802	1,732
Swaps	10,792	14,347	16,307	14,725	1,071	1,588
Options	9,597	12,748	14,701	10,466	388	597
IR	291,582	393,138	458,304	418,678	9,263	18,420
FRAs	18,668	26,599	39,370	39,262	88	153
Swaps	229,693	309,588	356,772	328,114	8,056	16,573
Options	43,221	56,951	62,162	51,301	1,120	1,694
Equity	7,488	8,469	10,177	6,494	1,146	1,113
Commodity	7,115	8,455	13,229	4,427	2,209	955
CDS	28,650	57,894	57,325	41,868	3,172	5,652

	Notional principal				Gross values	
	Dec-06	Dec-07	Jun-08	Dec-08	Jun-08	Dec-08
S–N CDS	17,879	32,246	33,334	25,730	1,889	3,695
M–N CDS	10,771	25,648	23,991	16,138	1,283	1,957
Unallocated	39,740	71,146	81,708	70,742	2,301	3,831
Exchange-traded	70,444	79,078	82,008	57,876		

The table shows the fairly dramatic slowdown and then drop during 2008, especially with equity, commodity and credit-related derivatives, but also the increase in gross value.

Maturity	FX	IRS
Under 1 year	65%	33% of total market
1–5 years	19%	33%
Over 5 years	16%	34%

The above table shows that the majority of FX derivatives, predominantly forwards, are under 1 year in maturity, interest rate derivatives are typically much longer, averaging between 5 and 10 years. The Eurozone, UK and US routinely now trade swaps out to 50 years. In terms of currencies, the major ones have little changed over the past 10 years. The main development is the increased rise in euro products, and the relative decline in USD.

Currency	Percentage of market share of IR derivatives
	Dec-08
USD	36.6%
Euro	38.7
Yen	14.1
GBP	7.4
Sw Fr	1.2
Can $	0.7
Sw Kr	1.3

1.4 THE EVOLUTION OF THE SWAP MARKET

The discussion below refers to the evolution of the early swap market in the major currencies during the 1980s. It is however applicable to many other generic markets as they have developed.

There are typically three phases of development of a swap market:

1. In the earliest days of a market, it is very much an arranged market whereby two swap end-users would negotiate directly with each other, and an "advisory" bank may well extract an upfront fee for locating and assisting them. This was obviously a slow

market, with documentation frequently tailored for each transaction. The main banks involved are investment or merchant banks, long on people but low on capital and technology as of course they were taking no risk. Typical counterparties would be highly rated, and therefore happy to deal directly with each other.

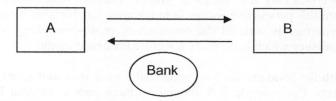

The first swap markets in the major currencies were even slower, as there was considerable doubt about the efficacy of swaps. End-users were dubious about moving the activities off-balance sheet, and there was apprehension that the accounting rules would be changed to force them back on-balance sheet. The World Bank–IBM swap (described above) played a major role in persuading people that the swap market was acceptable.

2. In the second phase, originally early to mid-1980s, commercial banks started to take an increasing role providing traditional credit guarantees.

The counterparties now would both negotiate directly with the bank, who would structure back-to-back swaps but take the credit risk, usually for an on-going spread not an upfront fee. The normal lending departments of the bank would be responsible for negotiating the transaction and the credit spread. The documentation is now more standardised and provided by the bank. This role is often described as acting as an "intermediary", taking credit but not market risk.

The role of intermediary may also be encouraged by external legislation. In the UK for example, if a swap is entered into by two non-bank counterparties, the cashflows are subject to withholding tax. This is not true if one counterparty is a bank.

3. The concept of a market-making bank originally developed by the mid to late 1980s, whereby a bank would provide swap quotations upon request. This would mean that they would be dealing with a range of counterparties simultaneously, and entering into a variety of non-matching swaps. With increased market risk, such banks required considerably more capital, pricing and risk management systems, and very standardised documentation. The swap market became dominated by the large commercial banks who saw it as a volume, commoditised business.

These banks would be typically off-setting the market risk by hedging in another market, usually the equivalent government bond market as this is the most liquid. Therefore banks with an underlying activity in this market are likely to be at a competitive advantage. Local domestic banks usually have close links with the local government bond market, and hence they are frequently dominant in the domestic swap market. Probably the only market where this is not the case is the USD market, where the markets are so large that a number of foreign banks can also be highly active and competitive.

It might be worth making the point here that banks frequently and misleadingly talk about "trading" swaps, as if a swap were equivalent to a spot FX transaction which is settled and forgotten about within two days. A swap is actually a transaction which has created a long-term credit exposure for the bank. The exposure is likely to remain on the bank's books long after the swap "trader" has been paid a bonus and has left the bank. From this perspective, swaps fit much more comfortably within the traditional lending departments with all the concomitant credit-controlling processes and not within a treasury which is typically far more lax about credit.

This link with the bond market has meant that a bank may well adopt different roles in different markets. For example, a Scandinavian bank such as Nordea Bank would be a market-maker in the Scandinavian and possibly some of the Northern European currencies. On the other hand, it would act as an intermediary in other currencies. For example, if a customer wanted to do a South African rand swap, it would enter into it taking on the credit risk, but immediately laying off the market risk with a rand market-making bank.

In this context, the 1996 EIB–TVA swap was interesting. The deal was brokered by Lehmann Brothers, but who played no role in the swap. At one point the swap had been out for tender from a bank but (rumour has it) the bid was a 1 bp spread. Why, asked the two counterparties, do we need to deal with a bank at all, especially given that we are both AAA which is better than virtually all banks? So they dealt directly! As the relative credit standing of banks declines, the market may well see more transactions of this nature—back full circle.

One cannot really talk about a "global" swap market. There are obviously some global currencies, notably USD, yen and the euro, which are traded 24 hours a day, and when it would be feasible to get swaps. But most swap markets are tied into their domestic markets, and hence available only during trading hours.

Swap brokers still play an important role in this market. Their traditional role has been to identify the cheapest suitable counterparty for a client, usually on the initial basis of anonymity. This activity creates liquidity and a uniformity of pricing, to the overall benefit of market participants. However, as the markets in the most liquid currencies continue to grow, the efficiency provided by a broker is less valued and their fees have been increasingly reduced to a fraction of a basis point. They are being forced to develop more electronic skills to survive.

1.5 CONCLUSION

The story of the swaps market has been one of remarkable growth from its beginnings only some 30 years ago. This growth has demonstrated that there is a real demand for the benefits swaps can bring, namely access to cheap funds and risk management, globally. Furthermore, the growth shows little sign of abating as swap markets continue to expand both geographically as countries deregulate and downwards into the economy. As we enter into 2009 and beyond, have derivatives suddenly become irrelevant?[4] In my view, certainly not. The measurement and management of risk, whether it be interest rate, foreign exchange rate, credit and so on, is, and will remain, critical for all organisations. To suddenly deny the main mechanism for managing these risks is simply irrational. What is, of course, important is to ensure that users of derivatives understand and can assess

---

[4] Or, as Warren Buffett famously described them, "toxic waste".

derivatives, or at least employ people that do. I very much hope that this book will play some small role in the continued use of derivatives, and assisting the orderly development of the market, by ensuring that people are well-trained in their understanding of the pricing, structuring and risk management of swaps and related derivatives.

2

Short-term Interest Rate Swaps

OBJECTIVE

The main objective of this chapter is to provide an introduction to the construction and pricing of short-term IRS using futures contracts. However, because a simple swap may be regarded as an exchange of two streams of cashflows which occur at different points in the future, extensive use is made of the concept of discounting. The chapter therefore begins with a brief discussion on the time value of money, and demonstrates how implied discount factors may be derived from the cash market. Because rates are only available at discrete maturities, interpolation is a necessary technique; and there are a number of different approaches which end up with different results. The chapter then discusses how to estimate forward rates, and how to price FRAs first off the cash market and then off the futures market. This leads naturally to the pricing and hedging of short-term IRS off a futures strip. Examination of the hedging reveals a convexity effect which is discussed in more detail in Chapter 7 and its Appendix. Finally, an alternative approach to pricing swaps without discounting is briefly discussed.

2.1 DISCOUNTING, THE TIME VALUE OF MONEY AND OTHER MATTERS

Today's date is Monday 4 February 2008; you have just been offered a choice of transactions:

> Deal 1: to lend $10 million and to receive 3.25% for 3 months;
> Deal 2: to lend $10 million and to receive 2.95% for 12 months.

Which do you find more attractive?

The current London rates at which you could normally deposit money are 3.145% pa and 2.89625% pa for 3 and 12 months, respectively;[1] we will assume that the credit-worthiness of the counterparty is beyond question. Comparing the transactions with these market rates, the 3-month deal is 10.5 bp above the market, whilst the 12-month deal is only 5 bp. Intuitively you favour the first transaction, but wish to do some more analysis to be certain.

---

[1] These market rates imply a negative curve, with long-term rates lower than short-term rates. This is unusual, as the cost of borrowing generally increases with maturity due to a charge for the loss of control of the money. But this inversion of the curve reflects a lack of supply at the short end, reflecting conditions following the current "credit crunch".

These market rates suggest that the following transactions are currently available:[2]

Dates	Days	3 mo. cash	12 mo. cash
4-Feb-08			
6-Feb-08		−10,000,000	−10,000,000
6-May-08	90	10,078,625.00	
6-Feb-09	366		10,294,452.08

where negative signs indicate payments, and positive or no sign receipts.

Note the following:

a. Whilst the rates are being quoted on 4 February, they are with effect from 6 February. In other words, there is a 2-day settlement period between the agreement of the transaction and its start. On 6 February, the counterparty's bank account would be credited with $10 million. This is the normal convention in the USD market, although it is feasible to organise a "same day" transaction. Conventions vary between markets; for example, the GBP convention is normally "same day".

b. Interest rates are invariably quoted on a "per annum" basis, even if they are going to be applied over a different period. It is therefore necessary to have a convention that translates the calendar time from, say, 6 May 2008 back to 6 February 2008 into years. The USD money market, in common with most money markets, uses an "Actual/360" daycount convention, i.e. calculates the actual number of days:

$$6 \text{ May } 2008 - 6 \text{ February } 2008 = 90 \text{ days}$$

and then divides by 360 to convert into 0.2500 years. The other common convention is "Actual/365", which is used in the sterling market and many of the old Commonwealth countries. The cashflow at the end of 3 months is given by:

$$\$10,000,000 * (1 + 3.145\% * 0.2500) = \$10,078,625.00$$

c. Payments can only be made on business days, and therefore a convention has to be applied to determine the appropriate date if the apparent cashflow date is a non-business day. The most popular is the "modified following day" convention, i.e. the operating date moves to the next business day unless this involves going across a month-end, in which case the operating date moves to the last business day in the month.

The concept of discounting will be used extensively throughout this book. The "time value of money" suggests that the value of money depends upon its time of receipt; for example, $1 million received today would be usually valued more highly than $1 million to be

---

[2] Please note that the calculations for all the numbers in this section are replicated in Worksheets 2.1 to 2.5.

received in 1 year's time because it could be invested today to generate interest or profits in the future. If C_t represents a certain cashflow to be received at time $t > 0$, then a discount factor DF_t relates this cashflow to its value today (or present value) C_0 by

$$C_0 = C_t * DF_t$$

Note that this does not presuppose any source or derivation of the discount factor.

The present value of each of these two market-based transactions may be easily calculated as:

$$-\$10,000,000 + \$10,078,625.00 * DF_3$$

and

$$-\$10,000,000 + \$10,294,452.08 * DF_{12}$$

where DF_3 and DF_{12} are the 3 and 12-month discount factors, respectively. The market rates are obviously freely negotiated, and we will assume that, at the moment of entering into the transactions, the transactions represent no clear profit to either party. In other words, at inception the transactions would be deemed to be "fair" to both parties, and hence have a zero net value. Hence, we can solve for the two discount factors, i.e. $DF_3 = 0.992199$ and $DF_{12} = 0.971397$, respectively. A general formula for discount factors from the money markets is:

$$DF_t = 1/(1 + r_t * d_t) \tag{2.1}$$

where d_t is the length of time (in years) and r_t is the rate (expressed as a % pa).

Turning back to the two original transactions, these will generate the following cashflows:

Dates	Deal 1	Deal 2
4-Feb-08		
6-Feb-08	−10,000,000	−10,000,000
6-May-08	10,081,250	
6-Feb-09		10,299,917
PV =	**2,604.52**	**5,308.28**

The present values are determined using the discount factors derived from the market rates. Thus we can see, perhaps against our intuition, that the second transaction would be the more profitable of the two. This is of course because the deal is longer: 10.5 bp over 3 months is roughly half of 5 bp over a year.

This is of course ignoring market realities such as bid–offer or bid–ask spreads (or "doubles" as they are frequently called). In practice, most analysis uses mid-rates, i.e. the arithmetic average between bid and offer, simply to enable the statement of "fairness" to be made, and subsequently adjusted for various spreads. These issues will be discussed in more detail later; for the current discussion they will be ignored.

The current money market data readily available is:

Today's date:	4-Feb-08	Rates
Start date:	6-Feb-08	
7-day	13-Feb-08	3.2175%
1-month	6-Mar-08	3.1813%
3-month	6-May-08	3.1450%
6-month	6-Aug-08	3.0975%
12-month	6-Feb-09	2.89625%

Discount factors at each of the maturities can be easily calculated as above, i.e.:

Today's date	4-Feb-08	Rate	DFs
Start date	6-Feb-08		
7-day	13-Feb-08	3.2175%	0.999375
1-month	6-Mar-08	3.1813%	0.997444
3-month	6-May-08	3.1450%	0.992199
6-month	6-Aug-08	3.0975%	0.984582
12-month	6-Feb-09	2.89625%	0.971397

You are now offered the opportunity to purchase today a riskless $100m due to be paid on 6 November 2008. What value would you place on this transaction? To answer this question, the discount factor on 6 November is required—but how to calculate it? The obvious approach is "interpolation", but this raises two questions:

- What is interpolated: cash rates or discount factors?
- How is the interpolation calculated: linear, polynomial, exponential, etc.? with associated questions "do the answers change the valuation?" and "are there any 'right' answers?". The simple answers to the latter questions are "yes" and "no, but some are better than others"! The results from some popular methods are shown below:

Calculation of the discount factor on 6-Nov-08

	Linear interpolation of rates	Cubic interpolation of rates	Linear interpolation of DFs	Cubic interpolation of DFs	Log-linear interpolation of DFs
	2.997%	3.027%			
	DFs	DFs			
	0.977699	0.977483	0.977989	0.977558	0.977967
PV =	97,769,912	97,748,286	97,798,944	97,755,783	97,796,722

where:

- "linear" is simply straight-line interpolation;
- "cubic" implies fitting a cubic polynomial of the form $a + b \cdot t + c \cdot t^2 + d \cdot t^3$ through the four neighbouring points and solving for $\{a, b, c, d\}$;
- "log-linear" is the straight line interpolation of the natural logarithm of the discount factors (this last one is often suggested as a discount curve is similar to a negative exponential curve).

The deal value fluctuates by some \$50,000 or roughly 5 bp, which, whilst perhaps not significant, is certainly worthwhile. It is more common practice to interpolate rates rather than discount factors at the short end of the curve. This is probably because it would be perfectly feasible to get a quote for a rate out to 6 November for depositing, and of course the two transactions should be arbitrage-free.

Cash rates are of course spot rates, i.e. they all start out of "today". The cash curve may be used to estimate forward rates, i.e. rates starting at some point in the future. For example, if we knew that we would receive \$100 million on 6 May 2008 for, say, 3 months, we could lock in the investment rate today by calculating the 3/6 rate.[3] Forward rates are usually estimated using an arbitrage argument as follows:

1. We could borrow \$100 million for 3 months at 3.1450%, the repayment cashflow[4] would be $100m * (1 + 3.1450\% * 0.250) = 100{,}786{,}250.00$.
2. The \$100 million could then be lent out for 6 months at 3.0975%, this would generate a cashflow of $100m * (1 + 3.0975\% * 0.506) = 101{,}565{,}958.33$.

At the end of the 3 months, the borrowing has to be repaid. Assume the repayment is to be financed by borrowing for another 3 months at the rate $r_{3/6}$, thus generating a new liability:

$$100{,}786{,}250.00 * (1 + r_{3/6} * d_{3/6})$$

where $d_{3/6} = 0.256$ is the length of time at the end of 6 months. For the transactions to break even:

$$100{,}786{,}250.00 * (1 + r_{3/6} * 0.256) = 101{,}565{,}958.33$$

The implied 3/6 rate is 3.0272%.

A general expression for a forward rate $F_{t/T}$, from t to T, is:

$$F_{t/T} = \{[(1 + r_T * d_T)/(1 + r_t * d_t)] - 1\}/(T - t) \tag{2.2}$$

However, to use this expression, the rates must be zero-coupon spot rates with maturities t and T. These are generally available when T is under 1 year, but are unlikely to be available for longer maturities. A more widely used expression for longer dated forward rates is:

$$F_{t/T} = \{(DF_t/DF_T) - 1\}/(T - t) \tag{2.3}$$

using discount factors estimated off the discount curve (which of course is synonymous for cash rates).

---

[3] Forward rates are conventionally quoted as "start/end" [or "start × end" or "start v end"] rather than "start/maturity".
[4] The lengths of time are shown rounded to only three decimal places.

Returning to the cash curve above, we want to estimate the 3-monthly forward rates, 3/ 6, 6/9 and 9/12. To do this, we need to estimate the 9-month discount factor DF_9. The table below shows it being estimated in a variety of ways, and the resulting forward rates.

Calculation of discount factor on 6-Nov-08					
	Linear interpolation of rates	Cubic interpolation of rates	Linear interpolation of DFs	Cubic interpolation of DFs	Log-linear interpolation of DFs
	2.997% DFs 0.977699	3.027% DFs 0.977483	0.977989	0.977558	0.977967
3 mo. forward rates					
3/6	3.0272%	3.0272%	3.0272%	3.0272%	3.0272%
6/9	2.7547%	2.8419%	2.6377%	2.8116%	2.6467%
9/12	2.5387%	2.4515%	2.6556%	2.4817%	2.6467%

The impact of the different methods on the forward rates is quite dramatic, showing differences of up to 20 bp. Contrast this with the difference in the discount factors, which in the previous example only reached 5 bp.

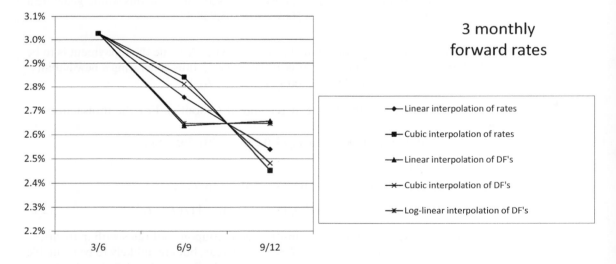

To understand why, rewriting eq. (2.3) as:

$$F_{t/T} = \{(DF_t - DF_T)/DF_T\}/(T - t)$$

highlights the fact that a forward rate is related to the gradient of the discount curve and is therefore much more sensitive to small differences in the estimates. To demonstrate this more clearly, the table below calculates a 15-day forward rate curve using all the five different methods of interpolation:

15-day forward curve

	Linear interpolation of rates	Cubic interpolation of rates	Linear interpolation of DFs	Cubic interpolation of DFs	Log-linear interpolation of DFs
6-Feb-08					
21-Feb-08	3.2043%	3.2023%	3.1899%	3.1958%	3.1910%
7-Mar-08	3.1528%	3.1535%	3.1637%	3.1609%	3.1632%
22-Mar-08	3.1456%	3.1253%	3.1077%	3.1416%	3.1136%
6-Apr-08	3.1237%	3.1120%	3.1117%	3.1224%	3.1136%
21-Apr-08	3.1019%	3.1080%	3.1157%	3.1033%	3.1136%
6-May-08	3.0802%	3.1075%	3.1198%	3.0843%	3.1136%
21-May-08	3.0667%	3.0673%	3.0078%	3.0785%	3.0175%
5-Jun-08	3.0474%	3.0496%	3.0115%	3.0588%	3.0175%
20-Jun-08	3.0282%	3.0312%	3.0153%	3.0361%	3.0175%
5-Jul-08	3.0091%	3.0113%	3.0191%	3.0105%	3.0175%
20-Jul-08	2.9900%	2.9895%	3.0229%	2.9820%	3.0175%
4-Aug-08	2.9710%	2.9650%	3.0267%	2.9505%	3.0175%
19-Aug-08	2.8560%	2.9372%	2.6769%	2.9160%	2.6896%
3-Sep-08	2.8067%	2.9057%	2.6254%	2.8785%	2.6392%
18-Sep-08	2.7712%	2.8697%	2.6283%	2.8380%	2.6392%
3-Oct-08	2.7358%	2.8287%	2.6311%	2.7945%	2.6392%
18-Oct-08	2.7005%	2.7821%	2.6340%	2.7479%	2.6392%
2-Nov-08	2.6654%	2.7293%	2.6369%	2.6983%	2.6392%
17-Nov-08	2.6303%	2.6697%	2.6398%	2.6457%	2.6392%
2-Dec-08	2.5954%	2.6027%	2.6427%	2.5900%	2.6392%
17-Dec-08	2.5606%	2.5278%	2.6456%	2.5312%	2.6392%
1-Jan-09	2.5259%	2.4444%	2.6486%	2.4694%	2.6392%
16-Jan-09	2.4912%	2.3518%	2.6515%	2.4044%	2.6392%
31-Jan-09	2.4567%	2.2496%	2.6544%	2.3364%	2.6392%

The average difference between the highest and lowest curves is 11.4 bp.

In practice, whilst there is no "right" method, most people interpolate the cash rates using either linear if the cash curve is relatively flat, or polynomial if the curve is quite steep.

2.2 FORWARD RATE AGREEMENTS (FRAs) AND INTEREST RATE FUTURES

A FRA is an agreement between two counterparties whereby:

- seller of FRA agrees to pay a floating rate interest and to receive a fixed interest rate;
- buyer of FRA agrees to pay the fixed interest and to receive the floating interest

on an agreed notional principal amount, and over an agreed forward period.

For example, a company is a payer of 3-month floating interest on $100 million of debt. The company is concerned about interest rates rising, and on 4 February 2008 it buys a $100 million 3/6 FRA at a fixed rate of 3.0272% from a bank. The following operations occur:

4 May 2008:   3 mo. $ Libor is fixed with effect from 6 May 2008
6 August 2008:   net cash settlement $(L - 3.0272\%) * \$100m * (6 \text{ August}-6 \text{ May})/360$
                     is paid.

This is shown from the point of view of the company, and will be positive if $L > 3.0272\%$ or negative if $L < 3.0272\%$. Hence, the company is locked into the fixed rate even if rates do rise over the period from 4 February to 4 May.

In practice, the net amount is discounted back to 6 May 2008 using the recent Libor fixing, i.e.:

$$\{(L - 3.0272\%) * 100m * (6 \text{ August} - 6 \text{ May})/360\}/[1 + L * (6 \text{ August} - 6 \text{ May})/360]$$

and paid then. The usual reason given for this market convention is a reduction in the credit exposure between the two parties:

a.   On 4 February, the current exposure is assumed to be zero, i.e. the FRA would have a zero valuation for both parties.
b.   However, there is a "potential future exposure" over the period from 4 February to 4 May which would fluctuate as the estimate of the Libor fixing on 4 May varies. If the estimate rises, then the FRA has a negative value for the bank and hence the company has a credit exposure on the bank; conversely, if the estimate falls, then the FRA has a positive value for the bank, and it has a credit exposure on the company.
c.   On 4 May, the official Libor fixing is known, which then fixes the net settlement amount and crystallises the residual credit exposure.
d.   The two parties could wait until 6 August with one of them having this known residual exposure. By making the payment immediately on 6 May, this 3-month residual risk is removed.

As banks are required to place capital against all credit exposures, and capital has a cost, retaining the residual exposure could be expensive. Discounting the net settlement amount therefore appears to favour the bank, as it implies that for a given credit limit and amount of capital, the bank could effectively do twice the total business in 3/6 FRAs. The impact of discounting on reducing the total credit exposure obviously declines as the time to the fixing date lengthens.

The benefit to the company is less clear. Whilst the value of the net settlement remains constant whether discounted or not, most companies neither mark-to-market nor are overly concerned about credit exposures. The cashflows from the FRA and from the underlying debt are not on the same dates, therefore creating a mismatch which may cause accounting and tax problems. It is highly unlikely that the company could reproduce the undiscounted net settlement, as it would not be able to deposit or borrow at Libor flat for an odd cashflow, irrespective of its credit worthiness. It is perfectly feasible for banks to provide non-discounted FRAs[5] at a price, but this is seldom done.

We saw in Section 2.1 how a forward rate may be created by spot money market transactions. However, FRAs are off-balance sheet whereas cash trades are on-balance sheet, which is not a good mix. If a liquid interest rate (or deposit) futures market exists, then this is much more likely to be used to price and to hedge FRAs. A brief reminder about futures contracts:

- equivalent to standardised FRA contracts, traded through exchanges;
- standardised notional principal amounts, maturity dates and underlying interest rates;
- futures are deemed to be credit risk-free as each contract is guaranteed by the exchange— to achieve this, when entering into a contract, each party must place an initial margin with the exchange (sufficient to cover an extreme movement in the market) plus a variation margin because each contract is valued and settled daily.

For example: the most liquid contract in the world is the 3-month Eurodollar traded on Chicago Mercantile Exchange:

- notional principal amount is $1 million;
- maturity dates: third Wednesday of a delivery month;
- delivery months: March, June, September and December;[6]
- in theory, 40 contracts (i.e. spanning the next 10 years) are open at any time; in practice, there is good liquidity in the near 16–20 contracts;
- underlying interest rate: 3-month USD Libor quoted on a "price" basis; on 4 February 2008, the quote for March 08 contract was 97.000, implying that the market was anticipating the 3-month Libor rate out of 19 March 2008 to be $(100 - 97.000)/100 = 3.000\%$;
- price movement is a minimum of half a tick, i.e. 0.005 with the exception of the nearest contract with a quarter-tick movement;
- initial margin: $1,013 per contract paid to the exchange; variation margin: $1,000,000 * 1\ \text{bp} * (90/360) = \$25$ per basis point movement per contract has to be paid or received daily (notice this simplistically assumes 3 months is equal to 0.25 of a year, and does not use Actual/360).

The current quotes for Eurodollar futures contracts are:

	Maturity date	Price	Implied rate
March 08	March 19	97.000	3.000%
June 08	June 18	97.410	2.590%

---

[5] Which could of course be thought of as a single-period swap!

[6] There are four so-called serial months. If today's date is 4 February 2008, then there would also be futures maturing in February, April, May and July 2008. The idea was to give traders more flexibility at the short end of the curve. In practice, the volume in the serial months tends to be very low, and their existence will be ignored.

Given these rates, we wish to price the FRA above by estimating the fair 3-month rate out of 6 May: this is usually done by simple linear interpolation between neighbouring implied futures rates as shown below (for full details see Worksheet 2.6):

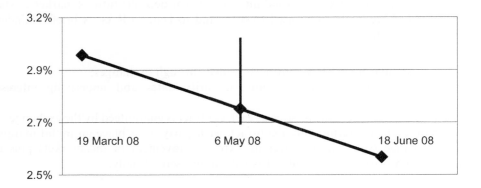

As:

$$6 \text{ May–19 March} = 48 \text{ days}$$

$$18 \text{ June–6 May} = 43 \text{ days}$$

linear interpolation gives:

$$(43/91) * 3.00\% + (48/91) * 2.59\% = 2.784\%$$

The reason for writing the interpolation in this fashion is that it provides a clear indication of the contribution of each futures contract, i.e. March provides 47%, June 53%, to the price estimate of the FRA. Leading on from that, it also provides a clear indication of the futures required to hedge the FRA; the bank has sold $100 million of a 3/6 FRA, therefore 100 futures contracts need to be sold to hedge it in the proportion of 47 March contracts, 53 June contracts.

Why do we sell futures, given that the bank has sold the FRA? The bank is paying the floating rate on the FRA, and is therefore concerned about rates rising. Futures are quoted on a price basis, i.e. the bank sells the March contract at 97.00. If rates then rise, the price will fall, and the bank can buy the contract back at a lower price. The profit gained—the variation margin—should hopefully offset the loss on the FRA.

How good is this hedge? This will be discussed conceptually first, and then in detail later. Consider first of all a 10 bp parallel shift in the 3-month forward rate curve. The bank would have to pay $10,000,000 * 10 \text{ bp} * (91/360) = \$25,555$ extra on the FRA. It would receive a total of $\$25 * 10 \text{ contracts} * 10 \text{ bp} = \$25,000$ from the two futures contracts. The small mismatch of $555 is due to the different daycount conventions. So the hedge is fairly effective; in theory, the size of the futures hedge could have been adjusted slightly, but this is obviously impractical.

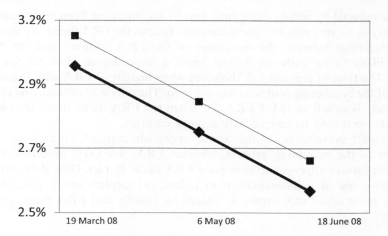

Next a rotational shift, pivoting around 1 May 2008. This results in the following shifts:

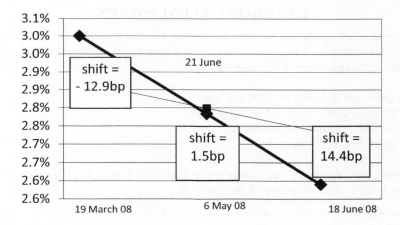

The impact can be calculated as:

March contract:	−12.9 bp	value = −$15,239
June contract:	+14.4 bp	value = +$18,989
FRA contract:	+1.5 bp	value = −$ 3,833
Net effect:		−$83

The hedge appears to be quite effective against both parallel and rotational shifts. However, if the curvature of the forward rate curve changes, for example both futures rates decrease but the FRA rate remains constant, then the hedge will fail.

As time passes, the hedge needs to be rebalanced as the proportions of the two contracts change. Eventually the March contract will expire, leaving the FRA hedged only with the June contract. This exposes the bank to rotational risk for the remainder of the contract.

This may be reduced by selling more June and by buying some September contracts, but this is unlikely to be very effective given the short time to the FRA fixing. By this, we mean that the correlation between the remainder of the FRA contract and the September contract is likely to be quite small, and hence a large degree of curve risk has been introduced. The time of greatest risk therefore when hedging a FRA with futures is when the shorter of the bracketing contracts has matured. The only way of removing this residual risk completely is to sell an IMM FRA, i.e. when the FRA fixing date falls on a futures maturity date, so it may be hedged with a single contract.

From a credit perspective, is the above approach correct? Futures are effectively risk-free due to the margining process, whereas FRAs are OTC products. Hence, are the rates from futures appropriate as implied FRA rates? In fact, OTC derivative markets make extensive use of collateralisation to reduce the implicit credit risk; this will be discussed in more detail in Chapter 3. Therefore, futures and FRA rates appear to be comparable.

2.3 SHORT-TERM SWAPS

There are some other issues that we need to discuss, and these will be done in the context of a more complex example. A money market swap is a short-dated swap typically priced and hedged using a futures strip. The swap will be:

- notional principal amount of $100 million;
- 1-year maturity, starting on 4 February 2008;
- to receive fixed F annual Actual/360;
- to pay 3-month Libor quarterly.

In this context, the "fair price" of a swap is the fixed rate F such that the net present value of the swap is zero. The structure of the swap is:

4 Feb 08	First Libor fixing ($=$ current 3 mo. cash rate 3.145%)
6 Feb 08	Start of swap (start of interest accruing on both sides)
4 May 08	Second Libor fixing
6 May 08	First floating payment $= \$100,000,000 * 3.145\% * (6 \text{ May}-6 \text{ Feb})/360$ $= \$78,625$
4 August 08	Third Libor fixing
6 August 08	Second floating payment $= \$100,000,000 * L * (6 \text{ August}-6 \text{ May})/360$
4 Nov 08	Fourth Libor fixing
6 Nov 08	Third floating payment
8 Feb 09	Final cashflow: fourth floating payment and single fixed receipt $= \$100,000,000 * F * (6 \text{ Feb 09}-6 \text{ Feb 08})/360$

Note that, whilst described in detail above, the distinction between the fixing date of a floating reference rate and the start of the accruing period will generally be ignored unless it has some special significance. Future examples will tacitly assume that the fixing takes place on the start date of each period.

The current market information out of 4 February 2008 is:

Cash rates		Futures prices	
6-Feb-08			
13-Feb-08	3.2175%	March 08	97.000
6-Mar-08	3.1813%	June 08	97.410
6-May-08	3.1450%	September 08	97.520
6-Aug-08	3.0975%	December 08	97.495
6-Feb-09	2.89625%	March 09	97.395

We will look at various ways of determining F, and then will return to hedging. As with all swaps, the main issue is what to do about the unknown forward floating rates?

Whilst there are a variety of approaches that may be used to address this, as we shall see later, using the futures to estimate the forward Libor rates as we did on the FRA and subsequently hedge them is a very natural choice. The first Libor is of course fixed today to be the current 3 mo. cash rate. The second Libor is none other than the 3/6 rate: we estimated this using the March and June futures above to be 2.784%. Similarly, we can estimate the other two Libor fixings, which are the 6/9 and 9/12 rates, respectively, off the futures strip as follows:

$$6/9: \quad [(42 * 2.590\%) + (49 * 2.480\%)]/91 = 2.531\%$$

$$9/12: \quad [(41 * 2.480\%) + (50 * 2.505\%)]/91 = 2.494\%$$

These calculations are shown in column [1] of Worksheet 2.7. Hence, floating cashflows can be constructed; see column [2].

The next step is to present-value the cashflows. This requires estimation of appropriate discount factors. The most obvious choice is to derive them from the cash rates as above, interpolating the rates as required; this values the floating side to be −$2,731,936 as shown in columns [3] and [4]. To calculate the fixed rate, we could either calculate it analytically or numerically:

- The value of the fixed side for $F = 1$ is simply:

  $$\$100,000,000 * [(6 \text{ Feb } 09\text{–}6 \text{ Feb } 08)/360] * 0.971397 = \$98,758,696$$

  For the swap to be fairly priced, $F = \$2,731,936/\$98,758,696 = 2.7663\%$. This will work in this situation as the present value of the fixed side is linear in terms of the fixed rate; this is true in many relatively simple structures, as we will see later.
- Alternatively, we could guess the fixed rate, construct the cashflow in column [6], calculate the present value of the fixed side, and if it is not the same as the floating PV, adjust the guess. A good starting point would be to use the average of the floating rates, i.e. 2.738% and adjusted from quarterly to annual using the formula $(1 + r_{qu}/4)^4 = (1 + r_{ann})$, i.e. 2.7666%; this gives a net PV of $28. But the starting point seldom matters as the iterations are well behaved. When pricing transactions in a spreadsheet, most people make extensive use of the Goal Seek or Solver functions to do this type of calculation. There are probably two reasons why this is so popular:

○ it directly generates the actual cashflows likely to happen under this swap, which is extremely useful for checking the structure;
○ the method may be easily modified to enable the pricer to calculate a fixed rate that will generate a desired profit (non-zero net PV) for the transaction.

As before, the hedges for the three unknown Libor fixings (it is assumed that the first Libor rate has already been fixed, and therefore cannot be hedged) may be calculated:

6/9: $(42/91) * 100 = 46$ June   and $(49/91) * 100 = 54$ September

9/12: $(75/91) * 100 = 45$ September   and $(16/91) * 100 = 55$ December

A total of 300 contracts are required, as shown in column [6].

Next, let us explore the effectiveness of this. For example, assume that the futures prices shift as shown below:

	Shift in futures prices (bp)
Mar-08	−25
Jun-08	−50
Sep-08	−100
Dec-08	−75

This will give rise to new Libor estimates, as shown in column [9], and the resulting change in the swap cashflows in [10]. The margin cashflows from the futures hedge are calculated in column [11]; for example:

March: 47 contracts $* -25$ bp shift in price $* \$25$ per bp $= \$29,375$ received

We can see that the total changes in the swap cashflows in column [10] sum to −$514,621, and the total receipts under the futures hedge in [11] sum to $503,750. The amounts are very similar, but not equal because of the differences in daycounts as discussed above (the resulting hedge ratio of 1.02 is roughly the ratio of the length of 3 months under the swap convention of Act/360 and under the futures convention being equal to $\frac{1}{4}$ of a year, which suggests that about 306 contracts are actually required) (see Worksheet 2.7).

However, column [10] ignores the timing of the cashflows and simply adds them up. The hedge is said to be a "cash hedge". In practice, the futures would pay the receipts on margin received today, whilst the additional payments under the swap would only occur on the payment dates. To make the results comparable, the changes in swap cashflows need to be discounted back, as in column [12]. In this case, the swap is very slightly overhedged, i.e. the changes in the value of the swap are smaller than the off-setting changes in the value of the futures receipts. The graph below shows the impact of a parallel shift in the futures prices, and it demonstrates that we are net short of futures contracts.

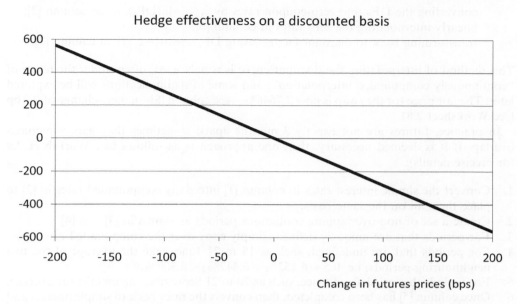

There is however a serious practical flaw in the model, in that it uses futures for estimating the future Libor fixings, and cash rates for deriving the discount factors. The hedge only protected against movements in the futures prices, and assumed that the discount factors remained constant. But both markets are providing information over the 12-month period; some of the information must therefore be complementary, and possibly contradictory. Shifts in the futures should also imply shifts in the cash rates, which has been ignored.

The discounting process is going to have to be rebuilt, this time using a set of non-redundant or parsimonious market information. Because futures, by definition, are not spot rates, we need at least one spot cash rate; this will ensure that the discount factors discount back to today. The more general approach is to use a cash-to-first-futures (CTFF) rate. This is a cash rate that matures, in this case, on 19 March 2008; by interpolating the cash curve, CTFF = 3.174%.

Define $DF(t_1, t_2)$ to be a forward discount factor that will discount a cashflow at time t_2 back to time t_1. Obviously $DF(t_1, t_3) = DF(t_1, t_2) * DF(t_2, t_3)$. Initially, assume that the implied futures rates apply from the maturity of one futures contract to the next one, eg. the implied March rate of 3.000% applies from 19 March until 18 June, the rate of 2.590% from 18 June until 17 September, etc. In this case we can build a discount curve as follows:

1. $DF(0, 19 \text{ March}) = (1 + 42/360 * 3.174\%)^{-1} = 0.996311$ (the usual simple DF).
2. $DF(19 \text{ March}, 18 \text{ June}) = (1 + 91/360 * 3.000\%)^{-1} = 0.992474$;
   $DF(0, 18 \text{ June}) = 0.996311 * 0.992474 = 0.988813$.
3. $DF(18 \text{ June}, 17 \text{ September}) = (1 + 91/360 * 2.590\%)^{-1} = 0.993496$;
   $DF(0, 17 \text{ September}) = 0.988813 * 0.993496 = 0.982381$, etc.

This cash & futures discount curve will now change as the futures prices shift. The following strategy can be adopted:

• Estimate the Libor fixings off 3 mo. cash and the futures strip as before.
• Calculate the DFs on the swap dates by interpolating the DFs from the futures dates by

○   converting the DFs into zero-coupon rates by $z_t = -\ln(DF_t)/t$, see column [2];
○   linearly interpolating the zero rates in column [6];
○   transforming back to discount factors using $DF_t = \exp\{-z_t . t\}$ in column [7].

This method of interpolating the discount curve is widely used, often under the name of "continuously compounded interpolation", and some of its implications will be explored later. The fair price for the swap is now 2.7646%—see column [8]—a mere change of 0.2 bp (see Worksheet 2.8).

In practice, futures are not exactly 3 months apart; sometimes they gap, sometimes overlap. If it is deemed necessary, then one approach is as follows (see Worksheet 2.9 for precise details):

1.   Convert the simple interest rates in column [1] into daily compounded rates in [2] to place them all on the same basis.
2.   Create a set of non-overlapping contiguous periods as shown in [3] and [4].
3.   For periods that are uniquely defined, simply copy over the compounded rates.
4.   For periods that are undefined, such as 15 to 21 June, take the average of the two neighbouring periods, i.e. $0.5 * (6.152\% + 6.447\%) = 6.300\%$.
5.   For periods that are defined twice, such as 20 to 21 September, again take the average.
6.   Once column [5] has been completed, then convert the rates back to simple interest and calculate the discount curve in the usual way; see columns [6] and [7].

The pricing difference in this case is negligible. However, such an approach can be invaluable for the estimation of short-dated forwards of FRAs over a gap or overlap.

An alternative way of pricing the swap (see Worksheet 2.10) is:

● estimate the Libor fixings off 3 mo. cash and the futures strip as before;
● calculate the DFs from the estimated Libor strip directly—this requires no interpolation.

The fair price is 2.7647%, a change of only 0.01bp. This approach is very efficient, but can only really be used when the cashflows are quarterly (as in this case), whereas the other approach is more general.

The alternative approaches, whilst more efficient and correct than the original model, have made no significant difference to the pricing. However, now return to the hedging of this swap. Because futures affect the swap through both the estimation and discounting processes, it is easiest to use numerical perturbation to estimate the impact of changing market conditions. In turn, each of the futures prices were perturbed downwards by 1 bp (equivalent to a rate increase of 1 bp, which is conventional), and the change in the value of the swap noted; see column [9] headed PV01 (Present Value of 1 bp, also known as PVBP) in either of the two above worksheets. This is often called "blipping" a curve, i.e. take a curve of rates, perturb one rate, note the change in value, return the perturbed rate to its original value and move on to the next rate. The hedge amounts are now calculated by dividing the PV01 by, in this case, $25 for a Eurodollar future to give the number of futures contracts required. The end result is frequently described as a value or "tailed" hedge.

The effectiveness of the hedge, in contrast with the previous one, is shown below. For small changes, the net effect is very close to zero, as expected. But, more interestingly, another phenomenon has arisen, namely that the net effect is always positive! The transaction plus hedge cannot lose irrespective of what happens to rates. This is an example of what is known as a "convexity (or gamma) effect".

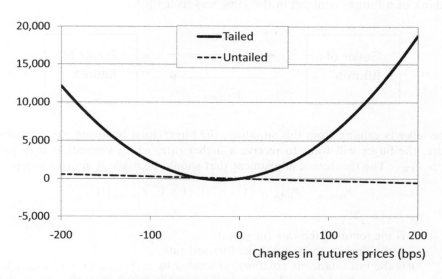

Hedge effectiveness

2.4 CONVEXITY BIAS IN FUTURES

How does this convexity bias arise? Consider a very simple situation, namely selling an IMM FRA at a rate of F_{FRA} and selling a single deposit futures at a rate of $F_{futures}$ to hedge. Obviously the tenor of the rates and the dates all match. So, would we expect F_{FRA} and $F_{futures}$ to match as well? Consider what happens when rates move. If, for example, rates go up, the FRA has to pay out a higher cashflow, whereas the futures will receive margin. But the key question is when? The futures margin is received immediately, but the increased FRA cashflow is only paid away at some date in the future. The longer the FRA, the greater the difference between the PV of the increased FRA cashflow and the margin cashflow.

Assume that we wish the cashflows to match dates; we will therefore invest the futures margin until the cashflow date on the FRA. But at what rate can we invest? As we surmised, rates have gone up, therefore at a high rate, which must be beneficial. The converse of this is true if rates drop—see diagram below.

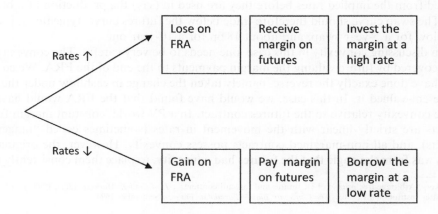

This is a second-order win–win situation, investing at high rates, borrowing at low rates. If we think of a futures contract in the same way as a FRA:

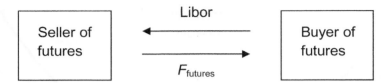

If the seller is gaining from this situation, the buyer must be losing. As compensation therefore, the buyer will want to receive a higher rate, which suggests that in practice, $F_{\text{futures}} > F_{\text{FRA}}$. The theoretical adjustment that should be made is approximately:

$$F_{\text{futures}} - F_{\text{FRA}} = (1 - e^{-\varphi}) \cdot (1 + \Gamma \cdot F_{\text{futures}})/\Gamma$$

where $\quad \varphi = \frac{1}{2}v^2 \cdot t^2 \cdot \Gamma$;

Γ is the tenor of the rate (in years);

t is the time to the *start* of the forward rate;

v is the instantaneous volatility, estimated by $\sigma \cdot F_{\text{futures}}/(1 + \Gamma \cdot F_{\text{futures}})$;

σ is the normal forward rate volatility usually taken from the cap market.

This expression was derived using the HJM approach—see later—and assumes continuous margining and constant volatility, i.e. no reversion. It is feasible to derive formulae with these effects, see for example Flesaker,[7] but they are negligible in practice.

The table on the opposite page shows that the adjustment is small for under say 2 years, and was therefore ignored by many people for quite a long time. In 1992, the spread between swaps and the unadjusted futures curve was very close to zero. However, as the Eurodollar futures market at the CME was extended to 10 years in 1993, and practitioners started pricing swaps off 5-year futures strips, the adjustments became exponentially sizeable and were taken into account.

The adjustment in the 5-year forward rate calculated above is approximately 18 bp. In practice, this adjustment was estimated to be in the range 12 to 22 bp over the period from 1989 to 1994 with an average of 17 bp.[8] Obviously, to use the futures rates in the estimation of Libor forward rates and swap discount factors, the adjustment factors should be deducted from the implied rates before they are used in (say) the production of a blended curve. The swap curve should therefore trade below the futures curve; typically, it is about 6 bp below for a 5-year swap, and about 18 bp for a 10-year one.

When discussing convexity in this case, one needs to be very careful. The convexity bias was discovered by future valuing the margin payments to the end of the FRA. We could of course have done exactly the reverse, namely taken the change in cashflow under the FRA and present-valued it. In this case, we would have found that the FRA would have had positive convexity relative to the futures contract. In a PV world, constant margin futures contracts are strictly linear with the movement in rates (sometimes called "tangential" contracts), and all non-margined contracts possess convexity. However, the original discussion was from the angle that the futures had convexity, to place them consistently into a

[7] B. Flesaker, "Arbitrage free pricing of IR futures and forward contracts", *J. of Futures Markets*, **13**(1), 1993, 77–91.

[8] Dean Witter Institutional Futures, *The Convexity Bias in Eurodollar Futures*, September 1994.

Futures	Futures price	Forward volatility	Adjustment (bp)
Mar-95	9254	9.71%	0.01
Jun-95	9334	10.09%	0.06
Sep-95	9315	10.97%	0.16
Dec-95	9310	12.49%	0.36
Mar-96	9302	13.70%	0.70
Jun-96	9296	14.55%	1.15
Sep-96	9287	15.04%	1.72
Dec-96	9290	15.13%	2.25
Mar-97	9286	15.36%	2.97
Jun-97	9283	15.73%	3.89
Sep-97	9276	16.26%	5.12
Dec-97	9277	16.94%	6.60
Mar-98	9272	17.29%	8.17
Jun-98	9269	17.29%	9.56
Sep-98	9261	16.95%	10.78
Dec-98	9262	16.26%	11.25
Mar-99	9257	15.73%	12.04
Jun-99	9252	15.36%	13.04
Sep-99	9244	15.15%	14.43
Dec-99	9245	15.10%	15.86
Mar-00	9238	15.05%	17.69
Jun-00	9232	15.00%	19.72
Sep-00	9224	14.95%	21.84
Dec-00	9225	14.89%	23.52
Mar-01	9218	14.83%	25.76
Jun-01	9212	14.76%	28.04
Sep-01	9204	14.70%	30.57
Dec-01	9208	14.63%	32.23
Mar-02	9292	14.56%	27.44

non-margined world. Convexity effects for more complex swaps will be discussed in Chapter 7.

2.5 FORWARD VALUING A SWAP

Before we finish with this structure, we are going to price the swap from a different point of view. The swap bank is paying the floating, receiving fixed. This implies that, at the end of the first quarter, it has to find $786,250 to pay away. Where does it get the money? Assume the money could be borrowed at Libor flat for a period of three months:

$$\$786,250 * (1 + 0.256 * 2.7837\%) = \$791,843$$

At the end of the period, the borrowing would have to be repaid, presumably by another borrowing. But of course another payment of $711,399 is also due. The new amount to be borrowed is $791,843 + $711,399 = $1,503,243. This process is then continued until the end of the year; at this point, a single fixed cashflow is received which can be used to repay all the borrowings. For the swap to be fair, the net cashflow on the maturity date should be zero. Solving for the fair fixed rate gives 2.7647%, exactly the same as before. This is a demonstration of a very important fact: discounting off a Libor curve is exactly the same as reinvesting at the implied forward rates (see Worksheet 2.11).

This approach permits a further consideration. An alternative view is that swap cash payments are tantamount to lending the counterparty money. What would be a fair rate for this counterparty, bearing in mind its relative creditworthiness? For example, if we assume that we would only lend to this particular counterparty at Libor + 100 bp, how should the pricing on the swap be adjusted? If we use this rate Libor + 100 bp as our effective borrowing cost in each period, then the new fair price for the swap can be calculated. In this case, the fixed rate rises by about 4 bp to 2.770%.

Conventionally, swap pricing assumes that banks can always fund themselves at Libor flat. In reality, this is seldom the case. This forward-valuing approach can be applied to embed the bank's funding cost into a swap. It will be applied to more complex transactions later.

3
Generic Interest Rate Swaps

OBJECTIVE

The previous chapter discussed short-term IRS, priced and hedged off a futures strip. Such a strip will not go out very far, and medium to long-term swaps are much more closely related to the bond market. This chapter first introduces a generic or "vanilla" swap, and shows how it may be regarded either as an exchange of cashflows, or as a link between two distinct markets. The pricing of a generic swap is then explored, first through the concept of comparative advantage, and then through the mechanism of hedging the two sides separately. During this latter process, we discuss a widely held belief in the swap market, namely the floating side of a generic swap including notional principals has no value. This leads us on to identification of the fixed side as a par bond, and to a discussion of the relationship between the bond and swap market. Hedging swaps with bonds to protect against interest rates changing adversely is quite common, but we also explore what would happen to such a hedge if the rates do not move: namely, cost-of-carry issues. Finally the chapter concludes with the description of various ways, some bad but popular and some good, to imply discount factors for a given set of generic market data.

3.1 GENERIC INTEREST RATE SWAPS

A generic or "plain vanilla" interest rate swap (a term probably first coined by the swap group at Salomon Brothers in the mid-1980s) is the simplest form of medium-term IRS. These constitute the vast bulk of interbank trading. Because of their maturity, they are associated far more with an underlying bond market than a deposit futures market for hedging. A generic USD swap is defined in Table 3.1.

The important elements of the definition are:

- The minimum maturity typically reflects the length of the liquid futures market: this is obviously currency-specific.
- The maximum maturity usually indicates the end of the very liquid swap market for which the bid–offer spread is tightest and constant. Brokers' quotes for US dollars are currently on a 3 bp spread out for 50 years—see screenshot overleaf—whereas sterling, for example, is on a 4 bp spread for the first two years, but then widens rapidly after that to 17 bp for 50 years. The bid–offer spreads quoted by an individual active trader would be much tighter than this; for the major currencies, typically down to 0.5 bp;
- The settlement date depends on the convention in the floating rate reference market. For example, in US dollars, euros and most currencies, this would be 2 business days after the trade date. For sterling and many of the old Commonwealth currencies, it is the same day, and so on.
- A generic swap is a "spot" swap, therefore the fixed rate is the current market rate.

Table 3.1   Generic US dollar swap terms

Maturity	5–50 years
Trade date	Date of agreeing to enter into the swap
Settlement date	2 business days after trade date

Fixed side

Fixed coupon	Current market rate
Frequency	Annual
Daycount	Act/360
Pricing date	Trade date

Floating side

Floating index	USD 3-month Libor
Spread	None
Payment frequency	Tenor of the floating index
Daycount	Act/360
Reset frequency	Tenor of floating index
First coupon	Current market rate for index
Premium/discount	None

```
GRAB                                              Curncy ICAU
200<Go> to view in Launchpad
 8:53  Intercapital  -  USD  Swaps           PAGE  1  /  2
    USD Swap Rates vs 3 Month Libor        USD Swap
    vs. LIBOR     Ask      Bid     Time    Spreads      Ask      Bid     Time
 1)  1 Year     2.638    2.608    8:53  18)  2 Year    86.250   83.250   8:36
 2)  2 Year     2.743    2.713    8:53  19)  3 Year    89.500   86.500   7:05
 3)  3 Year     3.066    3.036    8:53  20)  4 Year    92.500   89.500   8:38
 4)  4 Year     3.386    3.356    8:53  21)  5 Year    92.250   89.250   8:35
 5)  5 Year     3.671    3.641    8:53  22)  6 Year    96.250   93.250   7:05
 6)  6 Year     3.921    3.891    8:53  23)  7 Year    95.250   92.250   8:31
 7)  7 Year     4.121    4.091    8:53  24)  8 Year    91.000   88.000   7:05
 8)  8 Year     4.288    4.258    8:53  25)  9 Year    84.250   81.250   7:05
 9)  9 Year     4.429    4.399    8:53  26) 10 Year    75.000   72.000   8:34
10) 10 Year     4.546    4.516    8:53  27) 12 Year    94.000   91.000   8:34
11) 12 Year     4.738    4.708    8:53  28) 15 Year    92.500   89.500   7:37
12) 15 Year     4.932    4.902    8:53  29) 20 Year    87.250   84.250   7:36
13) 20 Year     5.088    5.058    8:53  30) 25 Year    72.000   69.000   7:05
14) 25 Year     5.143    5.113    8:53  31) 30 Year    53.250   50.250   7:05
15) 30 Year     5.163    5.133    8:53  32) 40 Year    53.750   50.750   7:05
16) 40 Year     5.168    5.138    8:53  Day Count: ANN ACT/360
17) 50 Year     5.158    5.128    8:53  33) EDU2 Curncy


Australia 61 2 9777 8600 Brazil 5511 3048 4500 Europe 44 20 7330 7500 Germany 49 69 9204 1210 Hong Kong 852 2977 6000
Japan 81 3 3201 8900      Singapore 65 6212 1000      U.S. 1 212 318 2000      Copyright 2008 Bloomberg Finance L.P.
                                                                              H178-644-0 15-Feb-08  8:53:44
```

Screen shot showing USD swap curve on 15 February 2008 (*source*: ICAP plc).

- The frequency of the fixed side usually matches the frequency of the coupon in the hedging government bond market; for example, sterling swaps are semi-annual reflecting the semi-annual coupons in the gilts market. But there are exceptions to this, such as USD where the swaps are usually quoted annually whilst the T-bond pays semi-annually, and the South African market where the swaps are quoted quarterly whilst the bonds pay semi-annually.
- The daycount convention on the fixed side again often but not invariably matches the underlying bond conventions. US T-bonds are Act/Act, the fixed side of the swaps is usually quoted Act/360; euro government bond are also Act/Act, but euro swaps are quoted 30/360; sterling uses Act/365 for both bonds and swaps. If the USD swap is quoted on an ACT/360 basis, then it is often described as being on a money market basis; if the convention is 30/360, it is said to be on a bond basis.
- The floating side almost invariably follows the convention in the domestic money market. For US dollars and Euribor, Libor is fixed two business days before the start of each floating or roll-over period, and paid at the end of the period using the Act/360 daycount convention. Therefore the first fixing is the current Libor rate.
- It is important that the tenor of the floating rate, its frequency of reset fixings, and the frequency of payment all match: for example, if the floating rate is 3 mo. Libor, then Libor is re-fixed at the beginning of each 3-month period and paid at the end of each 3-month period. It is perfectly feasible to get mismatch swaps, where these conditions are not true, such as using 6 mo. Libor but paying every 3 months as we shall see later, but these are not generic swaps. Some of the generic swaps traded in the domestic US market, with reference rates such as the weekly T-bill fixings, violate these conditions; these will be discussed later.
- Finally there is no spread on the floating rate, nor any lump sum payments, indicating that both counterparties deem the swap to be "fair", i.e. its initial value at mid-rates should be zero.

Interestingly, whilst the definition includes a statement on the range of possible maturities of a generic swap, it does not include any guidance as to the likely size of the underlying principal to which the interest rates are applied. Market practice would probably imply $10m–$50m; that is not to say that larger swaps could not be obtained relatively routinely, it is just that the bid–offer spread on the pricing might be slightly wider.

Table 3.2 shows the cashflows generated by a 7-year generic US dollar swap. Notice that, as in the earlier money market swap example, the periods are adjusted for non-business days, and the receipts on the fixed side of the swap reflect these adjustments. This is in contrast with the bond market, when interest will also only be paid on a business day but the amount will not vary. It is necessary to take these different conventions into account when structuring a bond–swap package, as we shall see later. The Libor values, other than the first fixing, are of course not known.

A generic swap is usually considered as an agreement to exchange two streams of cashflows, one calculated with reference to a fixed rate of interest and the other with reference to a floating rate. We can however change the frame of reference if we pretend that the notional principal amounts (NPA) are also exchanged at the beginning and end of the swap, as shown in Table 3.3.

The (pretend) exchange does not affect the economic reality of the swap, as the NPAs are assumed to be paid and received *simultaneously* at the start and end of the swap. However, the swap may now be thought of as:

- buying a fixed rate bond (albeit with slightly uneven coupon payments);
- either: issuing or selling a Floating Rate Note at Libor flat
  - or: borrowing money on the money markets.

In either case, it may be considered as an instrument that links together two distinct markets.

Table 3.2   Cashflows of a generic 7-year swap

Trade date:	4-Feb-08
Settlement date:	6-Feb-08
Notional principal:	100 million
Maturity:	7 years
To receive fixed rate:	3.885% ANN, Act/360
To pay floating rate:	3 mo. Libor
First Libor fixing:	3.145%

	Days (Act/360)	Fixed cashflows	Floating cashflows
6-Feb-08			
6-May-08	0.250		−786,250
6-Aug-08	0.256		−Libor
6-Nov-08	0.256		−Libor
6-Feb-09	0.256	3,949,750.00	−Libor
6-May-09	0.247		−Libor
6-Aug-09	0.256		−Libor
6-Nov-09	0.256		−Libor
8-Feb-10	0.261	3,960,541.67	−Libor
6-May-10	0.242		−Libor
6-Aug-10	0.256		−Libor
8-Nov-10	0.261		−Libor
7-Feb-11	0.253	3,928,166.67	−Libor
6-May-11	0.244		−Libor
8-Aug-11	0.261		−Libor
7-Nov-11	0.253		−Libor
6-Feb-12	0.253	3,928,166.67	−Libor
7-May-12	0.253		−Libor
6-Aug-12	0.253		−Libor
6-Nov-12	0.256		−Libor
6-Feb-13	0.256	3,949,750.00	−Libor
6-May-13	0.247		−Libor
6-Aug-13	0.256		−Libor
6-Nov-13	0.256		−Libor
6-Feb-14	0.256	3,938,958.33	−Libor
6-May-14	0.247		−Libor
6-Aug-14	0.256		−Libor
6-Nov-14	0.256		−Libor
6-Feb-15	0.256	3,938,958.33	−Libor

Table 3.3 Cashflows of a generic swap with notional exchange

	Fixed cashflows	Floating cashflows
6-Feb-08	−100,000,000	100,000,000
6-May-08		−786,250
6-Aug-08		−Libor
6-Nov-08		−Libor
6-Feb-09	3,949,750	−Libor
6-May-09		−Libor
6-Aug-09		−Libor
6-Nov-09		−Libor
8-Feb-10	3,960,542	−Libor
6-May-10		−Libor
6-Aug-10		−Libor
8-Nov-10		−Libor
7-Feb-11	3,928,167	−Libor
6-May-11		−Libor
8-Aug-11		−Libor
7-Nov-11		−Libor
6-Feb-12	3,928,167	−Libor
7-May-12		−Libor
6-Aug-12		−Libor
6-Nov-12		−Libor
6-Feb-13	3,949,750	−Libor
6-May-13		−Libor
6-Aug-13		−Libor
6-Nov-13		−Libor
6-Feb-14	3,938,958	−Libor
6-May-14		−Libor
6-Aug-14		−Libor
6-Nov-14		−Libor
6-Feb-15	103,938,958	−(Libor + 100,000,000)

3.2 PRICING THROUGH COMPARATIVE ADVANTAGE

There are various ways of pricing financial instruments. Probably the most common is to price an instrument relative to similar instruments already in the marketplace. But this begs the questions as to how do the first instruments receive their price. A second approach is to estimate the cost of replicating the instrument using financial instruments drawn from other, more liquid, financial markets. However, the oldest method is to identify a price which will provide both the seller and the buyer with some perceived economic benefit, i.e. an arbitrage price. This last method was most common in the early days of the swaps market, but as the market has grown in size and increased in speed, the first and second approaches are far more prevalent. Nevertheless it is important to understand the last, as fundamentally it is this rationale that drives the market.

Recall the EIB–TVA swap described in Chapter 1. Briefly, the EIB wished to borrow DEM, and the TVA USD; their funding costs are shown below:

	USD	DEM
EIB	$T + 17$	$B + 13$
TVA	$T + 24$	$B + 17$
Spread	7 bp	4 bp

We could use this information to price a swap. Remember, the upshot was that the EIB issued a USD bond at $T + 17$ bp, and the TVA issued a DEM bond at $B + 17$ bp as shown below. They entered into a swap, where m is the "price". What is a fair price?

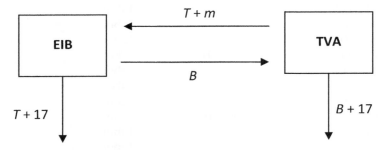

If we look at their net costs of funds:

	EIB	TVA
Cost of bond	$-(T + 17)$	$-(B + 17)$
Receipt on swap	$+T + m$	$+B$
Payment under swap	$-B$	$-(T + m)$
Net cost	$-(B + 17 - m)$	$-(T + 17 + m)$

To make the swap attractive to both parties, the net costs must be less than funding directly in the markets, i.e: $17 - m < 13$ bp for EIB, and $17 + m < 24$ bp for TVA.

The margin therefore must lie in the range of $4 < m < 7$. If the advantage were divided equally, then $m = 5\frac{1}{2}$ bp.

The underlying principle is that the two counterparties will both perceive a benefit from entering into a swap at some agreed price. It is important to stress that the key word is *perceive*, namely it is feasible for two parties to do a swap if they have strongly held but diametrically opposite views as to the future movement of interest rates. More likely however is when the parties have asymmetric advantages, for example different access to markets. It is frequently argued that such arbitrages will disappear as markets become more efficient. However, there are many sources that consistently distort markets such as governments with asymmetric taxation and cheap subsidisation, investors with arbitrary credit limits, capital regulations on banks with existing exposures, different perceptions of credit pricing, and so on, that suggest the arbitrages will continue.

It is possible to create a matrix of comparative advantage, which may be used to identify opportunities. Consider the following (simplified) US market data:

	Bond market	**Interbank money market**
US government	B	$L - 12\,\text{bp}$
Governmental agencies	$B + 3$	$L - 10\,\text{bp}$
Banks	$B + 25$	L
Financial institutions	$B + 35$	$L + 5\,\text{bp}$
Prime corporates	$B + 50$	$L + 10\,\text{bp}$
Lower credit corporates	$B + 100$	$L + 40\,\text{bp}$

This table conveys two main messages, namely that the cost of borrowing increases as the creditworthiness of the borrower decreases, and secondly that the relative cost of borrowing is typically much lower in the floating rate market than in the fixed rate market. There are a variety of reasons for this:

- Because the floating rates are reset periodically back to the current market rates, the potential credit exposure for the lender on fixed interest payments is considerably greater than on floating payments.
- Margins are in part determined by supply and demand, with the floating rate loan market usually being far larger and more liquid than the fixed rate bond market.

The second message can lead to potential swap opportunities. If we take an extreme (and totally unrealistic) situation, suppose:

- US Government wished to borrow floating;
- Lower-credit Corporate wished to borrow fixed.

If each went directly to the relevant market, this would cost a total of $(L - 12) + (B + 100) = B + L + 88\,\text{bp}$ (assuming that the basis points in the two markets are "additive"). However, the Lower-credit Corporate only pays 52 bp more than the Government in the floating market, compared to at least 100 bp in the fixed market. Therefore a cheaper way of raising the money would be for:

- Government to borrow fixed rate at B;
- Lower-credit Corporate to borrow floating rate at $L + 40\,\text{bp}$; and
- enter into a swap with each other

resulting in a total cost of $B + L + 40\,\text{bp}$, ie. saving 48 bp. The figure below shows the current arrangement:

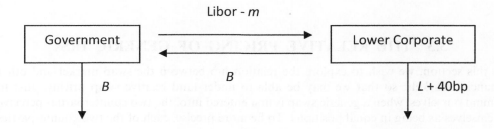

Using the same argument as above, namely "what margin m would make this transaction attractive to both counterparties?", we can calculate the net cost of funds for each party:

	Government	**Lower-credit Corporate**
Net cost of funds	$-(L - m)$	$-(B + 40 + m)$

To make this transaction attractive to them both, $12 < m < 60$. For example, assume that $m = 40$ bp. The net funding cost to the Government is $L - 40$ bp; a saving of 28bp. The Corporate funds itself at $B + 80$ bp; a saving of 20bp. Both parties achieve cheaper funding, with a total saving as expected of 48 bp divided between them.

The source of the saving is that the Government, as the stronger credit, is prepared to take a different credit view on the Lower-credit Corporate than the fixed rate market. This is tempered by the fact that the Government is not taking a risk on the principal amount of the borrowing, merely on the difference between the fixed and floating swap payments. In practice, the pricing of the swap would be by negotiation, and obviously the stronger credit has considerably more power. Also a bank would be typically acting as an intermediary and credit guarantor, and would require part of the savings.

Such an example is extreme and unrealistic. A more realistic matrix of comparative advantage may be as follows:

Table 3.4   Matrix of comparative advantage

	US government	Govern-mental agencies	Banks	Financial institutions	Prime corporates	Lower-credit corporates
US Government	—	1	13	18	28	48
Governmental agencies		—	12	17	27	47
Banks			—	5	15	35
Financial institutions				—	10	30
Prime corporates					—	20

where the figures are: (difference in fixed funding) less (difference in floating funding)

This suggests the apparent savings that may be made between pairs of counterparties; for example, a bank entering into a swap with a prime corporate credit might achieve an overall saving of 15 bp.

3.3   THE RELATIVE PRICING OF GENERIC IRSs

In this section, we wish to explore the relationship between the swap market and other financial markets, so that we may be able to understand relative swap pricing. Just to remind ourselves, when a generic swap is first entered into, the two counterparties perceive themselves as being in equal positions. To be more precise, each of the two counterparties perceive that the total value of the anticipated receipts is not less than the total value of the anticipated payments. If we assume the two counterparties use the same valuation process, and that they have the same access to the market, then this reduces to:

"Value of Receipts = Value of Payments"

or alternatively

"Net Value of Swap = 0"

If this equality were not true, then one party would deem itself to be disadvantaged and refuse to enter into this freely negotiated contract until the appropriate changes were made.

As we have already seen, a generic swap may be broken down into streams of cashflows, some generated with reference to a fixed interest rate, others possibly with reference to a variable rate. When we discussed the valuation of cashflows in money market swaps, we either discounted them back to the day of analysis, which is the commonest method, or future-valued them to the end of the swap. We will use discounting as the main method of analysis, and therefore the above expression may be modified to:

"Present Value of Receipts = Present Value of Payments"

We showed above how a generic swap may also be represented as two synthetic instruments, a fixed rate bond (with slightly uneven coupon) and a money market transaction involving principal cashflows at the beginning and end. Assume this swap has the maturity of T, and just consider the floating side, which we have assumed to be paying. The PV of the payments is (assuming a notional principal of 1):

$$+1 - \sum_k L_k * d_k * DF_k - DF_T \text{ summing from } k = 1 \text{ to } T$$

where d_k is the length of time from t_{k-1} to t_k;
          L_k is the forward rate fixed at t_{k-1} and paid at t_k.

The general formula for a forward rate—see Chapter 2—is:

$$L_k = [(DF_{k-1}/DF_k) - 1]/d_k$$

Substituting into the above:

$$PV = +1 - \sum_k (DF_{k-1} - DF_k) - DF_T = 0 \quad \text{as } DF_0 = 1$$

An intuitive interpretation of this result may be gained from the following. Consider the cashflows on the floating side:

a.   receive $100 million upfront;
b.   pays interest at Libor flat;
c.   repay the $100 million at maturity;

as shown below:

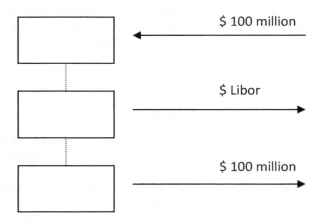

What do we do with the (notional) $100m received upfront. The obvious answer is to lend it out. Assume that we are a bank that can borrow or lend/deposit money at Libor ± margin within a marketplace, as shown below. The overall economic value of this floating transaction therefore depends solely upon the achievable margin, and not upon the particular levels of Libor. In particular, if the margin were zero, then the transaction would also have a zero value, which would lead in turn to the following statement:

"Value of a generic floating side of a swap, including the notional principals, is zero"

which was of course what we proved earlier:

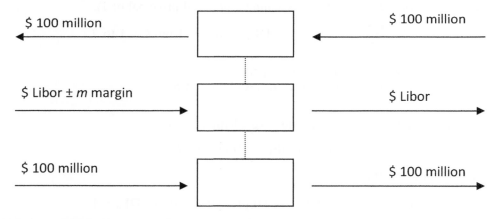

Understanding this aspect of swaps is absolutely key to the pricing of swaps. Suppose, in the example above, that the margin for depositing is −10 bp. The floating side would therefore be effectively making a running loss of $100m ∗ 10 bp = $100,000 pa or roughly $700,000 over the lifetime of the swap. This money would have to be recovered from the fixed side, which would have to be increased by (roughly) 10 bp above the current market, thus making it uncompetitive. Alternatively, if the $100m could have been lent out at a margin above Libor, then this value could have been used to subsidise the fixed side of the swap. So swap pricing should depend in part directly upon the abilities of banks to raise or to place money in their various local money markets; this in turn depends upon their creditworthiness and the liquidity of the market. For example, one highly rated European bank was able to raise funds a few years ago at an average cost of {Libor − 6 bp}, whereas for most of the 1990s, Japanese banks have been unable to borrow USD at Libor, but have had to pay a "Japanese premium" which ranged up to some 40 bp.

However, in practice, many banks assume, implicitly or explicitly, that the funding margin for the purpose of pricing swaps is Libor flat. The European bank above, for example, had instructed its swap desk to assume a funding cost of Libor flat for pricing purposes, so that the prices are not being subsidised by the bank's credit rating.[1] Many swap-pricing systems do not permit a true funding cost to be entered, but tacitly assume Libor flat.

It could be argued that if a swap portfolio is relatively flat, ie. the payments and receipts approximately balance, then this assumption is unnecessary. Unfortunately portfolios are seldom flat, unless they have been constructed over an entire economic cycle. When interest rates are perceived high, then most end users wish to pay floating and to receive fixed. The reverse is true when rates are low. Therefore demand for new swaps is frequently one-way round, creating an imbalance for a market maker.

A generic swap is a medium-term instrument; in this instance, the counterparties are committed to meeting their obligations for 7 years. How realistic is it to assume their creditworthinesses will remain constant, and hence their ability to raise or to deposit money, over the lifetime of the swap? The average funding cost for USD of one of the largest US banks increased to {Libor + 2 bp} during the height of the S&L crisis in the late 1980s. All its swap pricing—plus P&L and bonuses—had been calculated on the basis of Libor flat, so suddenly its (extremely large) swap portfolio started to haemorrhage profits!

Nevertheless, the assumption of zero margin is widely made, and we will (albeit with reservations) do the same for the remainder of this book. We will however show how to modify the pricing to include the funding cost for some structures later in the book.[2]

3.4 THE RELATIONSHIP BETWEEN THE BOND AND SWAP MARKETS

Turning to the fixed side of the swap, we can immediately therefore conclude that:

"Value of the fixed side of a generic swap, including the notional principals, is zero"

because the net value must equal zero. However, this synthetic "bond" satisfies three conditions:

- its current price is par, i.e. $100m;
- it is redeemed at par at maturity;
- the first period is a full period, or alternatively the accrued interest is zero.

Bonds that satisfy these conditions are known as par (yield) bonds, with the property that the yield to maturity equals the coupon of the bond. For the generic 7-year swap, the fixed rate is 3.885% ANN Act/360 whilst its yield is 3.884%—see Worksheet 3.2. The very slight difference is due to the impact of non-business days.

---

[1] At the time of writing this in late 2008, the short-term interbank had suffered considerable illiquidity, causing the spread over comparable rates such as Fed Funds to widen enormously relative to historic levels. This in turn meant that to fund the floating side on a swap could be extremely expensive, and hence highly unattractive. Ignoring the impact of funding on swap pricing during this time could be literally life-threatening for a swap desk.

[2] As indeed we have already done so for the money market swap using forward valuing.

Let us now turn the argument on its head. We are a swap market maker who has just been asked to make a price for a generic 7-year swap. We could turn to the bond market to identify the current yield of a 7-year par bond. Obviously such a bond will not be trading, but it can be estimated by interpolating the benchmark curve to give 3.051%.

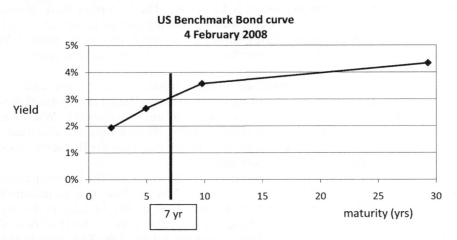

Unfortunately, the most liquid bond market in most countries is the governmental market, which is by definition deemed to be of a higher credit rating than the average interbank swap market, generally considered to be somewhere between AA− and A+. This implies that the equivalent bond yield is likely to be lower than that quoted in the swap market. Nevertheless, it is a starting point.

Bond yields are interpolated[3] from the benchmark bonds, the most liquid being 2, 5, 10 and 30 years maturity. The table shows mid-spreads and mid-swap rates.

US benchmark bonds

	Time to maturity	YTM sa	Spread	Yield + spread	ANN	Change daycount	Swap rates
06-Feb-08							
Jan-10	1.942	**1.94%**	87.00	2.8100%	2.830%	2.791%	2.795%
Jan-13	4.945	**2.66%**	86.00	3.5200%	3.551%	3.502%	3.505%
Nov-17	9.781	**3.58%**	70.00	4.2800%	4.326%	4.267%	4.265%
May-37	29.290	**4.34%**	48.00	4.8200%	4.878%	4.811%	4.815%
04-Feb-15	7.000	3.051%	85.00	3.9009%	3.939%	3.885%	3.885%

To convert from the bond yield, which is quoted on a semi-annual Act/Act basis, to a swap basis requires the following calculations:

- take the 7-year bond yield of 3.051%;
- add the spread of 85 bp = 3.901%;
- convert the bond to annual by $(1 + 0.5 * 3.901\%)^2 - 1 = 3.939\%$;
- convert the daycount by multiplying by $(360/365) = 3.885\%$.

(Note: there may be small differences due to rounding; see Worksheet 3.3 for more details.)

---

[3] The US Treasury currently uses a quasi-cubic Hermite spline function for interpolation—see *http://www.treas.gov/offices/domestic-finance/debt-management/interest-rate/yieldmethod.html* for details.

So the first and most important reason for the swap spread is the difference in credit between the underlying bond market and the interbank swap market. In the mid-1990s, the South African swap market was frequently quoted at very little spread off the government (and paristatal, i.e. quasi-governmental organisation) bond curve. One reason was the major financial institutions were perceived, locally at least, to be as creditworthy as the government. Indeed the long end of the swap was often significantly, i.e. 30 or 40 bp, below the bond curve. There was a similar situation in Italy at the same time, when certain Italian organisations could raise money more cheaply in the international bond market than the Italian government.

But there are other influences on the apparent spread. As we have already suggested, demand for paying or receiving swaps is seldom balanced, but depends upon the perception of the economic cycle. If rates are perceived to be low and therefore likely to increase, most end users want to pay fixed, receive floating. The market maker, observing the high demand for paying fixed, will in turn increase the fixed quote which is effectively equivalent to widening the spread. In this fashion the demand will be managed. Conversely, when rates are perceived to be high and will only come down, then the spread is reduced. An extreme case of this occurred in the early 1990s in Germany, when interest rates were increased substantially to fund the reunification, driving the swap spread down until at times it became negative! Obviously such an arbitrage situation is seldom sustainable for long periods. The spread in yen swaps often used to go negative in the run-up to the banking financial year-end of March, as Japanese banks would enter into swaps to pay floating, receive fixed from Western banks. For a normal, positive, swap curve, the floating rates would initially be below the fixed rate, and therefore the Japanese bank would make an immediate accrual profit.

A third major reason for the spread is the cost of hedging a swap portfolio. Consider a simple situation in which a bank has just entered into a swap to pay fixed, receive floating. The swap could be hedged by buying a specific bond, as follows:

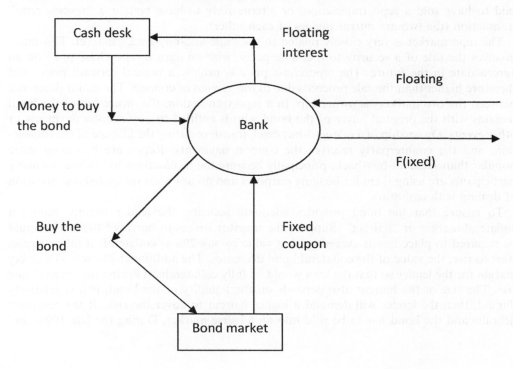

For reasons of liquidity, the bond is likely to be governmental. If interest rates fall, the swap loses in value, but the bond value increases. Hopefully, if the hedge is calculated correctly, one will off-set the other, as we shall see in Chapter 12.

But suppose rates do not change at all. Do we make money, lose money or remain flat? Over 1 day, we will:

- pay accrued interest F on the swap;
- receive accrued interest C on the bond;
- receive accrued floating interest L on the swap;
- pay accrued floating interest L on the borrowing.

Assuming the bond is trading close to par, in other words the nominal amount of the bond to be bought would be similar to the notional principal of the swap, then every day we would effectively lose $\{(F - C) * P * 1 - \text{day}\}$ where $(F - C)$ represents the swap spread, as the Libor cashflows would cancel. This carry-cost must be included in the pricing. In normal circumstances, such a hedge would only be held for a short period, so the total carry-cost over this period would then be spread over the lifetime of the swap, and as such would be fairly negligible. However, if the swap market was very illiquid, so that the hedge would have to sit in place for a long period, then the carry-cost would become very significant and would drive the fixed rate F closer to the bond coupon C. This is part of the argument in South Africa in the mid-1990s, as to why the swap spread was so close to zero.

In practice, the market maker is more likely to use the bond repurchase (or "repo") market than the cash market, as this allows practitioners to go long or short bonds more efficiently and cheaply. Briefly, the repo market operates as follows. Consider an investor who owns a bond. He can partially fund his bond position by borrowing money and providing the bond as collateral. Usually the interest charged on the borrowing, the repo rate, is lower than Libor, as the credit risks are lower due to the collateralisation. He is said to have sold a repo transaction, or alternatively to have bought a "reverse repo" transaction (the two are mirror images of each other).

The repo market is very closely related to the "sale-and-buy-back" market. This latter involves the sale of a security to a counterparty, with an agreed repurchase price on an agreed date in the future. The repurchase price is usually a neutral forward price, and therefore higher than the sale proceeds due to the accrual of coupon. The major difference between the two markets is ownership. In a repo transaction, the ownership of the bond remains with the original buyer of the bond who is entitled to any coupon payments or other events. Ownership in a sale-and-buy-back transfers during the lifetime of the transaction, and the counterparty receives the coupon payments. Repos are becoming more popular than sale-and-buy-back, principally because the transactions are cleaner as many participants are using them for hedging purposes and do not want the added complication of dealing with cashflows.

To ensure that the bond provides adequate security, the lender usually defines a collateral margin or "haircut". Suppose the investor wishes to borrow $100m. He would be required to place bonds exceeding that value by say 2% as collateral. If interest rates start to rise, the value of the collateral bond decreases. The additional 2% acts as a safety margin for the lender so that the loan would be fully collateralised during this interest rate rise. The size of the haircut also depends on the liquidity of the bond; if it is relatively illiquid, then the lender will demand a higher haircut to cover the risks if the borrower defaults and the bond has to be sold into an adverse market. During the late 1990s and early 2000s, the US and Western European governments moved into budget surpluses, with the concomitant decline in the size of their bond markets. Repo transactions were extended to non-governmental bonds, but with increases in the haircut.

Most repos are transacted on a general collateral (GC) basis, i.e. a general interest rate is applied irrespective of the security. If you wanted a specific bond as collateral, then this may be said to be "on special", whereby the interest rate may be higher or lower than the GC rate. For example, we describe below how inflation swaps may be hedged using index-linked bonds; these bonds are usually on special due to the limited supply and excess demand.

The repo market is highly liquid in many countries, but repo transactions are generally very short-term—approximately 80% of USD repos are overnight, and most European repos are under 14 days. Repo rates can be quite volatile, reflecting changes in supply and demand for the bonds.

Coming back to the swap, the bank could fund the bond position by buying a reverse repo transaction, i.e. borrowing the bulk of the money from the repo market and providing the bond as collateral. There is likely to be a small positive accrued gain on the floating transactions, because the collateralised repo rate is likely to be below Libor. Let us assume that the floating side of the swap is quarterly; 3-month Libor is therefore fixed at the beginning of the quarter, to be paid at the end. But the repo is short-term, and so would have to be rolled over if the hedge were to be held for the full quarter. Hence, even if repo rates are initially below the Libor fixing, it is possible for them to rise over the quarter and convert the gain into a further carry-cost. All of this adds to the risks of hedging, and hence to the cost.

It would be feasible to obtain a "term" repo, i.e. one agreed for a fixed period of time such as 3 months to match the Libor tenor. However, the rate on such a repo is likely to be higher than the GC rate, and nearer to Libor. Another aspect to consider is flexibility; does the bank really wish to hedge this swap fully for 3 months, or will the hedge change as additional swap transactions are done?

An additional source of risk is the "basis". The repo, bond and swap markets are all traded markets in their own rights, and whilst linked by arbitrage constraints, also have their individual characteristics. Basis risk is the term used to describe the risk of one market moving, possibly due to some internal factors, relative to the other markets. If a bank enters into a swap, it initially possesses a position which is open to the movement of both short and long interest rates. By then entering into a counter position in the bond market, the bank has attempted to reduce its long interest risk by substituting basis risk. In some circumstances, as we shall see later, basis risk may be greater than the initial interest rate risk, which suggests that that specific hedge is increasing overall risk not reducing it.

The concept of "comparative advantage" drives many capital market transactions. This was discussed in Chapter 1 and in Section 3.2, but briefly re-stated in this context it proposes that a bond issuer will issue a bond into the market where there is the greatest demand, hence pay the lowest yield or conversely receive the highest price, and subsequently swap it into the funds actually required. A bond is designed very much to meet the specific requirements of the investor community, and derivatives are then used to transform the bond into the specific requirements of the issuer. Very commonly, to assist the investors, newly issued bonds are quoted as a spread over some appropriate governmental reference bond. As we have seen above, swaps are also frequently derived as a spread over the bond curve. We can therefore have the following situation:

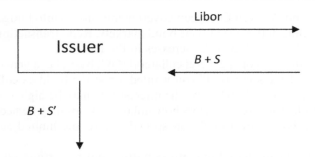

where S is the swap spread, S' the issuance spread. Concentrating just on the swap, and employing the following rather dubious manipulations (broadly correct but only exactly correct under certain circumstances):

- deduct the swap spread S from both sides;
- add the issuance spread S' to both sides;

we end up with a swap:

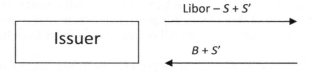

The objective of the issuer, as always, is to obtain cheap, i.e. sub-Libor, funding. This is true when $S > S'$, namely when the swap spread is wide and/or the issuance spread is tight. Under these circumstances, there will be a number of swapped bond issues. Simple supply and demand arguments suggest that the increased issuance will drive S' up, and the swap counterparty will reduce S, hence closing the issuance window.

Consider the plight of a potential bond issuer. The swap market is currently trading at a wide spread to the bond market, but for some reason the potential issuer will not be in a position to issue for another 3 months. However, if he waits that long, it is likely that the window will be closed. Therefore he would like to do a "spreadlock" swap today, which locks in today's spread S_0, but which starts in 3 months' time:

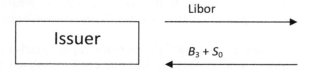

Notice that he does not care what happens to the bond yield B over the 3-month period, as that will be negated by the absolute level of the bond issue. To understand such a swap, we will examine it from the point of view of the counterparty, say a bank:

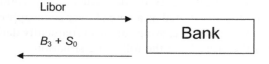

The bank has two sources of risk: Libor may drop over the lifetime of the swap, and the bond yield may rise over the next 3 months. The bank can hedge the first by entering into an off-setting generic swap today, matching the maturities:

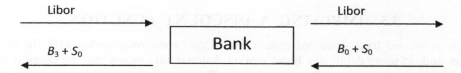

Note that this commits the bank to pay a fixed but unhedged Libor cashflow out at the end of the first period. Simultaneously, the bank does a (ideally 3-month) repo to lend money and to receive repo interest plus the reference bond as collateral. The bank then sells the bond into the market, with the intention of buying it back in 3 months' time.

Consider what may happen at the end of the 3-month period, when the repo terminates. First assume rates do not move. From the bank's perspective, it will:

- pay accrued Libor, but receive accrued repo;
- receive accrued fixed $= B_0 + S_0$, but pay accrued coupon on the bond when repurchased.

Remember that currently S_0 is quite wide, so it is likely that S_0 will exceed {Libor − repo}, and that the bank has a negative carry-cost.

Now assume rates do move over the period:

- If rates increase such that $B_3 > B_0$, the bond price will have decreased so that the bank can repurchase it cheaply and make a profit that should off-set the running loss from the two swaps.
- Conversely, if rates decrease so that $B_3 < B_0$, the running profit should off-set the increase in bond price.

The amount of bond to be repoed is determined by the need to match the bond gain or loss with the swaps' losses or gains. The nominal amount of the bond may therefore not match the notional principal of the swap, which will result in some accrued mismatches which must also be included in the pricing, i.e. some margin usually deducted from S_0 to compensate for the hedging costs.

Spreadlocks are often quoted in terms of this margin. For example:

Table 3.5   Spreadlock swaps as spread over mid-swap rates

Maturity	Treasuries (yield)	Mid-swap (bp spread)	Spreadlock swap rates Forward start period →				
			1 yr	2 yr	3 yr	5 yr	10 yr
1 yr	6.29%	112 bp	−9	−8	−6	−2	2
2 yr	6.79	72	16	15	14	14	12
3 yr	6.72	83	0	0	0	0	0
5 yr	6.65	99	7	6	5	4	3
10 yr	6.42	131	6	5	4	3	2
30 yr	6.15	156	8	7	6	4	2

Source: Prebon Yamane, owned by Tullet Prebon plc.

Spreadlocks only really occur during issuance windows for the reasons explained. As we shall see later, they should also be supplied during periods of investor demand, but for some reason the market does not appear to respond in that fashion.

3.5 IMPLYING A DISCOUNT FUNCTION

At this point, we have discussed generic swaps and their relationship with the money market and, in more detail, the bond market. Interest rate swaps may be thought of as the arbitrage hinge between the two markets. This idea will be explored in more detail when asset packaging is considered. We are now going to move on and assume that we can observe the various traded markets, and to discover what information we may imply.

Table 3.6   Current USD market data

Today's date: 4 February 2008
Spot: 6 February 2008

Libor cash Act/360				Mid swap rates		
7-day	11-Feb-08	3.218%	2 yr	08-Feb-10	2.795%
1-mo	04-Mar-08	3.181%	3 yr	07-Feb-11	3.035%
3-mo	04-May-08	3.145%	4 yr	06-Feb-12	3.275%
6-mo	04-Aug-08	3.098%	5 yr	06-Feb-13	3.505%
12-mo	04-Feb-09	2.896%	6 yr	06-Feb-14	3.715%
			7 yr	06-Feb-15	3.885%
Deposit futures			8 yr	08-Feb-16	4.025%
Mar-08	19-Mar-08	97.000	9 yr	06-Feb-17	4.155%
Jun-08	18-Jun-08	97.410	10 yr	06-Feb-18	4.265%
Sep-08	17-Sep-08	97.520	12 yr	06-Feb-20	4.435%
Dec-08	17-Dec-08	97.495	15 yr	06-Feb-23	4.615%
Mar-09	18-Mar-09	97.395	20 yr	07-Feb-28	4.755%
Jun-09	17-Jun-09	97.220	25 yr	07-Feb-33	4.805%
Sep-09	16-Sep-09	97.040	30 yr	08-Feb-38	4.815%
Dec-09	16-Dec-09	96.850	**ANN Act/360 against 3m Libor**		
Mar-10	17-Mar-10	96.665			
Jun-10	16-Jun-10	96.495			
Sep-10	15-Sep-10	96.340			
Dec-10	15-Dec-10	96.200			
Mar-11	16-Mar-11	96.060			
Jun-11	15-Jun-11	95.930			
Sep-11	21-Sep-11	95.800			
Dec-11	21-Dec-11	95.675			
Mar-12	21-Mar-12	95.565			

We have already seen how to estimate discount factors from cash and futures rates. Now consider the 2-year swap; the fixed cashflows including the notional principal at the beginning and end are:

Table 3.7   Fixed cashflows from 2-year generic swap

Trade date: 4-Feb-08
Settlement date: 6-Feb-08
Notional principal: 100 million
Maturity: 7 years
To receive fixed rate: 2.795% ANN, Act/360
To pay floating rate: 3 mo. Libor

Fixed cashflows

6-Feb-08   −100,000,000.00
6-Feb-09   2,841,583.33
8-Feb-10   102,849,347.22

As we have already discussed, the value of these cashflows should be zero:

$$-100,000,000 + 2,841,583.33 * DF_1 + 102,849,347.22 * DF_2 = 0$$

where DF_t is the discount factor at time t (in years). Because we know the cash and futures rates, we can estimate DF_1 from (one of) these markets, and hence solve the equation for DF_2. Which market would be better? Cash transactions are on-balance sheet, and usually carry some form of regulatory liquidity asset requirement; the rates therefore have to contain a component for this. Furthermore, as the majority of OTC swaps are collateralised, then futures or FRA rates are probably more appropriate. In detail, if $DF_1 = 0.972661$ from the futures market, then $DF_2 = 0.945423$.

This process may be repeated sequentially along the swap curve implying the annual discount factors. This is frequently called a "zero-coupon bootstrapping" process, and the phrase "bootstrapping a curve" is in common usage. It means:

- the initial discount factor is estimated from another market, usually the futures, FRA or cash depending what is available with good liquidity;
- the process then progresses sequentially up the swap curve.[4]

One necessary condition for the process is that swap rates must be known at annual intervals. Imagine the situation: we have just calculated DF_{10} and the next known rate is S_{12} as shown above. When we generate the cashflows for the 12-year swap, we will get the following:

	Daycount	Cashflow
11 year	6-Feb-19	4,496,597.22
12 year	6-Feb-20	104,496,597.22

---

[4] Bootstrapping is a term used in mountaineering; it describes how two climbers linked by a rope can scale a cliff.

i.e. two cashflows each with an unknown discount factor, but only one valuation equation. It is common therefore to "complete" the swap curve, estimating the missing points on the curve by some means of interpolation, usually either linear or some form of cubic.

A general bootstrapping expression can be easily derived. Assume we know DF_j for $j = 1, 2, \ldots, T - 1$, and now consider a generic swap of maturity T to receive floating, pay fixed:

1. The present value of the floating side is simply $1 - DF_T$ as shown above.
2. The present value of the (paid) fixed side is:

$$PV_{fixed} = -S_T * \sum_j \delta_j * DF_j = -S_T * Q_T$$

where δ_j is the appropriate fixed side daycount;
       $Q_T = \sum_j \delta_j * DF_j$ summed from $j = 1$ to $T = Q_{T-1} + \delta_T * DF_T$.

3. As the net value of the swap must be zero:

$$1 - DF_T - [S_T * Q_{T-1} + S_T * \delta_T * DF_T] = 0 \quad \Rightarrow \quad DF_T = (1 - S_T * Q_{T-1})/(1 + S_T * \delta_T)$$

Suppose we wish to construct the curve of 3-monthly forward rates (as this is the tenor of the floating side of generic USD swaps). We have annual discount factors, but need to estimate them every 3 months! Again, we need to interpolate in some fashion. There are of course many ways of interpolating, but three are popular:

• Linear interpolation of the DFs

    i.e. $DF_t = DF_{i-1} + \{(DF_i - DF_{i-1})/(T_i - T_{i-1})\} * (t - T_{i-1})$ for $i - 1 \leq t \leq i$

    or $DF_t = DF_{i-1} + \{gradient\} * (t - T_{i-1})$

• Linear interpolation of $\ln(DF)$—effectively assuming the discount curve follows a negative exponential.
• Linear interpolation of the equivalent zero-coupon rates. In turn these rates may be
    ○   continuously compounded: $DF_t = \exp(-z_t * t)$
    ○   discretely compounded: $DF_t = (1 + z_t/n)^{-t*n}$

We saw quite significant differences when we used different methods of interpolating short cashrates: the impact now will be even more dramatic. The results are summarised in the graphs below, generated in Worksheet 3.5.

The first graph shows linear interpolation of the swap curve followed by different methods for interpolating the discount curve. All three methods show large jumps in the forward curve; these are the result of poor interpolation on the original swap curve. Linear interpolation of the discount curve gives rise to the characteristic "Bart Simpson" curve with the regular fluctuations, whereas both zero-coupon and log-linear interpolation do appear to smooth these out. Continuously compounded zero coupon is probably the best of the three methods.

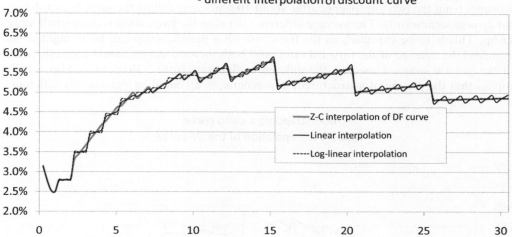

To understand why linear is so unacceptable, consider the following exaggerated simple situation:

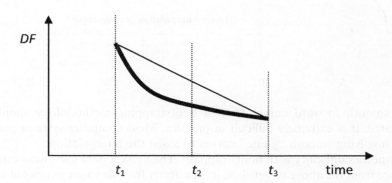

where a discount curve is known at time t_1 and t_3 but interpolated at t_2. Two methods of interpolation are shown: linear and non-linear. We calculate the forward rates from t_1 to t_2 and from t_2 to t_3 using:

$$F_{12} = [(\mathrm{DF}_{t_1}/\mathrm{DF}_{t_2}) - 1]/(t_2 - t_1) \quad \text{and} \quad F_{23} = [(\mathrm{DF}_{t_2}/\mathrm{DF}_{t_3}) - 1]/(t_3 - t_2)$$

Because $\mathrm{DF}_{t_2}^{\mathrm{L}} > \mathrm{DF}_{t_2}^{\mathrm{NL}}$ by construction, this means that:

$$F_{12}^{\mathrm{L}} < F_{12}^{\mathrm{NL}} \quad \text{and} \quad F_{23}^{\mathrm{L}} > F_{23}^{\mathrm{NL}}$$

If we accept that the non-linear approximation of the curve is more accurate, the forward rates from the linear interpolation will oscillate around the non-linear forwards, resulting in the characteristic zig-zagging.

The second graph shows a cubic Hermite[5] interpolation of the swap curve, followed by zero-coupon interpolation of the discount curve. The large jumps have been removed, and whilst the forward curve is perhaps better, it is still showing discontinuities. Worst still, the forwards from the two approaches after about 10 years may follow the same broad shape, but diverge significantly. The average difference between the two curves is quite small, only 0.6 bp. This is to be expected, as the fixed rate on a generic swap can be thought of as (roughly) the average of the forward rates, and both forward curves would correctly price all the generic swaps. However, the differences fluctuate from -30 bp to $+35$ bp, which implies that the pricing of a structured, non-generic, swap could be significantly different.

Bootstrapping a swap curve with Z-C interpolation of the DF curve

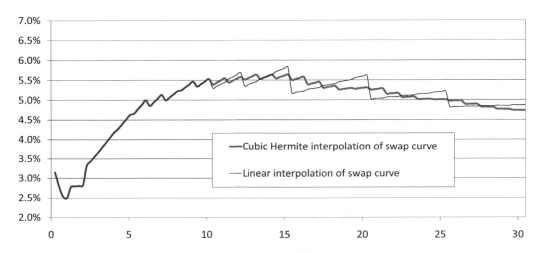

Producing smooth forward curves from a bootstrapping methodology should not be underestimated; it is extremely difficult in practice. Most computer systems use complex algorithms involving smooth "guide" curves to assist the interpolation.

There is another difficulty with bootstrapping. The market data used went out 30 years. As we can see from the above screenshot, it is perfectly feasible to get swaps out to 50 years in the major currencies. However, there is a problem. Using the bootstrapping formula, it is easy to show that:

$$DF_t = \{1 - (1 - DF_{t-1}) * (S_t/S_{t-1})\}/(1 + \delta_t \cdot S_t)$$

For $DF_t > 0$ as required, this means that $(1 - DF_{t-1}) * (S_t/S_{t-1}) < 1$. As t increases, $(1 - DF_{t-1})$ tends to 1. Therefore, if the curve is rising at the long end,[6] i.e. $(S_t/S_{t-1}) > 1$, it is feasible for $(1 - DF_{t-1}) * (S_t/S_{t-1}) > 1$ for some t less than the longest maturity, and hence $DF_t < 0$! For the USD market data above, as it is declining at the long

---

[5] Cubic Hermite interpolation is based on the following idea. Consider a function f whose values $f(x)$ and gradients $f'(x)$ are known at points t_1 and t_2. Fit a cubic to these four parameters, and then use the cubic to estimate the value $f(y)$ where $t_1 < y < t_2$. If this is being used to interpolate across different segments of curves, then the cubic segments are first-order continuous. There is a Hermite interpolation model in Worksheets 3.6 and 3.7.

[6] Suppose there were the following quotes: $S_{20} = 6.0\%$, $S_{30} = 6.2\%$ and $S_{50} = 6.3\%$. Naive interpolation would almost certainly guarantee $S_t/S_{t-1} > 1$, with subsequent failure.

end, this phenomenon does not occur. On the other hand it has been observed in some euro swap curves beyond 35 years. Unfortunately there is nothing inherent in the boot-strapping process that will guarantee that the discount curve will be asymptotic to the time axis. When it does occur, it is a serious problem as most systems cannot cope and break down.

The real difficulty is that the market provides information only at a small set of maturities. Unfortunately the bootstrapping algorithm requires all rates at the intervening maturities to be estimated, and then these estimated rates are treated as if they had exactly the same validity as the original rates from the market. Therefore the interpolation methodology is critical.

Most practitioners look at the forward curve as a measure of appropriateness. This is because the forward curve is effectively the gradient of the discount curve, so any small misalignment in the latter is magnified in the former. Looking at the forward curves above, the one using linear interpolation was rejected because it fluctuated so much. But the other two curves were little better, as they both had significant discontinuities. A measure of a "good" curve is often taken to be its overall smoothness, defined in some fashion.

These observations lead to an alternative approach to the derivation of discount and forward curves. Using the expressions above, we can write that the net present value of a swap with maturity T is:

$$\text{NPV}_T = S_T \cdot Q_T - (1 - \text{DF}_T)$$

which is of course a linear function in DFs. We know that:

$$\text{NPV}_T = 0 \quad \text{for all } T \in \{\text{original maturities}\}$$

Mathematically, how can we define a "good" forward curve? There are a variety of approaches, but a very simple one is to estimate the overall changes in the gradient of the curve, which may be approximated by

$$\text{Smooth} = \sum_i \{F(t_{i+1}, t_i) - F(t_i, t_{i-1})\}^2$$

Constraints on the discount factors such as $\text{DF}_t > \text{DF}_{t+1} > \text{DF}_{t+2} \cdots > 0$ could also be included, but in practice these should be unnecessary, indeed worrying if required.[7]

Worksheet 3.8 demonstrates one model for this approach, in which 3-monthly forward rates are treated as the unknown variables (except for the first four which are fixed off the cash and futures curves); see column [1]. A smoothing function is created as described above in column [2]. The discount factors and Qs are calculated from the forward rates in columns [3] and [4]. Finally the net value of each of the generic swaps is shown in column E. The objective is to ensure that all net values are zero whilst Smooth is minimised; the worksheet uses the Solver algorithm. The final forward curve is shown below, compared

---

[7] Using this definition of "good" implies that the forward curve would extrapolate flat. This is a common assumption, although one disputed by some historical evidence; see SM Schaefer et al., "Why do long term forward interest rates (almost) always slope downwards?", IFA Working Paper 299, 2000.

with the Hermite interpolated bootstrapping curve: this latter curve was used as the starting point for the optimisation. As one can see, it is considerably smoother than the boot-strapped curve, and yet remains arbitrage-free.[8]

Bootstrapping a swap curve

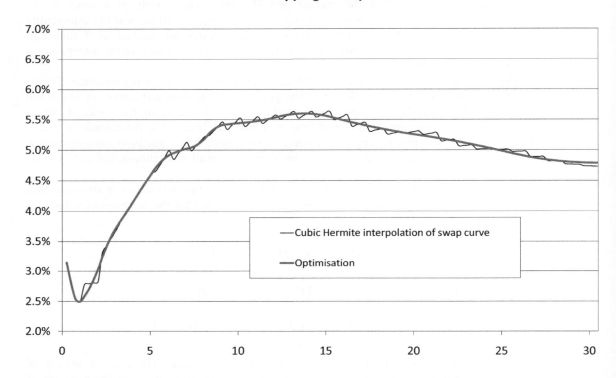

3.6 BUILDING A BLENDED CURVE

So far in this book we have seen a number of different financial instruments—cash, futures, swaps—being used to build discount curves. It is conventional in some countries, typically ones that do not possess a liquid futures markets, to incorporate FRAs as well. Furthermore it is feasible to use bonds and bond futures, although less likely due to the disparate implied creditworthiness and the limited range of maturities. In practice a group of traders and risk managers would build a curve from a mixture of instruments in segments—this is usually known as "blending", for example:

- cash for the first 3 months;

---

[8] Running the optimisation does take longer than bootstrapping, even with a good starting curve. One swap trader I know, Bo Nielsen currently at Nordea in Denmark, runs both the optimisation and the bootstrapping algorithms at the beginning of the day, and records the differences between the resulting forward curves. When any market point shifts, he then re-bootstraps the curve and then applies the differences to get a new smooth forward curve. If there is a substantial move in the curve, then he runs a new optimisation and starts afresh.

- interest rate futures for first 3 years;
- interest swaps from 2 years onwards.

The location of the breakpoints will depend upon liquidity and knowledge of when which instruments will be used for hedging. There are two different ways of tackling this problem of building a curve. First, the segments may overlap—see the cash and futures above, and the diagram below—and in that case some weighting information usually has to be provided about the relative importance of each market. The result is likely to be relatively smooth (especially if the weighting is applied gradually) but, and this is a big but, will not be arbitrage-free in the overlap portions. For example, any generic swap that matured in the overlap period between futures and swaps, and was used in the construction of the curve, would not be priced back to zero!

1. Overlap, weight and average   2. No overlap

cash   futures   **swaps**

The alternative is to remove the overlaps as shown in the second diagram. Arbitrage-freeness is maintained which from a market practitioner's perspective is highly desirable. But the problem now is how to achieve the handover between the segments in the smoothest possible fashion.

Developing a satisfactory balance between arbitrage-freeness and smoothness whilst using bootstrapping is extremely difficult, and many arcane multi-layer algorithms have been developed. The optimisation model described above however may be used to tackle the problem more directly.

For example, assume we wish to build a curve using the data above, namely short cash, a 3-year strip of futures and swaps from 2 years onwards. Note that there is a deliberate overlap between the futures and the swaps. The optimisation approach will be used to build two curves (see Worksheet 3.9 for details):

- An arbitrage-free curve. The worksheet builds a smooth forward curve whilst correctly pricing all the market data. Unlike the previous optimisation model (which used Value), an arbitrage error is defined as a mismatch between the market rates and the implied futures and swap rates.
- A smooth curve. The worksheet constructs a single objective function OF:

$$OF = w * SS + (1 - w) * Smooth$$

where $SS = \sum$ squared errors fitting the rates, and w is set to 90%. The definition of error as explained above ensures that SS and Smooth are comparable.

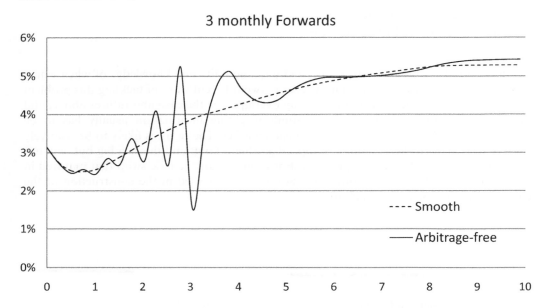

The ranges of the market data were specifically chosen so that constructing an arbitrage-free curve across all the data would be difficult. This is displayed in the spike around the 3-year point, as the futures come to an end, with the subsequent ripples along the curve as the algorithm tries to make the overall curve smooth. The smooth curve is no longer arbitrage-free: the average error across all rates is 0.15 bp. The example highlights the need to select the relevant market data extremely carefully, and indeed different traders may well want to use different sets of data for calibration. The optimisation approach removes the need for complex blending difficulties, and can make the tradeoff between arbitrage-freeness and smoothness quite explicit using a form of regression with multiple objectives. Whilst not easy to demonstrate within a spreadsheet formulation, probably the best overall approach is to model instantaneous forward rates rather than discrete tenor ones as above.

4

The Pricing and Valuation of Non-generic Swaps

OBJECTIVE

Given discount and forward curves, we can now start to price and value swaps that are structured for end-users. These are commonly known as non-generic, as they frequently possess aspects tailored to the user's requirements. Two common structures, namely forward start and amortising, plus a more complex one are analysed in some detail and three alternative approaches are described. In passing, a very real practical problem is observed and an alternative known as the "reference rate" method. Forward valuing as an alternative to discounting is then reintroduced. Finally swap valuation is discussed using two alternative approaches.

4.1 THE PRICING OF SIMPLE NON-GENERIC SWAPS: FORWARD STARTS

Whilst the vast bulk of swaps traded between banks, or at least between market-makers, are generic, most swaps conducted with non-banking counterparties are non-generic. Such swaps are usually structured to meet their specific requirements. In this chapter, we shall discuss how to price such swaps. We will start with some relatively simple structures, known as "par non-generic swaps" because, as we shall see, they can be cash-hedged with par generic swaps.

For example, suppose a company is currently paying quarterly floating interest on $100 million of debt maturing in 5 years' time. The treasurer believes that interest rates will continue to stay low for at least another year, but will continue to rise after that. Instead of entering into an ordinary 5-year swap to pay fixed annually, receive floating, she is considering a 1/5 forward starting swap. This means that the fixed rate would be agreed today, unlike the spreadlock swap, but the swap would only start in 1 year's time with a length of 4 years. Note that the usual convention for forward swaps is the same as for FRAs, namely {start/end}; an alternative is to use a phrase such as "1 into a 4-year swap"—if in any doubt, spell it out!

The cashflows from the swap would be as shown in Table 4.1 (from a bank's point of view).

The rate quoted, and remember this is a fair mid-rate so that the bank would be likely to add a spread onto the fixed rate, is some 16 bp higher than the current 5 year swap rate of 3.505%. Why is this, and how did the bank arrive at its quote?

There are a number of ways to approach this. First, let us consider how a bank might hedge such a transaction using generic instruments. Obviously its main concern is that Libor might rise over the lifetime of the swap. Libor could therefore be hedged by entering

Table 4.1   Cashflows of a 1/5 swap

Notional principal: USD 100m
Fixed rate: 3.671% ANN
Floating rate: Quarterly
Current 5-year swap rate: 3.505%
Current 1-year swap rate: 2.896%

Dates	Floating side	Fixed
6-Feb-08		
6-May-08		
6-Aug-08		
6-Nov-08		
6-Feb-09		
6-May-09	−Libor	
6-Aug-09	−Libor	
6-Nov-09	−Libor	
8-Feb-10	−Libor	3,742,196
6-May-10	−Libor	
6-Aug-10	−Libor	
8-Nov-10	−Libor	
7-Feb-11	−Libor	3,711,606
6-May-11	−Libor	
8-Aug-11	−Libor	
7-Nov-11	−Libor	
6-Feb-12	−Libor	3,711,606
7-May-12	−Libor	
6-Aug-12	−Libor	
6-Nov-12	−Libor	
6-Feb-13	−Libor	3,731,999

into two generic swaps:

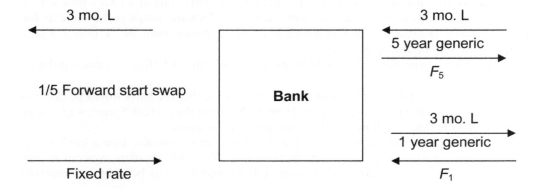

The 5-year generic swap offsets the Libor payments of the forward start, but also generates Libor receipts in the first year. The 1-year swap is required to offset these receipts.

The bank will be paying 3.505% ANN over 5 years, and receiving 2.896% in the first year. Thus there is a shortfall in the first year of 61 bp which will have to be recovered over the next four. Therefore we would expect the forward start swap rate to be approximately:

$$3.505\% + 61 \text{ bp}/4 = 3.657\%$$

crudely spreading the 61 bp over the 4 years. Worksheet 4.2 calculates this more accurately by taking the time value of money into account. Column [1] shows the fixed cashflows from the forward start, with the fixed cashflows from the two generic swaps in columns [2] and [3]. As we require the swap to have a zero value, we find that this is achieved by a forward rate of 3.671%.[1]

Pricing such non-generic swaps always revolves around what to do with the floating side. We saw in the discussion on bootstrapping that we would regard a money account that paid the floating reference flat as having no economic value. This applies equally to a forward starting money transaction as it does to a spot one. Assume that the bank exchanges the principal amount of $100 million with the swap counterparty twice, once at the start of the first floating period, and reverses the exchange on the last payment date, as shown in the box below:

	Money account	Counterentries
6-Feb-08		
6-May-08		
6-Aug-08		
6-Nov-08		
6-Feb-09	100,000,000	−100,000,000
6-May-09	−Libor	
6-Aug-09	−Libor	
6-Nov-09	−Libor	
8-Feb-10	−Libor	
6-May-10	−Libor	
6-Aug-10	−Libor	
8-Nov-10	−Libor	
7-Feb-11	−Libor	
6-May-11	−Libor	
8-Aug-11	−Libor	
7-Nov-11	−Libor	
6-Feb-12	−Libor	
7-May-12	−Libor	
6-Aug-12	−Libor	
6-Nov-12	−Libor	
6-Feb-13	−Libor − 100,000,000	100,000,000

Clearly these have no economic impact on the value of the swap. However, the floating side has now become equivalent to the money account (with zero value) plus the two remaining

---

[1] By using Goal Seek or Solver.

principal cashflows. The worksheet shows the swap consisting of the money account in column [1] and the counterentries in column [3]. The fair price of the swap is of course the same as before (see Worksheet 4.3).

The alternative and equivalent argument is, of course, that the value of the floating side is simply $1 - DF_{end}$.

Yet another approach would be to imply the Libor rates directly off the discount curve in the usual fashion. This is most straightforward, as shown in Worksheet 4.4). The implied rates are shown in column [1], and the resulting cashflows in [2]).

For a straightforward fixed–floating swap, the fixed rate may be thought of as some (albeit complex) average of the floating rates. For example, using implied 12-monthly forward rates, their simple average is close to the 5-year swap rate as shown below:

	Implied 12 mo. forward rates
Year 0/1	2.896%
Year 1/2	2.691%
Year 2/3	3.542%
Year 3/4	4.053%
Year 4/5	4.520%
Average over all 5 years	3.541%
Actual 5-year rate	3.505%

The forward starting swap rate must be approximated by the average over years 1 to 5 only, i.e. 3.702%. As the forward curve is rising, omitting the first rate will increase the average and hence the 1/5 forward swap rate will be higher than the 5-year spot rate.

The pricing of a forward start can also be estimated directly. From the previous chapter, the value of the fixed and floating sides of a unitary generic swap must be $F_n * Q_n$ and $1 - DF_n$, respectively. By extension, the value of the sides of a forward start must be $F_{s/n} * [Q_n - Q_s]$ and $[DF_n - DF_s]$. Therefore (see Worksheet 4.5):

$$F_{1/5} = [DF_5 - DF_1]/[Q_5 - Q_1] = [0.971397 - 0.838308]/[4.613187 - 0.987587] = 3.671\%$$

This is a very fast way of pricing forward starts, and will be used later.

We have seen three approaches to the pricing of this forward start swap:

• using hedging swaps to cancel the unknown Libors;
• converting the floating side into a zero-value money account by adding notional principal amounts to both sides;
• implying the Libor rates off the discount curve.

Each one is removing, in some fashion, the unknown floating rates. However, all three methods are consistent with each other.

Swap-pricing systems such as used by market-makers are likely to use the last two methods, fair pricing swaps at mid-rates for subsequent adjustment. Whilst the Notional Principal Amount (NPA) method is more traditional, harking back to the relationship with the bond market, the Implied Forward (IF) method which had its foundations in the futures market has probably overtaken it in popularity. IF is certainly more flexible and is also safer in the sense that it estimates what the actual cashflows would be if the curves remained valid. This may become more evident when we look at some more complex structures.

Many banks however act as an intermediary, particularly in foreign illiquid currencies. This involves doing a non-generic swap with a customer and therefore taking on the credit exposure, but immediately passing on most of the market risk by entering into hedging swaps with a market-maker. In this case, the hedging swaps would include a bid–offer spread which should then be reflected in the pricing of the non-generic swap.

There is however a very real practical problem. This is because the swap dates are all driven from the start date, whereas each period in the cash market is independent. The following is an extract from the swap dates (the 2-day settlement period is not mentioned as it does not affect this argument):

Swap dates	3 months later	Adjusted for business days
6-Nov-09	6-Feb-10	8-Feb-10
8-Feb-10	8-May-10	10-May-10
6-May-10	6-Aug-10	6-Aug-10

For example, consider what happens on 8 February 2010. The actual Libor rate fixed at that time in the cash market would be based on the period from 8 February 2010 until the end of the 3-month period, including non-business days, namely 10 May 2010. However, the swap cashflow would be calculated from the swap dates, i.e. from 8 February to 6 May 2010. The value of this cashflow would be:

$$\text{PV} = P * F(8 \text{ Feb}, 10 \text{ May}) * (t_{6\,\text{May}} - t_{8\,\text{Feb}}) * \text{DF}_{6\,\text{May}}$$

However, the NPA method implicitly assumes:

$$\text{PV} = P * F(8 \text{ Feb}, 6 \text{ May}) * (t_{6\,\text{May}} - t_{8\,\text{Feb}}) * \text{DF}_{6\,\text{May}}$$

which simplifies to $P * \{\text{DF}_{8\,\text{Feb}} - \text{DF}_{6\,\text{May}}\}$. Therefore, despite its wide popularity, the NPA approach is not entirely consistent with reality. Is this effect significant? Worksheet 4.6 has incorporated this, estimating the forward rates to match the cash market and then applying them over the swap dates. Columns [1] and [2] show the swap dates and the discount factors out of those dates, columns [3] and [4] the adjusted end dates for each period and associated discount factors. Column [5] calculates the tenor of each forward rate, and [6] the level of the forward rate. Finally the cashflows are calculated using the dates in [1] and the length of time shown in [7]. The new price for the forward swap is about 5.5 bp lower, highly significant given a 2 bp bid–offer spread.

A more theoretical statement of this problem is as follows:

• Calculate a set of dates $S_1, S_2, \dots$ 3 months apart out of the start date.
• Adjust these dates onto business dates, giving $S_1^a, S_2^a, \dots$ The length of time between these dates will sometimes be greater than 3 months, and sometimes shorter.
• Estimate the end of a 3 mo. rate out of the adjusted dates, i.e. $E_i = D_i^a + 3$ months.
• Adjust these dates to give $E_1^a, E_2^a, \dots$
• Implied 3-monthly forward rates would then be calculated from D_i^a to E_i^a; this estimate would be consistent with the physical cash market.

- But in the multiperiod instrument, it would be applied from D_i^a to D_{i+1}^a which is inconsistent.

For practical purposes, this approach is termed the "reference rate" methodology, as the forward rates follow the physical reference market. In contrast, the earlier method is to imply and then to apply forward rates over the period D_i^a to D_{i+1}^a; for obvious reasons this has been termed the "period date" approach. The reference rate method is theoretically correct; however, the period date method would appear to be the approach widely used in practice.

4.2 ROLLERCOASTERS

Another common structure is the "rollercoaster" swap. Consider again a company that is currently paying floating interest on some debt, and wishes to swap into fixed. Instead of the debt being a "bullet", i.e. being drawn down and subsequently repaid as a single lump sum, it is very common for the debt to have agreed drawdown and repayment schedules. Obviously the swap must have the same underlying principal structure. Common names for such structures are "step-up"—when the notional principal increases in steps, "step-down or amortising"—when the principal decreases. Rollercoaster is the general name suggesting the principal rising and falling.

It is important to note that the changes in the principal amount are defined in advance, and are not altered by subsequent events. There is a class of swaps, one example of which is "index amortising", where the principal amount changes as a function of some external events such as increases or decreases in the floating rate fixings. These will be considered later. To be specific, we will look at the pricing of a 5-year amortising swap, whereby the principal amount starts at $100 million and declines at the end of each year by $20 million as shown:

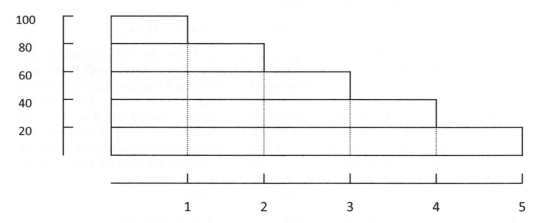

The bank will be receiving the fixed rate, paying Libor. It is shown like this because this also gives an idea how to hedge the Libor payments, namely by doing five swaps:

1. 20m 5-year swap to pay fixed @ 2.8963%, to receive Libor.
2. 20m 4-year swap to pay fixed @ 2.7950%, to receive Libor.
3. 20m 3-year swap to pay fixed @ 3.0350%, to receive Libor.

4. 20m 2-year swap to pay fixed @ 3.2750%, to receive Libor.
5. 20m 1-year swap to pay fixed @ 3.5050%, to receive Libor.

We can quickly produce a crude estimate of the fair amortising rate by averaging these generic swaps, i.e.

$$\frac{(5 * 3.5050\%) + (4 * 3.2750\%) + (3 * 3.0350\%) + (2 * 2.7950\%) + (1 * 2.8963\%)}{(5 + 4 + 3 + 2 + 1)} = 3.214\%$$

Notice that a weighted average was calculated, reflecting the total contribution of each hedging swap. A more precise calculation is shown in Worksheet 4.7: the amortising principal is shown in column [1], the cashflows using the estimated amortising swap rate in column [2], and the fixed cashflows from the hedging swaps in columns [3] to [7]. As usual, the estimated rate of 3.209% is such that the net cashflows have zero value.

To employ the NPA method, we have to do some more work. Under this approach, a stream of Libor payments $\{-L, -L, -L, \ldots\}$ can be replaced by $\{-P \cdots + P\}$, signifying a payment of the principal on the first fixing date and receiving the principal on the last payment date. We have the following structure on the floating side of the swap, as shown in the box on the left:

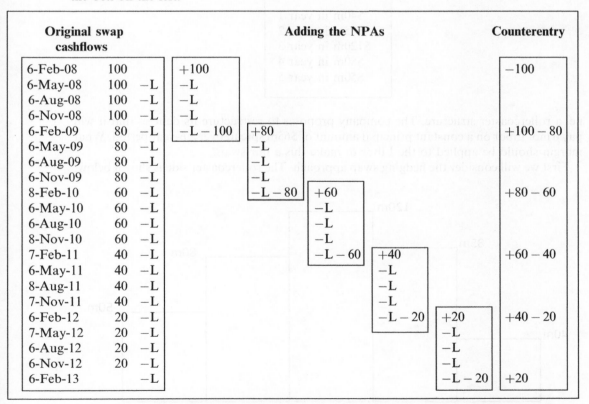

The first four cashflows are based on a principal of $100m. Add the principal amount on the first fixing day and subtract it on the last payment day as shown in the small box. A counterentry would have to be made to ensure that the swap value has not been changed.

Under our assumptions the cashflows in the small box have zero value, so we are left only with the counterentries. This process is then repeated throughout the lifetime of the swap, with the result that the floating leg has been completely replaced with a simple fixed cashflow, namely $\{-100, +20, +20, +20, +20, +20\}$. Worksheet 4.8 shows the swap reduced to two columns: column [1] is the cashflows on the fixed side of the swap, and column [2] the strip of principal amounts, with a total net value of zero.

The third approach is to use the implied forwards. These have been calculated in column [1] of Worksheet 4.9 in the usual way, the cashflows are then generated using the amortising principals and finally the net cashflows discounted and shown to have a value of zero.

4.3 PRICING OF SIMPLE NON-GENERIC SWAPS: A MORE COMPLEX EXAMPLE

Finally, to complete this section, we will apply these approaches to a slightly more complex swap. A company has some debt on which it is paying 6mo. Libor + 70 bp. The debt has the following principal structure:

$40m in year 1
$85m in year 2
$120m in year 3
$80m in year 4
$50m in year 5

i.e. a rollercoaster structure. The company proposes to restructure its debt so that it will pay 6 mo. Libor on a constant principal amount of $65m spread over a 6-year period. What margin should be applied to the Libor to make this a fair swap?

First we will consider the hedging swap approach. The rollercoaster side is shown below:

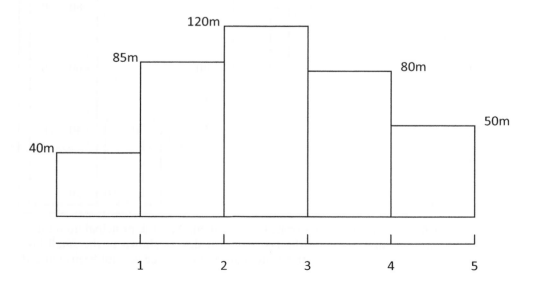

To decide how to hedge this, the trick is to always start at the far end and work backwards. From the bank's point of view, it has to pay Libor + 70 bp on this structure, therefore it could hedge the Libor payments by entering into:

5-year $50m swap to pay fixed, receive Libor

That will hedge the Libor payment it has to make in the final year. Working back, it will do

4-year $30m swap to pay fixed, receive Libor

and

3-year $40m swap to pay fixed, receive Libor.

We now have the following situation:

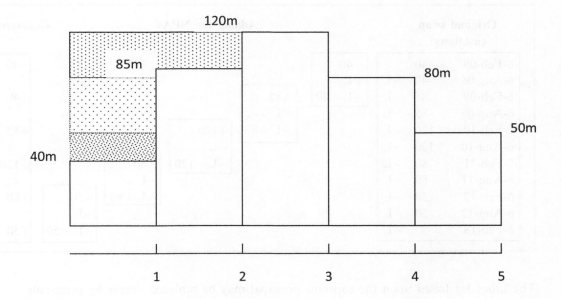

in which the Libor payments to be made in the last three years are matched, but the first two years are now overhedged. To rectify this, we will do:

2-year $35m swap to receive fixed, pay Libor

and

1-year $45m swap to receive fixed, pay Libor

so that now all the Libor payments to be made by the bank will be matched by Libor receipts. Turning to Worksheet 4.8, column [1] contains the cashflows for the 70 bp margin that has to be paid, whilst columns [2] to [6] are the fixed cashflows from the portfolio of five hedging swaps which have replaced the rollercoaster Libor payments.

The other side of the swap is more easily dealt with. The Libor receipts may be matched by a single 6-year swap to receive fixed, as shown in column [8], and the cashflows from the calculated balancing margin of 39.9 bp are shown in column [7]. The overall swap may be seen to be fair as its total discounted value is zero.

The NPA approach may be applied as follows. The rollercoaster side may be represented as shown below:

- the floating cashflows are broken up into strips, each based upon a constant principal amount;
- the NPAs are then added on the first fixing date of each strip, and subtracted on the last payment date, as shown in the boxes;
- counterentries have to be made to ensure that the value of the swap remains constant;
- we can then argue that the value of cashflows in each box is zero, so we are left just with the counterentries that are shown in column [1] of Worksheet 4.11.

Original swap cashflows			Adding the NPAs					Counterentry
6-Feb-08	40		+40					−40
6-Aug-08	40	−L	−L					
6-Feb-09	85	−L	−L − 40	+85				+40 − 85
6-Aug-09	85	−L		−L				
6-Feb-10	120	−L		−L − 85	+120			+85 − 120
6-Aug-10	120	−L			−L			
7-Feb-11	80	−L			−L − 120	+80		+120 − 80
8-Aug-11	80	−L				−L		
6-Feb-12	50	−L				−L − 80	+50	+80 − 50
6-Aug-12	50	−L					−L	
6-Feb-13		−L					−L − 50	+50

The Libor leg based upon the constant principal may be replaced simply by principals at the start and end of the swap: see column [3] of Worksheet 4.11.

The IF approach is, as usual, straightforward. Once the implied forwards are calculated, the two Libor cashflow streams may be constructed: see columns [1] and [3] of Worksheet 4.12.

4.4 FORWARD VALUING AS AN ALTERNATIVE TO DISCOUNTING—REVISITED

Consider the last structure. Based upon the IF approach, the accumulative net cash is shown in the graph below. It shows that the swap counterparty initially deposits money, but rapidly becomes a net recipient of nearly $4m.

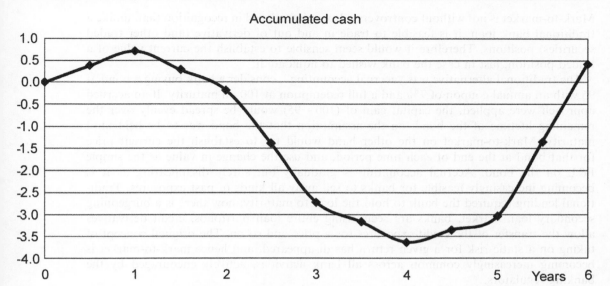

As discussed in Chapter 3, discounting off the swap curve is exactly equivalent to assuming that all money is deposited or lent at Libor flat. This is demonstrated in column [3]; each cashflow is rolled over at the appropriate Libor rate for the period, and the accumulated balance at the end of the swap is zero.

However, if we regarded the swap as effectively a financing vehicle for receiving money from and lending money to the counterparty, then we would be likely to inflict margins on these activities. Let us assume that:

- We would only pay Libor − 25 bp on deposits from this particular counterparty.
- We would expect to receive Libor + 50 bp on loans to this counterparty.

We could then use the forward-valuing approach discussed in Chapter 2 to estimate the new breakeven margin of 41.2 bp (see Worksheet 4.13).

This approach obviously has wide application, but in particular when there is a considerable disparity of credit rating between the two counterparties, and when there is a significant element of embedded loan or deposit.

This section has concentrated purely on embedded loans and deposits, and assumed that the implied forward rates also prevail in the future. Of course, the forward rates are stochastic, and hence the exposure that will actually occur depends upon the future movements of rates and is unknown. There are however techniques for estimating this "potential future exposure", and incorporating it into the pricing of a swap—these are discussed in Section 6.7.

4.5 SWAP VALUATION

The swap has been agreed, traded between the counterparties and recorded in a bank trading book. Banks are generally required by their regulators to mark their trading books to market every day. The main purpose of this is to establish the current value of a portfolio, so that the bank management has a clear idea of the trading assets and liabilities.

Mark-to-market is not without controversy. It was introduced in recognition that, unlike a traditional bank loan, it is feasible to trade in and out of derivative (and other traded securities) positions. Therefore it would seem sensible to establish the current value of a traded position, just in case the bank wished to liquidate it.

The traditional alternative was "accrual accounting"; consider a bank buying a bond at 95 with an annual coupon of 7% and a full redemption at 100 on maturity. If an accrued approach were applied, the capital gain of $(100 - 95)$ would be spread evenly over the remaining lifetime of the bond, on the assumption that the bond was to be held until maturity. Mark-to-market on the other hand would try to establish the current price for that bond at the end of each time period, and use the change in value as the simple P&L on the bond. Accrual accounting is gradually but surely disappearing as it is becoming increasingly feasible for banks to sell away all kinds of past exposures. Traditional lending required the bank to hold the loan to maturity; now there is a burgeoning secondary loan market, banks are securitising entire loan portfolios, credit derivatives allow the transfer of the credit exposures for a price and so on. The original concept of taking on a static risk for a given return has disappeared, and hence mark-to-market is becoming increasingly common across all bank activities, actively encouraged by the banking regulators.

However, the market in "old" or "seasoned" OTC derivatives is hardly active. It would be virtually impossible to obtain a price for a swap traded sometime ago, although obviously for unwinding purposes it is still feasible albeit seldom efficient. Therefore what passes for mark-to-market is usually "mark-to-model". This operates for a seasoned swap as follows:

1. Using the current market levels of generic instruments, build a discount curve.
2. Interpolate the discount curve to obtain discount factors on the relevant swap dates.
3. Value the swap

We shall see this below. This process raises a number of issues, such as:

*   What are the relevant market levels for this particular swap, and where are they?
*   As we have already seen, the process of estimating the relevant discount factors is not unique.
*   This process will produce a mid-valuation, which is unlikely to be achievable in the event of an unwind.

This suggests that different banks may well produce different daily valuations for the same transaction. There have been a number of well-publicised instances where P&L controllers, i.e. back-office people responsible for the daily P&L, have had to rely upon the traders of the original transaction to advise them as to the current levels of the relevant rates with disastrous consequences. Hardly the outcome originally envisaged by the advocates of mark-to-market! There are a number of market initiatives trying to overcome this, such as banks valuing each other's books, and closed or public clubs circulating market information.

As an example of swap valuation, we will consider the complex rollercoaster swap we have just priced above. Its details were, from the bank's point of view:

> To pay 6 mo. Libor + 70 bp on the following structure:
>
> $40m in year 1
> $85m in year 2
> $120m in year 3
> $80m in year 4
> $50m in year 5
>
> To receive 6 mo. Libor + 39.9 bp on $65m for 6 years

The swap was traded on 4 February 2008, and the first Libor fixing was 3.0975%.

Today's date is 4 March 2008. Over the 3-week period, rates have moved up slightly but because the swap is floating–floating, it is difficult to predict whether its value will be positive or negative.

As with swap structuring, the key to valuation is what to do about the unknown Libor fixings. Using generic swaps to cancel these is not feasible because of the mismatch in the dates. Therefore there are really only two common approaches:

1. Inserting the notional principal amounts to create a par FRN with zero value.
2. Implying the forward rates directly off the discount curve.

The first stage is to construct the new discount curve. This is shown in Worksheet 4.14. The discount factors on the relevant swap dates are then estimated by using zero-coupon interpolation—see columns [1] and [2].

Let us consider the two sides of the swap separately. The first Libor cashflow on the rollercoaster side is shown in column [3]; remember that this cashflow is to cover the interest over a full 6-month period, i.e. from 6 February to 6 August 2008, and the Libor fixing is known as it occurred at the beginning of the period. The remaining Libor fixings are unknown, but these may be replaced by notional principals in the usual fashion. For example, the Libor payment due on 6 February 2009 would have been fixed, ignoring the 2-day settlement, on 6 August 2008, i.e. the cashflow date of the previous fixing:

	Libor cashflows	Adding NPAs	Counterentries
6 August 2008	L fixing	+40m	−40m
6 February 2009	−40m $* L * 0.511$	−40m $* (1 + L * 0.511)$	+40m

By adding the NPAs, we have created a single-period money account with zero value, and with the above counterentries. This may be repeated throughout the lifetime of the swap, resulting in column [4]. Finally the margin cashflows in column [5] must also be paid (see Worksheet 4.15).

A similar analysis on the straight side of the swap produces columns [6]–[8]. Finally all the cashflows are netted and then discounted, using the DFs in column [4] of course, to produce a negative valuation of $762,456.

Using Implied Forwards is equally straightforward. The unknown Libors are estimated in the usual way: see column [3]. Columns [5] and [8] contain the implied Libor cashflows. All the cashflows may then be netted and discounted to produce the same valuation (see Worksheet 4.16).

Both methods produce mid-valuations and are therefore interchangeable. However, the NPA approach is the one embedded in regulatory capital calculations such as the BIS Accord and the EU Capital Adequacy Directive. This allows swaps, and similar derivatives, to be treated in a consistent fashion to bonds and other physical instruments. There is also another advantage to the NPA approach: consider the two Net Cashflow columns. As time progresses, and market rates change, the IF column changes daily, whilst the NPA column remains constant until the known Libor cashflows are actually made and a new fixing declared. Thinking about a large swap portfolio, it is possible to represent it by a relatively static "cash ladder"; this possesses numerous computational advantages for risk calculations.

5
Asset Packaging

OBJECTIVE

The previous chapter discussed so-called "par non-generic swaps", i.e. ones that can effectively be created from generic swaps. There are, of course, many complex swaps which cannot be created in that way. This chapter concentrates on the asset packaging or securitisation of securities, i.e. swapping the cashflows from the security into a different form. Only relatively simple interest rate asset swaps will be considered in this chapter; cross-currency and more complex swaps will be discussed in Chapters 9 and 11.

The first capital Accord, implemented by the major banks from 1988 onwards, introduced the requirement for banks to hold capital to act as a cushion against, initially, credit, and subsequently, market, risk. Let us define two types of capital:

- economic—the actual amount of capital required to act as an adequate (in some sense) cushion against credit risk;
- regulatory—the amount of capital required under the regulations.

The original Accord was extremely simplistic, and made no regulatory capital distinction between loans to very credit-worthy and to very credit-risky corporates, as shown below.

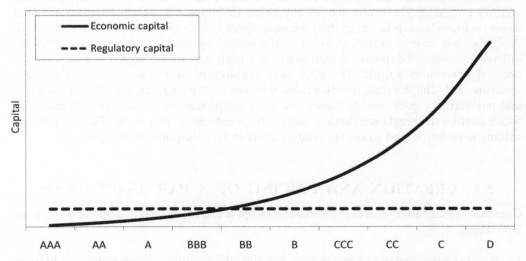

From a bank's perspective, a loan to a good credit has to be over-capitalised, and hence appears expensive. This anomaly provided an additional impetus, above the concept of comparative advantage as described in Chapter 1, to the growth in disintermediation, namely the raising of funds by the direct issuance of securities by good-quality organisations. Invariably, when such securities are issued, they are then swapped to meet the precise funding requirement of the issuer. For example: in October 2007, the EIB issued a bond linked to Ghanaian cedis. Did the EIB have a funding requirement for cedis? Probably not[1]; it was almost certainly swapped into floating euros, as shown below.

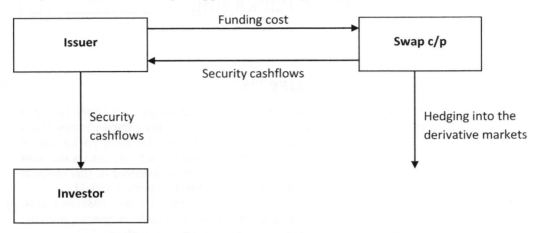

What's in it for the three parties? The investor is taking the risk–return profile of the security; in the example above, the high coupon of 10.75% pa in cedis may of course weaken. The issuer will swap the security into a desired currency whilst achieving a target funding cost. The swap counterparty will earn spreads/fees through the swap, plus potential returns through the hedging.

So far, only the swapping of new securities has been considered. There is also an active secondary asset swap market, in which investors buy securities cheaply, and then swap the cashflows into some desired profile such as a spread over the floating cost of funding the security purchase. There was a brief discussion in Chapter 3, which demonstrated that issuers achieved cheap funding when the swap spread was wider than the issuance spread. A similar but reverse argument holds in the secondary market, thus implying that the difference between the spreads should lie within a fairly narrow corridor, and arbitrage may occur if it ventures outside. The asset swap required in either case has the same basic structure. This chapter describes two main forms of asset packaging, namely par packages and par maturity packages. It shows how asset swaps may be reduced to a single form, which enables the breakeven funding margin to be calculated very easily. Finally, forward valuing is re-introduced to enable funding costs to be incorporated into pricing.

5.1 CREATION AND PRICING OF A PAR ASSET SWAP

Consider the secondary market. The basic concept is extremely simple, and occurs in three basic steps:

1. An "investor" borrows some money, say 100, at a floating reference rate plus margin.
2. The money is used to purchase a physical security; any excess or shortfall will be paid away or received under the swap.

---

[1] Although under the Cotonou Partnership Agreement of 2000, the EIB had been providing some African funding.

3. The "unwanted" cashflows from the security are paid away under a swap, to receive floating rate plus (hopefully, a larger) margin. At redemption, the capital sum is used to repay the borrowing, and again any excess or shortfall paid or received under the swap.

This process is shown below for a fixed coupon bond.

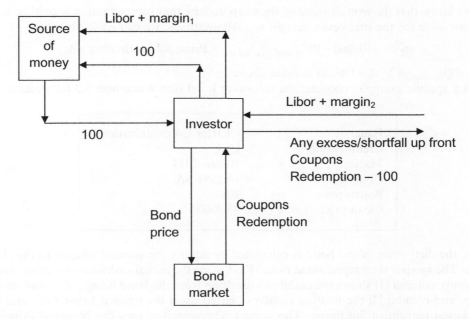

Consider the swap cashflows from the investor's point of view. In the left-hand swap, the actual cashflows that would occur are shown, where DP is the dirty (purchase) price of the security, including the estimated implied forward rates. Note the immediate lump sum of (100 − DP), which may be positive or negative, is paid upfront on the swap. The right-hand swap results by rearranging the swap cashflows, separating the floating principal of 100 and putting it on the other side.

$-(100 - DP)$			$+DP$		-100	
	$+L + m_2$				$+L$	$+m_2$
$-C$	$+L + m_2$		$-C$		$+L$	$+m_2$
	$+L + m_2$				$+L$	$+m_2$
$-C$	$+L + m_2$		$-C$		$+L$	$+m_2$
	$+L + m_2$				$+L$	$+m_2$
$-C$	$+L + m_2$		$-C$		$+L$	$+m_2$
	$+L + m_2$				$+L$	$+m_2$
$-C$	$+L + m_2$		$-C$		$+L$	$+m_2$
	$+L + m_2$				$+L$	$+m_2$
$-C$	$+L + m_2$		$-C$		$+L$	$+m_2$
	$+L + m_2$				$+L$	$+m_2$
$-C - (R - 100)$	$+L + m_2$		$-C - R$		$+L + 100$	$+m_2$

As we can assume that the cashflows in the dotted box have a zero value—as discussed earlier, the swap is therefore reduced to:

(a) the value of the security, $PV_{security}$;
(b) the value of the margin cashflows.

As we know that the overall value of the swap under either representation should be zero, we can solve for the breakeven margin m_2. Alternatively, we can write directly:

$$m_2 = -10,000 * PV_{security}/[Q_{floating} * \text{Principal on floating side}]$$

where $Q_{floating} = \sum d_t * DF_t$ as defined above.

As a specific example, consider the following bond (see Worksheet 5.3 for details):

Issuer		Charter Communications
Credit rating		CCC+
Maturity	=	10-Jan-2013
Coupon	=	10.25% SA
Redemption	=	100
Clean price	=	93.0000

First, the dirty price of the bond is calculated by adding the accrued coupon to the clean price. The swap is then represented twice. First using the actual cashflows occurring under the swap; column [1] shows the cashflows resulting from the bond being paid away on the swap, and column [3] the floating cashflows based upon the implied Libor rates and the breakeven margin of 766 bp pa. The second representation uses the Notional Principal approach; the bond cashflows are shown in column [2], and the breakeven margin cashflows alone in column [4]. Finally, the margin is also calculated directly using the above formula. Notice that in this model there is a short first floating receipt, from 6 February to 10 April which then lines up the subsequent cashflows and ensures that both sides of the swap, and hence the package, finish on the same date.

Consider the NP approach in a little more detail. If we were to wear a bond hat, i.e. discounting the bond cashflows using the YTM, then the pay side of the swap would value to zero. Hence the breakeven margin would also be zero. Asset packaging wouldn't work! But we have valued the bond cashflows off the IBOR curve, which is considerably lower and hence values the future bond cashflows more highly. The bond YTM reflects the CCC+ creditworthiness of the issuer, whilst the swap curve assumes a general credit rating similar to the IBOR market, namely about A+.

This discussion summarises the typical traditional approaches to credit within the two markets. The bond market has a well-developed sense of credit-adjusted returns as represented by the existence of multiple spread curves. Transactions in the interbank swap market are generally collateralised, as discussed in Section 6.7. Hence a dealer is much more likely to ascertain whether there is any spare credit capacity in the overall dealing limit with the counterparty, and if so make a price irrespective of the creditworthiness of the counterparty. Transactions with end-users may be based upon credit-adjusted swap pricing. Initially this met with little success as obviously the banks became uncompetitive, but following the economic crises in the Far East and Eastern Europe in 1997–9, and with the introduction of the new Accord, pricing has become more credit-sensitive. The modelling of credit-adjusted pricing will be discussed in Section 6.7.

At the end of the packaging process, typically performed by a professional, the investor will receive:

- details of the bond;
- identification of the swap counterparty;
- details of the swap plus resulting margin over Libor;

plus full supporting documentation on the bond purchase from say EuroClear, and an ISDA Master Agreement for the swap. The investor becomes the owner of the two separate components, which would enable one to be sold off later if required. Obviously the investor is responsible for the swap obligations if the bond defaults. It is feasible to find a third party such as a bank to take on the credit risks of the bond—as discussed later—but there would be a compensating charge.

Therefore asset packaging is to some extent an arbitrage between the two valuation approaches in the two markets. The margin being earned by the investor is not "profit", but a recompense for the risk that, if the bond defaults, he will still have to make the swap payments. Whether the margin is adequate or not is obviously a judgement which provides stimulus to the market.

5.2   CREATION AND PRICING OF A PAR MATURITY ASSET SWAP

The maturity of the above package matches the maturity of the bond, namely about 4 years and 11 months. In many cases, the investor does not want such an irregular maturity, but would want a regular maturity such as exactly 5 years long. In this case the argument is more subtle as the dates and maturity of the floating side of the swap do not match the dates and maturity of the bond cashflows. Using the above bond's dates, the bond redeems on 10 January 2013, whereas the package matures on 6 February 2013, a mismatch of about a month. Under the IF approach, this must also give rise to two additional swap cashflows: namely, the payment of the bond redemption amount on 10 January 2013, and the receipt of the par amount on 6 February 2013.

However, if we again assume a synthetic exchange of package principal, then the swap reverts back to the common form, namely the bond cashflows on the pay side, and the floating margin on the receive side. As the pay side of this swap is identical to the previous par swap, the value of the two receive sides must also be the same. The value of a receive side can be written as:

$$\text{PV} = m * \text{Principal} * \sum d_i * \text{DF}_i = m * P * Q_T = \text{constant}$$

As the maturity of the par maturity swap is greater than that of the par swap, hence $Q_{\text{par maturity}} > Q_{\text{par}}$, this implies that $m_{\text{par maturity}} < m_{\text{par}}$. Indeed, we could use this relationship to calculate the new margin approximately. As shown in Worksheet 5.4, the breakeven margin is 755 bp, a reduction of some 1.3%.

5.3 DISCOUNTING, EMBEDDED LOANS AND FORWARD VALUING

This relationship gives rise to another idea. Suppose the investor has a target margin to achieve. By reducing the principal amount provided by the investor, the margin must increase. But if the principal is lower than the dirty price of the bond, how can the packager buy the bond in the first place? Simple, embed the balance of the money as a borrowing from the swap counterparty!

For example, assume that the investor only provides 90 to buy the package. There is an immediate shortfall of 5.93, which is to be received upfront. At the maturity of the bond, the investor is repaid the 90, and the balance of 10 $(= 100 - 90)$ is paid away on the swap. Everything else follows as before, giving rise to a very handsome breakeven margin of 851 bp on a principal amount of 90 (see Worksheet 5.5).

Why does this work? Suppose the bond defaults, so that all future cashflows are lost. The investor argues that he will lose his investment, namely the 90, but no more!![2] There-fore the swap counterparty is taking on some of the credit risk of the bond issuer. What is the implied rate of interest on this embedded loan? Through the discounting process, it is IBOR flat. But that is the fair rate for an A+ exposure, not a CCC+. The counterparty is said to be subsidising the investor by absorbing some of the credit risk without receiving compensation. This is an example of a situation that arises in many structured swaps, namely they contain embedded loans and deposits. Consider a simpler example: the implied forward IR curve is positive, and you enter into a receiver's swap. This suggests that, near the beginning of the swap, you will be a net recipient of cash, whereas (if the forward rates remain constant as implied by the curve) you become a net payer of cash at the end. In another language, you borrow upfront and repay at the end; the implied rate of interest on the loan is IBOR flat. We can however employ the forward-valuing technique discussed in Chapter 3. Instead of discounting, any cashflow received has to be invested at some rate, and any cashflow paid has to be borrowed at a (typically different) rate. A money account is created, and the breakeven margin is calculated so that the balance of the account at the end of the package is zero. If the investment/borrowing rates are assumed to be a zero spread to the forward IBOR curve, then the margin is once again 846 bp. However, if the borrowing margin is set to IBOR + 50 bp (and zero for deposit margin), then the breakeven margin reduces to 846 bp (see Worksheet 5.6).

5.4 FURTHER EXTENSIONS TO ASSET PACKAGING

This chapter has concentrated on relatively simple asset packaging, and tried to introduce some basic structures such as par and par maturity packages. The chapter ended with the application of forward-valuing packages, as they often involve lumpy cashflows. The swapping of more complex securities, especially involving embedded options, is discussed in Chapter 11, where more advanced modelling techniques are introduced.

---

[2] In fact this is not entirely correct in this situation, because the investor also takes over responsibility for paying the cashflows under the swap, so the counterparty should still receive the 10 back at the end. But the broad argument is true.

6

Credit Derivatives

BACKGROUND AND OBJECTIVE

The modern credit markets, whereby organisations and individuals transfer credit risk, started in the late 1980s as the result of classic securitisation. Financial institutions in the US were granting residential mortgages, gathering them into large portfolios, and then selling the resultant cashflows to investors. Hence the credit risks on the mortgages were being transferred to the investors. When the economy turned down in the late 1980s, defaults started to rise, and investors become nervous. In response, total return swaps were developed. In essence these are very simple:

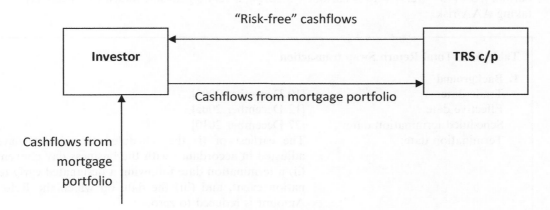

The mortgage-related credit-risky cashflows are paid away in return for "risk-free" cashflows.

In the US, there was a well-established and active secondary loan market. The loan documentation allowed banks to enter into a loan with a customer, and then sell the loan to a third party. Banks in Europe however had no such opportunities; loans had to respect customer confidentiality and were not transferable. The creation of TRSs enabled European banks to retain the loans on their balance sheets, whilst transferring the credit risk. This provided significant impetus to the development of the credit derivative market. This chapter starts by describing the first form of credit derivatives, namely total return swaps, and then its successor, single-name credit default swaps. Details of the market operations are provided, as this is a market with a number of unique conventions which are extremely important for users to understand. The relationship between CDSs and the corporate bond market are explored, and the pricing and hedging of generic CDSs developed. Based upon that, implied probabilities of credit events are then derived from CDS prices, which in turn permits the pricing of more complex structures such as forward start and amortising CDSs and CDS swaptions (see Chapter 10). Multiname CDSs are briefly discussed, and the Appendix describes a copula simulation approach for the modelling of credit portfolios. Finally, building upon this work, the credit-adjusted pricing of swaps is discussed.

6.1 TOTAL RETURN SWAPS

Table 6.1 summarises the termsheet of a TRS executed in December 2005 between two counterparties, A and B. Party A has bought the Reference Obligation, namely a 5-year AAA floating-rate note paying 3-month €uribor + 75 bp. The size of the purchase, defined as the initial Reference Amount, is €25 million.

Under Section 2, Party A pays to Party B any interest received on the note. In return, Party B will pay €uribor + 12.5 bp based on a principal equal to the Reference Amount. In addition, if the issuer of the note (partially or fully) defaults at any time so that the Reference Amount is reduced, Party B must make a payment equal to the reduction to Party A.

To ensure the risk-free nature of B's payments, under Section 6 collateral of €5 million has to be initially posted with A. This collateral will earn €uribor + 10 bp. Why does B want to enter into such a transaction? The return on the €5m collateral is €uribor + 5 * (75 − 12.5) + 10 = €uribor + 3.225%; a very significant return for effectively taking AAA risk.

Table 6.1   Total Return Swap transaction

1. Background

Trade date:	[10 December 2005].
Effective date:	[12 December 2005].
Scheduled termination date:	[27 December 2010].
Termination date:	The earliest of (i) the scheduled termination date, as adjusted in accordance with the business day convention, (ii) a termination date following a designated early termination event, and (iii) the date on which the Reference Amount is reduced to zero.
Reference Obligation:	Maturity: [27 December 2010].
Issued by a SPV	Coupon: 3-month €uribor + [0.75]%.
Indicative rating by S&P:	AAA.
Reference Amount:	EUR 25,000,000 subject to principal reductions under the Reference Obligation due to its terms and conditions.
Business days:	London, New York and TARGET settlement date.

2. Payments by Party A

Party A payment amount:	The amount of any interest (other than principal repayment or prepayment), if any, actually received by a holder of the initial Reference Amount of the Reference Obligation.
Payment dates:	Same business day on which Party A receives the Party A payment amount (if any), commencing on the first such date to occur after the effective date and ending on the termination date.

3. Payments by Party B

Party B first payments

Party B notional amount: Reference Amount.

Floating rate: 3-month €uribor + [0.125%].

Payment dates: [The 27th of each March, June, September and December].

Party B second payments

Party B second payment amount: Capital depreciation (if any).

Payment date: Each date when a capital depreciation occurs.

4. Capital depreciation   Any reduction in the aggregate principal amount of the Reference Obligation in accordance with its terms and conditions or any amount defined as capital depreciation under condition 5 (see below).

5. Early termination event   If the Reference Obligation is redeemed in whole or otherwise matures on any day prior to the scheduled termination date, then, notwithstanding the scheduled termination date, this transaction shall terminate on such day and such day shall be the termination date. The capital depreciation for this purpose shall be an amount equal to the then-outstanding aggregate principal amount of the Reference Obligation minus the actual amount paid by the obligor to holders of such Reference Obligation.

6. Documentation   Party B will enter into an ISDA master agreement and Credit Support Annex (CSA) with Party A, each to be governed by English law under the following terms:

(a) Party B shall agree to provide an amount of credit support to Party A on the effective date equal to 20% of the initial Reference Amount; this amount to be the minimum amount until the termination date.

(b) Party B agrees to pay additional amounts of credit support when the valuation plus [5.4]% of the initial Reference Amount exceeds the existing balance of credit support.

(c) The valuation will be calculated daily by Party A.

(d) The valuation shall be calculated using Party A's proprietary models.

(e) Party A will pay interest on Party B's credit support balance at the following rates:

     (i) First EUR 5m at 3-month Euribor + 0.10% and

     (ii) any additional amount at EONIA flat.

The above TRS is said to have a leverage of five, indicating the amount of protection being received by Party A. In the early and mid-1990s, the main counterparties were hedge funds. The financial markets over this period were very benign with few defaults, and TRSs with leverages of 10, 20 or even 30 were not uncommon!! The actual amount of protection being provided with these leverages should be, but seldom was, questioned. The Russian crisis in August 1998, and the subsequent collapse and rescue of the hedge fund Long Term Capital Management, put an effective end to such high leverage.

6.2   CREDIT DEFAULT SWAPS

However, the TRS market had already been dying for some years. The classic TRS involves an exchange of principal-based periodic cashflows plus the element of credit protection. The value of a TRS would fluctuate not only upon perceived changes in the riskiness of the Reference Obligation, but also on changes in the levels of interest rates, just like a corporate bond. Credit Default Swaps were developed in response to the demand for a cleaner form of credit transfer.

Based upon the situation above, a CDS could provide Party A with protection as follows:

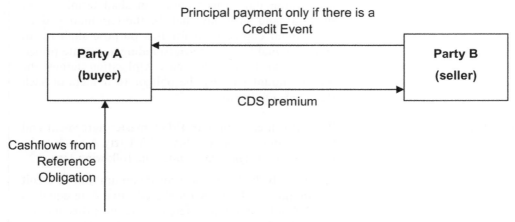

Party A buys a CDS from Party B; A pays a regular premium (in the above example, 62.5 bp) to B and in return, if the principal on the Reference Obligation is reduced, receives a principal payment to cover that loss. CDSs look, for all intents and purposes, and behave very much as insurance policies, providing protection if an Event occurs. Table 6.2 shows some example premiums: these are quoted on a per annum basis, and paid quarterly in arrears, usually on an ACT/360 basis. Once a payment has been made, then usually the swap stops; in other words, it is a one-claim instrument.

There are however some important conventions:

1. In December 2002, the CDS market moved to standardised payment (coupon) dates, namely 20th of March, June, September and December, or the next business day. This was to assist the trading of CDSs; if a trader sells a CDS on one day, and then buys a hedging CDS from a different counterparty a week later, the two premium dates will exactly match. Hence, if today's date is 4 February 2008, a 5-year swap would mature on 20 March 2013—note: the final maturity date does not have to be a business day.

Table 6.2 Example CDS premiums, 24 June 2005

ShortName	Tier	Av Rating	6m (%)	1y (%)	2y (%)	3y (%)	5y (%)	7y (%)	10y (%)	15y (%)	20y (%)	30y (%)	Recovery (%)
Hellenic Rep	SNRFOR	A		0.06	0.09	0.13	0.18	0.22	0.29	0.31	0.34	0.40	37.86
Russian Fedn	SNRFOR	BBB	0.43	0.49	0.63	0.77	1.01	1.21	1.40	1.60	1.65	1.71	28.84
Rep. South Africa	SNRFOR	BBB	0.15	0.15	0.25	0.38	0.61	0.78	0.94	1.12	1.15	1.25	28.23
Hong Kong Spl Admin Region	SNRFOR	A	0.06	0.07	0.08	0.10	0.15	0.18	0.22			0.30	32.50
People's Rep China	SNRFOR	A	0.12	0.13	0.18	0.22	0.30	0.37	0.47	0.57	0.56	0.65	31.13
Société Air France	SNRFOR	Unrated	0.19	0.23	0.32	0.43	0.64	0.79	0.98	1.06	1.07	1.11	39.12
ABN AMRO Bk NV	SNRFOR	AA	0.03	0.05	0.07	0.08	0.12	0.15	0.19		0.25		39.86
ABN AMRO Bk NV	SUBLT2	A		0.07	0.11	0.14	0.21	0.26	0.33		0.40		19.88
Ford Mtr Co	SNRFOR	BB	2.16	2.29	3.61	5.08	5.97	6.14	6.34	6.27	6.30	6.37	39.48
Gen Mtrs Corp	SNRFOR	BB	2.73	2.96	4.57	6.36	7.41	7.62	7.75	7.77	7.79	7.80	39.25

Source: Markit Group Limited—all data provided as is, with no warranties.

2. CDSs are traditionally traded on a $T + 1$ basis, namely protection starts at 00:01 on the next business day after the transaction date, and finishes at 23:59 on the maturity date. If the trade date is within 30 (calendar) days of the first coupon date, then no coupon is paid on that date, but the first coupon is paid on the second coupon date using a long first period (this is known as the stub convention).
3. If the underlying Reference Entity is so risky that the premium exceeds 10% pa paid quarterly, then the pricing conventionally switches to "upfront" with a running spread of 500 bp pa. For example, assume that the fair premium is deemed to be 12% pa; the buyer of the CDS would have to make an upfront payment of PV{700 bp pa over the anticipated lifetime of the CDS}[1] plus an additional 500 bp pa paid quarterly. If an Event occurs, then a "clawback" clause dictates how much of the upfront payment would have to be repaid by the seller to the buyer.

This market is rapidly growing, and currently covers about 5,000 Reference Entities. Most of the entities have a credit rating either in the lower part of the investment grade band or the upper part of the high-yield band—typically ranging from A to BB. Following the downgrading of Ford and General Motors in May 2005 out of investment grade, high-yield names have been expanding most rapidly. The depth of the market is extremely variable, and only the top 250 names or so maintain good liquidity. Supply and demand is a very important contributor to pricing in this market, and premium volatility is extremely high (possibly ten times greater than in the IR swap markets).[2]

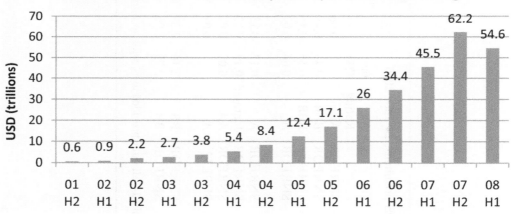

Whilst a CDS appears to be a relatively simple transaction, there have been three important difficulties with the market. First, a CDS is usually written on a specific Reference Entity, and not on a specific Reference Obligation. If the entity undergoes organisational restructuring (in the jargon, suffers a Succession Event), what might happen to the CDS? For example, in 2000 a UK company called National Power split itself into two separate companies, Innogy and International Power. Innogy took the majority of NP's assets,

---

[1] Usually discounted off the swap curve flat.
[2] Taken from ISDA. These numbers probably contain a high degree of double-counting; the DTCC Trade Warehouse has recorded about half this volume over H2 2008.

whilst IP took the majority of NP's obligations. NP then effectively became a risk-free shell company. What would happen to a CDS written on NP? Would it be cancelled? Remain on NP? Transfer to Innogy, or to IP, or split into two and transfer to both? The standard document in force at the time did not permit either cancellation or splitting under these circumstances. If the CDS remained on NP, then the buyer still has to pay the original premium but now on a shell that cannot suffer an event. If it transfers to Innogy, then the buyer has to pay the original premium on a company that is less risky than the old NP, whereas if it transfers to IP, then the buyer has now protection on a riskier company. The documentation was very unclear, and the self-interests of buyers and sellers were very much to the fore. The succession section was rewritten in 2003, but there have been unanticipated events subsequently (especially in 2005–7 as the result of the activities of private equity funds), that have caused disruptions to the market.

Second, has a publicly notifiable Credit Event actually occurred? The standard documentation recognises three Events for companies, namely bankruptcy, failure to payment (usually subject to a grace period and materiality threshold) and restructuring of one or more obligation; for sovereigns, moratorium and repudiation are recognised. Restructuring is defined as:

1. A unilateral change to material terms of any Obligation.
2. The mandatory exchange of Obligations for new Obligations with different terms due to a deterioration in the creditworthiness of the Reference Entity.

For example, in 2000 Conseco, an US insurer, renegotiated the terms of some maturing bank debt, pushing the redemption date out by 15 months whilst increasing the spread over Libor from 50 to 250 bp. Clearly an Event had occurred but at whose instigation? The banks or the company? Those banks participating in the renegotiations had not lost any money at that point, indeed it may be argued they were on better terms, and yet were able to make a claim. Non-banks often point to conflicts of interest around such an Event. Yet the vast majority of CDSs written on investment grade entities recognise restructuring; it is common practice not to recognise restructuring for high-yield entities. The Basel Accord also contributes here, only permitting a maximum of 60% capital relief if restructuring is excluded as an event.

Restructuring also introduces the opportunity of gaming, because the swap stops after a recognised Event. If a Restructuring has occurred, both the buyer and seller have to make a decision: is the Event to be recognised, or would it be better to wait for a hard Event to occur? If the buyer thinks the losses would be greater under a hard Event, then he would prefer to wait, whereas the seller would prefer to trigger immediately.

Third, once an Event has occurred, how is the size of payment to be determined? In 2007, about 75% of CDSs were physical-settled. Consider the example above, and assume the principal on the note had been reduced through an Event. The owner of the note could deliver the impaired value note to the seller of the CDS, and receive the full face value of €25 million in cash. Some 24% of CDSs were cash-settled. This would require the buyer and the seller of the CDS to agree the market value of the note after the Event, and then the buyer pays {€25m − Value} to the seller. A small proportion are fixed-settled, whereby the buyer and seller agree a fixed percentage of the principal—typically 60%—upfront that would be paid if an Event occurred.

In 2004, physical-settled CDSs represented nearly 90% of the market. Delphi, a large US car component manufacturer, went into bankruptcy in October 2005. Before the Event, its bonds had been trading at about 49% of face value; after the Event, they leapt to 72%!! This implied a net payment to the CDS buyer of 38% of the principal. Later Fitch estimated a fair price for the bonds was less than 10% of face value. Why did the bond price rise so dramatically? It has been estimated that about 90% of CDS buyers do not have the underlying exposure, but are merely speculating on price changes. When the Event occurred, all buyers of physical-settled CDSs must deliver an acceptable security to receive payment. The rule is very simple: no delivery, no payment—as some buyers have found to their cost. The impact of this "squeeze", as it is known, has been getting worse as the CDS market has been doubling in size each year, whereas the underlying stock of deliverable securities has been relatively static. The move towards cash-settled is hardly surprising; the current difficulty here is the length of time the buyer needs to wait after the Event until the market value of some Reference Asset has settled down following the fluctuations of physical settlement. Currently, these CDSs are taking over 3 months on average to settle, with some such as Parmalat over 6 months.

The Event at Conseco highlighted another difficulty. Whilst it was the maturing bank debt that was being renegotiated, Conseco also had some long-dated subordinate debt as well. The price of the renegotiated debt fell to 92% of face value, whereas the price of the subordinate debt fell to 68%. The buyer of a CDS can select, within certain fairly wide criteria, which physical security (or even portfolio of securities) to deliver. Not surprisingly, buyers of Conseco CDSs tried to deliver the subordinate debt, including the banks involved in the restructuring! After market discussions, the standard ISDA documentation was changed in 2003 to permit three alternative delivery clauses in the event of a restructuring:

- Modified Restructuring—the maturity of a deliverable security cannot exceed 30 months beyond the maturity of the restructured debt;
- Modified Modified Restructuring—the maturity of a deliverable security cannot exceed 60 months beyond the maturity of the restructured debt;
- Full (or complete) Restructuring—there is no maturity constraint.

In practice, most investment grade CDSs in the US are traded on a MR clause, whereas MMR is often used in Europe and FR in the rest of the world. This does give rise to parallel pricing; a FR CDS is likely to cost 10–20% more than a No-R CDS on the same name. Following extensive industrial discussions, some further conventions were agreed to be implemented on 8th April 2009 (so-called Big Bang day!). Some of these conventions were global, and some confined, at least in the first instance, to the US market. For example:

- The world was to be divided into five regions: Americas, Japan, Asia ex-Japan, EMEA, Australia/NZ. A Determination Committee (DC) consisting of 15 voting members, plus some non-voting, drawn from both the buy and sell sides of the industry, would be elected for each region.
- If you think a Credit Event has occurred within the last 60 days from today, then the DC must be approached for a decision. The implication of this move is that buying a CDS today gives you coverage from {Today − 60 days} all the way through until maturity date; note that coverage is no longer linked to the trade date. The implication of this new convention is that two swaps traded on different dates will now provide exactly the same coverage.

- Similarly, if you think a Succession Event has occurred within the last 90 days from today, then the DC must be approached for a decision and a statement about the outcome.

- Unhappiness over the settlement procedures led some market participants to take part voluntarily in a Credit Event Auction (CEA) process. This required market-makers in a relevant security issued by the Reference Entity to agree (through a complex bidding process[3]) an average price for that security some 30 calendar days after the Event. Buyers of the CDS would then either receive {100 − Price} as a cash settlement, or physical settlement, at their choice. The new convention is that CEAs will become compulsory for all CDS settlements.

- In the US, Restructuring will no longer be a recognised Event for normal CDSs, although it may still be possible to get an illiquid one with it. It is unlikely that Europe will follow this convention for various legal reasons, mainly that Chapter 11 bankruptcy (which allows an entity to restructure whilst under protection) does not really exist. In July, a Restructuring CEA was introduced; if the buyer has triggered the recognition of the Event, then there are maturity restrictions on which instruments are deliverable.

- In the US, payments for CDSs will be on an upfront basis, with 100 bp and 500 bp pa running spreads for investment grade and non-investment grade names, respectively. Due to the wider range of credits in Europe, running spreads are 25 bp, 100 bp, 500 bp and 1,000 bp pa, with also 300 bp and 750 bp spreads pemitted for recouponing an existing CDS (the objective is to ensure that the upfront payment is not too large).

One other problem, namely the slowness of agreed documentation and confirmations, which the FSA and Fed Reserve complained about in 2005, is being addressed, and increasingly standardised documentation and electronic-trading platforms are being used. The market has a target to get trades entered in the internal systems on the same day, and confirmations to be issued by $T + 5$, from mid-2009.

Whilst the original form of CDS permitted the delivery of any acceptable security, such as a bond or an assignable loan, in practice the market priced and hedged using traded bonds, as described in Section 6.3. But the bulk of corporate funding, especially in the non-US, is through bank loans. Loans are typically less risky than bonds for a variety of reasons: stronger covenants, closer bank relationships, material change clauses, higher recovery rates, and therefore the price of a CDS protecting a loan should be lower than that based on bonds. The loan CDS market started in November 2005, and has grown extremely rapidly. Entering into a swap, or buying an option, involved a potential credit exposure on the counterparty. The precise size of this exposure is unknown, as it depends upon movements in the financial markets, as discussed in more detail in Section 6.7. Contingent CDSs, providing credit protection over derivative transactions, have been available since 2002.

Reverting back to the earliest days of the credit markets, it is now feasible to get, especially in the US, Asset-Backed CDSs. These usually work on a pay-as-you-go basis. An investor buys an asset-backed security which would generate anticipated cashflows, and simultaneously buys an ABCDS for some regular premium. If the cashflow in any period is lower than anticipated for whatever reason, then the ABCDS seller makes good the shortfall, and the swap then continues.

---

[3] See, for example, *A CEA Primer* and *The Results of the Lehmann Brothers Auction*, both published by Creditex in October 2008, for further details.

6.3   PRICING AND HEDGING OF GENERIC CDSs

Assume a trader has just sold a CDS; she could hedge the transaction by selling a corporate bond issued by the same Reference Entity. How much of the bond should she sell? We will approach this question in a number of stages.

Imagine the following situation: you wish to value a cashflow of (say) 1 unit to be received at time T in the future. Obviously the simple answer is to discount it: $PV = 1 * DF_T$. If the cashflow is credit-risky, then the appropriate discount factor could be estimated from traded securities which carry similar risk. Thus the T-bond curve would give risk to credit risk-free DFs, whilst a BBB curve would generate credit-adjusted DF_{BBB}s. Assume that the riskiness of the cashflow is due to the possibility of an Event:

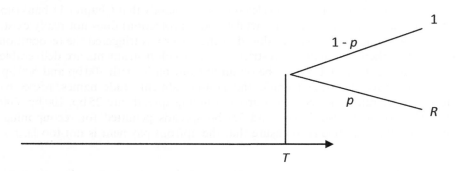

If p is the probability of an Event, and $R < 1$ the outcome when an Event occurs, then the expected outcome is $E\{1\} = p * R + (1 - p) * 1 = 1 - p * (1 - R)$. If we were to experience this situation many times, then $E\{1\}$ is the anticipated outcome; this is no longer uncertain, and therefore we can write $PV = E\{1\} * DF_{T,\text{risk-free}}$. Arbitrage suggests that the value of the cashflow should be the same using either approach; namely, $DF_{T,\text{BBB}} = E\{1\} * DF_{T,\text{risk-free}}$.

Now consider the properties of a generic Floating Rate Note, issued at par $= 100$, paying Libor flat on a periodic basis, and redeemed at par. If it is assumed that the note cashflows are discounted at Libor, using the above argument, then the value of the note immediately after the coupon payment must be par. Therefore consider any period of the note: assume this starts at time 0 and finishes at time 1. The value of the note at time 1 before the coupon payment is $100 * (1 + d_{01} * L_{01})$ where L is the Libor fixing at the beginning of the period and d the length of the period. The value of the note at some time t during the period is given by:

$$V_t = 100 * (1 + d_{01} * L_{01})/(1 + d_{t1} * L_{t1}) = \text{Clean price} + \text{Accrued}$$

The above trader does the following transactions:

1. Sells a CDS on some Reference Entity for a regular premium of m pa.
2. Buys a "risk-free" FRN with matching maturity for 100, generating Libor. (Of course, Libor is not really risk-free, but represents a prime interbank rate; this point will be addressed later.)
3. Sells a risky FRN for 100, assuming the same credit risk as under the CDS, generating Libor $+ s$ (spread)

If the CDS does not suffer an Event, then the Libor rates cancel and the net effect is an income of $(m - s)$ pa.

Now assume the Entity suffers an Event at time T. The CDS must be settled, and the FRNs unwound:

- For CDSs assume the risky FRN is delivered, therefore size of payment $= 100 - P_T$ where P_T is the clean price of the note. However, because the premium is paid in arrears, the buyer must pay the outstanding accrued of $100 * d_{0T} * m$.
- The risk-free FRN has to be sold for its clean price plus accrued, and the risky one bought back for its clean price of P_T plus accrued $\{L + s\}$. It can be easily shown that the net income here (to a first order) is $100 - P_T + \text{Accrued } s$, irrespective of what has happened to Libor since the fixing date.

Hence the net effect is simply accrued $\{m - s\}$ pa as before. This implies that, in the absence of riskless profits, the CDS premium m should equal the spread s over Libor for a FRN with the same maturity and issuer credit risk as the CDS. The spread can be estimated using the par maturity packaging techniques discussed in Chapter 5.

For example: suppose we wish to price a 5-year CDS, and the following bond is available:

Issuer:	xxx
Maturity:	23 July 2013
Coupon:	5.25% ANN
Clean price:	96.375

If today's date is 4 February 2008, a 5-year swap would mature on 20 March 2013 (remember—standardised roll dates), there would be 21 premium payments assuming no Event, and the first period would be a short stub. Worksheet 6.2 is constructed as before; the breakeven margin of 240 bp is calculated in three ways.

Note that the bond matures about 4 months after the CDS, which implies an embedded loan in the asset swap. Ideally, the funding and credit implications for this loan should be factored into the swap spread.

This margin can also be directly calculated using the asset-swapping formula from the previous chapter, namely:

$$\text{Margin} = -10,000 * \text{PV}_{\text{Security}}/(Q * \text{Principal}) = -10,000 * -11.455/(4.772 * 100)$$

$$= 240 \text{ bp}$$

This margin is called the ASW (asset swap) spread, and is widely available on trading screens.

As a quick-and-dirty approach approximation, traders often calculate the bond's Z-spread s, which is calculated from:

$$\text{Dirty price of bond} = \sum_t \text{CF}_t * \exp\{-(Z_t + s) * t\}$$

where Z_t is the (continuously compounded) zero-coupon rate for the appropriate cashflow time t implied from the swap curve (see Worksheet 6.3). As zero rates are spot rates, usually the Z-spread is higher than the ASW spread, but this depends upon the steepness of the curve. In this particular case, the breakeven Z-spread is 226 bp. As the Z-spread also ignores the actual maturity and frequency of the CDS, it is a gross approximation. There are other spreads sometimes quoted, such as:

- I-spread: YTM of bond–swap rate of correct tenor
- T-spread: YTM of bond–YTM of (interpolated) government bond.

How well does this model replicate the actual CDS prices quoted in the market? Define the CDS basis as: CDS premium – ASW spread; both are usually taken from the bid side of the two markets. There are various structural factors that have been ignored above that move the basis; the most important ones are probably:

- For a positive Basis:
    - the buyer possesses a delivery option for physical-settled CDSs;
    - the buyer may possess undisclosed information about the Reference Entity—this is often called the moral hazard premium;
    - corporate bonds may have material change clauses;
    - if the bond is trading below par, then the actual loss on the bond is likely to be less than the payout on the swap;
    - Libor is not a risk-free rate, hence the spread for good names may be small or even negative.
- For a negative Basis:
    - the credit risk between the buyer and seller of the CDS is asymmetric in favour of the seller—although many CDSs are collateralised;
    - the funding cost for many traders is above Libor, whereas the asset-packaging techniques, as discussed in Chapter 5, often implicitly assume a Libor-flat cost;
    - shorting corporate bonds usually means borrowing the bond under a repo agreement; these tend to be highly illiquid and hence expensive.

The net effect of these factors is that the Basis has tended over the years to average at about 10–20 bp above zero. But, as mentioned above, supply and demand does play a major role, and the volatility of premiums is very high, causing the basis to fluctuate significantly. Beta is a concept drawn from the Capital Asset Pricing Model, and measures relative volatility; the CDS market is said to have a high beta relative to the cash (physical bond) market. An example of a typical beta trade would be, if the trader thinks that the creditworthiness of an Entity is likely to deteriorate, to:

- buy a CDS;
- buy a corporate bond.

If the trader is correct, the value of the CDS would rise faster than the drop in the value of the bond.

There have been a number of recent studies about the efficiency of the CDS market. The following graph was published in a working paper from the Bank of International

Settlement.[4] The topmost line shows the basis (for 5-year CDSs) as defined above; ignoring the hiatus at the end of 2001, the basis fluctuates a lot, but is on balance positive. The other curves are spreads over different T-bond curves; the fact that all of these are permanently skewed away from zero provides evidence that Libor is used as the base risk-free rate.

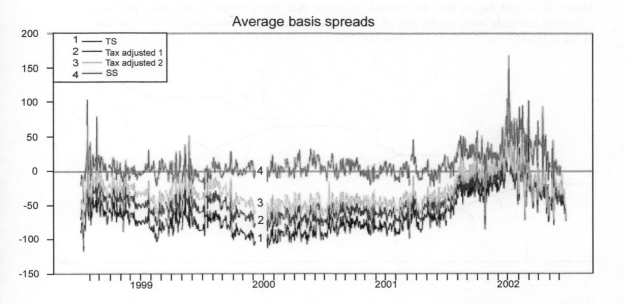

The main events at the end of 2001 were the collapses of Enron and Worldcom; the reaction of the market demonstrates the high beta of the CDS market relative to the cash market.

There is one further reason why the basis is, on average, positive. Assume that the basis is significantly negative; a risk-less[5] profit could be made by buying an asset package and simultaneously buying a CDS to hedge the credit risk. In theory, a risk-less profit could also be achieved if the basis was positive, but shorting packages is far less efficient.

As this market has developed, increasingly investors of non-governmental securities have been arguing that the return on the security (as a swap spread) must exceed the risk-free return plus the CDS premium. Such activity naturally brings the basis into line.

Just as generic IRSs are priced off the governmental bond curve, as discussed in Chapter 3, so are generic CDSs priced off the corporate bond market. However, in each case, there is no perfect relationship between them, which is why, at the end of the day, trading is an art and not merely a science.

How might a trader hedge a CDS using a corporate bond, albeit accepting basis risk? If the margin shifted by 1 bp, the risky FRN and hence the CDS increased in value by

---

[4] *An Empirical Comparison of Credit Spreads between the Bond Market and the Credit Default Swap Market*, BIS Working Paper 160, August 2004. The BIS does not warrant or guarantee the accuracy, completeness or fitness for purpose of the BIS material and shall in no circumstances be liable for any loss, damage, liability or expense suffered by any person in connection with reliance by that person on any such material. The original text is available free of charge from the BIS website (*www.bis.org*).

[5] In practice, arbitrage profits are never risk-less. The CDS will not exactly hedge the asset package due to technical differences in documentation and market conventions, but should be close.

$47,723 per $100m nominal. A similar shift caused the bond price to reduce by $47,678. Hence the hedge ratio is: $100m $* 47,723/47,678 = 100.1$m to be sold (see Worksheet 6.4).

6.4 MODELLING A CDS

Consider a bought CDS of some maturity T. Subdivide its maturity up into time slices, Δt. These slices can be as fine as desired. Assume that both credit events and premium payments can only occur at the end of a time slice.[6] Under these circumstances, the lifetime of the CDS is:

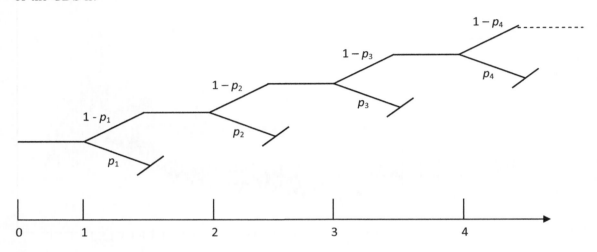

Define:

- p_k as the probability of an Event occurring at the end of period k, as shown. This will be called a Forward Default Probability (FDP) to fit in with the conventions of credit modelling, although strictly it is an Event probability.
- S_k as the probability that the CDS survives at least to the end of period k:

$$S_k = \prod_j (1 - p_j) = S_{k-1} * (1 - p_k), \quad \text{where } S_0 = 1$$

- H_k as the conditional probability that the CDS survives until period $k - 1$, but suffers an Event at the end of period k (often called Hazard[7]): $H_k = S_{k-1} * p_k$.

Assume, for the moment, that the FDPs are known, and that the anticipated payout on the CDS if an Event were to occur is $(1 - R)$. R is conventionally currently set to 40% of the notional principal P for investment grade names in the CDS market. The expected kth cashflows on the two sides of the swap are:

- Premium$_k$: $P * m * \Delta t_k * S_{k-1}$;
- Payment$_k$: $P * (1 - R) * H_k$.

---

[6] It is feasible, but not common, to get "postponed" CDSs, where the payout is delayed until the next standardised roll date. There is full premium payment on the last roll date.

[7] Many people use the Hazard as their base, and derive the FDPs from that. There is some justification for this from insurance modelling.

Notice that S_{k-1} is the probability of paying the kth premium; that is because premiums are paid in arrears, and accrued premium has to be paid. Hence, the breakeven premium[8] is given by:

$$m = (1 - R) * \sum_k H_k * \mathrm{DF}_k / \sum_k \Delta t_k * S_{k-1} * \mathrm{DF}_k$$

where the DF_ks are "risk-free" discount factors taken off the IBOR curve. See Worksheet 6.5 where a time slice is assumed to be a quarter of a year; for the given FDPs in column [1], first the Survival and Hazard rates are calculated, and then the expected cashflows are discounted. The breakeven margin is 741.4 bp pa (this may seem very high, but was in fact taken from a General Motors curve as discussed below.

Obviously, assuming an Event can only occur at the end of a quarter is unrealistic. How would the model change if we assume, for example, shorter time periods such as monthly? The diagram shows the CDS over a quarter:

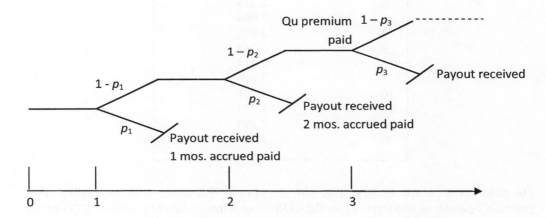

There is a probability of H_1 that there will be an Event at the end of the first month; in this case, both a payout would be received but also 1 month's accrued has to be paid. Similarly, there is a probability of H_2 that there will be an Event at the end of the second month; in this case, 2 months' accrued has to be paid. At the end of the quarter, the premium has to be paid with probability S_3, irrespective of whether an Event occurs or not. If there is an Event, then a payout would be received as before. More generally, if we assume that a quarter is divided into Q slices, the expected value on the premium side for a given quarter is:

$$m * \left\{ \sum_{q=1 \text{ to } Q-1} d_q * H_q * \mathrm{DF}_q + d_Q * S_{Q-1} * \mathrm{DF}_Q \right\}$$

where d_q is the length of time from the start of the quarter until the end of the qth slice. The payment side of the swap is simply summed over all slices for all quarters as before (see Worksheet 6.6).

The JP Morgan model is becoming an industry standard. This assumes that Events will only occur, on average, at the middle of a quarter. Under this assumption, the expected

---

[8] There is a tacit assumption here that credit event rates and interest rates are independent.

values are:

on the premium side: $\quad m * \{0.5 * d_Q * H_Q * \mathrm{DF}_{Q-\frac{1}{2}} + d_Q * S_Q * \mathrm{DF}_Q\}$

on the pay side: $\quad (1 - R) * H_Q * \mathrm{DF}_{Q-\frac{1}{2}}$

The difference in end-result between the two approaches is a small fraction of a basis point.

How are the FDPs estimated? It is common practice to imply them from the quotes in the CDS market, just as implied forward rates are taken off the IRS curve. A General Motors modified restructuring strip will be used as an example, see Table 6.2.

Table 6.2	GM CDS prices
Maturity (years)	**CDS prices (%)**
0.5	2.728
1	2.964
2	4.572
3	6.362
5	7.414
7	7.619
10	7.751
15	7.770
20	7.790
30	7.800

The most common approach, just as with the normal IRS curve, is bootstrapping. This generally operates in two steps. First, the CDS curve is interpolated to estimate CDS prices on a quarterly basis—Hermitian interpolation (as discussed in Chapter 3) has been used in the examples below to do this. Quarterly is used because that is the normal payment frequency of the premium. Second, a modelling frequency has to be selected. Initially, as above, choose a quarterly frequency, and assume that the $\mathrm{FDP}_k, k = 1, \ldots, N - 1$, have been estimated. Using the formula:

$$m * \sum_k \Delta t_k * S_{k-1} * \mathrm{DF}_k = \sum_k (1 - R) * H_k * \mathrm{DF}_k$$

it can be easily solved for p_N, as H_N is the only term that depends upon it (see Worksheet 6.7).

However, if we wish to model Q slices per quarter, then the basic model described above can be used. However, the CDS prices off the curve cannot be estimated more finely than quarterly because the premium frequency must be retained. Therefore the bootstrapping has too many degrees of freedom, and another assumption is required. It is common to assume that either the FDP or the Hazard rate[9] remains constant over all slices in a given

---

[9] Constant instantaneous Hazard functions are probably most commonly used in theory. This has the mathematical advantage that credit-risky continuously compounded forward rates are the sum of the equivalent risk-free continuously compounded rate plus the Hazard (or intensity). In practice, however, most implementations fall back on discrete slices, as these are more readily implied from market data.

quarter. Using the above formula, given we have already estimated S_{N-1}, we guess a single constant value p_N for all the p_q's, estimate H_q and S_{Q-1}, and hence solve for the breakeven premium of CDS_N. But, as this premium is already known off the curve, the correct value for p_N can be found. Worksheet 6.9 demonstrates this on a monthly basis using Hermitian interpolation, and there is a daily model on the CD (Worksheet 6.10).

Adopting such a piecewise constant approach must result in first-degree discontinuities. Other approaches are perfectly feasible, such as piecewise linear or optimisation (see Worksheets 6.11 and 6.12), as described in Chapter 3—see graph below. Instead of constructing an arbitrage-free probability curve, some banks build regression curves such as Nelson–Siegel instead—see Worksheet 6.13.

Estimating FDP curves using GM data

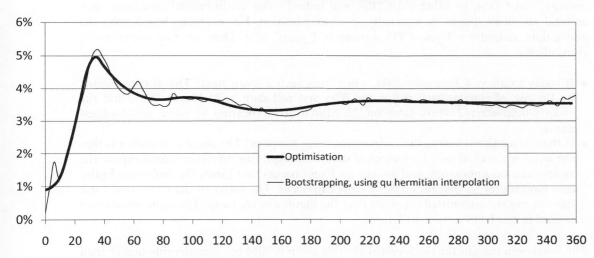

Does the use of Q slices per quarter make a significant difference to the eventual pricing? Provided that the FDPs are implied consistently from the market curve, then pricing differences in structured CDSs is generally less than 1 bp. Worksheets 6.5 and 6.6 referred to above priced a 5-year GM swap, once quarterly and once monthly. As they were using implied probabilities from the same curve, the swaps produced exactly the same premium.

Are these implied probabilities good predictors of real-world events? In the same way that implied forward IRs are poor predictors of future spot IRs, or FX forwards are poor predictors of future spot FXs, numerous studies[10] have concluded that the default probabilities are not good real-world predictors. From a purely trading perspective, that is irrelevant as only relative prices are important; the same applies to hedging as the probabilities do reflect the true cost. But for an end-user, buying or selling long-term credit protection, the implication is important. Increasingly, with the implementation of the

[10] For example: I. Marsh, *What Central Banks Can Learn about Default Risk from Credit Markets*, BIS Paper 12, August 2002; P. Houweling et al., *An Empirical Comparison of Default Swap Pricing Models*, Erasmus University, June 2002; or J. Amato, "Risk aversion and risk premia in the CDS market", *BIS Quarterly Review*, December 2005. More recent studies have suggested that the inclusion of other factors such as stochastic volatility or discrete jumps in asset values may provide an explanation for this apparent divergence between the CDS spreads and the real world: see, for example, B. Zhang et al., *Explaining CDS Spreads with Equity Volatility and Jump Risks of Individual Firms*, BIS Working Paper, September 2005, or R. Anderson, *What Accounts for Time Variation in the Price of Default Risk?*, an early draft working paper from the LSE in London, August 2008.

Internal Rating Based (IRB) approach in the new Basel Accord in many countries from 2008, which requires banks to estimate validated probabilities and recovery rates, cheapness/dearness analysis of CDS prices based upon real-world evidence is becoming more common. This in turn may drive a convergence of the CDS market to the real world. But whilst the estimated percentage of speculators in the CDS market remains extremely high, such a convergence is unlikely.

6.5   PRICING AND VALUING NON-GENERIC CDSs

Once the FDPs have been estimated from a given CDS strip, they may then be used to price non-generic CDSs, such as forward-starting and amortising CDSs as well as options[11] on CDSs, to value old CDSs, and indeed other credit-related structures such as total return swaps, in an internally consistent fashion. For example, based upon the above data, consider a 3-year CDS starting in 2 years' time. There are two questions on conventions:

- If today's date is 4 February 2008, when does such a swap start? This is complicated by the use of standardised roll dates. The first roll date is 20 March 2008, and the swap would start 2 years later on 22 March 2010 (bearing in mind non-business days).
- If there is an Event before the swap starts, what happens? The usual convention is that the swap is knocked out, i.e. cancelled with no obligations on either side. Suppose the swap was a no-knock-out, and assume an Event occurs that forces the Reference Entity into bankruptcy so that no further events can occur. The buyer of the CDS would still have to pay the committed premium over the lifetime of the swap! The same convention is used in the CDS option structures.

The breakeven margin for the forward-starting swap is 1056 bp, considerably higher than the spot 5 year swap, but that reflects the steepness of the forward curve over the first 5 years (see Worksheet 6.14).

To model the no-knock-out version, the Hazard rates remain as before, but the probability of survival on 22 March 2010 is 100%. Using $S_N = S_{N-1} - H_N$, the remaining Survival rates can be estimated; the breakeven margin is now 854 bp. The reduction reflects the probability of 15.68% that GM will suffer an Event before the swap starts, but the buyer would still have to pay the premium—see Worksheet 6.15.

Other structures such as

- FRNs which pay Libor plus a spread with redemption of principal at maturity, but where the note cashflows may cease;
- CDSs where the premium is not fixed over the lifetime, but is refixed at the beginning of each period—see Worksheet 6.16 for an example (not surprisingly, the "floating" version of a generic CDS has a zero margin);
- constant maturity CDSs, where the premium of each period is linked to a longer term CDS rate (just like a yield curve swap). As expected, just like a yield curve swap, this swap may

---

[11] These will be briefly discussed in Chapter 10.

also possess considerable convexity.[12] Worksheets 6.17 and 6.19 price such a CDS without and with convexity adjustment, respectively.

- contingent CDSs, where the underlying exposure on the Entity is itself a derivative, and therefore is subject to fluctuations in the financial markets;
- total return swaps, which consist of an exchange of risk-free and risky cashflows;

may all be handled using the implied FDPs.

The valuation of old CDSs is easier than the valuation of IRSs because of the standardised roll dates. Consider, for example, a 5-year $100m GM CDS traded on 15 August 2006, with a premium of 650 bp pa. This swap will mature on 20 September 2011. From today's date of 4 February 2008, there are 15 periods left. By using today's implied FDP and discount curves, the expected cashflows can be built as before, and the net valuation is $1,152,169 (see Worksheet 6.20).

6.6 BASKET AND PORTFOLIO CDSs

The discussion above has revolved around single-name CDSs. It is also feasible to obtain basket and portfolio CDSs. The difference between a basket and a portfolio is mainly semantic, a basket is a small portfolio with generally less than a dozen entities, whereas a portfolio CDS can be written on a portfolio of several hundred or thousands of entities. The main products are different:

- First-to-Default is probably the most common form of basket CDS: if any one of the entities in the basket suffers an Event, then a payout is made and the CDS stops. These are generally sold as providing cheaper protection than buying a set of individual single-name CDSs, on the assumption that more than one event is highly unlikely. There are also N-to-Default CDSs, which will make N payouts before stopping, and Nth-Loss CDSs, which only pay on the Nth event. These structures are probably less common now than 10 years ago.
- A portfolio CDS is equivalent to an N-to-Default CDS, where N is equal to the number of entities in the portfolio. As the portfolio is large, the probability of all entities suffering an Event, and hence the swap stopping prior to maturity, is remote. These CDS are generally tailored to provide protection over a large portfolio, with no secondary market. They are an integral part of the synthetic CDO market, used by banks to transfer credit risk from a portfolio to buyers of CDO tranches.

Since June 2004, products based upon credit indices have been the largest and fastest growing part of the credit transfer market. These indices are based upon the performance of a standardised portfolio of entities. The most liquid indices are the iTraxx Europe and the US CDX, plus various subindices—see box for further details.

The modelling and pricing of portfolio products is a significant topic in its own right. An

---

[12] The adjustment is calculated as follows (see D. Brigo, *CM CDS Pricing with Market Models*, Working Paper, Banca IMI, December 2004, for full details). If the CMS rate of length L fixed at time t is $P(t, L)$, then this may be expressed as a function of single period forward rates P_i, $i = t, \ldots, L - 1$. The expected value of P_i observed at the fixing date t:

$$P_i(t) = P_i(0) * \exp\left\{ T_{i-1} * \sigma_i * \sum \rho_{i,k} * \sigma_k * d_k * P_k(0) / [d_k * P_k(0) + (1 - R)] \right\}$$

where σ_i and $\rho_{i,k}$ are the volatilities and correlations between the one-period rates (estimated in theory from the CDS options market—see Worksheet 6.18), and the summation k is over t to i.

outline of the commonly used underlying theory and methods is described in Section 6.8 (Appendix).

Credit indices

In June 2004, the formation of iTraxx Europe and the US CDX indices was announced. This has been followed by indices in other regions such as Japan, Asia ex-Japan, Australasia, Emerging Markets and so on. Each index was based upon a carefully constructed portfolio with the following criteria:

- 125 entities drawn in a specified number from seven industrial sectors;
- each entity must be investment grade;
- each entity must have been actively traded in the CDS market over the previous six months.

As entities may be downgraded, or their trading reduces, each composition of the portfolio is "rolled" every 6 months, in March and September, to ensure the index is up to date. The level of each index is fixed everyday as the equally weighted average of the single-name CDS prices on each entity. There are currently four fixings, based upon 3, 5, 7 and 10-year CDS maturities. The graph below shows iTraxx Series (Roll) 8, based on 5-year quotes:

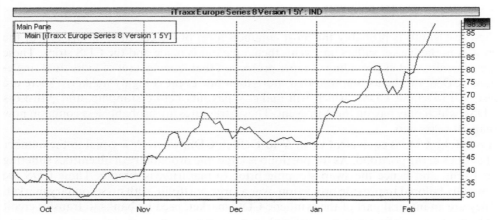

There are also subindices, formed from the entities in each industrial sector (and with two indices representing senior and subordinated debt for the financial sector). There is also a cross-over index which is made up of 50 names which are BBB or worse, active in the CDS market and on Negative Outlook by a rating agency.

There are three main products available which may be bought on any given day:

- Index-linked notes: these pay 3m €uribor + level of index on purchase day quarterly. The notional principal is reduced by 0.8% (= 1/125) each time an entity suffers an Event.
- Index-linked CDSI: the seller receives level of index on purchase day quarterly, but has to make a payment of 0.8% when an Event occurs. These are, in theory, physically settled, but given the squeezes in 2005 onwards, may well become cash-settled.

- Tranches of the index portfolio: different slices of the portfolio can be purchased. Each will pay a quoted rate over, typically, a 5-year period, but losses on the portfolio may reduce the notional principal.

Index-linked products are popular because they represent a wide cross-section of credit exposures within the region, and also possess good market liquidity at least in the current series.

6.7 CREDIT EXPOSURE UNDER SWAPS

When a generic swap is first agreed with a counterparty, its value is zero. As time passes, and rates move, the value will change to be either positive or negative. If the value is positive, then we have a credit exposure on the counterparty. If he (or she) does not fulfil his obligations under the swap, then the positive value cannot be realised. A distinction is made between the current credit exposure (CCE) to a counterparty and the potential future exposure (PFE). When a swap is first agreed, the CCE = 0, but there is still a PFE linked with the potentially favourable movement in rates in the future. This distinction is in the Basel Accord, which requires capital to be allocated against both CCE and PFE. This will be discussed in this section.

Associated with this concept is the use of credit-adjusted pricing, i.e. adjusting the price of a derivative to incorporate some margin that reflects the potential loss if the counterparty defaulted at some stage during the derivative's lifetime. In the early days of the derivatives market, when counterparties all tended to be of good credit, such adjustments were seldom made. During the earlier part of this century, credit-adjusted pricing became more common for transactions that were not collateralised. But even then, competitive pressures were sufficiently large that it is possible for a poor-credit counterparty to access flat unadjusted prices. Nevertheless, as more countries adopt the second Accord, with its risk-based capital approach,[13] there is increasing pressure to impose credit-adjusted pricing.

The accountants have also made an impact; FAS 157 requires banks to deduct the expected loss (known as the Credit Value Adjustment) due to counterparty credit risk from the fair valuation of derivative positions. Most banks have adopted two approaches:

1. Charge traders for the incremental CVA at the time of the transaction.
2. Create a central Credit Portfolio Management activity, which has responsibility for levying the above charge, and then managing the overall credit risk; this CPM is often a profit centre.

Some banks have taken the concept further, and charge for unexpected losses (i.e. tail losses greater than expected—see Section 6.8 (Appendix) for further details). The concept of CVA questions the widespread use of credit limits—are limits redundant provided all credit exposures are properly priced? However, for a number of reasons, such as:

- it is computationally extremely challenging to estimate CVA in real time;
- the credit models have known limitations;

---

[13] The Accord introduced a separate charge for counterparty credit risk in July; see *Guidelines for Computing Capital for Incremental Risk in the Trading Book*, published by Basel Committee on Banking Supervision, July 2009.

- the credit markets are not sufficiently liquid, especially after the crisis in 2007–9, to enable all credit risks to be hedged efficiently;
- the use of CVA increases potential pro-cyclical risk, namely a lower charge in a rising economy;

the demise of limits is premature.

We will consider one simple approach to measure PFE, and to introduce credit-adjusted pricing based upon a generic IRS. Assume we have a current curve of forward interest rates $F_0 = \{F_{0,0}, F_{0,1}, F_{0,2}, \ldots\}$ where $F_{0,T}$ is the estimate today of the forward rate that fixes at time T. We also assume a known volatility curve $\sigma_{0,T}$—this is an ATM curve of volatilities of the forward rates, implied from the cap market. If we assume that the forward rates follow a log-normal process,[14] we can write:

$$F_{t,T} = F_{0,T} * \exp\{(\mu_T - \tfrac{1}{2}\sigma_{0,T}^2) \cdot t + \sigma_{0,T} \cdot \sqrt{t} \cdot \varepsilon\}$$

This describes the possible evolution of the Tth forward rate through time, where ε is a unit normal random variable. The drift μ_T is small in practice for interest rates, and will be ignored for this discussion but see Section 11.4 for more details. As it is assumed that ε is drawn from a unit normal distribution, $\pm 5\%$ probability bounds can be constructed:

$$F_{t,T}^{\text{up}} = F_{0,T} * \exp\{-\tfrac{1}{2}\sigma_{0,T}^2 \cdot t + 1.645\sigma_{0,T} \cdot \sqrt{t}\}$$

$$F_{t,T}^{\text{down}} = F_{0,T} * \exp\{-\tfrac{1}{2}\sigma_{0,T}^2 \cdot t - 1.645\sigma_{0,T} \cdot \sqrt{t}\}$$

These imply that there is a 5% chance that the "actual" forward rate will lie above $F_{t,T}^{\text{up}}$, 5% that it will lie below $F_{t,T}^{\text{down}}$ and hence 90% that it will lie in between.

Worksheet 6.22 has taken the current 12-month forward curve out for 20 years, and evolved it through time using a volatility curve. Obviously, as time passes, the forward rates are fixed and then drop off. The graph below shows the new forward curves evolving:

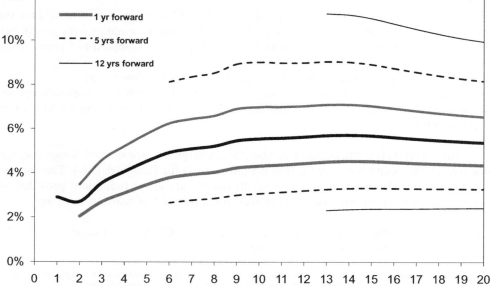

14 See the discussion on Libor-based simulation in Section 11.4 for more details.

These are usually called "95% curves" for reasons explained later. Box 1 in Worksheet 6.9 "Modelling forward exposure" shows the evolution over the first year: column [5] shows the expected evolution of the curve, and columns [4] and [6] show the upper and lower bounds.

The next step is to calculate how the valuation of a swap would change. Consider a vanilla swap to pay fixed which matures at T; its value at time t is $\{(1 - \mathrm{DF}_{t,T}) - S_{0,T} * Q_{t,T}\}$. So, given the current swap curve, we can take the forward curve which has been evolved out for 1 year, calculate the new discount curve $\mathrm{DF}_{1,T}$ and values of $Q_{1,T}$, and hence calculate the value of the swaps. This is demonstrated in Box 2 of Worksheet 6.9 "Modelling forward exposure". The valuation is done after net payment of the cashflows at the end of the first year, hence the 1-year swap has zero value. It may be more valid to include this payment in the valuation on the grounds that, if a default were to occur, it is likely to occur before payment; the model would be simple to modify.

It is a valid assumption that I am only concerned with my exposure on the counterparty, and not the exposure of the counterparty on me. Hence, if rates rise, the swap will gain in value for me, and so will my PFE. The evolution of the swap value through time can be tracked based on the 5% evolved curves, producing the 95% potential future exposure (PFE) envelope, i.e. there is a 5% chance that *my* exposure may exceed this. The graph below demonstrates the classical exposure (expressed in terms of Notional Principal Amount) rising as rates rise, and then dropping back to zero by maturity due to the continued receipt of cashflows. From the graph, the maximum exposure for the 12-year swap is about 22% of the NPA: this is often called the Peak Exposure Limit (PEL).

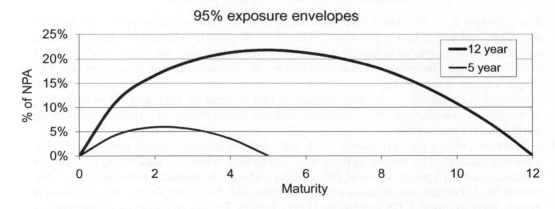

Worksheet 6.24 contains an extract from a Bank of England report,[15] estimating the PELs for an IRS and a CCS under a range of maturities and probability envelopes—these data are graphed in Worksheets 6.25 and 6.26. These results formed the foundation for the capital setting in the first Basel Accord published in 1987.

The 95% anticipated loss in the tth period under this swap, following the envelope, is $H_t * \mathrm{PFE}_t$ where H_t can be estimated either from the CDS market as above or using historic data: Worksheet 6.27 uses historic cumulative default data published by Moody's. The PV of expected losses across the lifetime of the swap is $\sum H_t * \mathrm{PFE}_t * \mathrm{DF}_t$. The expected PV of 1 bp received through the lifetime of the swap is $\sum S_t * d_t * \mathrm{DF}_t / 10{,}000$ expressed as a percentage of NPA.[16] Therefore, the required adjustment in the price—and

---

[15] Report 1361d: *Potential Credit Exposure on IR and FX Related Instruments*, Bank of England, 1987.
[16] The term $S_t * \mathrm{DF}_t$ is often referred to as a credit-adjusted discount factor or CADF.

note that this assumes that only the counterparty is likely to default: I will not adjust my prices to take into account the probability that I might default—is:

$$10,000 * \sum H_t * \mathrm{PFE}_t * \mathrm{DF}_t / \sum S_t * d_t * \mathrm{DF}_t$$

This adjustment was calculated on the basis that the margin had to be sufficient to cover a 95% loss: the results are summarised in Worksheet 6.29. This is quite pessimistic; the first Basel Accord operated on the basis of a 50% loss, i.e. the adjustment should cover the average credit loss. This also ignores any possibility that the swap might have a current mark-to-market loss, in which case the counterparty has a credit exposure on you. But this follows the regulations, which state that the credit exposure has to be calculated as:

$$\max\{0, \text{current exposure}\} + \mathrm{PFE}$$

It would be straightforward to change the model for the adjustment to reflect $\max\{0, \text{current exposure} + \mathrm{PFE}\}$.

The new Basel Accord permits this approach directly through the use of Expected Positive Exposure (EPE) which is defined as the average of the PFE over the lifetime of the swap. The EPE is then used to determine the regulatory capital charge for counterparty credit risk.[17]

6.8   APPENDIX: AN OUTLINE OF THE CREDIT MODELLING OF PORTFOLIOS

The objective is to provide a brief outline as to how credit-sensitive portfolios may be modelled, and hence how a portfolio CDS might be priced. What makes this modelling difficulty? As a portfolio is merely a collection of entities, and we know how to model individual entities from Section 6.4, then can we simply just combine them together? The simple answer is no; we know that the behaviour of entities is not independent of each other, but is correlated. It is the existence of this correlation that makes the modelling of portfolios considerably more difficult, and the performance of products written on portfolios less predictable.

There are two main approaches used, full random simulation and semi-analytic (or quasi-simulation). The second approach is widely used when the underlying portfolio is sufficiently large (typically, at least 100 entities) and well diversified, so that appeals to the central limit theorem and hence normality are justified. For example, the methodology is usually used to model CDS written on iTraxx indices. Details of this class of approaches really fall outside the scope of this book.[18]

We will approach full simulation in a number of stages. First, for a given time horizon T, we will assume that we know, for each entity k in the portfolio:

- The size of exposure E_k.
- The probability of the entity defaulting within the time horizon, $P_{k,T}$. This may, of course, be implied from the single-name CDS market if available.

---

[17] See pp. 260–262 of *International Convergence of Capital Measurement and Capital Standards* and p. 14 of *The Application of Basel II to Trading Activities and the Treatment of Double Default Effects*, published by Basel Committee of Banking Supervision in June 2006 and April 2005, respectively.

[18] See, for example, P. Schonbucher, Section 10.4 in *Credit Derivatives Pricing Models*, Wiley, 2003, for a detailed discussion.

- The scale of the loss if a default occurs, $LGD_k = 1 -$ Recovery rate$_k$, expressed as a percentage.

Hence, the Expected Loss over the time horizon, in monetary terms, is $E_k * P_{k,T} * LGD_k$.

We also introduce the concept of asset growth over this time. If the entity has assets of value $V_{k,0}$ at time T, and these assets have grown or shrunk to $V_{k,T}$, then the growth g_k is given by:

$$V_{k,T} = V_{k,0} * \exp\{g_k * T\} \quad \text{or} \quad g_k = \ln[V_{k,T}/V_{k,0}]/T$$

The reason for using a continuously compounded definition for growth, rather than a simple definition, is that $V_{k,T} > 0$ for all (positive or negative) values of g_k.

We assume that a distribution for the growth rate over the period T can be estimated. This would be based in part upon historical performance, and in part upon subjective views about the future. An example of such a distribution is shown below (for this particular entity, it is very dependent upon receiving a large contract; if it does, it will do well, and if not, it will shrink):

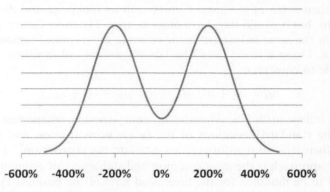

Note that, obviously, there is no attempt to assume normality, or indeed any theoretical distribution. Given we know $P_{k,T}$ for this entity, we can locate a line on the distribution, so that the area to the left is $P_{k,T}$.

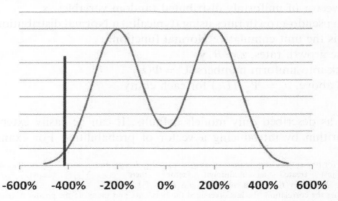

Define the cumulative distribution function from this distribution as $\Psi_k(X) =$ Prob$\{g_k \geq X\}$. Therefore, if we generate a uniformly distributed random variable U_k between 0 and 1, then the implied growth rate is $g_k = \Psi_k^{-1}(U_k)$. Hence, the location of the line on the distribution is at $\hat{g}_k = \Psi_k^{-1}(P_{k,T})$. The performance of this entity can now be modelled:

1. Randomly generate U_k.
2. If $g_k \geq \hat{g}_k$ (or, alternatively, if $U_k \geq P_{k,T}$) then there is no default.
3. If $g_k < \hat{g}_k$, then the entity defaults with $\text{Loss}_k = E_k * \text{LGD}_k$.

This basic idea could be easily extended to all entities in the portfolio. After repeating a large number of times (S&P typically run 500,000 scenarios), a loss distribution may be constructed.

But we still have not yet tackled the problem of correlation. Ideally, we want to use default correlation; namely, if one entity defaulted, what is the likelihood of a second one defaulting? But the historic data for such events is very limited, so we fall back on asset growth correlation. Why does correlation arise? Assume that the fortunes of an entity are driven by a number of underlying factors $F_1, F_2, \ldots$ For example, if the entity were a car manufacturer, then some of the relevant factors are likely to be the broad state of the economy, the price of fuel, disposable income, price of steel and so on. If another entity is, say, an airline, then some of the same factors such as fuel price and disposable income would be relevant, but it would then have other factors. The more factors in common, e.g. two companies in the same industrial sector or same geographical region, the higher the likely correlation. Using historic data (the last 60 monthly observations is common), it might be possible to construct:

$$g_k = \alpha_k + \beta_{F_1} \cdot g_{F_1} + \beta_{F_2} \cdot g_{F_2} + \cdots + \varepsilon_k$$

where ε_k is an independent idiosyncratic or entity-specific component. If we assume knowledge of the standard deviations of the factor growth rates, and the correlations between them, then it is straightforward to estimate the correlation[19] between (say) g_k and g_h. A factor approach is the most common and stable way of estimating correlations, but it does need to be modified for the forecasted level of the business cycle.[20]

We now assume we have a full correlation matrix C between entity growth rates. Decompose the matrix (see the discussion in Section 11.4 for details) into $B \cdot B^{\text{Transpose}}$. The method proceeds as follows:

1. Generate a vector of uniformly distributed random variables, $\mathbf{x}$.
2. Convert into pseudo-growth rates using (typically) a Normal distribution,[21] $\mathbf{y} = \Phi^{-1}(\mathbf{x})$ where $\Phi(y)$ is the unit cumulative Normal function.
3. Modify these growth rates, $\mathbf{z} = B \cdot \mathbf{y}$.
4. Convert back into uniform numbers, $\mathbf{U} = \Phi(\mathbf{z})$.
5. Continue as above, $g_k = \Psi_k^{-1}(U_k)$ for each entity.

The algorithm as described only models defaults. It can be easily extended into a full migration algorithm by introducing a vector of probabilities. For example, define the

---

[19] If the relationships for two entities are summarised as $g_k = \alpha_k + \sum_j \beta_{F_j} \cdot g_{F_j}$ and $g_h = a_h + \sum_i b_{F_i} \cdot g_{F_i}$, where the idiosyncratic components are just treated as additional factors, then $\rho_{k,h} = \sum_{i,j} b_i \cdot \beta_j \cdot \text{cov}(F_i, F_j) / S(g_k) \cdot S(g_h)$ where $S^2(g_k) = V(g_k) = \sum_{i,j} \beta_i \cdot \beta_j \cdot \text{cov}(F_i, F_j)$ and $\text{cov}(F_i, F_j) = S(F_i) \cdot S(F_j) \cdot \rho_{F_i, F_j}$.

[20] Obviously, the higher the correlation, the less diversified the portfolio, and therefore the greater potential credit risk. Rating agencies often use minimum base correlations, derived from periods of stress, in addition to factor-derived correlations—see p. 7 of *Global Rating Criteria for Corporate CDOs* published by Fitch, April 2008.

[21] We are tacitly applying a Gaussian copula; it is perfectly feasible and often argued desirable to apply other distributions such as a t-distribution. Probably the original reference is *On Default Correlation: A Copula Function Approach* by David Li, RiskMetrics Group Working Paper 99-07, April 2000.

probability of the kth entity moving from its current credit state to state YY by the end of the time horizon $P_{k,T,YY}$ where $\sum_{YY} P_{k,T,YY} = 1$. The generated growth rate g_k can then be compared against the set of cut-off rates $\hat{g}_k$ and the implications recorded.[22]

The current algorithm does however have one serious practical deficiency. Defaults are implicitly assumed to occur only at the end of the time horizon. If the time horizon is fairly short, then the practical implication may be negligible. But for long time horizons, such as 5 years, defaulting near the beginning or near the end could have markedly different effects on the timing of cashflows. To overcome this, we can use the following approach. Assume that, for differing time horizons $t_1 \le t_2 \le t_3 \le \cdots \le t_n = T$, we know the accumulative default probabilities $P_{k,t_1} \le P_{k,t_2} \le P_{k,t_3} \le \cdots \le P_{k,t_n} = P_{k,T}$ (again, potentially implied from the CDS market, or from historic rating-agency data, or from internal sources. We can then sample U_k as described above:

- if $U_k \ge P_{k,T}$, then there is no default.
- if $U_k < P_{k,T}$, then find the pair of probabilities such that $P_{k,t_{j-1}} \le U_k \le P_{k,t_j}$.
- find the time of default by interpolating between t_{j-1} and t_j.

The basic assumption is that the worse the growth rate, the earlier the default. The entity may default later than time T, but that is irrelevant for this discussion.

There is a spreadsheet "Modelling a Portfolio CDS" that demonstrates much of this discussion. The portfolio consists of 100 assets with credit ratings of A, BBB or BB; its total size is $3.2bn. The time horizon is set to be 5 years. The PD, either to maturity or to 5 years whichever is the shorter, and LGD for each asset are known, giving an Expected Loss of 1.83%. This suggests that the CDS premium should be approximately $1.83\%/Q_5 = 40$ bp pa. The assets are spread across five industrial sectors, with known betas to the sectors, so a full 100×100 correlation matrix can be constructed. Accumulative default probabilities at 3-monthly intervals are known for each asset (from S&P).

The heart of the model is in Worksheet 6.35. This first generates a set of uniformly distributed $(0, 1)$ random variables, which are converted into growth rates using either a Normal or a t-distribution (if the latter, then degrees of freedom also need to be set). These growth rates are then modified by the decomposed correlation matrix, and then converted back into uniform variables U; see columns [1]–[4] for details. If $U_k < PD_k$, then the asset will suffer a default; the accumulative probabilities can be used to determine when the default will occur (the model assumes that defaults occur at the beginning of each period, but it would be simple to modify it so that the default time would be interpolated across the period). Finally, the size of each payment to be made under the CDS is determined, and present-valued to give the total payments as a percentage of the size of the portfolio; see columns [5]–[7]. There is also an antithetic worksheet, which uses $(1 - \text{Random variable})$ as the basic input (see Worksheet 6.36).

Finally, Worksheet 6.37 runs 500 scenarios, putting the PV of payments into a table. The average PV is consistently close to 1.7% ($\approx 1.83\% * DF_{2\frac{1}{2}}$), thus giving a more accurate estimate for the premium of 37 bp pa. A full loss distribution is also constructed, and a Weibull distribution fitted to it, as shown below. The theoretical distribution may be used to calculate tail properties; for example, there is a 20% chance that the total payments will exceed 3% of the size of the portfolio.

---

[22] This methodology forms the basis for the CreditMetrics algorithm, see for example G. Gupton et al., CreditMetrics, Technical Document, Morgan Guaranty Trust Co, 1997.

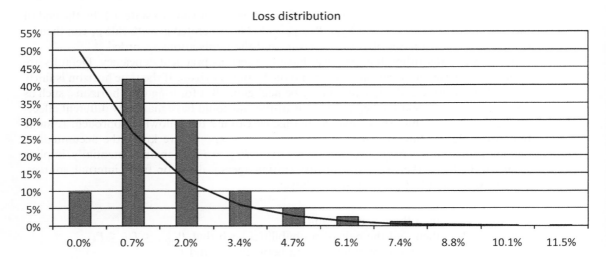

Worksheet 6.37 also contains a correlation parameter. If ξ_0 is the base correlation between two industrial sectors, or alternatively is the beta coefficient between an asset and its sector, then define:

$$\xi_\lambda = \xi_0 + (1 - \xi_0) * (1 - \exp\{-\lambda\})$$

as a shifted value dependent upon a value of $\lambda > 0$. This enables the reader to experiment with changing values of correlations and betas, and to see the impact on the loss distribution and most importantly on the tail properties.

7

More Complex Swaps

OBJECTIVE

The swaps discussed in the book so far have been fairly basic. This chapter introduces a range of more complex swaps called mismatch swaps. These are swaps where the usual conventions on the floating side are violated. A range of examples are presented in some detail: in-arrears, average rate, compound and finally yield curve swaps. The concept of convexity is re-introduced (see Chapter 2), and various approaches are described in Section 7.6 (Appendix).

7.1 SIMPLE MISMATCH SWAPS

Consider the process of determining the cashflow corresponding to a generic floating rate fixing:

1. The rate L has a tenor τ.
2. It is fixed at the start of a period, at time t.
3. The cashflow is paid at the end of the period T, where $T = t + \tau$.
4. The cashflow is calculated by $P * L * \tau$.

We could write a more general statement:

1. The rate L fixes at time t.
2. The cashflow is calculated by $P * L * q$ where q is some length of time in years.
3. The cashflow is paid at time $T \geq t$.

In the generic case, $q = \tau = T - t$.

But there is no necessity for this relationship to be true. A mismatch swap is defined as one where the relationship does not hold. A simple example is an "in-arrears" swap, where the floating rate is both fixed and paid effectively at the end of the period, hence $T = t$. These swaps arise when a user wishes to take a view on the movement of interest rates. Receiving conventional floating rates means that the first cashflow is fixed from the outset; hardly desirable if you wish to take an open position on the rates moving. Receiving in-arrears means that the first fixing is not until the end of the first period, therefore giving some opportunity for the rate to move.

Pricing such a swap is straightforward using implied forwards. For example, consider the following swap:

Maturity:	5 years
Principal:	100 million USD
To receive:	3 mo. Libor in arrears
To pay:	3 mo. Libor + 7.52 bp in advance

First the implied forward rates are estimated; see column [1] of Worksheet 7.2. For a single period, say from t_1 to t_2, the in-arrears cashflow is constructed by:

$$P * F_{23} * (t_2 - t_1)$$

i.e. the forward rate for the next period applied backwards as shown in column [2]. Finally the conventional cashflow, including the margin, is calculated; see [3]. The swap is shown to have a zero fair value; see [4].

The margin can be roughly anticipated. The spot 3 mo. rate is 3.145%, and the final rate out of 6 February 2013 is 4.711%, giving a spread of 165 bp. All the other rates effectively cancel. As we are receiving the high rate, and paying the low rate, the swap counterparty needs to receive some compensation. This is crudely approximated by 165 bp divided by 20 periods, giving 7.83 bp; obviously this ignores the timing of the cashflows.

7.2 AVERAGE RATE SWAPS

In-arrears swaps are a very simple, but seldom used, example of mismatch swaps. A more common application, because it has a firmer practical foundation, is the class of average rate swaps. We will consider two different types, arithmetic average rate used by end-users, and overnight average rates used mainly by banks (see Section 8.1 for details).

Consider a company that has the following debt structure:

1.   3 mo. Libor + 25 bp on $100m, out of 20 February.
2.   3 mo. Libor + 35 bp on $50m, out of 7 March.
3.   3 mo. Libor + 30 bp on $75m, out of 21 March.
4.   3 mo. Libor + 25 bp on $100m, out of 3 April.
5.   3 mo. Libor + 50 bp on $25m, out of 15 April.

All the debt has a long time to maturity. The company would like to swap the debt from floating to annual fixed for the next 3 years.

Obviously one way to do this is to enter into a series of five individual swaps. However, it had recently constructed a 3-year budget with funding assumptions based upon an average value of 3 mo. Libor. Therefore an alternative structure would be:

● to pay an annual fixed rate;
● to receive Libor, based upon a weighted average, for 3 years

on a principal of $350m. This is constructed in Worksheet 7.3. First the appropriate dates for each of the debt is constructed; see columns [1], [4], [7], [10] and [13]. This includes the date of the last fixing as shown. From the discount curve, the last fixing plus the implied forward rates have been constructed in columns [3], [6], [9], [12] and [15]. The weights to be applied to each debt are calculated, i.e. for debt 1, we get $100/(100 + 50 + 75 + 100 + 25) = 28.57\%$, etc.

The 3-year swap is priced out of 4 January 2000 from a bank's point of view. The cashflows at the end of each quarter are:

- to receive $\sum w_i * L_i$ based upon the implied Libor fixings: columns [18] and [19];
- to pay Fixed rate $= 3.0185\%$ ANN Act/360: column [20].

7.3 COMPOUND SWAPS

Compound swaps are another family of swaps related to average rate swaps. Consider the following swap:

- to receive F annually;
- to pay Libor quarterly.

Even if we assume rates do not change from those implied at the beginning, obviously the fixed rate receiver has an accumulating credit exposure which is effectively reset annually. Compound swaps were developed to reduce this exposure, and have proven to be remarkably popular in some countries such as Canada. The simplest form is as follows:

Time (months)	Fixing	Implied cashflow	Compounded cashflow
0	$L_{0/3}$		
3	$L_{3/6}$	$CF_3 = P * (1 + d_1 * L_{0/3})$	$CF_{3-acc} = CF_3$
6	$L_{6/9}$	$CF_6 = P * (1 + d_2 * L_{3/6})$	$CF_{6-acc} = CF_6 + CF_{3-acc} * (1 + d_2 * L_{3/6})$
9	$L_{9/12}$	$CF_9 = P * (1 + d_3 * L_{6/9})$	$CF_{9-acc} = CF_9 + CF_{6-acc} * (1 + d_3 * L_{6/9})$
12		$CF_{12} = P * (1 + d_4 * L_{9/12})$	$CF_{12-acc} = CF_{12} + CF_{9-acc} * (1 + d_4 * L_{9/12})$

Each floating cashflow is re-invested at the new Libor rate flat for the next period. Eventually a single cash payment is made at the end of the year, matching the frequency of the fixed side, and thereby reducing the credit exposure substantially. The main complication with compound swaps is the existence of spreads. For example, there may be a spread on:

- the original Libor fixing that determines the implied cashflows;
- the Libor rates used for reinvestment;
- the final (overall) implied compounded Libor rate;

or any combination thereof. The specification of the contract needs to be carefully defined to avoid confusion and error.

Worksheet 7.4 shows a swap paying 3 mo. Libor $+ 25$ bp against a fair annual fixed rate of 3.741%. If the floating side is compounded up at Libor $- 25$ bp, the fixed rate reduces to 3.737%.

7.4 YIELD CURVE SWAPS

At the beginning of 1994, short-term USD interest rates were at a historic low, had been for most of 1993 and, despite the steep positive implied forward rate curve, nobody was forecasting any increase. Money market investors were therefore actively searching for ways to enhance their returns. Three strategies were popular:

1. Liquidation and re-investment in foreign assets: DEM were extremely popular as their curve was inverted at the time due to the substantial borrowing to fund re-unification.
2. Liquidation and re-investment further up the USD curve.
3. Structured speculation based upon interest rate expectations.

Strategies 1 and 3 will be discussed under cross-currency and embedded option structures, respectively. Implementing strategy 2 would require a full liquidation of the short-term assets followed by the purchase of long-term assets such as bonds, obviously involving substantial cashflows plus fairly wide dealing spreads.

Alternatively investors could enter into a yield curve swap such as shown below:

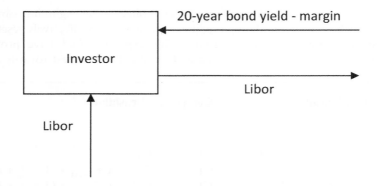

where the long-term rate merely acts as a floating reference rate, traditionally re-fixed in advance at regular intervals and the cashflow paid at the end of each period. The margin is determined so that the initial value of the swap is set to zero. This is of course simply another form of basis swap.

In theory any reference rate could be used, but in practice yield curve swaps typically use either the Treasury or the Swap curve. The former are probably more common in the US, whereas the latter are common across Europe (probably reflecting the relative liquidities of the bond and swap markets). Government organisations such as the US Treasury provide daily standardised bond reference rates. Averaged fixings of standardised swap reference rates (e.g.: 1 to 10, 12, 15, 20, 25, 30 years in both euros and USD) are provided daily by ISDA across six major currencies (see their webpage ISDAFIX for further details).

These swaps allow fund managers and other investors to change the duration of their investments efficiently, as the dealing costs are much lower than through the cash markets. Typically the bid–offer spreads for standard reference rates are about double those for generic IRSs. Combined swaps such as:

● to pay 2 yr swap rate;
● to receive 10 yr swap rate – margin;

where both reference rates are re-fixed regularly, are popular and allow investors to take a position on the relative steepness of the curve.

One other advantage is that, unlike a physical instrument which will shorten with the passage of time, these reference rates do not shorten (this is often described as "not rolling down the curve").

As an example, we will price, i.e. find the breakeven margin, for the following:

Trade date:	4 February 2008
Maturity:	4-year USD swap
Principal:	$100 million
To pay:	6 mo. Libor sa
To receive:	{5 year sa Act/360 swap rate – margin} sa

This means that the long-term reference rate is the 5-year semi-annual Act/360 swap rate, and that the cashflows for the actual swap are themselves semi-annual on both sides. Obviously there is no relationship between the frequency of the cashflows on the fixed side of the underlying reference swap and the frequency of the actual cashflows.

This is an example of a C(onstant) M(aturity) swap, where the structure of the underlying swap reference rate does not change over the lifetime of the swap. These are the most common type, and would normally be abbreviated to CMS, indicating the CM nature and the use of the Swap curve as a reference. CMTs would use the Treasury curve. VM (variable maturity) structures, where the length of the reference rate changes, do exist; for example, consider an investor who already possesses a portfolio with an average maturity of, say, 10 years, and wishes to swap it into a constant 5-year yield. As time passes, the reduction in the maturity of the physical portfolio needs to be reflected on the pay side of the swap.

The actual sequence of events on the two sides of the example swap are:

- at the beginning of each 6-month period, there are fixings of the two rates;
- at the end of each period, there is a net cash payment.

Using FRA notation, we can represent the first yield curve fixing as $FS(0, 5)$, the second as $FS(\frac{1}{2}, 5\frac{1}{2})$, the third as $FS(1, 6)$ and so on. We know from Chapter 4 that forward swap rates can be estimated by:

$$FS(t, T) = (DF_t - DF_T)/(Q_T - Q_t)$$

where it is important that the Q represents the correct frequency of the underlying reference swap rate. In Worksheet 7.5, the Q column [2] is calculated on a semi-annual basis, reflecting the frequency. Applying the formula, for example, to the fixing on 6 August 2009, resulting in a cashflow on 8 February 2010:

	DF	Q
6 August 2009	0.959112	1.476473
6 August 2014	0.778986	5.865882

gives $FS(start, end) = (0.959112 - 0.778986)/(5.865882 - 1.476473) = 4.1037\%$. It is conventional that all the swap cashflows are then discounted using the usual Libor DFs. The margin in column [7] could be estimated in the usual fashion, namely what margin would set the net present value of the swap to zero? However, in a simple case like this, pricing can be done dynamically by using the following equation:

$$\text{Net PV} = \text{PV(Libor)} + \text{PV(CMS)} + \text{PV}(m) = 0$$

$$\text{PV}(m) = P * m * Q_{end} = -[\text{PV(Libor)} + \text{PV(CMS)}]$$

which enables the margin m to be estimated directly. The breakeven margin is 91.8 bp, which is of course very close to the difference between the average of the CMS fixings (4.245%) and the average of the Libor fixings (3.309%). This highlights the fact that these swaps are not providing a "free" pick-up, but really represent an open position on the steepness of the curve.

If the underlying reference frequency switches to quarterly, then the compounding of Q must also switch to quarterly, as shown in column [2] of Worksheet 7.6. The CMS rates are estimated semi-annually based upon the quarterly Qs, and then the rest of the worksheet is as before. Because quarterly rates are lower than semi-annual rates, hence the spread of the CMS curve is tighter to the Libor curve, the CMS margin has reduced from 91.8 bp to 88.9 bp.

If the underlying reference frequency is retained as semi-annual, but the payment frequency on the swap itself is quarterly, then Q has to be calculated more carefully. The first CMS estimate is calculated from a semi-annual Q starting on 6 February 2008. The second CMS estimate uses semi-annual Q starting on 6 May 2008. Effectively, therefore, there are two series of semi-annual Qs which do not overlap but are a quarter apart, as shown in column [2] of Worksheet 7.7. The remainder of the worksheet is similar to before, but obviously with quarterly cashflows. The spread of quarterly CMSs over 3 mo. Libor has widened slightly, giving a higher breakeven margin of 97.1 bp.

An alternative to the normal form of CMS is termed a "participation CMS". In this case, a breakeven multiplier on the CMS rates is calculated, instead of a margin. For the original CMS discussed, the multiplier is 78.1% (see Worksheet 7.8 for more details).

The risk management characteristics of CMS swaps are interesting. We have been discussing a 4-year swap, but it obviously has exposure out to 8.5 years on the curve. If the underlying swap curve follows a parallel shift, then, like all basis swaps, both sides move and the change in the net value is likely to be very small. On the other hand, if the curve rotates around, say, the 4-year point, then the two sides change value in the same direction resulting in a large net change. These effects are in direct contrast to a generic fixed–floating IRS, which has high sensitivity to parallel shifts but low to rotations. This will be discussed in more detail in Chapter 12.

7.5 CONVEXITY EFFECTS OF SWAPS

Consider the generic 30-year USD swap out of 6 February 2008; the current rate is 4.815% ANN. Assume we are receiving fixed on a notional of USD1m. If this swap is valued off the current forward curve, its value is (of course) zero. If the forward curve is subject to a parallel shift of +100 bp, then its value drops to −$142,345. Conversely, if the curve has a −100 bp shift, the value rises to +$179,299 (see Worksheet 7.9 for details). The fixed rate receiver is said to be benefitting from a convexity effect of $370 per bp shift. A similar effect may be seen in the CMS, where equal shifts in the forward curve result in unequal changes in value (see Worksheet 7.10 for details).

More formally, consider the implied forward method for pricing some new swap. We can write the discount factors as functions of forward rates $\mathbf{F}_w$. Therefore our pricing approach has been to determine (say) the fixed rate F such that:

$$\text{PV}_{\text{fix}}[F, \mathbf{F}_w] - \text{PV}_{\text{floating}}[\mathbf{F}_w] = 0 \tag{7.1}$$

Obviously in reality the forward rates are unknown (except for the initial fixing), and therefore could be regarded as random variables subject to some generating process. Hence the PVs are themselves random variables, and of course the above expression, equating a random variable on the left-hand-side to a constant on the right-hand-side, is not appropriate. A more correct expression would be to take expectations with respect to some distribution; that is:

$$E\{\text{PV}_{\text{fix}}[F, \mathbf{F}_w]\} - E\{\text{PV}_{\text{floating}}[\mathbf{F}_w]\} = 0 \tag{7.2}$$

What is this expression saying? We don't know how the forward rates will behave in the future, but on average the swap should be fair (i.e. have a zero value) to both counterparties. The implied forward method effectively estimates the expected forward rates, and then calculates F_{IF} from:

$$\text{PV}_{\text{fix}}[F_{\text{IF}}, E\{\mathbf{F}_w\}] - \text{PV}_{\text{floating}}[E\{\mathbf{F}_w\}] = 0 \tag{7.3}$$

If F_{IF} is substituted into eq. (7.2), would we get zero? No: if we consider a function $f(x)$, where x is a random variable under some distribution, then $E\{f(x)\} = f(E\{x\})$ only if the function is linear. As we know that discount factors are non-linear functions of forward rates, then eq. (7.2) cannot be expressed as a linear function, and therefore the expected value of eq. (7.2) is non-zero. This implies, of course, that using F_{IF} will therefore, on average, benefit one of the two counterparties and penalise the other. This benefit is broadly called the "convexity (or curvature)" effect as we need to consider higher order terms when trying to quantify it.

Convexity effects arise from a variety of sources. Non-linearity between value and the market factors is one, as above. Another was described in Section 2.4, resulting from the failure to discount the variation margin of futures. It can also arise through timing mismatches, where the normal floating convention of fixing a rate at the beginning of a period, and paying the cashflow at the end is violated, as in in-arrears and average rate swaps. Section 9.11 (Appendix) describes the "quanto adjustment", which is another convexity effect.

Are convexity effects important? In theory, yes, because a swap is supposed to be a fair transaction between two counterparties, and convexity biases the outcome in favour of one of them. In practice, less so; the convexity effect for short-dated swaps is fairly negligible. The table below measures the convexity effect for $1m notional of generic swaps for a 100 bp parallel shift in the forwards.

Convexity effect for different maturities		
Maturity	USD	USD per yr
2	451	225
5	2,413	483
10	7,959	796
15	14,874	992
20	22,262	1,113
25	29,691	1,188
30	36,954	1,232

For the 30-year swap, this implies a bias of roughly 0.12 bp per basis point shift per annum. But in some currencies such as euros, GBP and to a lesser extent USD, 50-year swaps are becoming more common. The table below shows an extract from the USD curve in February 2008:

Extract from USD curve: 15 February 2008	
Maturity	Midpoints
20	5.073%
25	5.128%
30	5.148%
40	5.153%
50	5.143%

Notice how the long end of the curve turns down; this is almost certainly a convexity adjustment reducing the benefit to the fixed rate receiver.

How can the convexity effect be modelled? There are a number of different approaches. Probably the most appropriate would be to use the Libor-based model, described in detail in Chapter 11. This permits the forward curve to be randomly simulated, so the scale of the effect could be assessed.[1] But the general form of the model does not give rise to closed-form equations. It would be feasible to restrict the changes in the forward curve to parallel shifts, and then derive some approximate formulae.[2] There is a separate spreadsheet, Ch 7 Measuring the convexity effect in an IRS using BGM, which demonstrates this approach.

A widely used approach is to adopt a different set of market factors. A discount bond is a zero-coupon bond that pays 1 at maturity T. Its price today is given by the discounted

---

[1] There is a small technical problem using this model to assess the convexity effect. As described, the effect arises from the asymmetry of change in value as rates move up and down. This model assumes that percentage changes in rates follow a normal distribution, so that changes in rates themselves follow a log-normal distribution. But a log-normal distribution is itself not symmetric; large increases in rates are more likely than large decreases. Blindly using the Libor model to assess the impact of changing forward rates on the value of a generic swap would give rise to an apparent negative convexity effect for the fixed rate receiver. It all depends what is meant by the phrase "rates move up and down"!!

[2] See, for example, Model 3 in P. Hagan "Convexity conundrums: Pricing CMS swaps, caps and floors", Issue 3 of *Wilmott Magazine*, Wiley, January 2003.

value of the cashflow, i.e. $p_T = 1.DF_T = DF_T$. We can therefore think of DFs as being themselves tradeable discount bond prices, with their own market behaviours, volatilities, correlations, etc.

Consider the generic swap: its net value can be expressed as:

$$PV_{fix} - PV_{floating} = P * F * Q - \{1 - DF_{end}\}$$

i.e. the net value is a linear function of DFs. In words, if we work in a world of discount bond prices, then generic swaps (i.e. all those described in earlier chapters) do not possess convexity effects, and hence eqs. (7.2) and (7.3) are equivalent.[3] However, for more complex swaps such as all those described in this chapter, their net values cannot be described in linear terms of the DFs. Section 7.6 (Appendix) contains the derivation and details of models that permit the calculation of the convexity adjustment for these more complex swaps.

Another approach is to view the fixed side of the swap as a bond, and resort to bond mathematics. This is commonly used to assess the convexity effect in CMSs. These formulae are derived in Section 7.6.3 (Appendix).

7.6 APPENDIX: MEASURING THE CONVEXITY EFFECT

This Appendix describes a range of different approaches that have been used in practice to estimate the theoretical size of the adjustment, depending upon the specific type of swap. The Appendix first describes two approaches applicable to a range of swaps, and shows some results for a range of swaps. The convexity effect in yield curve swaps is then considered separately, as this produces some particular problems. The analytic results will then be compared with simulated values.

7.6.1 Two approaches to measuring the convexity effect

The first approach is simple and crude, but effective in many circumstances and makes few underlying assumptions. The second approach is more generally applicable, but is based upon a specific stochastic generating process. However, it is demonstrated that the two approaches are in fact consistent with each other, and produce the same results for a range of swaps.

Approach 1

Consider a normal floating swap payment on nominal principal of $1:

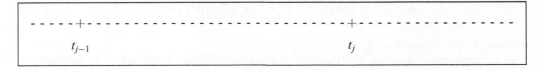

---

[3] If this puzzles the reader, then consider a normal fixed-coupon bond. As every textbook shows, the relationship between price and yield is both inverse and curved. If you own the bond and rates rise, then the price will drop. But it will drop slowly due to the curvature. Conversely, if rates fall, the price will rise fast due to the curvature. The owner of the bond is benefitting from convexity. Now, write the price of the bond as: Price $= \sum_T CF_T * DF_T$. If any one of the DFs moves up or down, the price shifts by the same amount—what's happened to the convexity?

The fixing of the floating rate $r(t_{j-1}, t_j)$ takes place at t_{j-1}, and the payment at t_j. The value of the cashflow at time t_j is:

$$V(t_j, t_j) = r(t_j) * d_j \quad \text{where } d_j = t_j - t_{j-1}$$

Define $p(t_{j-1}, t_j)$ to be the price of a discount bond at time t_{j-1} matures to 1 at t_j. We can write:

$$p(t_{j-1}, t_j) = 1/[1 + r(t_j) * d_j]$$

that is:

$$V(t_j, t_j) = [p(t_{j-1}, t_j)^{-1} - 1] \tag{7.4}$$

The value of the cashflow at time 0 is given by:

$$V(0, t_j) = V(t_j, t_j) * \text{DF}(t_j) \tag{7.5}$$

We can express $\text{DF}(t_j)$ as a sequence of compounded discount bond prices; that is:

$$\text{DF}(t_j) = \prod p(t_i, t_{i+1}) \quad \text{where } i = 0 \text{ to } j-1 \tag{7.6}$$

Combining (7.4), (7.5) and (7.6) together, we get:

$$V(0, t_j) = \text{DF}(t_{j-1}) - \text{DF}(t_j) \tag{7.7}$$

which is of course a well-known result.

If we repeat the same analysis for an in-arrears fixing, using the same notation, we get:

- the fixing takes place at t_j, and is given by $r(t_{j+1})$;
- the payment is also at t_j;
- i.e. $V(t_j, t_j) = r(t_{j+1}) * d_j$ where $d_j = t_j - t_{j-1}$;
- or $V(t_j, t_j) = [p(t_j, t_{j+1})^{-1} - 1] . (d_j/d_{j+1})$;
- and

$$V(0, t_j) = [p(t_j, t_{j+1})^{-1} - 1] . (d_j/d_{j+1}) * \text{DF}(t_j) \tag{7.8}$$

which does not simplify as before.

Consider a function $y = f(x_1, \ldots, x_n)$ where the xs are random variables. We can use the following approximation:

$$E\{y\} = f(E\{x_1\}, \ldots, E\{x_n\}) + \frac{1}{2} \sum_i \sum_j (\partial^2 f / \partial x_i \, \partial x_j) . s_i . s_j . \rho_{ij}$$

where s_i is the standard deviation of x_i, and ρ_{ij} the correlation between x_i and x_j.

If we assume all the xs are independent, then this reduces to:

$$E\{y\} = f(E\{x_1\}, \ldots, E\{x_n\}) + \frac{1}{2} \sum_i (\partial^2 f / \partial x_i^2) . v_i \tag{7.9}$$

where v_i is the variance of x_i.

If we apply eq. (7.9) to eq. (7.7) above, treating the discount bond prices as the random variables, we get:

$$\partial \text{DF}(t_j) / \partial p(t_{i-1}, t_i) = \text{DF}(t_j) / p(t_{i-1}, t_i) \quad \text{and} \quad \partial^2 \text{DF}(t_j) / \partial p(t_{i-1}, t_i)^2 = 0$$

i.e. no convexity effect.

Applying (7.9) to the in-arrears expression (7.8), we get:

$$\partial V(0, t_j)/\partial p(t_j, t_{j+1}) = -\mathrm{DF}(t_j) \cdot p(t_j, t_{j+1})^{-2} \cdot (d_j/d_{j+1})$$

and

$$\partial^2 V(0, t_j)/\partial p(t_j, t_{j+1})^2 = 2 \cdot \mathrm{DF}(t_j) \cdot p(t_j, t_{j+1})^{-3} \cdot (d_j/d_{j+1})$$

Thus:

$$E\{V(0, t_j)\} = [p(t_j, t_{j+1})^{-1} - 1] \cdot (d_j/d_{j+1}) * \mathrm{DF}(t_j) + \tfrac{1}{2} \cdot 2 \cdot \mathrm{DF}(t_j) \cdot p(t_j, t_{j+1})^{-3} \cdot (d_j/d_{j+1}) \cdot v_j$$

If we assume that each p is distributed log-normally, the relationship between variance and volatility is given by (where it is assumed also that the expected discount bond price is given by the implied price):

$$v_j = p(t_j, t_{j+1})^2 \cdot \{\exp[(\sigma_j)^2 \cdot t_j] - 1\}$$

Substituting and re-arranging:

$$E\{V(0, t_j)\} = [p(t_j, t_{j+1})^{-1} \cdot \exp[(\sigma_j)^2 \cdot t_j] - 1] \cdot (d_j/d_{j+1}) * \mathrm{DF}(t_j) \qquad (7.10)$$

where the volatility σ_j is on the forward bond price. This of course is very similar to eq. (7.8) but with the convexity factor $\exp[(\sigma_j)^2 \cdot t_j]$. If the volatility is set to zero, then this factor is equal to 1, and the convexity adjustment disappears.

Approach 2

This approach is based upon Heath–Jarrow–Morton (HJM) modelling, and can produce more general results.[4]

As before let $p(t, T)$ be the price of a discount bond at time t which matures at time T to a par value of 1. We assume that the price follows the process:

$$dp(t, T)/p(t, T) = r(t) \cdot dt + \sigma_p(t, T) \cdot dW$$

For convenience, only one stochastic Wiener source has been assumed, although the results may be easily extended. Because the bond is a traded security in a risk-neutral world, its expected return is given by $r(t)$. The bond price volatility is $\sigma_p(t, T)$, with of course $\sigma_p(t, t) = 0$. Using Ito's lemma, we get:

$$d[\ln p(t, T)] = [r(t) - \tfrac{1}{2} \cdot \sigma_p(t, T)^2] \cdot dt + \sigma_p(t, T) \cdot dW$$

Define the continuously compounded forward rate from t to T observed at time t_0 as $f(t_0, t, T)$. This will satisfy the relationship:

$$p(t_0, T) = p(t_0, t) * \exp\{-f(t_0, t, T) * (T - t)\}$$

that is:

$$f(t_0, t, T) = [\ln p(t_0, t) - \ln p(t_0, T)]/(T - t)$$

that is:

$$d[f(t_0, t, T)] = \frac{[\sigma_p(t_0, T)^2 - \sigma_p(t_0, t)^2]}{2 \cdot (T - t)} \, dt + \frac{\{\sigma_p(t_0, t) - \sigma_p(t_0, T)\}}{(T - t)} \, dW$$

---

[4] Following discussions with Stuart Turnbull, 1994–5.

As $t \to T$, then $f(t_0, t, T) \to f(t_0, T)$, i.e. a forward rate of infinitesimal tenor at time T. This is given by:

$$d[f(t_0, T)] = \sigma_p(t_0, T) \cdot \sigma(t_0, T) \cdot dt + \sigma(t_0, T) \cdot dW \qquad (7.11)$$

where $\sigma(t_0, T) \equiv \partial \sigma_p(t_0, T)/\partial T$. Integrating this last expression, we get

$$\sigma_p(t_0, T) = \int_{t_0}^{T} \sigma(t_0, \tau) \cdot d\tau$$

An obvious interpretation of $\sigma(t_0, T)$ is an *instantaneous* volatility. There are two common assumptions:

a. Constant instantaneous volatility σ which gives $\sigma_p = \sigma \cdot T$. In practice, we might observe the volatility of a 3-month bond price to be 0.25–0.5% pa which would imply σ to be within the range 1–2%.
b. Reverting instantaneous volatility $\sigma \cdot e^{-\lambda \tau}$ which gives $\sigma_p = (\sigma/\lambda) \cdot [1 - e^{-\lambda T}]$ where λ is some reversion factor.

Note that this definition of an instantaneous forward rate clearly shows a link between the drift and the variance of the instantaneous rate, as given in eq. (7.11).

We can now go back and price a forward discount bond in terms of the instantaneous forward rate:

$$p(t, T) = \exp\left[-\int_{t}^{T} f(t_0, u) \cdot du \right]$$

and also a money account:

$$B(t) = \exp\left[\int_{t_0}^{t} r(u) \cdot du \right]$$

where $r(t) = f(t, t)$, the riskless rate of return.

HJM show that $Z(t, T) = p(t, T)/B(t)$ is a unique martingale under conditions of no arbitrage, which implies $Z(0, T) = E^Q\{Z(t, T)\}$ where the Q indicates expectation with respect to risk-neutral probabilities. This leads to:

$$B(t) = \frac{1}{p(0, t)} \cdot \exp\left[-\frac{1}{2} \int_{0}^{t} b(v, t)^2 \cdot dv - \int_{0}^{t} b(v, t) \cdot dW^Q(v) \right] \quad \text{where } b(v, t) = -\int_{v}^{t} \sigma(v, u) \cdot du$$

and W^Q is a Wiener process, and to

$$p(t, T) = \frac{p(0, T)}{p(0, t)} \cdot \exp\left[-\int_{t}^{T} \int_{0}^{t} \sigma(v, s) \int_{v}^{s} \sigma(v, u) \, du \cdot dv \cdot ds - \int_{t}^{T} \int_{0}^{t} \sigma(v, s) \, dW^Q(v) \cdot ds \right]$$

Now let's consider an in-arrears swap: as before the fixing takes place at t_j, i.e. $r(t_{j+1})$, and the payment at t_j, that is:

$$V(t_j, t_j) = r(t_{j+1}) * d_j = [p(t_j, t_{j+1})^{-1} - 1] \cdot (d_j/d_{j+1}) \quad \text{where } d_j = t_j - t_{j-1}$$

Discounting back using the money account, and also the fact that this is a martingale, we can write:

$$\frac{V(0,t_j)}{B(0)} = V(0,t_j) = E^Q\{V(t_j,t_j)/B(t_j)\} = E^Q\left\{\left[\frac{1}{p(t_j,t_{j+1})\cdot B(t_j)} - \frac{1}{B(t_j)}\right]\cdot(d_j/d_{j+1})\right\}$$

If we make some assumption about the shape of $\sigma(v,u)$ as discussed above, then we can take expectations by:

1. Substituting for $p(t_j, t_{j+1})$ and $B(t_j)$.
2. Evaluating the integrals.
3. Taking expectations over the Wiener process dW^Q using the result that:

$$E\{\exp(x)\} = \exp\{\mu_x + \tfrac{1}{2}(\sigma_x)^2\}$$

$$E\{\exp(-x)\} = \exp\{-\mu_x + \tfrac{1}{2}(\sigma_x)^2\}$$

to get:

$$V(0,t_j) = p(0,t_j)\cdot\left\{\frac{p(0,t_j)}{p(0,t_{j+1})}e^\varphi - 1\right\}\cdot(d_j/d_{j+1})$$

This is the standard result but with an adjustment factor e^φ. If we assume $\sigma(v,u) = \sigma$, i.e. constant with no reversion, then $\varphi = \sigma^2\cdot t_j\cdot(d_{j+1})^2 = \sigma_p(t,T)^2\cdot t_j$, i.e. the same result as under the first approach. See Section 7.6.2 for a fuller statement of φ.

In the main text, we priced a 5-year swap to receive 3 mo. Libor in arrears, and to pay 3 mo. Libor + 7.52 bp in advance. The margin was positive because of the rising forward curve. Applying the above formula, if $\sigma = 1\%$ and $\lambda = 2\%$, then the margin is increased to just over 8 bp. Worksheet 7.12 has been slightly re-arranged from the earlier one, and uses the relationship $PV_{\text{in-arrears}} + PV_{\text{in-advance}} + m * Q = 0$ to estimate m dynamically.

The graph below shows how the margin increases with volatility:

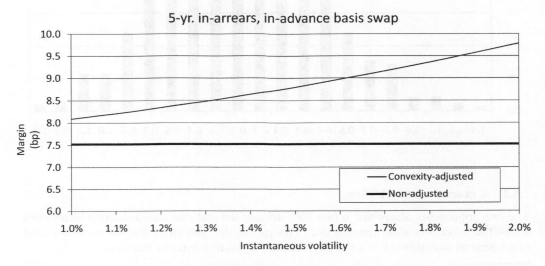

Is the adjustment appropriate? Worksheet 7.13 is built as follows:

[1]:	contains the usual IBOR DFs
[2]:	quarterly discount bond prices
[3]:	simulated bond prices using the formula

$$p_t = p_0 * \exp\{-\tfrac{1}{2}.(\sigma_p)^2.t + \sigma_p.\sqrt{t}.\varepsilon\} \quad \text{where } \varepsilon \text{ is } N(0,1) \text{ and } \sigma_p = 1\%$$

[4]:	re-calculated DFs
[5]:	implied forward rates from the new DFs
[6]:	in-arrears cashflows
[7]:	in-advance cashflows including 7.52 bp margin

The adjustment in the fair margin, away from 7.52 bp, is calculated by present valuing columns [6] and [7] and then using the formula $10,000 * \text{Net PV}/100 * Q$. The example shows that the in-arrears side is still valued above the in-advance side, with an average convexity adjustment of 0.54 bp compared with a theoretical one of 0.66 bp using a bond price volatility of 1% and no reversion. The chart below shows the results of the simulation:

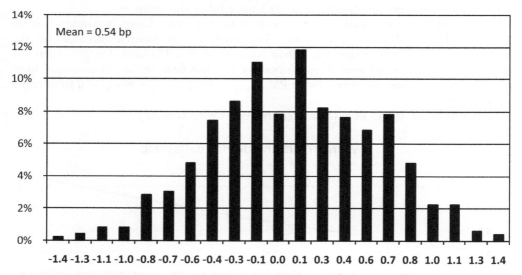

In -arrears simulation showing distribution of convexity adjustments

7.6.2 A general mismatch swap

The two approaches above are in fact very similar; the first one uses a discrete framework whilst the latter uses a continuous one. This means that the latter may be used to model more general situations. For example, consider a floating interest payment[5]:

---

[5] As discussed in Section 7.6.

Let r_j be an interest rate fixed on time t_j
r_j has a tenor of Γ_j
interest is payable calculated over a period q_j
interest is paid at time $T_j \geq t_j$

This is a very general statement as to how the value of a cashflow resulting from a floating reference rate may be estimated.

The value of the cashflow at T_j is given by, as before:

$$V(T_j, t_j, T_j) = r_j \cdot q_j = \left[\frac{1}{p(t_j, t_j + \Gamma_j)} - 1 \right] \cdot (q_j/\Gamma_j)$$

Thus, we can write the present value of this as:

$$V(0, t_j, T_j) = E^Q \left\{ \left[\frac{1}{p(t_j, t_j + \Gamma_j)} - 1 \right] \cdot \frac{1}{B(T_j)} \right\} \cdot (q_j/\Gamma_j)$$

Using the same approach as before, we find:

$$V(0, t_j, T_j) = p(0, T_j) \cdot \left\{ \frac{p(0, t_j)}{p(0, t_j + \Gamma_j)} \cdot e^\varphi - 1 \right\} \cdot (q_j/\Gamma_j)$$

where:

$$\varphi = \tfrac{1}{2} \cdot (\sigma^2/\lambda^3) \cdot (1 - \exp[-\lambda\Gamma_j]) \cdot (1 - \exp[-2\lambda t_j]) \cdot \{\exp[-\lambda(T_j - t_j)] - \exp[-\lambda\Gamma_j]\}$$

If $\lambda = 0$, then φ reduces to $\sigma^2 \cdot \Gamma_j \cdot t_j \cdot (t_j + \Gamma_j - T_j)$.

Some special cases follow:

a. If $\sigma = 0$, then there is no volatility and hence no convexity.
b. For a conventional fixing and payment, $T_j = t_j + \Gamma_j$, i.e. φ reduces to zero as expected.
c. For an in-arrears payment, $t_j = T_j$, i.e. φ simplifies to

$$\tfrac{1}{2} \cdot (\sigma^2/\lambda^3) \cdot (1 - \exp[-2\lambda t_j]) \cdot (1 - \exp[-\lambda\Gamma_j])^2$$

and for $\lambda = 0$, φ reduces to $\sigma^2 \cdot \Gamma_j^2 \cdot t_j$ as shown in Section 7.6.1.

Consider an average rate swap, which may be described in the following terms:

• partition a period of the time $[t, \tau]$ into k slices $t = t_1 < \cdots < t_k = \tau$;
• define an average payment that has to be paid at time T_j, not necessarily the same as τ, by:

$$\text{AV}(0, T_j) = \sum_{i=1}^{k} w_i \cdot V(0, t_i, T_j)$$

where the vector $\mathbf{w}$ contains the known averaging weights that sum to 1.

An average rate swap was priced in the main text. Its convexity adjustment is shown in the box in Worksheet 7.14. The adjustment is extremely small, only a fraction of a basis point; this is hardly surprising as the timing difference $(t_j + \Gamma_j - T_j)$ is relatively small for each fixing. If we wish to value the average part-way through a period, then we could partition the time slices into $\{1, \ldots, j\}$ and $\{j+1, \ldots, k\}$ where the fixings on the first partition have already been observed. Obviously the convexity effect will then disappear for $1, \ldots, j$.

The convexity effects for in-arrears and average rate swaps is relatively small. Turbo or power swaps—e.g. swaps that pay fixed rate and receive (Libor)^n where n is usually set to 1.5 or 2—have a much greater effect. The same analysis as above produces the following result:

$$\varphi = \tfrac{1}{2} . (\sigma^2/\lambda^3) . (1 - \exp[-2\lambda t_j]) . (1 - \exp[-\lambda d_j)])^2$$

or for $\lambda = 0$,

$$\varphi = (\sigma . d_j)^2 . t_j$$

Notice that this expression is exactly the same as for the in-arrears, but the jth cashflow is given by:

$$V(T_j, T_j) = [1 + \tfrac{1}{2} . \{n . (n-1)/(1-p)^2\}(e^\varphi - 1)] * L^n/100 * d_j \quad \text{where } p = p(t_j, T_j)$$

Turning to Worksheet 7.15:

[1]:	calculate the Q of the fixed side of the swap
[2]:	calculates the turbo Libor rate; notice that this is calculated by raising the rate expressed as a whole number, e.g. 3.145, to the power and *then* converting to a percentage
[3]:	the cashflows are calculated in the usual way, and the fixed rate is then estimated using $\text{PV}_{\text{floating}} + F * Q = 0$
[4]:	calculates φ with reversion
[5]:	calculates the convexity adjustment as given above
[6]:	hence the PV of the adjusted floating side, and the fair fixed margin

This is repeated in columns [7] to [9] for zero reversion; the impact is relatively small. The following table shows the theoretical size of the fair fixed rate for a 4-year qu/qu swap:

Power	No convexity adjustment	Convexity adjustment Volatility → 1.0%	1.2%	1.4%	1.6%	1.8%	2.0%
1.0	3.235	3.235	3.235	3.235	3.235	3.235	3.235
1.2	4.105	4.189	4.226	4.270	4.321	4.378	4.442
1.4	5.215	5.467	5.578	5.709	5.860	6.031	6.222
1.6	6.633	7.185	7.429	7.716	8.048	8.423	8.844
1.8	8.446	9.508	9.975	10.528	11.165	11.887	12.695
2.0	10.766	12.659	13.491	14.475	15.611	16.897	18.335

As we can see, the adjustments are large and highly sensitive to the volatility. Turbo swaps have a convexity comparable with interest rate options such as caps, and may be risk-managed together.

Why would anybody enter into these swaps, other than for speculation? Consider a typical company paying floating debt; as rates rise, obviously there is an adverse impact. But also, as rates rise, this has a dampening effect on the economy and therefore is likely to reduce demand. The likely impact on the company's bottom line (P&L or cashflow) is not linear with rate movement but greater, roughly $L^{1.2}$.

7.6.3 Yield curve swaps

As one may expect from the above discussion, yield curve swaps also require convexity adjustments. We could apply the same formula as above, but this would be incorrect as the reference rate is not a zero-coupon rate as tacitly assumed. Traditionally the financial markets have approached this in a very different manner from the analysis above, so we will first discuss the market method, and then try to understand whether it is realistic.

Consider a typical fixed-coupon bond; there is obviously a non-linear relationship between the bond price P and its yield to maturity y given by:

$$P = \sum_t CF_t * (1+y)^{-t} \quad \text{where } CF_t \text{ represents the bond cashflows}$$

Assume we are buying the bond at time T in the future, so that the actual bond price will be P_T and the forward bond yield y_T. For a given bond curve today, we can imply $P_0(T)$ and $y_0(T)$. We can approximately write:

$$P_T = P_0(T) + [y - y_0(T)] \cdot P_0(T)' + \tfrac{1}{2} \cdot [y - y_0(T)]^2 \cdot P_0(T)''$$

Taking expectations:

$$E\{P(y)\} - P_0(T) = [E\{y\} - y_0(T)] \cdot P_0(T)' + \tfrac{1}{2} \cdot E\{[y - y_0(T)]^2\} \cdot P_0(T)''$$

where $P_0(T)'$ and $P_0(T)''$ are the first and second derivatives with respect to yield at $y_0(T)$.

If we assume that $E\{P(y)\} = P_0(T)$, i.e. a world that is forward risk-neutral with respect to bond prices, then:

$$E\{y\} = y_0(T) - \tfrac{1}{2} \cdot E\{[y - y_0(T)]^2\} \cdot P_0(T)''/P_0(T)'$$

As we can write $E\{[y - y_0(T)^2\} \approx y_0(T)^2 \cdot (\sigma_y)^2 \cdot T$, the expected yield is

$$E\{y\} = y_0(T) - \tfrac{1}{2} \cdot y_0(T)^2 \cdot (\sigma_y)^2 \cdot T \cdot P_0(T)''/P_0(T')$$

Therefore, for a yield curve swap, we can regard the forward swap as equivalent to a forward par bond, estimate the forward rate off the current curve, but then apply the adjustment.[6] ATM swaption volatility of the appropriate forward time and underlying length is typically used in the adjustment.

As the Convexity of a bond $= P_0(T)''/P_0(T)$, and the modified Duration $= P_0(T)'/P_0(T)$, the ratio $P_0(T)''/P_0(T)'$ is equivalent to C/D which increases with the maturity of the bond. Hence the size of the adjustment depends upon:

- the tenor of the underlying reference rate;
- the volatility of the reference rate;
- the time to the fixing.

[6] A fuller description is given in many texts, such as J. Hull, *Options, Futures and Other Derivatives*, Fourth Edition, pp. 547–55 and Appendix 20A.

In the main text, we priced a 4-year CMS which was receiving the 5-year swap rate less 91.8 bp. If we assume the volatility curve is a flat 20% pa then the convexity adjustment can be seen in the new worksheet, with an overall margin of 94.7 bp. The size of the convexity adjustment is 3.6 bp. The convexity details are (see Worksheet 7.16):

---

[5]:	unadjusted CMS yield
[6]:	calculates $(1 + y_0(T)/2)^{-1}$; remember that the reference swap is semi-annual
[7]-[-9]:	these columns calculate P' and P'' having differentiated the general bond formula
[10]:	finally the convexity adjustment in basis points is calculated using the above formula

---

Hagan[7] develops a very similar model, with an adjustment factor of:

$$-y_0(T)^2 \cdot [Q_{\text{end}} - Q_{\text{start}}] \cdot [\exp\{\sigma_y^2 \cdot T\} - 1] G_0(T)'$$

where, in the simplest case, $G_0 \approx y_0 \cdot u^d/(1 - u^N)$ where $u = (1 + d * y_0)^{-1}$, d is the daycount fraction (assumed to be 0.5) and N is the number of periods in the reference CMS rate. The convexity adjustment for the same volatility is 3.5 bp (see Worksheet 7.17 for details).

Despite being widely used, this approach however has some practical shortcomings in that it concentrates purely on adjusting the CMS fixing. For example, the swap reference rate fixes in advance at the beginning of each period, but the cashflow is received only at the end of the period. This late payment is likely to reduce the benefit to the CMS receiver. Hull[8] suggests an additional adjustment term to compensate for the discounting from the payment date back to the fixing date:

$$-y_0(T) \cdot F \cdot d \cdot \sigma_y \cdot \sigma_F \cdot \rho_{y_F} \cdot T/(1 + F \cdot d)$$

where F is the forward interest rate from the fixing date to the payment date;
          d is the tenor of the forward rate (daycount fraction);
          σ_F is the volatility of the forward rate;
          ρ_{y_F} is the correlation between the CMS rate and the forward rate.

He suggests a correlation of 70%, which seems a touch high between a long and short rate. Applying this adjustment term reduces the convexity adjustment to 3.1 bp (see Worksheet 7.18 for details).

Hagan also introduces other, more sophisticated, expressions for G representing a wider range of potential movements.

Pugachevsky[9] has criticised these approaches, suggesting that they actually over-estimate the convexity benefit quite considerably because fluctuations in the rates would affect not only the CMS side of the swap, but also the Libor side as well. He developed an alternative approach which resulted in significantly lower adjustments.

Furthermore, we would like to be consistent in our approach to convexity, and earlier we used independent discount bond price volatilities which are related to cap volatilities. There is obviously a theoretical relationship between cap and swaption volatility which could be

---

[7] Ibid.
[8] Ibid., pp. 554–5.
[9] D. Pugachevsky, "Forward CMS rate adjustment", *Risk*, March 2001, pp. 125–8.

used.[10] Alternatively we could simulate the swap as before. The end-result appears very different when we assume:

- that only the CMS fixing is stochastic;
- that the Libor fixing and discounting are also stochastic.

Worksheet 7.19 shows that, for a parallel shift in the discount bond curve, the convexity effect (if only the CMS fixing is adjusted) is more than 16 times greater than the effect if all rates are adjusted—this is understandable as we know that CMS swaps have very little overall sensitivity to parallel shifts. Worksheet 7.20 performs the same calculations using random simulations of the discount bond curve; the resulting convexity effects are closer to Pugachevsky's results. This demonstrates that concentrating on the convexity effect inherent in the CMS fixing alone, and not on the convexity in the overall value of the swap, may be misleading.

---

[10] See R. Rebonato, *Interest Rate Options*, Wiley.

8

Cross-market and Other Market Swaps

OBJECTIVE

A cross-market swap is one that links together two different financial markets. Yield curve swaps, linking short-term Libor with long-term swap or bond yield rates is one example. As there are many other financial markets, then many other structures are feasible. This chapter discusses some of the more common ones, such as overnight indexed swaps, CP swaps, equity and commodity swaps, and also demonstrates how implied forward curves from these other markets can be built.

Swaps arising from other markets are also growing in popularity, for example inflation swaps and volatility swaps. The chapter discusses some of the common structures, and how they may be modelled and priced.

8.1 OVERNIGHT INDEXED SWAPS

These are average rate swaps that are being increasingly used by banks themselves for hedging. During a normal business day, a bank will make a large number of cash payments and receipts. These will ultimately flow down to the cash desk within the Treasury, who will have the final responsibility to fund the net payments or lend out the net receipts. At the end of each working day, the desk will ensure that its books, either in separate currencies or all netted back to a single home currency, are square within limits. Given the estimated future cash requirements of the bank, part of the expertise of the desk is to decide how much money will be borrowed or lent, and for what period of time. The remaining balances are invariably sourced into the bank overnight market on an uncollateralised basis. The overnight rates available in this market depend upon the net positions of all the contributing banks, and can fluctuate violently from day to day.

Most financial centres publish an official overnight rate, usually calculated by averaging the observed rates reported by the commercial banks. For example, 41 banks spread across the Eurozone (plus 7 non-Euro international banks) supply their overnight rates to the European Central Bank by 6 pm CET each business day; the ECB then publishes an arithmetic average called the Euro OverNight Index Average (EONIA) by 7 pm. Other rates include the Sterling OverNight Index Average (SONIA), the US Fed Funds Effective rate, the SA Rand Overnight Deposit (ROD), the Japanese Mutin and so on.

In order for the banks to perform some limited risk control over the fluctuations, Overnight Indexed Swaps (OISs) have been developed. This is the generic name for a class of swaps that:

- pay some temporal average of the overnight rate;
- receive a fixed rate;

for some notional principal amount at the end of a pre-specified period. Most OIS swaps have a maturity of less than 1 year, although longer ones are obtainable. Structured swaps such as forward starts and rollercoasters are also available.

The precise structure of an OIS varies from centre to centre, and generally reflects the detailed market operations. For example, the table below shows an extract from the average rate side of a 1-month EONIA swap traded on 2 January 2008 on a fixed rate of 3.750% (see Worksheet 8.2 for full details):

	EONIA fixing	Daycount	Principal accruing
4-Jan-08	4.087%		1
7-Jan-08	4.107%	3	1.000341
8-Jan-08	4.119%	1	1.000455
9-Jan-08	4.174%	1	1.000569
10-Jan-08	4.053%	1	1.000685
11-Jan-08	3.883%	1	1.000798
14-Jan-08	3.881%	3	1.001122
15-Jan-08	4.078%	1	1.001230
16-Jan-08	4.041%	1	1.001343
17-Jan-08	4.018%	1	1.001455
18-Jan-08	3.968%	1	1.001567
21-Jan-08	3.984%	3	1.001898
22-Jan-08	3.989%	1	1.002009
23-Jan-08	3.994%	1	1.002120
24-Jan-08	4.003%	1	1.002231
25-Jan-08	4.015%	1	1.002343
28-Jan-08	4.018%	3	1.002678
29-Jan-08	4.055%	1	1.002790
30-Jan-08	4.135%	1	1.002903
31-Jan-08	4.187%	1	1.003018
1-Feb-08	4.114%	1	1.003135
4-Feb-08	4.082%	3	1.003479
5-Feb-08		1	1.003593

Note that it starts at $T+2$, and finishes 1 day later, resulting in a 32-day swap. The first rate, 4.087% applies from 4th to 7th January, a period of 3 days given that 4 January was a Friday. Based on a principal amount of 1, the principal and interest on 7th January is:

$$1 * (1 + 4.087\% * 3/360) = 1.00034058$$

The P&I is then accrued from 7th to 8th January:

$$1.00034058 * (1 + 4.107\% * 1/360) = 1.00045471$$

This process is continued through the swap until the end of the swap on 5th February.

The total accrued interest is given by $P\&I - P = 0.0035926897$ or €359,268.97 on a principal of €100m. This can then be converted into an average rate:

$$0.0035926897 * 360/32 = 4.042\%$$

One practical point to note is that invariably the daily compounding calculations are done to a pre-specified number of decimal places, usually rounded to six. This can be significant over the full lifetime of the swap.

There would be a net cash settlement at the end of the swap, taking the difference between the average rate and the constant fixed rate:

$$€100m * \{4.042\% - 3.750\%\} * 32/360 = €25,935.63$$

calculated on a simple basis, where P is the actual principal amount. If the swap were longer than 1 year, then multiple settlements are common.

Most other markets follow a similar compounding process, although there are exceptions. For example, the ROD swaps take an arithmetic average of the overnight rates compiled by the South African Financial Exchange during each calendar month, and then compound up that average for each month.[1]

When an OIS is first entered into, obviously the overnight fixings are unknown and need to be implied off a forward curve. Not knowing where the overnight rates are likely to be, in the early days of this market banks typically used the IBOR curve as a reference, recognising that this is not ideal but they possessed little else. Use of a governmental curve is likely to be worse, and repo rates are of course collateralised. The unknown average rate for an EONIA swap may be easily estimated from a Libor curve using:

$$P\&I = \prod_i (1 + r_i * d_i) \quad \text{where } r_i = [DF_s(i)/DF_e(i) - 1]/d_i$$

$$= \prod_i DF_s(i)/DF_e(i) = 1/DF_{end}$$

The average rate is

$$\left(\frac{1}{DF_{end}} - 1\right) \times \frac{360}{d_{0,end}}$$

which is equal to $r_{0/end}$. In practice, in normal times the EONIA rate would be some 6–8 bp below the equivalent Libor rate.

Today, there is a full separate EONIA swap curve quoted—see graph below—that would enable the overnight forward rates to be implied. For an EONIA swap that was entered into some time previously, valuation would consist of real compounding using the rates already determined in the past plus the estimated forward rates off the curve.

[1] To make matters confusing, the South African Reserve Bank publishes a SAONIA rate each date. It is also feasible to get j-ROD swaps, where the compounding follows the EONIA convention.

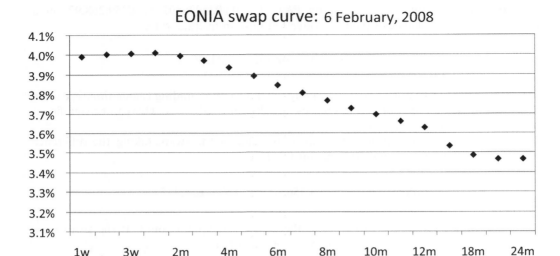

EONIA swap curve: 6 February, 2008

EONIA swap rates are generally, but not always, below the Euribor rates of the same
tenor, with the spread widening in times of stress, such as the sub-prime defaults of 07/08.
A typical trading strategy might therefore be to deposit for 1 year at Euribor, but pay the
daily EONIA through a swap, taking advantage of a positive curve.

8.2   CROSS-MARKET BASIS SWAPS

Interest rate basis or floating–floating swaps are intrinsically straightforward. However,
their pricing can be complex, which is why they are being discussed in this section.

There are two classes of IR basis swaps. The first class use the same reference index but of
different tenors. For example:

To pay	1 mo. Libor
To receive	12 mo. Libor

In theory the fair mid-price of such a swap should be zero. In practice, there is usually a
small margin on one side representing the relative supply and demand in the two cash
markets, their liquidities and the inherent credit exposure. The last point is very evident in
the above swap, as the bank will be making 12 monthly payments before the annual receipt.
These swaps are generally used only by market professionals to risk-manage the floating
sides of their portfolios.

Related to these swaps are yield curve swaps, which typically use short-term Libor on
one side and a very long-term rate on the other. These are an extremely important structure
of swap, and were discussed in some detail in Chapter 7.

The other major class of basis swap uses two reference rates, one typically Libor and the
other a floating rate from a completely different market, and is often called a cross-market
swap. There are a variety of such swaps available, especially in the US, due to the large
number of possible reference rates. Some example reference rates are:

Commercial paper: Rate of interest paid on short-term securities issued by corporates to fund their working capital requirements (obviously the level depends upon their credit rating)

Municipal: Rate of interest paid on securities issued by state and local government agencies

Prime: Rate of interest at which a commercial bank in the US would lend to its most creditworthy domestic customers (*Note*: this is effectively a regulated domestic rate, and should not be confused with Libor which is effectively an unregulated international rate. Base rate would be the UK equivalent.)

Fed Funds: Federal Funds are non-interest-bearing reserves deposited by member banks at the Federal Reserve. The Fed Funds rate is the rate of interest charged by banks trading these reserves, and is closely monitored by the Fed

T-Bills: Rate of interest paid on short-term government securities

```
GRAB                                                              CurncyPREB
PREBON YAMANE
                                              Page 1 of 1              22:08 GMT
FF vs 3M LIBOR    Prime vs 3M LIBOR        CP vs 3M LIBOR   T-Bills vs 14-Feb-08
TERM  BID   ASK    TERM   BID     ASK      TERM  BID   ASK   TERM  BID    ASK
 3M 51.38 55.38     3M -259.13 /-254.13     3M 42.50 57.50    3M 92.50 132.50
 6M 48.75 52.75     6M -261.75 /-256.75     6M 37.50 52.50    6M 85.00 125.00
 9M 45.13 49.13     9M -264.38 /-259.38     9M 32.50 47.50    9M 77.50 117.50
 1Y 42.38 46.38     1Y -267.13 /-262.13     1Y 27.50 42.50    1Y 72.50 112.50
18M 35.88 39.88    18M -271.63 /-266.63    18M 24.50 39.50   18M 67.50 107.50
 2Y 33.00 37.00     2Y -272.50 /-267.50     2Y 24.50 39.50    2Y 65.00 95.000
 3Y 28.50 32.50     3Y -276.00 /-271.00     3Y 22.50 37.50    3Y 62.00 92.000
 4Y 26.25 30.25     4Y -277.25 /-272.25     4Y 17.50 32.50    4Y 70.00 90.000
 5Y 24.75 28.75     5Y -278.75 /-273.75     5Y 15.00 30.00    5Y 64.00 84.000
 7Y 23.00 27.00     7Y -278.50 /-273.50     7Y 15.00 30.00    7Y 62.50 82.500
10Y 20.50 24.50    10Y -281.00 /-276.00    10Y 15.00 30.00   10Y 62.50 82.500
                                           15Y 12.50 27.50   15Y 60.00 80.000
                                           20Y 12.50 27.50   20Y 60.00 80.000
                                           25Y 12.50 27.50
                                           30Y 12.50 27.50

   All Prices are indicative. For Firm Prices Please Call +1 201 557 53633
Australia 61 2 9777 8600 Brazil 5511 3048 4500 Europe 44 20 7330 7500 Germany 49 69 9204 1210 Hong Kong 852 2977 6000
Japan 81 3 3201 8900    Singapore 65 6212 1000    U.S. 1 212 318 2000    Copyright 2008 Bloomberg Finance L.P.
                                                               H178-644-0 15-Feb-08  8:41:37
```

Source: Prebon Yamane, owned by Tullett Prebon plc.

All the above quotes are shown in basis points, added to the non-Libor reference rate. For example a bank would therefore provide a 10-year swap to pay 3-month Libor, and to receive 1-month CP + 30 bp.

Forward curves can be constructed from each of the basis swap curves, using the current Libor forward curve and Libor discount factors on each side. For example, consider a CP swap with maturity n:

$-L$	$+CP$	$+m_n$
$-L$	$+CP$	$+m_n$
$-L$	$+CP$	$+m_n$
$-L$	$+CP$	$+m_n$
$-L$	$+CP$	$+m_n$
$-L$	$+CP$	$+m_n$
$-L$	$+CP$	$+m_n$
$-L$	$+CP$	$+m_n$
$-L$	$+CP$	$+m_n$
$-L$	$+CP$	$+m_n$
$-L$	$+CP$	$+m_n$
$-L$	$+CP$	$+m_n$
$-L$	$+CP$	$+m_n$

If we put the principals in on both sides, the left-hand-side will have a zero value and so we could write:

$$-1 + \sum_t (CP_t + m_n) * d_t * DF_t + DF_n = 0$$

Given we know the quoted margins, we can therefore estimate the implied forward CP rates. This could be either by bootstrapping—i.e. estimate m_j for $j = 1, 2, \ldots$ by interpolation from the market quotes and then calculate CP_j sequentially—or using an optimisation approach.

Worksheet 8.4 uses an optimisation approach. One-month CP rates, which are probably the most common tenors, are used; the same approach could easily be adapted for CP rates of other tenors. Given that one can get estimates for CP rates out for a year, it would be quite easy to estimate the first few forward rates off this physical market, but this has not been done in the worksheet. Instead we have adopted a slightly different tack. The CP curve is effectively a spread curve off Libor, so if we define $CP_t = L_t - m_t$ we can work in terms of the spreads $\{m\}$. First, 1-month Libor rates are estimated from the current swap curve. The spread curve $\{m\}$ is estimated in column [1], and the final values of the mid-rate CP − Libor swaps in column [6], using the above equation:

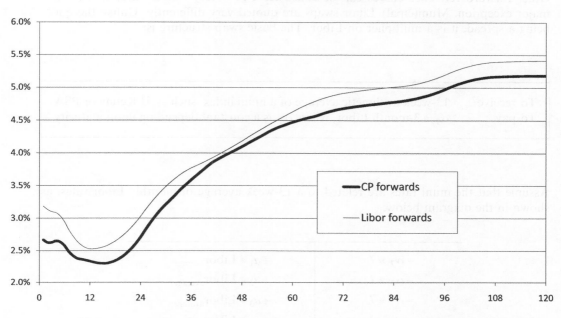

Term	Bid	Ask	Time		Bid	Ask	Time		Bid	Ask	Time
	Percentage of Libor				Quarterly Bond Rate				BMA Muni Bond Index Spread		
	vs BMA Muni Index				vs BMA Muni Index					vs Libor	
1Y	1) 71.6250	73.6250	2/14	12) 1.881	1.934	2/14	23) 0.69	0.75	2/14
2Y	2) 71.6875	73.6875	2/14	13) 1.958	2.013	2/14	24) 0.72	0.77	2/14
3Y	3) 72.0625	74.0625	2/14	14) 2.191	2.251	2/14	25) 0.79	0.85	2/14
4Y	4) 72.1250	74.1250	2/14	15) 2.430	2.498	2/14	26) 0.87	0.94	2/14
5Y	5) 72.2500	74.2500	2/14	16) 2.642	2.715	2/14	27) 0.94	1.01	2/14
7Y	6) 72.8750	74.8750	2/14	17) 2.987	3.069	2/14	28) 1.03	1.11	2/14
10Y	7) 73.3750	75.3750	2/14	18) 3.325	3.415	2/14	29) 1.12	1.21	2/14
12Y	8) 73.6875	75.6875	2/14	19) 3.475	3.570	2/14	30) 1.15	1.24	2/14
15Y	9) 74.6875	76.6875	2/14	20) 3.666	3.764	2/14	31) 1.14	1.24	2/14
20Y	10) 75.7500	77.7500	2/14	21) 3.834	3.935	2/14	32) 1.13	1.23	2/14
30Y	11) 76.7500	78.7500	2/14	22) 3.947	4.050	2/14	33) 1.09	1.20	2/14

Source: Prebon Yamane, owned by Tullett Prebon plc.

Other forward reference curves can be constructed in a very similar fashion, with one major exception. Muni(cipal)–Libor swaps are quoted very differently. Unlike the quote being a spread, it is a multiplier on Libor. The basic swap structure is:

To receive	13-week arithmetic average of a muni index, such as JJ Kenny or PSA
To pay	$\alpha_T * $ 3-month Libor, where α_T is a constant depending upon maturity

Assume that the muni rates are related to a 13-week average of monthly Libor rates, as shown in the diagram below:

$-\alpha_T * L$	$+a_1 * \text{Libor}_{\text{average}}$
$-\alpha_T * L$	$+a_2 * \text{Libor}_{\text{average}}$
$-\alpha_T * L$	$+a_3 * \text{Libor}_{\text{average}}$
$-\alpha_T * L$	$+a_4 * \text{Libor}_{\text{average}}$
$\vdots$	$\vdots$
$-\alpha_T * L$	$+a_{T-2} * \text{Libor}_{\text{average}}$
$-\alpha_T * L$	$+a_{T-1} * \text{Libor}_{\text{average}}$
$-\alpha_T * L$	$+a_T * \text{Libor}_{\text{average}}$

Therefore, we can estimate the average of the Libor rates, and then solve for the forward multipliers $\{a_1, a_2, \ldots\}$ using the following formula for a swap of maturity T:

$$-\alpha_T + \sum_t a_t * \text{Libor}_{\text{average}-t} * d_t * \text{DF}_t + \alpha_T * \text{DF}_n = 0$$

Note that the daycount fraction d_t is on a 30/360 basis. In Worksheet 8.5, smoothing is applied to the forward multipliers.

The worksheet estimates the implied muni rates by first calculating 1-month implied Libor rates at weekly intervals; see columns [1] through [8]. The next step is to calculate the 13-week average Libor rate; see column [9] and summarised in column [10]. Using the same optimisation approach, we now estimate the forward multipliers to be applied to these average rates to arrive at the average 3-month muni rate[2] so that the values of the quoted swaps are zero: see column [11].

---

[2] An alternative construction would be to apply the multipliers to the 1-month Libor rates before averaging, and then proceed as before.

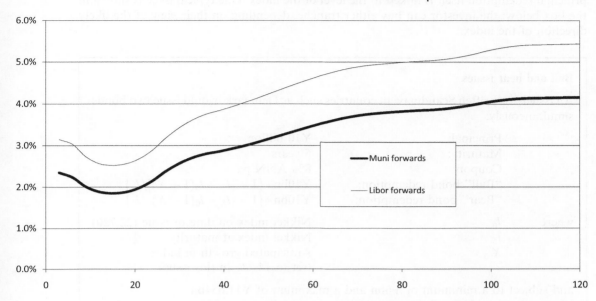

This section has described the existence of various basis swaps, and how the implied forward rates may be estimated based upon the market quotes. Most other basis swaps are priced as either a spread or a multiplier. Because they are effectively a link between two markets, the conventions may however appear unusual for people only familiar with Libor markets but of course they have to be consistent with the practice in the non-Libor market. Prime (and base) swaps are another good example. Because these are quite regulated, the rates do not change from day to day, but typically only after a signal by the government. A time-series of Prime therefore consists of a series of relatively large step changes, typically multiples of 25 bp. Most people model Prime as a function of forward Libor, but based upon confidence bands. For example, Prime is held constant whilst Libor remains within a band; when Libor moves outside the band, then both Prime and the band are adjusted. So Prime typically lags Libor changes, although there can be asymmetry going up and down depending upon government policy.

8.3 EQUITY AND COMMODITY SWAPS

Equity derivatives, traditionally written on the individual stock, have a long history. They have been frequently used in association with the raising of capital in the guise of:

- convertible bonds, i.e. bonds that are convertible into equity, usually at the option of the bond-holder;
- equity warrants, i.e. long-dated equity call options;

and so on. Modern equity derivatives are very often written on equity indices, for example a bond that pays coupon according to the rise in a particular index is targeted at a traditional investor who does not wish to risk capital in the equity market but is prepared to take a view on the index. For the more adventurous, there are structures where the principal redemption itself is linked to the level of the index. One typical issue is shown in the box below; the investor can buy either tranche, depending on their view of the likely direction of the index.

Bull and bear issues

An issuer, very often Scandinavian countries such as Denmark, would issue two bonds simultaneously:

Principal:	¥10 billion
Maturity:	5 years
Coupon:	8% ANN pa
"Bull" bond redemption:	$¥10bn * \{1 + [I_5 - I_0(1 + X)]/I_0\}$
"Bear" bond redemption:	$¥10bn * \{1 - [I_5 - I_0(1 - X)]/I_0\}$

where
I_0	Nikkei index on date of issue (22,720)
I_5	Nikkei index at maturity
X	Anticipated growth in index (set to 14.7% in this issue)

and subject to a minimum of ¥6bn and a maximum of ¥11.054bn

The coupon is above the current market level, as compensation for the equity risk. The factor X can be used to ensure that there is sufficient demand for both tranches. From the issuer's point of view, the total redemption amount to be paid for both bonds is simply $2 * (1 - X)$. In this case, $X = 14.7\%$ of the redemption amount is the compensation for paying the higher coupon.

There seems to be a general perception that equity derivatives are widespread, possibly because of the raised profile they receive through embedded structures. In reality, they typically constitute less than 2% of the derivative market.[3]

There are a number of different ways in which an equity index may be constructed from an underlying portfolio of stocks:

- An unweighted average of the quoted share prices, such as the Nikkei 225.
- A weighted, usually by market capitalisation, average of the share prices, such as the main FTSE 100.
- A free-float index, where the share prices are weighted not by total share issuance, but only by the number of the shares available to trade.
- A stock investor will make money through both the growth in the share price and also through the receipt of dividends. When a company pays a dividend, its share price and hence any one of the above indices are likely to drop accordingly. A total return index is based upon both components. Many stock exchanges offer total return indices as part of the broad offering.

Equity swaps are a relatively new invention, and currently represent only 20% of the total

---

[3] See *Global OTC Derivative Report*, BIS, November 2000.

equity OTC derivative market. But it is the fastest growing part because they can be an efficient means of moving investments between the equity and interest markets. For example, suppose an investor is currently receiving USD Libor on some assets, but believes that the stock market is about to rise. He could liquidate his investment and re-invest in stocks, but that is likely to incur considerable transaction costs, or he could enter into an equity swap:

To pay	USD Libor on a notional principal
To receive	The return on an equity index applied to a notional principal

An equity swap is really a cross-market swap:

Trade date:	4 February 2008
Notional principal:	$100m
Maturity:	2 years
To receive:	USD 3 mo. Libor
To pay:	S&P 500 Index quarterly + 10 bp pa

Some typical cashflows are shown in Worksheet 8.6.[4] Hypothetical future values of the index and Libor are shown in columns [1] and [2], respectively. Therefore the return on the index over each period can be calculated as $r_t = (I_t - I_{t-1})/I_{t-1}$: for example, the return over the first period is

$$(1,454.13 - 1,380.82)/1,380.82 = 5.31\%$$

Note that this return may be either positive or negative, depending on the movement in the index. The index-related cashflow to be paid at the end of the first quarter is:

$$\$100m * \{5.31\% + 10\,\text{bp} * 0.253/10,000\} = \$5,309,241 + 25,000 = \$5,334,241$$

as shown in columns [4–6] of the example box of the worksheet. Note that the return does not use a daycount fraction, whereas the margin is quoted on a per annum basis as usual and therefore uses the fraction. The Libor cashflows are calculated in the usual fashion, and finally a net cashflow is settled, as shown in column [8].

Such a swap could be priced by estimating future values of the index using a cost-of-carry argument:

$$I_t = I_0 + \text{Expected growth} - \text{Expected dividends}$$

and after adjustments for share issues, splits, etc. However, a rather simpler approach is to consider how such a swap might be hedged. At the beginning of the swap, assume we borrow $100m at 3 mo. Libor flat. These interest payments will exactly match the Libor receipts on the swap. We will then buy $100m of the components of the index; this does not

---

[4] The spreadsheet contains two versions of each worksheet. One version randomly generates the index, interest and FX rates to demonstrate that the hedges will work successfully under any movements. However, for discussion purposes, this randomness has been removed from the other "fixed" version.

mean buying every component of the index, but sufficient to act as a reasonable tracker. At the end of the first quarter, the index has risen by 5.31%, i.e. the holding is now worth $105,309,241. The increased amount of $5,309,241 is sold off, thereby generating a cash-flow to meet the payment on the swap and simultaneously re-balancing the principal investment in the index back to $100m. This process is then repeated each quarter. At the end, the investment in the index is totally liquidated, and the Libor borrowing re-paid (see hedging box of Worksheet 8.6).

An alternative would be to use eurodollar and S&P 500 index futures to hedge the swap, in a very similar fashion to the method employed in money market swaps. Unfortunately there is only good liquidity in (at the most) the three nearest index futures contracts, so using these futures to price and to hedge a longer swap would involve quite a lot of basis risk, potential roll-over costs, as well as the funding of the initial and daily variation margins which will create convexity issues.

So, in theory as with most basis swaps, a Libor–equity swap should be priced very close to flat. The existence of the margin reflects supply and demand, the bank's efficiency replicating the index, the bank's ability to fund in the interbank market, various costs of running the portfolios and of course the required return on capital employed.

The above swap is called a "fixed notional" swap; each cashflow is estimated using the constant notional principal of $100m. The hedging of such a swap is not very efficient because it involves selling or buying potentially small amounts of the components of the index each quarter. A more common structure is a "variable notional" which avoids this (see Worksheet 8.8).

At the end of the first quarter the index has risen by 5.31%. Instead of liquidating part of the index investment, we borrow the money required to pay under the swap, namely $5,309,241: columns [8] and [9] show the periodic borrowings or repayments and the total effect. To match the future Libor interest payments, the notional principal of the swap is also increased by 5.31% as shown in column [3]. The swap cashflows are therefore calculated based upon the notional principal at the beginning of each period. At the end of the swap, the original index investment is liquidated and used fully to repay the accumulated Libor borrowing, as shown in columns [8] and [11].

Cross-currency equity swaps have also been included in the spreadsheet (see Worksheets 8.10 to 8.13). The structure of these will be discussed in Chapter 9.

In summary, equity swaps are used to simulate the exposure to an index but without having to actually make the physical investment. The variable notional versions in particular mimic the cashflows that would have occurred.

8.3.1 Commodity swaps

These are very similar in structure to equity swaps and have two main types:

- fixed-for-floating commodity price swap;
- floating price against floating interest swap;

with other types of swaps being generated from these basic ones. Fixed-for-floating are popular "natural" multiperiod structures used by commodity producers and users to lock in common prices. Price–interest swaps would on the face of it also appear to have a natural purpose. For example, commodity producers are naturally long the commodity and short interest rates, and should therefore be prepared to pay the price and to receive Libor as a hedge against rising borrowing costs. But in practice this link between interest payments and production costs is not so simple, and hence such swaps are less popular. Overall, OTC commodity derivatives constitute about 0.5% of the total market[5] and are not growing particularly rapidly.

Typical fixed–floating commodity swap

Trade date:	4 February 2008
Notional quantity:	100,000 bbl
Commodity:	WTI Light Sweet Crude
Maturity:	6 August 2008
Frequency:	Monthly
Period end date:	6th day of each month
Settlement date:	5 days after period end
To pay:	$97.8 per bbl
To receive:	Arithmetic daily average of reference price over each period
Settlement method:	Net cash payment

Commodity swaps are usually priced off commodity futures or by estimating the forward price of the commodity. The former can involve considerable basis risk as the range of reference commodities under futures contract is considerably restricted compared with the possible references for OTC contracts, although frequently the dates are matched to reduce the basis risk.[6] Forward-pricing is in theory relatively simple to calculate as a commodity may be purchased today (spot) and held until the fixing date[7]:

$$\text{Current price} + \text{Cost of funding position} + \text{Cost of physical storage}$$

This suggests that the Forward price > Spot price, i.e. said to be in "contango". Unfortunately supply and demand, especially for seasonal commodities, can distort this relationship quite considerably, and it is feasible to observe "backwardation", i.e. when the Forward price < Spot price. Some producers, wishing to entice consumers to commit to forward purchases and hence provide a guaranteed demand, will offer a "convenience yield" or discount on the theoretical forward price which also needs to be taken into account. Commodity prices do exhibit high volatility, and simplistic forward-pricing carries a very real risk.

There is a range of practical commodity swaps. Swaps involving oil prices are probably the most common, but it is feasible to get OTC swaps against most commodities. Currently an increasing market is weather derivatives, trading such structures as fixed–floating

---

[5] BIS, ibid.

[6] The activities of the US subsidiary of the German company Metallgesellschaft is a widely debated example of the basis risk. In summary, MG offered customers long-dated (up to 10 years) contracts to supply gas and oil at fixed prices. MG hedged its exposure to rising prices by buying short-term commodity futures. Unfortunately the prices dropped, and whilst the customer contracts were showing a theoretical profit, MG had to pay out real cash margins. The cash drain on the company became so large that the Board ordered all positions to be unwound; it was estimated that the total losses were about $1.3bn.

[7] Except for commodities which cannot be stored such as electricity.

temperature or rainfall. Another one that fluctuates in popularity are property swaps; for example trading the percentage change in a property index over a period against Libor.

Other forms of structured swaps include:

- basis swaps with reference to the spread between two linked commodities such as Brent and WTI crude oils;
- spread swaps with reference to either side of production such as WTI crude oil against a refined product like jet fuel or kerosene;
- curve–lock swaps, which lock in the backwardation/contango spread (very similar to spreadlock swaps described above).

8.4   LONGEVITY SWAPS

On average, people are living longer and longer; for example the life expectancy for men aged 60 is 5 years longer in 2005 than in 1980. This is creating significant risks for pension providers if they underestimate this lengthening. Many governments in the developed world, such as the UK's Government Actuary's Department, publish regular mortality indices. There are also an increasing number of OTC longevity indices published, such as:

- Longevity Index by Credit Suisse. This started in 2006, and produces an annual estimate of actual life expectancy based on US data.
- LifeMetrics by JP Morgan. This started in 2007, and produces annual estimates for the US, the Netherlands and England and Wales.
- Xpect by Deutsche Börse. This will be a monthly index based upon live feeds from undertakers in the UK and Germany, and is anticipated to launch late in 2008.

The first mortality bond was issued by Swiss Re in December 2003. It was for 3 years, paying Libor + 135 bp, on a principal of $400m. The principal started to reduce if a broad-based mortality index across five countries rose to 130% at the end of the 3 years, and was completely exhausted if the index exceeded 150%.[8] This is really an example of a catastrophe bond, as the mortality rate during WWII did not hit these levels, which would only be triggered by some event such as a pandemic.

In 2004, BNP Paribas suggested that EIB should issue a 25-year £540m longevity bond. The bond paid a coupon of £50m $* S(t)$. The starting point was a cohort of people who were 65 years old on the issue date. $S(0)$ was defined as 100%, and $S(t)$ their continued survival rate as published by the Office for National Statistics. The bond was an annuity, with no redemption principal, to provide a hedge for pension funds. A swap had to be organised, funding the EIB at 3-month Euribor − 20 bp. Eventually the bond was never issued, as the EIB became concerned about reputational risk. But longevity bonds started to come back again in 2006/7.

Longevity swaps have been under discussion for some 5 years. The two sides of such a structure would typically be:

- pay an income stream based upon current longevity expectations;
- receive an income stream, usually based upon changes in one of the OTC indices.

---

[8] See D. Blake *et al.*, *Living with Mortality: Longevity Bonds and Other Mortality-linked Securities*, presented to the Faculty of Actuaries, 16 January 2006, for further details.

For example, the UK insurer Lucida did a longevity swap with JP Morgan in February 2008; this was the first one based upon the LifeMetrics index. The transaction was thought to be for 10 years based on a notional of GBP100 million, whereby Lucida received money if people initially based in the 60 to 69-year age band lived longer than anticipated. Interestingly, the swap was to hedge Lucida's exposure to the Irish population; the basis risk between the English and Welsh base of LifeMetrics and the Irish was thought to be negligible.

Interest in longevity transactions is increasing, as institutions recognise their exposures and endeavour to hedge themselves. The absence of any significant market removes the possibility of liquid-hedging and easy price discovery. These derivatives, not only swaps but also options, are at the stage of the IRS market in the early 1980s, which was a negotiated market between end-users.

8.5 INFLATION SWAPS

Over the past decade or so, governments around the world have been trying to bring inflation under control, with varying degrees of success. Fears that inflation might get out of control again have spurred the significant growth in the inflation swap market. There are two main types:

- fixed-for-floating inflation;
- real-for-nominal (i.e. Libor) interest rates;

where the cashflows on one or both sides are calculated with reference to future inflation.

However, before we can discuss inflation swaps, it is important to understand the mechanics of inflation. Virtually every country publishes some form of consumer price index. This is set to 100 on an arbitrary date.[9] Price information across a large shopping basket of retail products is usually gathered at the end of each month from a range of locations in the country. The average, weighted by the relative amount of each item purchased, annualised price growth g is then calculated based upon the price of the basket 1 year earlier. The new level of the index is calculated using this price growth, and published some 4–6 weeks later.

For example, the Eurozone publishes the Harmonised Index of Consumer Prices (HICP). Each member country calculates its CPI based upon 12 standardised divisions of consumer consumption. The HICP is based upon a weighted arithmetic average of these CPIs.

Inflation-linked securities ("linkers") have been issued by a number of organisations, including governments. There are primarily two reasons for their issue:

1. When investors are concerned about extremely high future inflation (or hyper-inflation), and are therefore unwilling to bear this risk. Governments such as Brazil, Mexico, Israel and Argentina have all found it necessary to issue short-dated inflation-linked securities regularly as the only way they could attract investors.
2. With inflation apparently stable and under control across much of the developed world (at the time of writing), an increasing number of governments have been issuing index-linked bonds. There are three reasons for this:

---

[9] The UK Retail Price Index was rebased to 100 in February 1987.

○ In such circumstances, traditional fixed-coupon bonds are unattractive to investors. Because of the low coupon, a small increase in inflation will result in a large decrease in bond price, i.e. the bond's price elasticity with respect to inflation is high.

○ Governments frequently set themselves inflation targets; by issuing these bonds, they can act as a form of penalty if inflation is allowed to get out of control.

○ They broaden the range of potential investors in the government securities, which is likely to reduce the overall cost of debt. This is also why many supranationals such as the World Bank and EIB have issued linkers.

The first major market of the latter form was started in the UK, whose government has issued linkers ever since 1981. The table below summarises the major government-issued linker markets as of January 2008. Many of the European bonds are linked to the HICP, and not to the national CPI. Some Australian states have also issued linkers, but often tied to commodity price indices.

Country	Market value ($ US billion)	Number of linkers	Longest maturity
Australia	8	3	2020
Canada	37	5	2041
France	209	11	2040
Germany	23	2	2016
Greece	24	2	2030
Italy	100	6	2035
Japan	75	14	2017
Sweden	37	5	2028
UK	320	14	2055
USA	492	23	2032

Source: UK DMO March 2008

The mechanics of these linkers are very similar. For example, consider the UK linker below:

Issue date:	23 September 2005
Maturity date:	22 November 2055
Coupon:	1.25% sa
Dirty price:	136.78 on 4 February 2008

The modern convention is to use a 3-month inflation lag as the reference. The base index I_0 for this bond would be the RPI on 23 June 2005. The UK RPI was:

1 June 2005	192.2
1 July 2005	192.2 (pure coincidence that they are the same number)

The base index is estimated by linear interpolation:

$$\mathrm{RPI}_{23\text{-June-}05} = \mathrm{RPI}_{1\text{-June-}05} + (22/30) * (\mathrm{RPI}_{1\text{-July-}05} - \mathrm{RPI}_{1\text{-June-}05}) = 192.2$$

where 22 is the reference date of 23rd − 1 and 30 is the number of days in the month of September.

For a cashflow at time T, the reference index I_T, namely with a 3-month lag as described above, and hence the index ratio $\{I_T/I_0]$ are calculated. If the face value of the bond at issue was P_0, then:

Coupon at time T	$c_T = 0.5 * 1.25\% * P_0 * \{I_T/I_0\}$
Principal redemption at maturity	$P_{\mathrm{Maturity}} = P_0 * \{I_{\mathrm{Maturity}}/I_0\}$

There is one small problem with this approach. Assume today's date is 4 February 2008; the next coupon is to be paid on 22 May 2008, nearly four months away. This coupon is currently unknown because the February and March RPIs have not yet been published, and therefore accrued coupon for pricing cannot be calculated. The convention is to use the index ratio for 4 February as an estimate for the correct index ratio, knowing that the estimate will converge as time passes.[10]

The main investors in these bonds have been pension funds, using the bonds as hedges against their inflation-linked liabilities. But the bonds are not ideal, as the cashflow from a pension is an annuity, with no large linked redemption payment. Therefore banks have been increasingly providing inflation swaps to investors, and then hedging themselves with the bonds.

The most basic form of inflation swap is a zero-coupon swap. Assume today's date is 4 February 2008, and a bank is quoting 3.17 bid for a 10-year zero on £25m. This means that the bank would:

- pay £25m $* [(1 + 3.17\%)^{10} - 1]$ on 5 February 2018 (the 4th is a non-business day);
- receive £25m $* [I_{10}/I_0 - 1]$ on 5 February 2018.

Sterling zero swaps use a 2-month lag convention with no interpolation, therefore I_0 would be the December 2007 index, and I_{10} the December 2017 index. This zero market has become increasingly liquid in the major indices in recent years, and prices are readily available on trading screens.

---

[10] Prior to 2005, the UK linker market was unique in using an 8-month lag. Even with the publication lag, the coupon would then have been known with certainty before the start of the semi-annual coupon period. However, this convention was criticised by investors as not providing sufficiently close inflationary protection.

```
05:52 01MAY06     ICAP                              UK69580     ICAPINFLATION
Please call +44 (0)20 7532 3050 for further details  Page Fwd <ICAPINFLATION2>
      HICPXT             HICP              FRCPI            UKRPI            USCPI
     BID ASK           BID ASK          BID ASK          BID ASK          BID ASK
  1y 2.29-2.49      1y 2.19-2.39     1y 1.88-2.08     1y 2.49-2.79     1y 2.90-3.10
  2y 2.25-2.39      2y 2.34-2.48     2y 2.00-2.14     2y 2.50-2.74     2y 2.69-2.93
  3y 2.21-2.35      3y 2.33-2.47     3y 2.06-2.20     3y 2.56-2.80     3y 2.72-2.96
  4y 2.18-2.32      4y 2.30-2.44     4y 2.09-2.23     4y 2.61-2.85     4y 2.76-3.00
  5y 2.16-2.30      5y 2.29-2.43     5y 2.10-2.24     5y 2.66-2.90     5y 2.80-3.04
  6y 2.15-2.29      6y 2.28-2.42     6y 2.12-2.26     6y 2.69-2.93     6y 2.81-3.05
  7y 2.14-2.28      7y 2.30-2.44     7y 2.14-2.28     7y 2.73-2.97     7y 2.81-3.05
  8y 2.14-2.28      8y 2.30-2.44     8y 2.15-2.29     8y 2.76-3.00     8y 2.80-3.04
  9y 2.15-2.29      9y 2.27-2.41     9y 2.17-2.31     9y 2.80-3.04     9y 2.81-3.05
 10y 2.15-2.29     10y 2.27-2.41    10y 2.18-2.32    10y 2.83-3.07    10y 2.80-3.04
 12y 2.11-2.35     12y 2.23-2.47    12y 2.15-2.39    12y 2.87-3.11    12y 2.85-3.09
 15y 2.13-2.37     15y 2.25-2.49    15y 2.17-2.41    15y 2.90-3.14    15y 2.91-3.15
 20y 2.16-2.40     20y 2.27-2.51    20y 2.19-2.43    20y 2.93-3.17    20y 2.97-3.21
 25y 2.18-2.42     25y 2.30-2.54    25y 2.19-2.43    25y 2.97-3.21    25y 3.04-3.28
 30y 2.20-2.44     30y 2.36-2.60    30y 2.20-2.44    30y 2.97-3.21    30y 3.14-3.38

      Jan               Jan              INT              Feb              INT
   100.62223         100.65000       112.23129        194.20000        198.72858
   01-Jan-06         01-Jan-06       03-Feb-06        01-Feb-06        02-Feb-06
   20060101          20060101        20060203         20060201         20060202
ICAP Global Index <ICAP>                    Forthcoming changes <ICAPCHANGE>
```

The picture above (*source*: ICAP plc) shows, from left to right, zero-coupon quotes for HICP eX-Tobacco, HICP, French CPI, UK RPI and US CPI. The base indexing dates and indices are shown at the bottom; notice that the French and US swaps do interpolate the base index whereas the others do not. HICP-related indices use a 3-month lag, reflecting the long potential publication lag, whereas all the others use 2-month.[11] HICPXT is the most common Eurozone reference index, probably because many governments have been deliberately inflating the price of tobacco, and hence distorting HICP to a small extent.

Clearly, given the quotes, a forward inflation index curve can be implied. Forward inflation can also be implied off the physical (cash) markets in two different ways. The traditional approach is to imply a forward inflation curve from a set of linker bonds by:

1. Deriving bond-based DFs from normal on-the-run bonds.
2. Guessing a forward inflation curve, usually in the form of inflation growth rates.
3. Building the linker bond cashflows based on this curve.
4. Pricing the linker bonds by discounting using the DFs.
5. Adjusting the guess until the theoretical prices match the market prices.

Full details are in the spreadsheet entitled "Inflation swap models". In outline, the first part of the spreadsheet is organised as follows:

- Static and current market data on non-linkers and linker bonds, as well as a Libor curve, are entered in Worksheets 8.14 to 8.17.
- The input yield of the non-linker bonds is converted into a price in Worksheet 8.18.
- Step 1 above is performed twice. First, a smooth DF curve is constructed by fitting a parametric Nelson–Siegel curve to the non-linker bonds; see Worksheets 8.19 and 8.20.

---

[11] As 1 May is a widespread bank holiday, the base months hadn't been updated.

Second, arbitrage-free DFs are estimated by bootstrapping (see Worksheets 8.21 and 8.22). The two results are compared in Worksheet 8.23.

- The "guess" is performed three ways. First, by fitting another Nelson–Siegel curve to the inflation growth rates (see Worksheets 8.24 and 8.25). Second, by bootstrapping a piece-wise constant inflation-growth curve (see Worksheets 8.26 and 8.27). Third, by using optimisation (as described in Chapter 3); this is performed in a separate linked spread-sheet "Building an inflation curve by optimisation" with the final results shown in Worksheet 8.31.

The end result for UK gilt data is shown below.

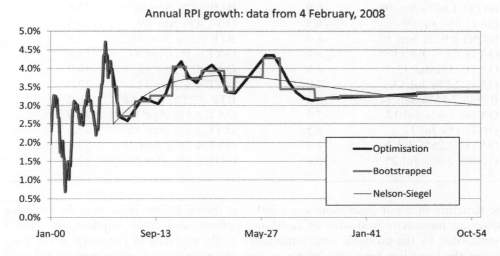

Annual RPI growth: data from 4 February, 2008

The resulting inflation curves from the zero swap and the cash linker markets are shown below.

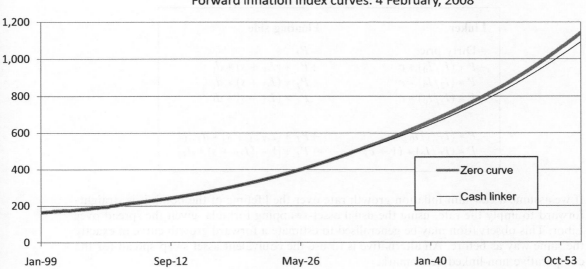

Forward inflation index curves: 4 February, 2008

There is very good agreement between the two curves for the first 30 years; the implied zero growth rate from the cash market is within 2 bp of the swap market. The difference increases with maturity, probably reflecting the limited supply of linker bonds at the longer end plus the on-balance sheet requirements of physical instruments.

Alternatively, there is a fairly liquid asset swap market for both normal and linker bonds. The table below shows a euro curve on 4 February 2008:

Linker	Par asset swap spread	Comparative benchmark	Par asset swap spread	Relative spread
BTP€i 1.65% Sep 08	−6.0	BTP 3.5% Sep 08	−13.0	−7.0
OATi 3% Jul 09	−6.5	OAT 4% Apr 09	−18.0	−11.5
BTP€i 0.95% Sep 10	−1.0	BTP 5.5% Nov 10	−4.0	−3.0
OATi 1.6% Jul 11	−6.0	OAT 6.5% Apr 11	−14.0	−8.0
OAT€i 3% Jul 12	−8.0	OAT 5% Apr 12	−14.0	−6.0
OATi 2.5% Jul 13	−7.0	OAT 4% Apr 13	−12.0	−5.0
BTP€i 2.15% Sep 14	10.5	BTP 4.25% Aug 14	6.0	−4.5
OAT€i 1.6% Jul 12	−7.0	OAT 3.5% Apr 15	−12.0	−5.0
OATi 1% Jul 17	−5.5	OAT 3.5% Apr 15	−12.0	−6.5
OAT€i 2.25% Jul 20	−11.5	OAT 4.25% Apr 19	−13.0	−2.5
GGB€i 2.9% Jul 25	16.0	GGB 5.9% Oct 22	12.0	−4.0

The structure of a par asset swap for a linker is shown below. Note that the structure implies an immediate mismatch of cashflows upfront with credit implications. This is compensated by the probable contra-mismatch at the maturity of the swap. If the dirty price of the bond is a long way from par, then the asset swap is often constructed on a "proceeds" basis, where the principal on the floating side P_L is set to the dirty price of the linker.

Linker	Floating side
+Dirty price	$-P_L$
$-P * (I_1/I_0) * c$	$+P_L * (L_1 + s) * d_1$
$-P * (I_2/I_0) * c$	$+P_L * (L_2 + s) * d_1$
$-P * (I_3/I_0) * c$	$+P_L * (L_3 + s) * d_1$
$\vdots$	$\vdots$
$-P * (I_{T-1}/I_0) * c$	$+P_L * (L_{T-1} + s) * d_{T-1}$
$-P * (I_T/I_0) * (1 + c)$	$+P_L * [1 + (L_T + s) * d_T]$

If we assume a constant inflation growth rate over the lifetime of the bond, it is straightforward to imply the rate, using the usual asset-swapping formula, given the spread over Libor. This observation may be generalised to estimate a forward growth curve in exactly the same way as before. An alternative is to use the equivalent asset swap spread for the comparative non-linked benchmark.

Year-on-year (YoY) inflation swaps are also fairly liquid, but less than inflation asset swaps. The basic structure is to:

- pay $P * (I_T/I_t - 1) * d_{t,T}$;
- receive $P * F * d_{t,T}$.

where P is the principal amount, t and T are the beginning and end of a reference period, $d_{t,T}$ is the relevant daycount fraction, and F is a fixed percentage. Usually the period is annual, corresponding to quoted growth rates so that $(I_T/I_{T-1} - 1)$ is equal to the forward growth rate $g_{T-1,T}$. In this case, the daycount fraction is set to 1; fractions are usually only calculated for periods shorter than a year.

It is tempting to estimate the forward growth rate off the forward index curve using the usual arbitrage argument (see Worksheet 8.34).

But the situation is complicated by the fact that neither I_t nor I_T are known at the beginning, unlike a zero swap. The unknown indices may be hedged by entering into a pair of zero-coupon swaps of maturities t and T, respectively. But the hedge would generate a cashflow at time t which would then have to be re-invested until time T when the YoY swap would pay. As the size and sign of this cashflow would be dependent upon I_t, the re-investment rate $r_{t,T}$ could not be easily hedged. Therefore there is a convexity effect arising from the joint behaviour of I_t and $r_{t,T}$.

We want to estimate $E_T\{I_T/I_t\}$ under some measure, where we already know $E_t\{I_t\}$ and $E_T\{I_T\}$ from the zero market. Mercurio[12] developed the following approach. Define:

$$\exp\{D_T\} = E_T\{I_T/I_t\}/[E_T\{I_T\}/E_t\{I_t\}]$$

where $D_T \approx t * \sigma_t * [\rho_{I,r} * \sigma_B + \sigma_t - \rho_{t,T} * \sigma_T]$;

σ_T, σ_t are the B&S volatilities for I_T and I_t, respectively;

σ_B is the B&S volatility for a forward ZC bond price at time t, maturing at time T [this can be estimated from cap vols: $d_{t,T} * r_{t,T} * \sigma_r/(1 + d_{t,T} * r_{t,T})$ where $d_{t,T}$ is the length of the forward rate r fixing at time t, paying at time T];

$\rho_{I,r}$ is the correlation between the forward nominal IR and the CPI index;

$\rho_{t,T}$ is the correlation between I_{t-1} and I_t.

Hence the payside is $P * \{[E_T\{I_T\}/E_t\{I_t\}] * \exp\{D_T\} - 1\} * d_{t,T}$ (see Worksheet 8.36).

There is a small but growing market for inflation-linked options. These options can arise in a number of guises:

- Stand-alone caps. For example, a 10-year option with a payout of $\max\{0, I_{10}/I_0 - 125\%\}$. Re-writing this as $\max\{0, [I_{10}/I_0 - 1] - [(1 + 2.2565\%)^{10} - 1]\}$ immediately shows that the cap is indeed an option on a payer's zero swap.
- Hybrid securities. For example, the following was issued in 2005:
  - 25-year note in euros;
  - coupon in year 1, $C_1 = 4\%$;
  - $C_t = \max\{0, \min\{1.7 * g(t), 4.5\%\}\}$ for $t = 2, \ldots$ where $g(t) = I_t/I_{t-1} - 1$ and I is the HICPXT index;
  - redemption at 100, and callable on any coupon date from year 2 onwards

---

[12] Fabio Mercurio, *Pricing Inflation-indexed Derivatives*, working paper from Product and Business Development Group, Banca IMI, 2004.

- In the UK, many pension liabilities are inflation-linked but with a cap/floor collar on YoY inflation growth. Typical bounds for the collar are 0% to 5% or, more recently, 1% to 3%. The related swap is known as a Limited Price Index (LPI) swap, with, clearly, embedded options. Typical payout would be:

$$\text{LPI}_t = \text{LPI}_{t-1} * [1 + \max\{\text{Floor}, \min\{g(t), \text{Cap}\}\}]$$

Such structures are path-dependent and hence best modelled by simulation, as discussed below.

Given the existence of these, albeit limited, products, it is feasible to imply volatilities. However, because many of the option structures are very driven by demand, the reliability of the implied estimates is questionable, and the completion of an entire volatility surface is pretty unrealistic. Estimates of correlations are even more unreliable, suggesting that both the convexity adjustment and the option pricing is subject to considerable error; see Belgrade for a more detailed discussion.[13] One approach is to calibrate the parameters by simulating a known inflation swap with no embedded options, and then use that swap as a control variate (see the discussion on LPI swaps below).

End-user-driven inflation swaps have even more interesting features. For example, consider the one below:

Typical end-user fixed–floating inflation swap

Trade date:	4 February 2008
Start date:	1 September 2015
Maturity date:	1 September 2034
Principal (P):	GBP5.335 million
To receive:	Fixed inflation growth rate of 4.7866% pa quarterly cashflow$_T = P * (1 + 4.7866\%)^T$
Uplift frequency:	5 years
To pay:	Floating inflation quarterly cashflow$_T = P * \{I_T/I_0\}$
Uplift frequency:	Annual
Reference lag:	3 months
Base indexing date:	1 June 2014

This is a long-dated forward starting swap designed to hedge the revenue stream of a major infrastructure project. Because of the forward start, I_0 is unknown and therefore there is a convexity effect. Whilst the cashflows are quarterly on both sides, the frequency of changing the inflation reference is different. On the floating side, the inflation index is only uplifted annually, whilst on the fixed side, the power of the growth rate is only changed once every 5 years. Nevertheless, the basic swap-pricing principles remain true, and the rate of 4.7866% is the breakeven rate that gives a net value of zero (see Worksheet 8.37).

Path-dependent LPI swaps were briefly described on the previous page. The annual growth rate is usually collared. Worksheet 8.40 in spreadsheet "LPI Inflation Swap"

---

[13] See N. Belgrade *et al.*, *Reconciling YoY and ZC Inflation Swaps: A Market Model Approach*, CDC IXIS CM working paper, August 2004. This paper shows how to produce a consistent correlation structure from ZC swap quotes and implied YoY volatilities.

contains an LPI model. The swap being priced is a fixed–floating 20 yr structure, starting in approximately 18 months' time with quarterly cashflows and annual uplifts on both sides. The annualised growth rate is collared to lie within the band 1–3%.

The worksheet prices two swaps simultaneously. First, an unconstrained RPI swap is modelled both analytically and by simulating the future growth rate. The volatility used for the growth rate is adjusted until the average price from the simulation matches the analytic price; in the worksheet, the difference is only 0.04 bp. Simultaneously, the LPI swap is also modelled, using the same random growth rates as for the RPI, and obviously observing the collar. Because the price is a non-linear function of the value of the swap, columns [BN to BT] approximate the function as a cubic, solve for the price, and then use a delta approximation to refine the answer. The average LPI price is then adjusted by the 0.04 bp difference.

The other main, albeit less common, end-user structures are real-nominal swaps. The cashflows on one side are related to a nominal interest rate such as Libor, whereas the other side is an inflated fixed real rate.

Typical inflation Libor swap

Maturity:	5 years (typically shorter than 30 years)
Principal (P):	£100 million
To receive:	$P * 3$ mo. Libor $*$ year fraction quarterly
To pay:	$P * 4.62\% * \{I_T/I_0\}$ sa $*$ year fraction quarterly
Reference lag:	2 months

Worksheet 8.41 demonstrates that the breakeven rate is indeed 4.62%.

There is one remaining major topic that needs to be discussed. Consider the graph of historic inflation growth below.

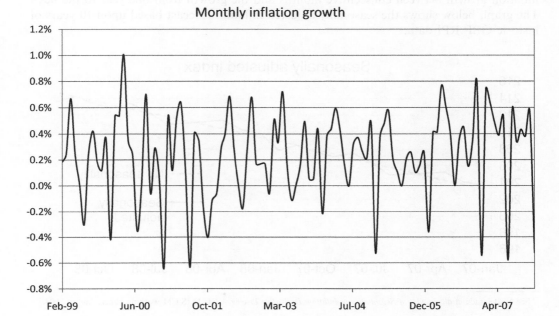

Monthly inflation growth

It clearly demonstrates seasonal fluctuations in inflation. Negative growth usually occurs from December to January and from June to July due to sales, and may also occur in October due to an excess of seasonal produce, or in the winter due to higher energy costs. Flow seasonality can also occur. For example, all the long UK linkers pay coupons on 22 May and 22 November; if these are asset-swapped, then supply and demand suggests that market-makers will reduce the z-c fixed rates for the reference months of (mainly) March and September, and hence the implied breakeven indices. Another example is that the French index is often distorted as the Livret A inflation-linked savings accounts use the May and November index fixings.

Consider the 10-year mid-zero rate above of 2.95%; this implies a breakeven index $I_{10} = I_0 * (1 + 2.95\%)^{10} = 259.72$ where I_0 is the February 2006 index of 194.20. The implied fixed growth for the same swap, but referencing different base indexing dates, changes significantly:

Indexing month	Fixed rate	I_0	I_{10}	Difference (bp)
Feb-06	**2.95%**	194.20	259.72	
Jan-06	2.99%	193.40	259.72	4.25
Dec-05	2.96%	194.10	259.72	0.53
Nov-05	2.98%	193.60	259.72	3.19
Oct-05	3.00%	193.30	259.72	4.78

The fixed rates for the other months were all based upon a constant I_{10}. Calendar spread trades are common, where a trader will (for example) pay the fixed rate on a z-c swap with a 2-month lag, and receive on a z-c swap with a 3-month lag.

Whilst some sophisticated models for seasonality do exist,[14] most people estimate the seasonality adjustment required based upon the historical difference between annualised inflation growth between consecutive months and the growth from one year to the next. The graph below shows the seasonally adjusted inflation forecast based upon 10 years of historic GBP RPI data.

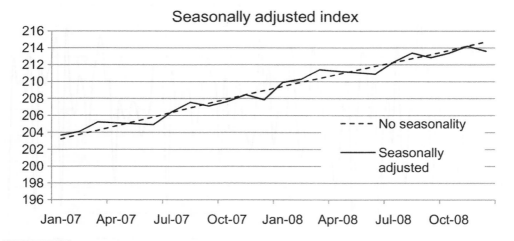

This was estimated using the Buys–Ballot model,[15] which is of the form:

$$X_T = \sum_k a_k * T^k + b_j + \varepsilon_T$$

where $\qquad X_T$ is the index [or the logarithm] at time T;

First expression: a polynomial in time;

Second expression: b_j is a "bump" for month $j, j = 1, 2, \ldots, 12$ where $\sum_j b_j = 0$ summing over all 12 months

The model was fitted by minimising the least squares of the residuals ε. There are two models available in spreadsheet "Ch 8 Inflation–Seasonality Adjustments": Worksheet 8.44 fits to the RPI curve, and Worksheet 8.45 to the ln(RPI).

8.6 VOLATILITY SWAPS[16]

A swap is effectively an exchange of cashflows between two counterparties. There is a wide range of different ways in which these cashflows may be calculated, as we have already seen. One family of swaps are the volatility and variance swaps, whereby the cashflows are calculated with reference to the volatility or variance of some market entity. For example:

- If σ is the annualised volatility (standard deviation of returns) of some dynamic measure such as share price, FX rate, etc. then a single period volatility swap, also known as a "realised volatility forward contract", has a payoff at expiry of:

$$N * \{\sigma_T - F_{\text{vol}}\}$$

where $\qquad \sigma_T$ is the realised volatility over the lifetime of the swap;

N is the notional amount of the swap in \$ per annualised volatility point; and

F_{vol} the annualised fixed volatility (volatility delivery price).

Consider a 1-year volatility receiver's forward on IBM's stock price for \$250,000 per point and a fixed rate of 30%. If the observed volatility over the year was 25%:

$$\text{Payout} = 250,000 * (30\% - 25\%) = 1,250,000$$

Option traders are often described as "trading volatility", but in practice this is not entirely true as the price of an option depends upon many other factors as well. On the other hand, a volatility swap is very close to being a pure play on volatility! But apart from the directional trading of volatility levels, these swaps may also be used to trade volatility spreads.

They may also be used as a hedge against a volatility exposure, possibly arising from an option portfolio. Dynamic delta-hedging of option portfolios[17] is common but is subject to a tracking error as the hedge is usually changed after the market (and therefore the portfolio delta) has moved. These tracking strategies are more active in periods of high

---

[15] See Chapter 2 in C. Gourieroux *et al.*, *Time Series and Dynamic Models*, published by Cambridge University Press 1997.

[16] Much of this section is drawn from "A guide to volatility and variance swaps" by K. Demeterfi *et al.*, *J. of Derivatives*, Summer 1999, pp. 9–32.

[17] See Chapter 10.

volatility, hence incurring greater costs with less accuracy. Other exposures to volatility are less direct. For example, market relationships such as spreads are notoriously less stable during periods of high volatility; therefore running a spread strategy has an indirect exposure to volatility. Equity prices are generally negatively correlated to volatility, i.e. as equity drops volatility rises. which can act as a diversification strategy. The volume of volatility and variance swaps is relatively small but has been growing rapidly; by mid-2008, several million of notional principal were being traded each day— but see the end of the section. This section is included to indicate how the swap markets are continually evolving.

Obviously it is critically important to specify calculation of the volatility quite precisely. Some of the relevant factors are listed below:

- Source and observation frequency, e.g. daily close of S&P 500 index.
- If OTC, how is it defined?
- Derivation of return, e.g. simple or compounded?
- Calculation of standard deviation: assumption about mean return? Usual assumption: zero mean (less argument and also permits easier risk management).
- Conversion factor (or formula) from observed standard deviation to annualised, e.g. no. of days in year?

Variance swaps are closely related to volatility swaps, but defined by:

$$\text{Payoff: } N * \{(\sigma_T)^2 - F_{\text{var}}\}$$

where N and F_{var} are defined in terms ($ per annualised volatility point squared). They obviously have less direct application but they are theoretically simpler to price and to hedge than volatility swaps.

For example, consider a variance swap:

- which starts at $t = 0$ and finishes at $t = T$, and covers m_T observations;
- define the simple return $r_i = (S_i - S_{i-1})/S_{i-1}$ and hence define

$$v_{0T} = (\sigma_{0T})^2 = \left\{\sum (r_i)^2 / T\right\} \quad \text{summing from 1 to } m_T$$

Suppose we now stand at time $0 < \tau < T$. We can write:

$$v_{0T} * T = v_{0\tau} * \tau + v_{\tau T} * (T - \tau) \quad \text{or} \quad v_{0T} = \lambda_\tau * v_{0\tau} + (1 - \lambda_\tau) * v_{\tau T}$$

where $\lambda_\tau = \tau/T$. We know $v_{0\tau}$, hence the mark-to-market value of the swap is

$$N * [\lambda_\tau * \{v_{0\tau} - F_{\text{var}}\} + (1 - \lambda_\tau) * \{v_{\tau T} - F_{\text{var}}\}] * \text{DF}_{\tau T}$$

These swaps are similar to average rate swaps, so that delta $\to 0$ as $\tau \to T$. The existing swap could be hedged by using $(1 - \lambda_\tau)$ of a new off-setting swap. Unfortunately, none of these simple results apply to volatility swaps.

In this section (which is considerably more complex than most of the book), we will first discuss the pricing and hedging of variance swaps, and then briefly discuss how volatility swaps might be approached. As usual, a fair price for the swap when it first starts would have a (risk-neutral) expectation of zero, that is:

$$F_{\text{var}} = E\{v_{0T}\} = E\{(\sigma_T)^2\}$$

We therefore need to estimate σ_T. This could either be historically (unconditionally or conditionally) measured, or we could use an implied volatility from the options market. If we used the latter, we would also want to use the option for hedging. Consider a normal call option with maturity T. If we define variance $v = \sigma^2 . T$, we can easily calculate the variance sensitivity, that is:

$$\partial C/\partial v = \tfrac{1}{2} . T/(2\pi v)^{1/2} . S . \exp\{-\tfrac{1}{2}(d_1)^2\}$$

It would be feasible to delta-hedge the variance sensitivity of the swap with a single option. Unfortunately the hedge would need frequent re-balancing as the variance sensitivity of the option is also a function of the underlying, as shown in the graph below (see Worksheet 8.46), which would not affect the swap. So a simple hedge such as this is unlikely to be very efficient as it brings along other exposures as well.

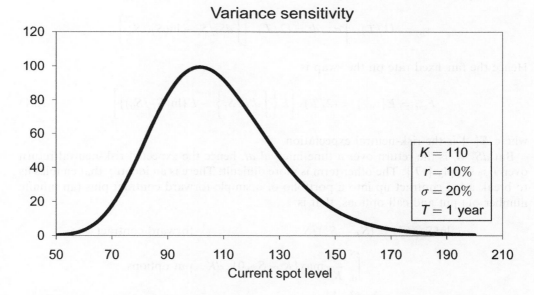

Suppose we create a weighted portfolio of options with strikes $K_1, K_2, \ldots$ as follows:

$$\Pi = \sum_i f(K_i) * C_i * \delta K$$

where δK are the steps between the strikes and $f(\ )$ is the amount of the ith option. The portfolio variance sensitivity is:

$$V_\Pi = \sum_i f(K_i) * \{\partial C_i/\partial v\} * \delta K$$

If $f(K_i) \propto 1/(K_i)^2$ then we find that V_Π becomes increasingly independent of S as the number of options in the portfolio increases.[18] We could, at least in theory, create a robust delta hedge. If all the options were priced off the same volatility, then that would be our best estimate for the swap volatility.

But unfortunately this result ignores any smile effects, so we need to go back to basics. Assume a stock price evolves as:

$$r_t = dS_t/S_t = \mu \cdot dt + \sigma \cdot dz_t$$

where the drift μ and continuously sampled volatility σ are functions of time (and other parameters). Using Ito's lemma:

$$d \ln(S_t) = \{\mu - \tfrac{1}{2}\sigma^2\}\, dt + \sigma \cdot dz_t$$

Therefore, by subtraction, we get

$$dS_t/S_t - d \ln(S_t) = 0.5 * \sigma^2 \cdot dt$$

If we integrate from 0 to T, we get:

$$v_{0T} = (1/T) \cdot \int \sigma^2 \cdot dt = (2/T) \cdot \left[\int dS_t/S_t - \ln(S_T/S_0) \right]$$

Hence the fair fixed rate on the swap is

$$F_{\text{var}} = E\{v_{0T}\} = (2/T) \cdot \left[E\left\{ \int dS_t/S_t \right\} - E\{\ln(S_T/S_0)\} \right] \tag{8.1}$$

where $E\{\ \}$ is the risk-neutral expectation.

But dS_t/S_t is the return over a time interval dt, hence the expected risk-neutral return over T is simply $\{rT\}$. The other term is more difficult. There is an identity that enables us to break a log-contract up into a portfolio of a simple forward contract plus (an infinite number of) put and call options, that is:

$$\ln(S_T/S^*) = (S_T - S^*)/S^* \qquad\qquad \text{forward contract}$$

$$- \int_0^{S^*} \frac{1}{K^2} \max\{K - S_T, 0\} \cdot dK \quad \text{put options}$$

$$- \int_{S^*}^{\infty} \frac{1}{K^2} \max\{S_T - K, 0\} \cdot dK \quad \text{call options}$$

---

[18] Substituting for $\{\partial C_i/\partial v\}$ we get

$$V_\Pi = \tfrac{1}{2} T/(2\pi v)^{1/2} \cdot \sum_i f(K_i) * S \cdot \exp\{-\tfrac{1}{2}(d_i)^2\} * \delta K_i$$

Define $x_i = K_i/S$, we can write:

$$V_\Pi = \tfrac{1}{2} T/(2\pi v)^{1/2} \cdot \sum_i [f(K_i) * (K_i/x_i)^2] \cdot \delta x_i \exp\{-\tfrac{1}{2}(d_i)^2\}$$

where d_i is now a function of x_i only. We wish:

$$\partial V_\Pi/\partial S = 0 \quad \Rightarrow \quad \partial V_\Pi/\partial K_i \cdot \partial K_i/\partial S = \partial V_\Pi/\partial K_i \cdot x_i = 0$$

Differentiating the term $[f(K_i) * (K_i/x_i)^2]$ with respect to K_i, we get:

$$\partial f/\partial K_i * (K_i/x_i)^2 + 2 \cdot f \cdot K_i \cdot (1/x_i)^2 = [\partial f/\partial K_i * K_i + 2 \cdot f] \cdot K_i \cdot (1/x_i)^2$$

The expression $[.]$ is zero if $f(K_i) \propto 1/(K_i)^2$.

for any given value S^*. If we set $S^* = E\{S_T\} = S_0 e^{rT}$ (i.e. ATM forward), then

$$E\{\ln(S_T/S_0)\} = \ln(S^*/S_0) + E\{\ln(S_T/S^*)\}$$

$$= rT - e^{rT} \int_0^{S^*} \frac{1}{K^2} P(K) . dK - e^{rT} \int_{S^*}^{\infty} \frac{1}{K^2} C(K) . dK$$

or

$$F_{\text{var}} = (2/T) . \left\{ e^{rT} \int_0^{S^*} \frac{1}{K^2} P(K) . dK + e^{rT} \int_{S^*}^{\infty} \frac{1}{K^2} C(K) . dK \right\}$$

Notice that each integral is effectively a portfolio of increasingly OTM puts and calls which will rapidly decline in value as they move further OTM.

Unfortunately, this can't work in practice either, as options are only traded at finite steps and it is highly unlikely that there is an option traded with a strike S^* exactly equal to $E\{S_T\}$, so we need to approximate. We can re-write eq. (8.1) as:

$$F_{\text{var}} = (2/T) . [rT - (S_0 e^{rT} - S^*)/S^* - \ln(S^*/S_0)] + f(S_T)$$

where

$$f(S_T) = (2/T) . E\{(S_T - S^*)/S^* - \ln(S_T/S^*)\}$$

The function $f(S_T)$ may be replicated at time T by a portfolio of calls and puts expiring at time T:

$$\Pi_T = \sum_i w_{ip} * P_T(K_{iP}) + \sum_i w_{ic} * C_T(K_{iC})$$

where it is assumed that:

$$\text{Put strikes:} \quad S^* = K_0 > K_{1P} > K_{2P} > \cdots$$
$$\text{Call strikes:} \quad S^* = K_0 < K_{1C} < K_{2C} < \cdots$$

Therefore:

$$E\{f(S_T)\} = e^{rT} . \Pi_0 = e^{rT} . \left[\sum_i w_{ip} * P_0(K_{iP}) + \sum_i w_{ic} * C_0(K_{iC}) \right]$$

For example, we want to estimate the expected variance for use in a 1-year swap. We can observe a strip of 1-year options, trading on a spot of 100, as shown in the table below. We will initially assume that all these options are priced using a constant option volatility of 20% pa, together with a risk-free rate of 10% pa. Therefore $E\{S_T\}$ is calculated to be 110.52, and we select $S^* = 111$, and will use strike steps of 5. The shape of the function $f(S_T)$ is given below (see Worksheet 8.47):

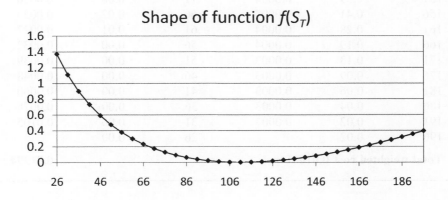

Shape of function $f(S_T)$

The ws can be estimated sequentially due to the asymmetric nature of the option payoff function, that is:

$$w_{0c} = [f(K_{1C}) - f(K_0)]/[K_{1C} - K_0]$$

$$w_{1c} + w_{0c} = [f(K_{2C}) - f(K_{1C})]/[K_{2C} - K_{1C}]$$

$$w_{1c} + w_{1c} + w_{0c} = [f(K_{3C}) - f(K_{2C})]/[K_{3C} - K_{2C}], \text{ etc.}$$

For example:

- for $111 \leq S_T \leq 116$, only the first call option is in the money, with a value of $C_0 = 5$ when $S_T = 116$
  ○ $f(111) = 0$ by construction, and $f(116) = 0.00197$;
  ○ therefore $f(116) = w_{0C} * C_0$;
  ○ which gives $w_{0C} = 0.00197/5 = 0.00039$;
- for $116 \leq S_T \leq 121$, the first two call options are in the money with values $C_0 = 10$ and $C_1 = 5$, respectively, when $S_T = 121$
  ○ $f(121) = 0.00766 = w_{0C} * C_0 + w_{1C} * C_1 = 0.00039 * 10 + w_{1C} * 5$;
  ○ this can also be written as:

$$f(121) - f(116) = w_{0C} * C_0(121) + w_{1C} * C_1 - w_{0C} * C_0(116) = (w_{0C} + w_{1C}) * C_1$$

  ○ which gives $w_{1C} = 0.00074$, as shown in the table below.

Call strikes	Call value	Weights	Put strikes	Put value	Weights
111	7.77	0.0004	111	8.20	0.0004
116	5.92	0.0007	106	5.93	0.0009
121	4.44	0.0007	101	4.07	0.0010
126	3.28	0.0006	96	2.64	0.0011
131	2.39	0.0006	91	1.59	0.0012
136	1.71	0.0005	86	0.88	0.0014
141	1.22	0.0005	81	0.44	0.0015
146	0.85	0.0005	76	0.20	0.0017
151	0.59	0.0004	71	0.08	0.0020
156	0.41	0.0004	66	0.02	0.0023
161	0.28	0.0004	61	0.01	0.0027
166	0.19	0.0004	56	0.00	0.0032
171	0.13	0.0003	51	0.00	0.0039
176	0.09	0.0003	46	0.00	0.0048
181	0.06	0.0003	41	0.00	0.0060
186	0.04	0.0003	36	0.00	0.0078
191	0.02	0.0003	31	0.00	0.0105
196	0.02		26	0.00	
Total weighted cost 0.01661					**0.01994**

The approximate value of $E\{f(S_T)\}$ is estimated to be

$$e^{rT} * (0.01661 + 0.01994) = 0.0403915$$

This gives:

$$F_{\text{var}} = -0.0000190 + 0.0403915 = 0.0403725 = 4.04\%$$

and volatility $= 20.09\%$. This is slightly higher than the input volatility due to the linear interpolation of the log function over the finite step size. The results have been generated in Worksheet 8.48.

Now suppose however that the strip was subject to a smile as shown below, generated in Worksheet 8.49:

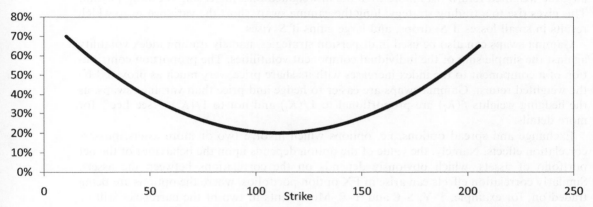

In this case, F_{var} increases as expected to 6.46%, and therefore the "average" volatility to 25.42%, as shown in Worksheet 8.50.

In summary, this section has shown how "correct" variance and volatility may be implied out of the options market, and how a static replicating hedge for the swap may be constructed so that:

- changes in volatility do not force the hedge to change;
- the hedge is model-independent;
- the hedge does not protect against jumps in the stock price.

We have concentrated on variance swaps. Volatility swaps are much more difficult because there is no simple, i.e. linear, relationship between an observation and volatility. This means that there is no simple replication strategy, and the swap would have to be dynamically hedged.

Define $f(x) = x^{1/2}$. We can therefore write, using a Taylor's expansion:

$$f(v) \approx f(v_0) + (v - v_0).f' + \tfrac{1}{2}(v - v_0)^2.f''$$

This gives:

$$f(v) \approx \{(v + v_0)/2v_0^{1/2}\} - \{(v - v_0)^2/8v_0^{3/2}\}$$

If we expand $f(\ )$ around $v_0 = E\{v\}$, we get:

$$E\{v^{1/2}\} \approx E\{v\}^{1/2} - \text{Var}\{v\}/8v_0^{3/2}$$

Thus the expected volatility is less than the square root of the expected variance as calculated above, i.e. there is a convexity adjustment. To estimate the size of the adjustment, we need a more complex model of the volatility process, and there can be no simple replicating hedge.[19]

An interesting variation on variance swaps is a gamma swap. Assume, for ease, that the underlying reference is a single stock price; if the price crashes due to some significant adverse event, the variance (or volatility) spikes. To reduce the impact of the spike, variance swaps often contain an embedded cap to protect the seller from "crash" risk. A gamma swap weights the periodic squared return $\ln(S_t/S_{t-1})^2$ by $[S_t/S_0]$. If S_t drops close to zero, the squared return becomes extremely large, but the weighted return approaches zero, obviating the need for the cap. Of course, if the share price rises dramatically, the weighted return rises more than the unweighted one, increasing the swap payout. This gives rise to a trading strategy: long the gamma swap, short the variance swap which results in small losses if S_t drops, and large gains if S_t rises.

Gamma swaps can also be used in dispersion strategies, namely trading index volatility against the simple sum of the individual component volatilities. The proportion contribution of a component to the index increases with its share price, very much as provided by the weighted return. Gamma swaps are easier to hedge and price than variance swaps, as the hedging weights $f(K_i)$ are proportional to $1/(K_i)$ and not to $1/(K_i)^2$—see Lee[20] for more details.

Exchange and spread options, i.e. options which involve two or more assets, possess correlation effects. Namely, the value of the option depends upon the behaviour of the net portfolio of assets, which obviously depends on the correlations between the assets. Similarly correlation effects can arise in FX option portfolios, where the options are being traded on, for example, $-¥, $-€ and ¥-€. Movements in two of the currencies will be reflected in the third, and hence its volatility must reflect both the volatilities of the other two plus their correlation. Such correlation risks would not be controlled by straightforward "Greek" hedging. In a very similar fashion to above, it is feasible to design covariance and correlation swaps that would enable these risks to be managed. As before, covariance swaps are relatively straightforward, correlation swaps are less so.[21]

Following the collapse of Lehman Brothers in September 2008, volatility in the markets spiked dramatically. For example, the volatility of the S&P 500 index was 21.5% at the beginning of 2008, 79.2% by early December, and still 43.5% by April 2009. The volatility of Citibank shares was considerably worse: 47%, 213% and 229% on those three dates, respectively. Banks were large sellers of volatility, often in the form of variance swaps which are a levered version of a volatility swap, suffering losses as volatility rose despite attempts to hedge. At the time of writing (mid-2009), the single-stock market was effectively dead, and bid–offer spreads on index-linked swaps have widened considerably.

---

[19] See O. Brockhaus *et al.*, "Volatility swaps made simple", *Risk*, January 2000, pp. 92–95 for some results using some models.
[20] R. Lee, *Gamma Swap*, working paper from University of Chicago, December 2008. See also H. Buehler's dissertation on volatility markets from the Technical University in Berlin, June 2006.
[21] See Brockhaus *et al.*, ibid.

9

_____ Cross-currency Swaps _____

OBJECTIVE

This chapter re-introduces cross-currency swaps. It starts by discussing that most fundamental building block, namely the cross-currency basis swap, and considers its pricing, hedging and its role in creating a proper foreign currency discount curve. Subsequently fixed–floating cross-currency swaps are described in the context of swapping a fixed-coupon bond into a floating in another currency. In particular, the impact of changing the terms of the swap on the floating margin is explored. Diff and quanto diff swaps are then introduced, as examples of cross-currency swaps without exchange of principal. Section 9.11 (Appendix) describes the necessary quanto adjustment effect arising from the interaction between FX spot rates and IRs. Fixed–fixed swaps are then discussed, of which the best-known example is long-term FX forwards. Finally, cross-currency swap valuation is considered in some detail. Because of the principal exchange at the end of the swap, this creates a large potential credit exposure due to movements in the future FX spot rate. It is common practice to re-balance the principals in the swap regularly, by settling the change in the value of the principals.

The chapter concludes by a brief look at some rarer structures, such as dual and multi-currency swaps, including power reverse duals, and cross-currency equity swaps.

9.1 FLOATING–FLOATING CROSS-CURRENCY SWAPS

Cross-currency swaps (CCSs) were briefly discussed in Chapter 1. Generic CCSs all have the same fundamental three-part structure betraying their back-to-back loan origins:

- the initial exchange of principal amounts;
- periodic exchanges of interest payments;
- re-exchange of the principal amounts at maturity.

A floating–floating or cross-currency basis swap (CCBS) possesses this structure where both of the reference interest rates are floating. Consider the following example, based on an actual swap executed some years ago. From party A's point of view:

- at start, pay USD100m and receive GBP30m;
- every 3 months, receive 3 mo. USD Libor on $100m, and pay 3 mo. GBP Libor on £30m;
- at maturity, receive back USD100m and pay GBP30m.

If the two sides of the swap are considered separately, then each one is effectively a rolled money account (or par FRN depending on your perspective) which has, as argued in Chapter 3, zero economic value. Therefore in theory a CCBS with no spreads on either side should have a zero value. If we took two discount curves, one USD and the other GBP, created from the relevant IRS markets, calculated the implied Libor rates, created the cashflows and discounted, we would indeed get zero values on both sides. In practice, as we shall see in the next two sections, CCBSs are not quite as simple as this.

When this swap was freely entered into, the prevailing spot exchange rate was $1.7/£. Therefore we can see that the initial exchange is considerably away from the spot rate. Does this matter? From the point of view of market "fairness", in other words does the swap have an initial value of zero?, the answer must be that the exchange rate is irrelevant. By breaking the swap into the two FRNs, each of which is fair in its own right, the combination must also be fair. Of course, as soon as the swap starts, the first Libors are fixed and then the exchange rate becomes important at least to net-value the known cashflows as the markets move. Obviously also, if the swap included any margin on either side, then the exchange rate is relevant from the beginning.

What about from a credit perspective? This is a very different story. Imagine a situation in which, immediately after the initial exchange, counterparty B absconds! Counterparty A is effectively out [$100m − £30m * 1.7] = $49m. To make the swap credit fair as well, the principal amounts should be $51m and £30m. Suppose we re-write this swap as shown below:

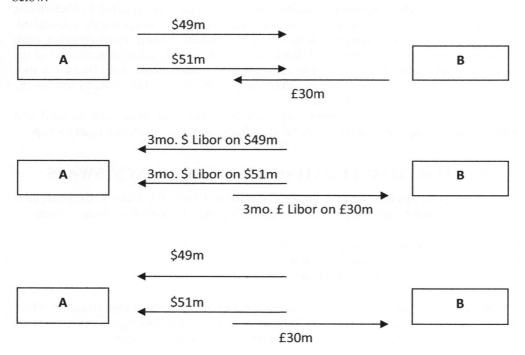

Then we can see that it is actually made up of $51m "at-market" swap plus a $49m loan. The swap is said to be "off-market" with the relationship:

$$\text{Off-market} = \text{At-market} + \text{Loan or deposit}$$

but effectively off-balance sheet. The majority of CCSs are slightly off-market, usually to ensure that the principal amounts are both round amounts. The above example is an obvious exception, and was in fact used to conceal the embedded loan.

Coming back to the original swap for a moment, and thinking of it as back-to-back rolled money accounts, there is no natural maturity to the contract. The arrangement could last in perpetuity provided that the two counterparties are happy with the ongoing credit exposures. In the late 1980s there were at least two banks in London that used to offer "perpetual swaps", i.e. CCBSs with no contractual maturity. Either counterparty could declare, at the time of a floating rate fixing, that the swap would terminate at the next payment date with a re-exchange of the principal amounts.

Whilst there is a reasonably active market in CCBSs, it is estimated that some 75% of the CCS market have a fixed–floating (usually USD Libor) structure. But CCBSs are extremely important as a fundamental building block, as we can construct a fixed–floating swap using a CCBS plus a simple IRS:

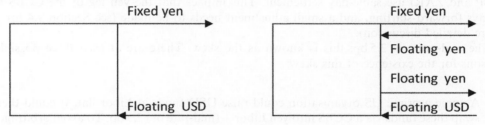

As a theoretical CCBS swap is priced at Libor–Libor flat, this suggests that the market rates in the fixed–floating CCS market should be very close to those in the IRS market. For pairs of highly liquid currencies, this is generally true, although distortions do occur. The suggested bid–offer spread should be wider than in the IRS market because CCBSs carry quite a high potential credit exposure due to the terminal principal exchange, and hence a much higher capital charge than IRSs.

9.2 PRICING AND HEDGING OF CCBSs

The table below shows quotes for freely available CCBSs:

	JPY (Act/360)		GBP (Act/365)		Euro (Act/360)	
1	2.00	−1.00	−1.25	−5.25	−5.125	−7.125
2	3.00	0.25	−1.25	−5.25	−3.250	−5.250
3	4.00	1.00	−0.75	−4.75	−2.750	−4.750
4	5.00	2.00	−0.75	−4.75	−2.375	−4.375
5	6.00	3.00	−0.75	−4.75	−1.875	−3.875
7	7.00	4.00	−0.75	−4.75	−1.125	−3.125
10	7.75	4.75	−0.75	−4.75	−0.375	−2.375
15	7.50	4.50	−1.00	−5.00	1.875	−2.125
20	7.00	4.00	−1.00	−5.00	2.625	−1.375
30	6.50	3.50	−1.00	−5.00	3.125	−0.875
40			−1.00	−5.00	3.250	−0.750
50			−1.00	−5.00	3.375	−0.625

All 3 mo. rates against 3 mo. USD Libor on 4 February 2008.

The quotations are showing the basis point spread on the non-USD Libor side. For example, the 3-year yen swap is $\{4, 1\}$ meaning that:

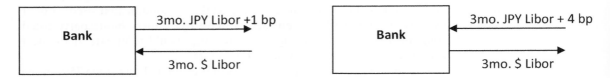

Cross-currency swaps follow the usual convention in the FX market, namely that there is a 2-day settlement period, as in the US. However, yen interest rates (as well as, for example, GBP and ZAR) use same-day settlement. This implies that the yen leg of the CCBS is 2-days forward starting, and a small adjustment needs to be made (see Section 9.4 for a more detailed discussion).

The mid-point is 2.5 bp; this is known as the skew. There are at least three possible reasons for the existence of this skew:

1. Assume a prime US organisation could raise USD funds at Libor flat. It could then swap these funds via a CCBS into yen Libor + (mid-rate of) 2.5 bp. To avoid arbitrage, the skew should be a measure of the relative access the organisation has to the two money markets.
2. An imbalance in the supply and demand for CCBSs. If the market was perfectly balanced, the bid-offer prices would be equi-distant from zero.
3. Very often, short-term FX forwards are used to hedge CCBSs, as described below. These forwards themselves are subject to skews, namely a distortion away from the theoretical value determined by interest rate differentials. The table below shows that the skew in the short-term $/¥ market, measured in terms of basis point adjustments to the yen rates, is not trivial relative to the CCBS spread (see Worksheet 9.3).

The relative importance of these reasons depends upon the actual currencies involved and the current market conditions:

Today's date: 04-Feb-08		Spot rate:	106.601			
	Mid-JPY	Mid-USD	Theoretical forwards	Quoted forwards	Implied yen rate	Skew (bp)
06-Feb-08						
06-May-08	0.809%	3.083%	105.9998	105.987	0.7608%	−4.85
06-Aug-08	0.858%	3.035%	105.4457	105.458	0.8816%	2.33
06-Feb-09	0.933%	2.834%	104.5986	104.554	0.8906%	−4.24

In practice therefore it would be argued that the CCBS at the mid-rate of $\{2.5\,\text{bp}\}$ would have zero value—not quite the theoretical argument used before. The following approach may be used to hedge a CCBS, and hence produce an estimate of the cost-of-carry. In practice, as hedging would be done on a portfolio basis, this estimate is likely to be far too high unless the portfolio was completely one-sided. Consider the 3-year swap quoted above, but assume we don't know the spread s:

Time	USD	JPY
0	+1m	−106.601m
3	−Libor	+(Libor + s)
6	−Libor	+(Libor + s)
9	−Libor	+(Libor + s)
⋮		
36	−Libor	+(Libor + s)
	−1m	+106.601m

Re-write it as a series of 3-monthly forward FX swaps, i.e. with a principal exchange every 3 months. The first swap could be hedged using a reverse spot 3 monthly swap as shown:

Cross-currency basis swap		
Time	USD	JPY
0	+1m	−106.601m
3	−Libor	+(Libor + s)
	−1m	+106.601m
3	+1m	−106.601m
6	−Libor	+(Libor + s)
	−1m	+106.601m
6	+1m	−106.601m
9	−Libor	+(Libor + s)
	−1m	+106.601m
⋮		
33	+1m	−106.601m
36	−Libor	+(Libor + s)
	−1m	+106.601m

First hedge		
Time	USD	JPY
0	−1m	+106.601m
3	+Libor	−(Libor + sk)
	+1m	−106.601m

where sk is the implied skew. Hence the net yen cashflow at the end from the first contract plus hedge is $+(s − sk) * 106.601 * \$1m * 0.25$.

Consider the second contract. We could think of hedging this using a forward–forward FX swap; this strategy might work in this case because it is only 3 months out, but forward–forward contracts are unlikely to be available as we consider contracts further out. Suppose we do nothing for 3 months, and then hedge with another spot 3-month forward swap, that is:

Second CCBS contract		
Time	USD	JPY
0	+1m	$-S_{0,0}$
3	−Libor	+(Libor + s)
	−1m	$+S_{0,0}$

Second hedge		
Time	USD	JPY
0	−1m	$+S_{3,3}$
3	+Libor	−(Libor + sk)
	+1m	$-S_{3,3}$

where $S_{0,0}$ and $S_{3,3}$ are the observed spot rates in 0 and 3 months' time, respectively. It is assumed that the skew has remained constant. There is obviously a yen principal mismatch at the beginning due to the movement in the spot rate. If:

$$(S_{3,3} - S_{0,0}) > 0$$

then we have excess yen to be deposited at Libor + m_d (the margin is likely to be negative):

$$(S_{3,3} - S_{0,0}) < 0$$

then we have a yen shortfall to be funded at Libor + m_b.

Therefore the cashflow at the end is (*Note*: the Libor cashflows cancel.):

$$\{s * S_{0,0} - sk * S_{3,3} + (S_{3,3} - S_{0,0}) * m_x\} * \$1m * 0.25$$

where x depends on the sign of $(S_{3,3} - S_{0,0})$. If the future spot rates could be estimated, then all the cashflows at the end of each quarter could be calculated, and hence the cost of the hedge.

It is of course a foolish person who would try to predict future spot rates. Assume that the relative change in the spot S follows a normal process:

$$dS_t/S = \mu . dt + \sigma . \sqrt{dt} . \varepsilon$$

where μ is the drift, σ the volatility and ε is $N(0, 1)$ or:

$$S_{t,0} = S_{0,0} * \exp\{(\mu - \tfrac{1}{2}\sigma^2) . dt + \sigma . \sqrt{dt} . \varepsilon\} = E\{S_{t,0}\} * \exp\{\sigma . \sqrt{dt} . \varepsilon\}$$

Market practice varies for the next step, because there are no good real predictors for the future spot rate: different approaches use:

- $E\{S_{t,0}\} = S_{0,0} * \exp\{(\mu - \tfrac{1}{2}\sigma^2) . dt\}$ as shown, where $\mu = (\check{r}_Y - \check{r}_\$)$ and $\check{r}$ is a continuously compounded rate estimated from the market curves;
- $E\{S_{t,0}\} = F_{t,0}$, the forward rate quoted at time 0;
- $E\{S_{t,0}\} = S_{0,0}$, as various studies have shown that the current spot rate is as good a predictor of future spot rates as anything else.

We can estimate a probability range for $S_{t,0}$. For example, there is a 75% probability that a normally distributed variable will lie within ±1.15 standard deviations, that is:

$$E\{S_{t,0}\} * \exp\{-\sigma . \sqrt{dt} . 1.15\} \leq S_{t,0} \leq E\{S_{t,0}\} * \exp\{+\sigma . \sqrt{dt} . 1.15\}$$

This can be used to generate a probability envelope as shown below[1]:

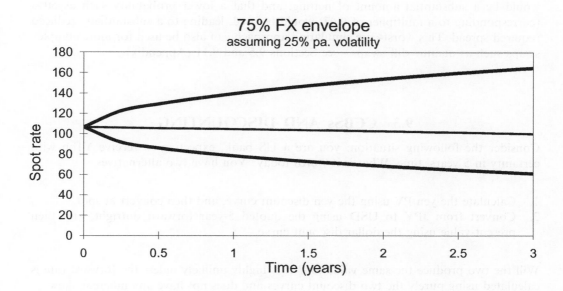

75% FX envelope
assuming 25% pa. volatility

where the central line is the anticipated forward rates. Worksheet 9.4 calculates this graph as follows:

- columns [1] and [2] are the current discount curves;
- $F_{t,0}$ is estimated by $S_{0,0} * (\mathrm{DF}_t^\$/\mathrm{DF}_t^\yen)$ in column [3];
- columns [4] and [5] calculate the upper and lower curves.

Suppose the future spot rate followed the upper curve.[2] According to the construction above, there would be a continual excess of yen that would have to be deposited for 3 months—see column [6]. The worksheet has assumed a skew of 2 bp and a negative deposit margin of 5 bp pa, and calculated the total PV of the cost of hedging to be just over ¥137,000 on a principal of ¥106.6m based on an annualised volatility of 25%. This can be converted into a spread of 4.3 bp pa by dividing the cost by the 3-year quarterly Q, which is estimated in column [9].

The process is then repeated following the lower curve with a funding margin of 3 bp, giving a PV of ¥37,000. In the real world, we don't know what path the spot rate will take in the future. However, we know that the cost of any path lying wholly within the envelope (and indeed any reasonable path extending below the lower curve) must be less than the worst case of the two curves. Therefore the cost of hedging is estimated to be 4.3 bp pa with a 25% chance that this might be exceeded.

---

[1] This methodology is applied by the risk department of a major bank in London. It made an interesting practical observation. If $E\{S_{t,0}\}$ is estimated by $S_{0,0} * \exp\{(\mu - \tfrac{1}{2}\sigma^2) . dt\}$, the upper curve will start to turn down again at $t^* = \{\tfrac{1}{2}\varepsilon\sigma/(\mu - \tfrac{1}{2}\sigma^2)\}^2$. For example, if $\varepsilon = 1.65$, $\mu = 0$ and $\sigma = 50\%$ (say for a commodity), then t^* is just under 11 years. This is one argument for using a different estimator for $E\{S_{t,0}\}$; alternatively it is suggested that the upper curve is held constant for $t > t^*$.

[2] This is a very similar approach to that used to estimate the PFE of a swap, and hence its credit-adjusted price—see Section 6.7.

The approach described above is for micro-hedging, and hence pricing, a single CCBS very conservatively. In practice, a portfolio is likely to be reasonably balanced, so there would be a substantial amount of netting, and that a lower probability such as 50% (corresponding to a multiplier of 0.67) would be used, leading to a substantially reduced required spread. This worst-case simulation approach can also be used for more complex swaps such as quanto–diff swaps—see Sections 9.5 and 9.11 (Appendix).

9.3 CCBSs AND DISCOUNTING

Consider the following situation: you are a US bank, expecting to receive ¥1bn with certainty in 5 years' time. What is it worth today? You have two alternatives:

1. Calculate the yen PV using the yen discount curve, and then convert at spot.
2. Convert from JPY to USD using the quoted 5-year forward outright, and then present-value using the dollar discount curve.

Will the two produce the same valuation? It is highly unlikely unless the forward rate is calculated using purely the two discount curves and does not have any inherent skew.

CCBS		Yen IRS	
$-P_\$$	$+P_¥$	$-P_¥$	$+P_¥$
$+L_\$$	$-(L_¥ + s)$	$+L_¥$	$-F_¥$
$+L_\$$	$-(L_¥ + s)$	$+L_¥$	$-F_¥$
$+L_\$$	$-(L_¥ + s)$	$+L_¥$	$-F_¥$
$+L_\$$	$-(L_¥ + s)$	$+L_¥$	$-F_¥$
$+L_\$$	$-(L_¥ + s)$	$+L_¥$	$-F_¥$
$+L_\$ + P_\$$	$-(L_¥ + s) - P_¥$	$+L_¥ + P_¥$	$-F_¥ - P_¥$
Net value $= 0$		**Net value $= 0$**	

Consider a generic mid-rate CCBS and a generic mid-rate yen IRS to which has been added the notional principals. Each is freely traded in the financial markets, and will initially have zero value. Being a US bank, we assume that you can access your domestic money market efficiently, and are able to fund or deposit USD at Libor flat; this is the same assumption as in earlier chapters. Therefore the USD leg of the CCBS above has a zero value, and hence the JPY leg including the spread must have zero value as well. But if this is true, we can no longer argue that the floating leg of the yen IRS including the notional principals has zero value (except in the trivial case when $s = 0$) to the US bank. Quietly ignoring potential difficulties such as differences in frequencies and daycount conventions, the CCBS spread could be added to both sides of the IRS without affecting its net value. Both individual sides would now value to zero, and it would be feasible to repeat the bootstrapping process to derive the CCBS-adjusted discount curve.

$$
\begin{array}{cc}
\multicolumn{2}{c}{\textbf{Yen IRS}} \\
-P_{¥} & +P_{¥} \\
+(L_{¥}+s) & -(F_{¥}+s) \\
+(L_{¥}+s) & -(F_{¥}+s) \\
+(L_{¥}+s) & -(F_{¥}+s) \\
+(L_{¥}+s) & -(F_{¥}+s) \\
+(L_{¥}+s) & -(F_{¥}+s) \\
+(L_{¥}+s)+P_{¥} & -(F_{¥}+s)-P_{¥} \\
\multicolumn{2}{c}{\textbf{Net value}=\textbf{0}}
\end{array}
$$

However, bootstrapping requires a CCBS-adjusted zero-coupon rate to start the process off. A better and more general approach is to model the CCBS directly having already estimated the Libor rates off the unadjusted curve (see Worksheet 9.2 "Building an adjusted yen curve" on the accompanying CD for details).

We want to estimate a smooth discount (or forward curve) that will value all the CCBSs to zero. One way to do this[3] is as follows:

- Column [4] shows the correct dates for the two sides of the CCBS, including the 2-day settlement period.
- Columns [5] and [6] show the interpolated yen z-c rates and the unadjusted 3-month forwards calculated for those dates.
- Column [2] shows a guessed spread curve over the unadjusted forward curve.
- Therefore, a new forward curve is built in column [8] by interpolating this spread curve, followed by an adjusted DF curve in column [9]. In the worksheet, the spread curve is linearly interpolated in column [7], but some other form could easily be used.
- Column [10] values the market-quoted CCBSs, using the expression:

$$
V_k = -1 + \sum_i L_i * d_i * \mathrm{DF}_i + s_k * \sum_i d_i * \mathrm{DF}_i + \mathrm{DF}_k
$$

where L_i are the unadjusted yen Libor rates, and DF_i the adjusted DFs.
- The objective is to calculate the new spread curve in column [2] so that the CCBSs are all zero-valued, and that the new forwards are as smooth as possible. Column [11] contains the smoothing conditions.

This procedure is easy to implement in practice, and yet provides good forward and discount curves.

---

[3] There are alternative and more complex approaches; see, for example, E. Fruchard *et al.*, "Basis for change", *Risk Magazine*, October 1995, **8**(10), pp. 70–75.

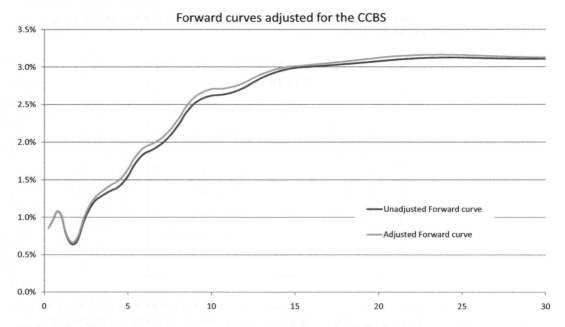

Forward curves adjusted for the CCBS

To see the adjusted curve in use, we will asset-package a USD bond into a 5.5-year par maturity JPY package; the bond details are shown below:

Today's date	=	04-Feb-08
USD bond details:		
Maturity	=	15-Sep-13
Coupon	=	3.75% sa
Redemption	=	100
Clean price	=	96.00
Fraction of year	=	0.104 to next coupon
Accrued interest	=	3.3596
Dirty price	=	99.3596
Current spot rate	=	106.601

First, let us assume we are going to swap the bond into a par 5.5-year USD 3 mo. Libor package. Using the techniques described in Chapter 5, the bond can be swapped into a synthetic FRN paying USD Libor + 47.65 bp (see Box 1 of Worksheet 9.6).

We now want to swap this package into JPY. Box 2 of the worksheet swaps the bond into yen in two stages. It first builds the floating yen side of a cross-currency swap as {Libor + margin} off the IRS curve using the implied forward rates. The margin is calculated by ensuring that the value of this leg is equal to the value of the USD leg above: this gives a margin of 47.73 bp. Second, we now recognise the existence of the CCBS. The 5.5-year CCBS margin of 4.75 bp (estimated by interpolating the CCBS curve) is added to the 47.7 bp margin, giving a net margin of 52.5 bp.

An alternative approach is to use the adjusted discount curve, as shown in Box 3 of the worksheet. Notice that the discount factors in columns [1] and [3] are different; however, the implied yen Libor rates must be the same because these are only quoted once—see columns [2] and [4]. We now calculate the {Libor + margin} cashflows as before. The margin is set so that the value of this leg is again equal to the USD value, but of course this time using the adjusted discount curve. The resulting margin is again 52.5 bp, albeit fractionally different.

Which approach is "correct"? Probably (although it is not clearcut to me) the first as it uses a tradable spot instrument, but the second is much easier to implement in a system and to apply to a portfolio, and therefore is more commonly applied.

The vast majority of CCBSs have a USD Libor leg. This is reducing in a similar way to the spot FX market, namely crosses are becoming more common as Europe and the Far East increasingly use EUR and JPY reference rates, respectively, instead of USD. If your domestic currency is not USD, then the above discussion needs to be modified to ensure that adjustments are made to the valuations of all non-domestic cashflows.

9.4 FIXED–FLOATING CROSS-CURRENCY SWAPS

Whilst CCBSs are fundamental financial instruments, some 75% of the CCS market is fixed–floating, in many cases as above originating from swapping a bond issue into a floating reference currency.

When swapping a bond issue, the issuer requires the entire bond structure to be reflected in the swap, so that there is no residual exposure to the issuance currency. Some typical examples of the types of manipulations will be discussed through an example, which is based upon a real bond issue by a German bank in the late 1990s. The issuer had a target to:

- raise USD40m;
- at Libor – 25 bp or better.

Notice that the bond was issued with a coupon below the current swap rate. This was possible because, being a German issuer, it was sold into the retail base in Germany, Switzerland and Benelux who cannot access the SA swap market very efficiently.

Date:	7 June 1999
Details of bond issue:	
Size:	ZAR250m
Term:	5 years
Coupon:	13.75% ANN 30/360
Issue price:	101.25
Fees:	2%
Expenses:	0.25%
Payment:	4 weeks from issue
Details of swap:	
Type:	ZAR fixed, USD floating
All-in swap:	13.935% qu Act/365
Current spot exchange rate:	1USD = ZAR6.108

There are a number of issues to be dealt with, such as:

1. Bond proceeds are raised 4 weeks after issue
   - therefore the initial exchange has to be delayed although the swap starts today.
2. Net bond issue at $101.25 - 2.25 = 99$
   - i.e. raises ZAR247.5m;
   - but of course has to repay ZAR250m on maturity;
   - so there is a principal mismatch.
3. Issuer only wishes to raise USD40m
   - although at the current spot rate ZAR250m is worth USD40.93m;
   - hence long USD0.93m which could subsidise the margin.
4. Bond proceeds are raised 4 weeks after issue
   - but the German bank wants USD40m immediately the bond issue is underwritten;
   - effectively requiring a 4-week loan.

The issuer wants all these taken into account in the swap structure, and to receive an estimate of the sub-Libor margin.

As a starting point, assume that the bond is issued today (7 June 1999) at par. The bond has a value of ZAR8,060,748 or USD1,319,703 as shown in Box 1 of Worksheet 9.7. This is equivalent to a USD stream based on a principal of USD250m/6.108 = USD40.93m. The fair margin is 75 bp pa below USD6m Libor.

Is this correct? The current 5-year ZAR swap rate is 13.935% quarterly. This converts into 14.680% using the quick and dirty formula $(1 + \frac{1}{4} * r_{qu})^4 = 1 + r_{ann}$ or 14.700% if the discount curve is used; see Box 2 of the worksheet. The bond has therefore been issued at $14.70\% - 13.75\% = 95$ bp below SA curve. So, 1 bp annual coupon on the sa side is worth $(DF_1 + \cdots + DF_5) = 3.39$ bp upfront. The equivalent calculation of USD 1 bp sa is worth $Q_5 = 4.30$ bp. Hence ZAR 95 bp $* (3.39/4.30) =$ USD 75 bp sa so the margin appears correct. The ratio $(3.39/4.30) = 0.789$ is called the "conversion factor" and indicates how much 1 bp in ZAR is worth in USD. Conversion factors depend upon the two curves and the maturity, which change frequently. Their main use is to calculate the impact of changes in the issuance level of the bond on the funding margin.

However, the principal exchange does not happen for 4 weeks: What is the impact? This may be estimated in two parts:

+ Late receipt of ZAR250m costs the swap counterparty ZAR250m $* (1 - DF_{1\,month})$

$$= 250m * (1 - 0.9894) = Z2,645,015 = \$433,041$$

+ Late payment of \$40.93m benefits the swap counterparty \$40.93m $* (1 - 0.9962)$

$$= \$154,392$$

The net balance of \$278,650 is a cost to the counterparty. The value of 1 bp on $40.93m = 40.93m * Q_5 * 1$ bp $= \$17,607$; therefore the balance corresponds to a margin of 278,650/17,607 or 15.8 bp (see Box 3 of the worksheet).

Box 3 confirms this result. The principal amounts are now exchanged on 5 July 1999. The value of the ZAR cashflows has reduced quite significantly, and this is compensated by a smaller sub-Libor margin on the USD side.

However, the issuer only wants to raise $40m, not $40.93m, i.e. a reduction in the USD principal of 2.3%. As the SA leg hasn't changed, the USD margin should increase by the same amount, i.e. from 59 bp to $59 * (1 + 2.3\%) = 60.4$ bp. (*Note*: this is only approximate as principal exchange is not at start of swap.) Box 4 of the worksheet confirms this argument, increasing the margin to 60.3 bp.

Next the issuer wants the USD40m upfront, although he will not have ZAR bond proceeds for 4 weeks. The cost of this effective loan to the swap counterparty is $\$40m * (1 - DF_{1\,month}) = \$150,884$. The value of 1 bp on $40m = 40m * Q_5 * 1$ bp $= \$17,207$, therefore this cost is equivalent to a reduction in the margin of $150,884/17,207 = 8.7$ bp, as shown in Box 5 of the worksheet.

Finally the issuer does not receive the par value of the bond, but only 99%, i.e. ZAR247.5m. The cost to the swap counterparty of being 1% short in 4 weeks time is $ZAR250m * 1\% * (1 - DF_{1\,month}) = ZAR2,473,550$ or $404,969. This will reduce the margin by $404,969/17,207 = 23.54$ bp (see Box 6 of Worksheet 9.7).

The objective of this section was to demonstrate how a cross-currency swap may be manipulated, and in particular how the impact of actions may be quickly verified.

9.5 FLOATING–FLOATING SWAPS CONTINUED

As we have already described, investors at the short end of the US curve were having a torrid time in 1993, especially as the year drew to a close, rates fell and no increase was anticipated. The same investors saw a very different picture in Germany. The need to fund re-unification and to support the deutschmark had inverted the curve, with short-term money rates at about 9%, some 600 bp above the US ones. But how could they take advantage of this situation?

The obvious way is to liquidate the US investment, convert the money into DEM and re-invest. However, the same outcome may also be achieved by entering into an at-money CCBS to pay US Libor and receive DEM Libor (plus or minus a small margin which will be ignored in the following discussion). Because the initial exchange is done at the current spot rate, it has no economic value and can be omitted; the spot rate being used to determine the relative principals for the interest payments and the final exchange. The cashflows are as shown in the diagram below:

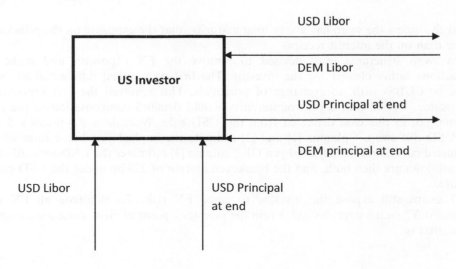

Whilst less extreme at the time of writing, a Japanese investor might well look across at the USD curve, and see an initial positive spread, in excess of 200 bp, widening out to 300 bp in 5 years' time. The investor could pay away JPY Libor plus JPY principal at the end, and receive USD Libor plus USD principal.

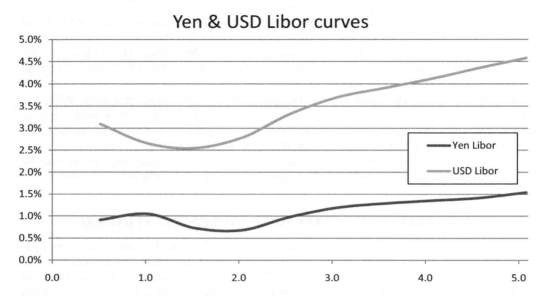

The Japanese investor is now receiving a higher rate of interest, but has entered into two sources of FX exposure:

1. Exposure on the principal exchange at the end. Because US interest rates are higher than yen rates, theoretically the USD would be expected to weaken against the yen during the swap, and therefore the USD principal received at maturity is likely to be worth less than the JPY principal paid away.
2. Exposure on the periodic receipts of USD interest.

It is likely, unless the swap has a very long maturity, that the exposure on the principal is greater than on the interest receipts.

Two swap structures were devised to remove the FX exposures and make the transactions rather cleaner for the investor. The first were called differential or "diff" swaps, or CCBSs with no exchange of principals. This removed the first exposure to the investor, but of course the counterparty would demand compensation in the form of a margin, in this case deducted from the USD side. Worksheet 9.8 prices a 5-year JPY–USD diff swap. Columns [1] and [2] estimate the implied yen Libor rates off the unadjusted curve, and the adjusted yen DFs; column [3] estimates the USD forward rates. The cashflows are then built, and the breakeven margin of 228 bp under the USD curves estimated.

Diff swaps still expose the investor to some FX risk. To eliminate all FX risk, "quanto–diff" swaps were devised. From the investor's point of view, these are extremely simple, that is:

To pay	Yen Libor on $P_¥$
To receive	($ Libor − margin) on a yen principal $P_¥$

Because the currency of the cashflow is determined by the principal, this is really a single-currency swap, albeit using a foreign USD reference curve. The next worksheet has the same structure as the previous one, but applies the USD Libor rates to the JPY principal. The fair margin is 237 bp. This is higher than before as expected, but the difference of only 9 bp confirms the earlier statement that the FX exposure on the principal is likely to be greater than on the interest cashflows (see Worksheet 9.9).

Notice the difference between the diff and the quanto–diff curves. In the former, the investor is still paying away the stronger currency, and hence the USD curve less margin is mainly above the yen curve. But with the quanto swap, the yen and {USD − margin} curves are on average equal, and the investor is effectively taking a view on the relative movement of them. If they are roughly parallel, then there is no immediate return enhancement, and hence little demand. If the curves are substantially non-parallel, as was the case in 1993, then the US investor would receive a return enhancement albeit at the expense of potential losses later. More recently (in 1995), the Japanese–Australian curve spread was wider at the short end than the long end, and there was some investor interest.

The table below summarises the position:

Swap →	CCBS	Diff	Quanto–diff
USD margin (bp)	0	−230 bp	−239 bp
Risks			
IR	✓	✓	✓
FX on principal	✓	×	×
FX on interest	✓	✓	×

Now consider the quanto–diff swap from the point of view of the swap counterparty. How might he hedge it? The yen Libor side and the margin are routine and will be ignored:

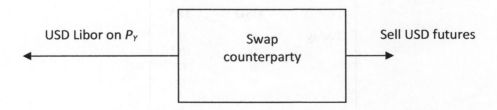

Assume the quanto leg is to be hedged by selling USD deposit futures. If USD rates rise, the USD-related payment on the swap increases, but the futures margin is received. Conversely, if rates fall, the swap payment is less but margin has to be paid. But of course the swap payments are in JPY, whilst the margin is in USD. So the hedge will offset fluctuations in the swap payments, but in the wrong currency, i.e. the counterparty has an FX exposure in addition to the interest rate exposure.[4] This is difficult to hedge in any static fashion because its size and direction depends on the movement in interest rates. Furthermore, FX rates and interest rates are generally correlated, so shifts in the correlation structure will impact hedge efficiency. The normal practice is to dynamically hedge in a similar fashion to FX options, but recognising that this carries a substantial amount of basis risk which should be reflected in the pricing. Two revised formulae and some sample results are outlined in Section 9.11 (Appendix); note that for the example above, the margin is further increased indicating the possible impact of these effects.

9.6   FIXED–FIXED CROSS-CURRENCY SWAPS

Conceptually these are very straightforward, simply consisting of two known cashflows in different currencies which have a net value of zero. Each cashflow may be derived by reference to a fixed rate of interest, i.e. 6% Act/360 annual on $100m with or without principal cashflows, or simply be a stream of cashflows possibly determined by some other activity. They are widely used, but very often as part of a larger structure. An exception to this are long-term FX forward contracts (LTFXs).

Consider a normal FX outright contract such as the one discussed above:

6 mo. FX out of 4 Feb 2008:	
To sell	$100m on 6 Aug 2008
To buy	¥105.458m

This was priced theoretically off the two money market curves, and the skew estimated to be 2.33 bp on yen Libor. The structure of the outright, using swap terminology, is two zero-coupon legs with bullet payments at the end of each. But when the maturity of this outright is increased beyond 12 months, zero-coupon cash rates seldom exist and we must resort to swap techniques.

For example, a 5-year LTFX would have the following structure:

	USD	JPY
Today	0	0
	0	0
	0	0
	0	0
	⋮	⋮
	0	0
Year 5	+1	$-S_5$

---

[4] Hardly surprising as the exposure was removed from the investor, and had to go somewhere.

namely, to buy USD and to sell JPY in 5 years' time at the rate of yen S_5 per USD. If S_0 is the current spot rate, then $1 * \mathrm{DF}_5^{\$} * S_0 - S_5 * \mathrm{DF}_5^{¥} = 0$, i.e. $S_5 = S_0 * \mathrm{DF}_5^{\$}/\mathrm{DF}_5^{¥}$ where the yen discount factor is off the CCBS-adjusted curve. From Worksheet 9.12, this gives:

$$S_5 = 106.601 * 0.838308/0.942304 = 94.836$$

Pricing LTFX and similar structures is relatively simple. Because they are often very large one-off transactions, they may be priced and hedged as a single deal rather than merely managed within a portfolio. A technique that is widely used is as follows.

First consider the USD side on its own: we will be receiving (say) $1m in 5 years' time as shown in column [2] of Worksheet 9.10. What transactions can we do today that will create a matching liability in 5 years?

a. Suppose we borrow some money $\$P_5$ at, given we are still a US bank, $ Libor flat.
b. Simultaneously enter into a 5-year swap to receive floating, and to pay $\$F_5 = 3.505\%$ annual Act/360—this effectively converts the borrowing from floating to fixed.
c. The amount to be borrowed is:

$$\$P_5 = \$1m/(1 + 1.017 * 3.505\%) = \$965,592$$

where (6 Feb 13–6 Feb 12)/360 = 1.017. At the end of the last period, the liability = $\$P_5 * (1 + 1.017 * 3.505\%) = \$1m$.
d. Of course, interest has to be paid in each of the earlier periods; this gives rise to negative cashflows as shown in column [3].
e. The net effect is in [4], where it can be seen that the 5-year cashflow of the LTFX has now been reduced to an upfront transaction plus only four future cashflows.
f. The steps are now repeated: as the fourth net cashflow = −$34,220 is negative, we deposit $34,220/(1 + 1.011 * 3.275\%) = \$33,123$ which generates principal plus interest receipts in the last period which exactly offset the fourth cashflow: see column [5], and so on.

At the end of the process, we have effectively entered into five money market transactions and five IR swaps with differing maturities. The net amount of money to be borrowed upfront is $838,308 (see column [12]) which is of course equal to $\$1m * \mathrm{DF}_5^{\$}$.

In practice, it would work somewhat differently, and Worksheet 9.11 demonstrates this.

The swap principals may incidentially be estimated rather more easily than above:

• create a matrix A such that $\{a_{ij} = 0$ if $i < j$, $a_{ij} = S_i * d_j$ if $i > j$, and $a_{ij} = 1 + S_i * d_i$ if $i = j\}$, where S_i is the ith swap rate, d_j the length of the jth period;
• $\mathbf{P} = A^{-1} . \mathbf{CF}$ where $\mathbf{CF}$ is the vector of original USD cashflows arising from the LTFX (column [2]).

This result is shown in column [3]. We can replicate the transaction by:

• Borrow $838,308 at 12 mo. Libor for 5 years and simultaneously enter into the swaps. At the end of the first year

○ interest has to be paid based upon the current 12 mo. rate of 2.89625%: this is $24,684—see column [4];
○ the swaps will generate a surplus or deficit—in this case a deficit of only $5,836[5] in column [5];
○ therefore there is a total cash shortfall of $30,520 as in [6], which will be funded by a new Libor borrowing.

• The new Libor rate is also fixed at the end of the first year. This is of course currently unknown, and the worksheet calculates a forward rate from the implied curve using:

$$F_{t,1/2} = F_{0,1/2} \cdot \exp\{\sigma \cdot \sqrt{t} \cdot \varepsilon\}$$

where $F_{t,1/2}$ is the 1/2 forward rate observed at time t, σ the annualised volatility and ε a random sample from a unit normal. The new forward curve is in column [1]. The worksheet on the CD will permit the Libor curve to be randomly simulated, to demonstrate the hedge working under a range of situations.

At the end of the second year:

• as before, interest has to be paid based on $F_{1,1/2}$;
• the new swap surplus or deficit is generated;
• the cash shortfall is rolled over.

Notice that the total cash shortfall at this point is constant; as $F_{1,1/2}$ changes, fluctuations in the interest payments are exactly offset by the cash generated by the swaps. At the end of 5 years, the total shortfall is $1m, i.e. precisely matching the inflow from the LTFX.

The above discussion has assumed mid-swap rates, and all borrowing and lending takes place at Libor flat. Very often bid–offer spreads are included in the swap rates, especially if the transaction is being hedged at arm's length. It is quite simple to modify the calculations accordingly.

We have agreed that we needed to borrow $838,308 upfront to create a liability which exactly offsets the $1m that will be received in 5 years' time. But what shall be done with the borrowed money? We can enter into a spot FX transaction to sell the USD and receive JPY $S_0 * 838,308 = 89,364,451$, and then deposit these proceeds using the yen money market. Using the same technique, yen IRSs may be used to guarantee the value of the asset in 5 years' time (see column [8] of Worksheet 9.12).

The quoted forward rate is therefore:

$$S_5 = \text{Value of JPY asset in 5 years' time} / \text{Value of USD liability in 5 years' time}$$

If it is assumed that the yen deposit will earn Libor flat, then $S_5 = 94.624$ calculated either using the method above or directly from $S_0 * \text{DF}_5^{\$}/\text{DF}_5^{¥}$ using of course the unadjusted yen DFs.

---

[5] For the kth period, given by $d'_k * L_k * \sum P_j - d_k * \sum(P_j \cdot S_j)$ where d'_k and d_k are the lengths of the kth period on the floating and fixed side of the swaps, the swaps may differ due to daycount conventions and the summation for $j \geq k$.

USD spot sale of 838,308		$ IR swaps	USD borrowing of 838,308	JPY deposit of $S_0 * 838,308$		¥ IR swaps	JPY spot buy of $S_0 * 838,308$
			Periodic $ Libor interest payments	Periodic ¥ Libor interest receipts			
USD forward receipt of 1,000,000		USD liability of 1,000,000		JPY asset of $S_5 * 1,000,000$			JPY forward payment of $S_5 * 1,000,000$

The structure of the transaction plus hedge is shown diagrammatically above. The spot and forward transactions are shown on the outside, then the two sets of IRS hedges, and finally the two money market transactions are shown in the middle. But we know that back-to-back money market transactions can be replicated by a structured CCBS, which is effectively rolled over each period. Hence the total hedge for an off-balance sheet forward would also off-BS.

However, we know from the 5-year CCBS market that a bank capable of raising money at USD Libor flat would pay (a mid-spread of) 4.5 bp above yen Libor. Incorporating this reduces S_5 to 94.765—the margin may be entered into the worksheet as indicated. In these circumstances the first CCBS transaction is:

- to receive a USD principal of 838,308;
- to pay a yen principal of 89,364,451; and
- to pay $ Libor and to receive ¥ Libor + 4.5 bp, respectively;

the cashflows are shown in columns [1] and [9] of Worksheet 9.12 (in Boxes 1 and 2). The periodic cashflows plus the surpluses or shortfalls from the two IRS strips, see columns [3] and [11], respectively, are then also paid into CCBSs, all of which mature on 6 Feb 2013. The overall outcome is a USD liability of 1 million and a JPY asset of 94,765,153. Notice that there is a very small difference between the yen asset used to estimate the size of the IRS hedge and the resulting balance on the money market account of some ¥500. This is because the argument here is circular, and only converges to within a small error.

If the adjusted yen discount factors are used in $S_0 * DF_5^{\$}/DF_5^{¥}$, as discussed above, we get a very similar result, namely $S_5 = 94.765$. The latter is, as before, a very quick method for pricing LTFXs whilst still reflecting the relative costs of funds.

9.7 CROSS-CURRENCY SWAP VALUATION

This is very similar to interest rate swap valuation, namely each side of the swap is valued separately in its own currency in the usual fashion; these values are then netted by converting into a single currency using the current spot FX rates. In theory, either the notional principal or the implied forward method may be used to value the floating side if there is one. If an adjusted foreign curve is being used for discounting, then only the implied method is appropriate. For example, Worksheet 9.13 values a 5-year CCBS which was originally traded at:

To pay	3 mo. USD Libor
To receive	3 mo. JPY Libor $+ 4.5\,$bp

Discounting off an adjusted curve, this swap initially has a zero value, as shown in columns [1] and [2] of the worksheet.

Worksheet 9.13 then simulates what might happen after one year. It takes the two existing forward curves, and randomly simulates them using the formula:

$$F(\tau, t, T) = F(0, t, T) * \exp\{\sigma_t . \sqrt{\tau} . \varepsilon_t\}$$

where τ is the length of time moving forward;
          σ is the forward rate volatility (actually taken off cap curves—see Chapter 10);
          ε is a unit normal random variable[6];

as well as the spot rate. Finally, the new cashflows are calculated in columns [3] and [4]; note that the valuation is being done on 6 February 2009, but immediately after the Libor cashflows on that date have been completed. The two sides of the swap are then discounted and the JPY side converted into USD at the current spot rate. The USD side, being both estimated and discounted off the same curve, is always valued at $100m, but the value of the yen side fluctuates (see New market data box of Worksheet 9.13).

However, CCSs are often treated differently to IRSs in one important aspect. The potential credit exposure of a CCS is much higher than an IRS due to the large re-exchange of principals at the end, which of course an IRS does not possess. This was briefly discussed in Section 6.4. This is recognised in the Basel Accord, which requires ten times as much capital for a CCS with a maturity greater than one year than for an equivalent IRS. Therefore many CCSs are traded on the condition that the principals will be adjusted to new current spot rates at regular intervals, such as annually.[7]

Consider a simple generic CCBS with no margin, as shown below. It will be initially assumed that both estimating and discounting are off the same yen curve:

Time	USD	JPY
0	$+100$m	$-10,660$m
3	$-L_\$$	$+L_{¥}$
6	$-L_\$$	$+L_{¥}$
9	$-L_\$$	$+L_{¥}$
12	$-L_\$$	$+L_{¥}$
15	$-L_\$$	$+L_{¥}$
18	$-L_\$$	$+L_{¥}$
$\vdots$		
60	$-L_\$ - 100$m	$+L_{¥} + 10,660$m

---

[6] The worksheet actually uses correlated sampling. First a vector of independent unit normal random variables φ is generated, and then a correlated vector $\varepsilon = A . \varphi$ where $A . A' =$ correlation matrix—see Chapter 11 for more details. There are two worksheets: 9.13 has had the simulation removed, but 9.14 will still run the simulation

[7] The Accord has a cutoff, whereby a 1% capital charge is imposed for up to and including 1 year, 5% up to 5 years and 7.5% beyond. Hence a long swap with annual revisions will, in theory at least, only carry a 1% charge. However, the regulators are somewhat wary of this, and usually demand more than a paper revision.

At the end of year 1, the current value of the yen side is simply ¥10,660m. But the spot rate has shifted from $S_0 = ¥106.601$ to $S_1 = 94.97$, therefore valuing the yen side at ${10,660m/94.97} = $112,248,604. The swap has a positive net value of $12,248,604, which is a credit exposure—see column [1]. More generally, the net value is given by:

$${(S_0/S_1) - 1} * P_$$$

The swap could therefore be settled by paying this amount, and re-started at the new exchange rate by paying $¥S_1 * P_$$, receiving $P_$$. Equivalently, by simply receiving the payment of $¥{S_0 - S_1} * P_$$, the swap is now re-balanced at the new exchange rate, as shown in column [2]. This process could be repeated each year, receiving $¥{S_{t-1} - S_t} * P_$$, and re-balancing the swap to the new exchange rate (see New market data box of Worksheet 9.16).

When a swap has a fixed rate or a margin, then the process is not quite so simple. If the margin of 4.5 bp was included, but the discounting and estimation were still done off the same curve, then the present value of the margin on the change in principal, that is:

$$PV \text{ of } ¥{S_0 - S_1} * P_$ * (4.50 \text{ bp}) * d_t$$

see column [3] of Worksheet 9.18—has to be included in the payment to be made on the re-balancing date.

Finally, if the valuation uses different estimation and discounting curves, then a further allowance has to be made for this. Worksheet 9.20 shows the actual valuation of the yen cashflows, including the margin, off the adjusted curve to be ¥10,653,188,080 or at the new spot rate $94,800,797. This may be replicated by an upfront payment of:

(1) $¥{S_0 - S_1} * P_$ = -¥577,344,835$—see column [2].
(2) $PV_{adjusted}$ of $¥{S_0 - S_1} * P_$ * (4.50 \text{ bp}) * d_t = -¥1,029,804$ as shown in column [3].
(3) The change in value due to the use of the adjusted rather than the unadjusted curve: this is calculated by:
    a. $PV_{adjusted} - PV_{unadjusted}$ of {yen cashflows using new principal $S_1 * P_$$};
    b. $PV_{adjusted} - PV_{unadjusted}$ of ${¥{S_0 - S_1} * P_$ * (4.50 \text{ bp}) * d_t}$;
    c. $PV_{adjusted} - PV_{unadjusted}$ of {yen cashflows using old principal $S_0 * P_$$}.
    The total change in value = a + b − c = −¥1,404,150.

This gives a net receipt of $-¥577,344,835 - 1,029,804 + 1,404,150 = -¥576,970,489$. This receipt plus the re-balanced cashflows are shown in column [4] of the New market data box of Worksheet 9.20. The PV of this new stream of cashflows is, of course, exactly the same as the PV of the original swap.

9.8 DUAL-CURRENCY SWAPS

Investing requires a judicious balance between return and risk, whilst issuance is almost invariably about raising money as cheaply as possible. Securities are structured to meet the risk-return requirements of a group of investors, but almost inevitably swapped into simple debt for the issuer. Dual-currency issues are a perfect example of this.

Consider the dilemma of Japanese investors since the crash of the Nikkei in 1989. Equity has given very poor returns, and the 10-year benchmark bond yield has been considerably below 2%. During the next 10 years, a number of dual-currency bonds have been issued. For example:

Issuer:	**Asfinag (German autobahn financing company)**
Maturity:	20 years
Principal:	¥20bn
Coupon:	Either A$5.70% or DM5.31% ANN
	(the issuer had option to select currency before first coupon payment)
Principal	Repaid in ¥
Issuer:	**SNCF (French Railways)**
Maturity:	3 years
Principal:	¥10bn
Coupon:	¥5.65% ANN
Principal	Repaid in A$

In both cases, the issuer then swapped the bond into plain USD Libor less a margin.
    There are two main types of dual-currency bond:

- coupon is paid in a foreign currency, but the principal is repaid in the domestic (i.e. currency of issue);
- reverse dual: coupon is paid in the domestic currency, but the principal is repaid in a foreign currency.

Generally, unless the bond is extremely long, the latter are considerably riskier than the former as the principal itself is at risk.
    Consider the French issue: this was paying about 400 bp over the curve to the investor for taking on the currency risk that the A$ will weaken against ¥. The ¥/A$ exchange rate in 1996 was about 76.4, and based on the interest rate differentials was expected to weaken to 59 over the 3 years. In other words, losing about 22% of the principal amount whilst only gaining a total of 12% in coupon. Hardly surprising that this swaps into a substantial margin below Libor (see Worksheet 9.22).
    Looking at the worksheet, the bond cashflows are shown from the point of view of the bond issue, i.e. receiving the principal, and then paying away the coupons and redemption as shown in columns [1] and [2]. This has a total positive value to the issuer of just over $10m. If this is given away on the swap, the issuer would expect a substantial margin of 376 bp below Libor on a USD principal of 100 million.
    The "fair" breakeven coupon, i.e. the coupon that gives the bond a zero value, is 9.51% suggesting that the issued coupon is some 400 bp too low, as we have already surmised. What happened over the 3 years? The AUD actually strengthened for most of the time, and the lucky investors received both the high coupon plus a valuable principal.
    As we can see from the Asfinag issue, these complex bonds frequently contain embedded options. That issue only contained a single 1-year option, whether to select to pay the PV{AUD stream} or PV{DEM stream}. Other bonds of this type have FX-related options on each cashflow, very often both protecting the issuer from paying large amounts, and protecting the investor from ever receiving effectively a negative payment.[8]

---

[8] A good source describing many of the different structures is *Structured Notes and Hybrid Securities* by Satyajit Das, published by Wiley in 2001.

In recent years, power reverse dual-currency (PRDC) structures have been extremely popular with Japanese investors, with some $60bn outstanding in 2008. For example, the following was issued by the EIB in July 2005, and swapped into 3 mo. Euribor less a margin. Notice the fairly small size of issue: this is very common, as many of them are sold entirely to a single investor such as a regional pension fund. The note pays a highly attractive guaranteed coupon in the first year, but thereafter the coupon is subject to the vagaries of the AUD/JPY spot rate. If the yen strengthens, i.e. the rate drops, then the investor will receive a low coupon for the next 29 years plus redemption in a weakened currency. If the yen weakens, then the coupon will rise, but the trigger will ensure early redemption with the yen principal being repaid. Early redemption is the best outcome for the investor, and is often (if wrongly) assumed.

Power Reverse Dual with trigger issued by EIB

Issue date: July 2005
Size: ¥1bn
Maturity: July 2035
Issue price: 100
Coupon: Paid sa in yen
                 10% in year 1
                 $26\% * (S_T/S_0) - 18.7\%$ thereafter
                 where S is JPY/AUD spot rate
                     S_0 is rate 10 days before issue
                     S_T is rate 10 days before coupon date
                 Subject to a non-negativity constraint
Redemption: AUD1,666,667
Trigger: B_1 (set on July 2006) = 84.10
                 $B_T = B_{T-1} - 1$ each year
                 If $S_T \geq B_T$ on any coupon date, then mandatory redemption is in yen

---

These complex structures often cause a moral debate, as it is very hard for typical investors to assess their "fairness", and there is no doubt that some issues are overly complex to obscure their true value. On the other hand, they could be viewed as the high-risk–high-return component of a diversified portfolio which is relatively easily to buy. If they did not exist, the range of investing opportunities would be significantly reduced.

Many of these structures were linked to the JPY–USD exchange rate. As the USD started to weaken significantly in 2008, these structures lost a large percentage of their value, and early redemption became highly unlikely. To make matters even worse, the spread in the 30-year JPY–USD CCBS turned sharply positive, implying that investors would find it very expensive to attempt (I think that is the best word, as there is no genuinely effective way[9]) hedging their FX risk.

---

[9] See P. Tucker, "A perspective on recent monetary and financial system developments", published in *BoE Quarterly Bulletin*, **Q2**, 2007 (footnote on p. 312 for one of many warnings issued by BoE on PRDCs). See also the article "Storm over Japan bonds shows bank worries were prescient", published in *Financial Times* on 1 May 2008.

The PRDC described above was swapped into Euribor. There are therefore three relevant FX rates, and of course three discount curves. It may be modelled in a simplistic fashion by building a JPY/AUD FX tree, in a very similar fashion to the IR trees constructed in Chapter 11, plus externally provided discount curves. But this ignores correlation effects, and so it may be necessary to build multi-currency trees—as described in Section 11.5 (Appendix)—or simulation.[10]

9.9 CROSS-CURRENCY EQUITY SWAPS

We saw in the previous chapter how equity swaps may be constructed. It is perfectly feasible to extend the construction into cross-currency swaps.

Trade date:	4 January 2000
Notional principal:	$100m
Maturity:	2 years
Current FX rate:	102.985
To receive:	Yen 3 mo. Libor
To pay:	S&P 500 index quarterly

At the current spot rate, the yen principal is ¥10.2985bn, i.e. we are assuming an at-market swap. The cashflows are calculated in the same way as before, but notice that there is a final exchange of principals at the original spot rate (see columns [7] and [8] of Worksheet 8.10). The hedging is also very similar: the yen principal is borrowed at yen Libor flat, converted into USD and invested in the index. At the end of each period, the hedge is re-balanced to $100m and the surplus or shortfall paid to the counterparty.

This hedge suffers from the same problem, namely it requires odd index-based transactions at the end of each quarter which may be inefficient, and so a variable notional structure may be more appropriate. However, because of the need to exchange principals and the movement in the FX rate, the CCVN structures are more complex. Consider how it might work. Over the first quarter, the index rises by 5.52% implying a payment of $5,523,707. In the single-currency version, this payment is funded by increasing the Libor principal by the same amount. In the cross-currency version, we do the same but in JPY which has to be converted into USD at the prevailing FX rate, that is:

$$\$5,523,707 * S_1 = ¥560,537,884 \quad \text{using } S_1 = 101.48$$

Therefore the yen principal is increased by this amount (see Worksheet 8.12).

Turning to the worksheet, columns [4] and [7] show the USD principal and cashflow for a hypothetical series of index movements. Column [5] shows the new JPY principals

---

[10] See for example F. Bailly *et al.*, *ANR Grid Computing—Benchmark—PRDC Pricing*, published by Calyon Quantitative Research in December 2006, or Y. Osajima, *FX-IR Hybrid Modeling* from Mitsubishi Derivatives Research, presented at Osaka University Workshop in December 2005, for details of three-factor and two-factor models, respectively.

calculated by:

$$P_{\yen,i} = P_{\yen,i-1} + P_{\$,i-1} * (1 + r_i) * S_i$$

and column [8] the resulting cashflows. Note that there is an exchange of principals at the swap maturity.

The swap can be hedged by borrowing $100m $* S_0$ in JPY at Libor flat, converting the proceeds to USD and investing in the index. Each period, the yen borrowing is increased or decreased by $P_{\yen,i} = P_{\yen,i-1} + P_{\$,i-1} * (1 + r_i) * S_i$, as shown in column [9]. The interest being paid in column [11] exactly matches the interest received in column [8]. At the end, the index investment is liquidated, converted to yen at the prevailing spot rate and used to repay the total borrowing.

However, the CCVN do expose the investor to movements in the FX rate as well as movements in the index. It is feasible to get currency-protected ("quanto") swaps where both sides would be denominated in, say, USD. These are either dynamically delta-hedged or hedged using simple quanto instruments such as FX forwards—see Section 9.11 (Appendix).

9.10   CONCLUSION

This chapter has discussed the construction and pricing of cross-currency swaps. Whilst the market for them is considerably smaller than for IRSs, it is still an extremely important market. CCSs are extensively used by organisations who borrow in a "cheap" currency, and then swap the proceeds into their desired currency. Exchange rates have become more volatile over the last 50 years due to the abolition of many fixed rate regimes, and demand for currency exposure management has increased accordingly. The use of CCSs, and particularly long-term FX forward contracts which are merely a special type of CCS, to provide medium to long-term risk management is increasing each year on the back of increasing currency deregulation.

9.11   APPENDIX: QUANTO ADJUSTMENTS

Quanto structures were introduced in Section 9.5. The difficulty of hedging a quanto structure was described because of the joint exposure to interest rates in the foreign currency as well as to the FX rate.

A general approach is to use the HJM methodology, as outlined in Section 7.6 (Appendix). The following results are based upon the assumptions[11]:

1.   The domestic term structure has one source of uncertainty: call it W_1.
2.   The foreign term structure has two sources of uncertainty, W_1 and W_2: i.e. one source in common plus an additional one.
3.   The spot FX rate $S(t)$ has three sources of uncertainty, W_1, W_2 and W_3: i.e. the FX rate is related to the two term structures plus one additional source.

This permits three correlations between the two term structures and spot rate.

---

[11] Details are given in S.M. Turnbull, "Pricing and hedging diff swaps", *J. of Financial Engineering*, **2**(4), 1993, pp. 297–333.

Using the same notation as in Section 7.6 (Appendix), the expected present value of a domestic payment at time t_{j+1} based on a foreign reference rate may be written as:

$$V(0, t_{j+1}) = E^Q\left\{\frac{1}{p_f(t_j, t_{j+1}) \cdot B_d(t_j)} - \frac{1}{B_d(t_j)}\right\}$$

i.e. constructing the foreign discount bond $p_f(t_j, t_{j+1})$, but applying a domestic money account $B_d(t_j)$. By evaluating the integrals, we get:

$$V(0, t_{j+1}) = p_d(0, t_{j+1}) \cdot \left\{\frac{p_f(0, t_j)}{p_f(0, t_{j+1})} \cdot e^\varphi - 1\right\}$$

This is the usual expression with an adjustment term e^φ, where φ consists of the following expressions:

$$\varphi = a_{f_1} + a_{f_2} + a_{d_f} + a_{f_s}$$

$$a_{f_i} = \tfrac{1}{2}(\sigma_{f_i})^2 \cdot (\lambda_{f_i})^{-3} \cdot (1 - \exp[-\lambda_{f_i} \cdot t_j]) \cdot (1 - \exp[-\lambda_{f_i} \cdot d_{j+1}])^2 \quad \text{for } i = 1, 2$$

$$a_{d_f} = -\sigma_{d_1} \cdot \sigma_{f_1} \cdot (\lambda_{d_1} \cdot \lambda_{f_1} \cdot \lambda_{f_1})^{-1} \cdot (1 - \exp[-\lambda_{f_1} \cdot t_j]) \cdot (1 - \exp[-\lambda_{f_1} \cdot d_{j+1}])$$

$$* \left\{1 - \frac{\lambda_{f_1}}{\lambda_{f_1} + \lambda_{d_1}} \cdot \frac{(1 - \exp[-(\lambda_{f_1} + \lambda_{d_1})t_j])}{(1 - \exp[-\lambda_{f_1} t_j])} \cdot \exp(-\lambda_{d_1} \cdot d_{j+1})\right\}$$

$$a_{f_s} = -\sum_i \delta_i \sigma_{f_i} \cdot (\lambda_{f_i})^{-2} \cdot (1 - \exp[-\lambda_{f_i} \cdot t_j]) \cdot (1 - \exp[-\lambda_{f_i} \cdot d_{j+1}])$$

If the lambdas = 0, i.e. there is no reversion:

$$a_{f_i} = \tfrac{1}{2}(\sigma_{f_i})^2 \cdot t_j \cdot (d_{j+1})^2 \quad \text{for } i = 1, 2$$

$$a_{d_f} = -\sigma_{d_1} \cdot \sigma_{f_1} \cdot t_j \cdot d_{j+1} \cdot t_{j+1}$$

$$a_{f_s} = -\sum_i \delta_i \sigma_{f_i} \cdot t_j \cdot d_{j+1}$$

If the input data are the following:

1. Volatility of domestic term structure, in terms of discount bond prices, σ_{d_1}, plus reversion factor λ_{d_1}.
2. Volatility of foreign term structure, σ_f, plus reversion factors λ_{f_1} and λ_{f_2}.
3. Spot FX rate vol., σ_{FX}.
4. Correlations between the three components, i.e. ρ_{d_f}, $\rho_{d_{FX}}$ and $\rho_{f_{FX}}$.

Then the parameters for the above formulae are calculated by:

$$\sigma_{f_1} = \rho_{d_f} \cdot \sigma_f$$

$$\sigma_{f_2} = \sigma_f \cdot [1 - (\rho_{d_f})^2]^{1/2} \qquad \text{i.e. from } (\sigma_f)^2 = (\sigma_{f_1})^2 + (\sigma_{f_2})^2$$

$$\delta_1 = \rho_{d_{FX}} \cdot \sigma_{FX}$$

$$\delta_2 = (\rho_{f_{FX}} \cdot \sigma_{FX} \cdot \sigma_f - \delta_1 \cdot \sigma_{f_1})/\sigma_{f_2} \quad \text{i.e. from } \text{covol}(f, FX) = \delta_1 \cdot \sigma_{f_1} + \delta_2 \cdot \sigma_{f_2}$$

In the main text, we priced a JPY–USD QDS to have a margin of −237 bp on the USD side. Worksheet 9.24 contains the following data:

	Volatility	Lambda 1	Lambda 2
Domestic IR:	15%	10%	
Foreign IR:	15%	10%	10%
FX rate:	20%		
	$d-f$	$d-\text{FX}$	$f-\text{FX}$
Correlation:	0.5	0.3	−0.3

The margin increased by 8 bp to −241 bp. Worksheet 9.24 also contains sensitivity graphs with respect to the main parameters (see the CD). The biggest impact, not surprisingly following the discussion about the difficulty of hedging, is to the FX/foreign IR correlation.

Based upon the above sensitivity findings, a widely used approximation[12] is to consider the last term only, which gives:

$$V(0, t_{j+1}) = p_d(0, t_{j+1}) \cdot F_f \cdot d_{j+1} \cdot \exp\{\rho_{F,\text{FX}} \cdot \sigma_{\text{FX}} \cdot \sigma_F \cdot t_j\}$$

where F_f is the foreign forward rate from t_j to t_{j+1} (see Worksheet 9.25). Notice that the correlation in this model is between the spot FX rate and a forward rate, unlike the previous model which is between the spot rate and a discount bond price. This means that the two correlations will have opposite signs.

---

[12] See, for example, Hull, ibid., pp. 518–520 for a more detailed discussion.

10

OTC Options

OBJECTIVE

Many banks trade, i.e. price and hedge, a range of options on both forward interest rates and forward swaps alongside swaps themselves. It is therefore appropriate to discuss the more common forms of these options, especially in the context of the swap market.

The chapter starts by very briefly discussing the Black option-pricing model, the one that is universally used for the pricing of European interest rate options. The practical estimation of volatility from both historic data and implied from an existing options market is described, including smile surfaces. Section 10.13 (Appendix) discusses the SABR model, which is probably the most popular for modelling and interpolating smile surfaces. The concepts of par and forward volatilities are introduced, and various approaches for transforming between them discussed. Different forms of caps, floors and collars are described, including examples of digital and embedded swap structures.

The terminology and pricing of swaptions are then looked at, especially when embedded in swaps such as extendible and retractable. As before, swaption spaces are discussed. The relationship between cap and swaption volatility is explored with some examples. Finally, there is a brief section on FX options, looking at their pricing and replication.

More complex non-European structures are discussed in Chapter 11.

10.1 INTRODUCTION

Interest rate options have been widely traded over-the-counter (OTC) since the mid-1980s, following the growth in the swap market. The "first" generation of options, as it is often described, constituted European options such as caps/floors and swaptions on the *level* of forward interest rates and swap rates. They are invariably priced using Black's 1976 formula, which provides a closed-form pricing model requiring a small number of market inputs. The formula is "single"-factor, implying that the level is the only source of uncertainty.

Second and third-generation options, possessing path dependency and barrier characteristics, respectively, have now been developed to take more complex views on the movement of interest rate curves, such as rotation (steepening) or twisting. The variety of such options is extremely wide, and being extended daily. The pricing and hedging of such instruments requires multifactor models, which are capable of incorporating the correlation effects along a curve. The wide practice however of hedging these options with a portfolio of single-generation options has resulted in many unexpected losses. A number of these structures will be discussed in Chapter 11.

Let us establish some boundaries. First, this is not a book primarily about options; therefore it will not attempt to discuss the wide variety of options that are now at least theoretically available. Second, most of this chapter will concentrate on the practical

implementation of first-generation options, and especially in conjunction with swaps and
other securities. Third, it is assumed that all readers are familiar with simple Black and
Scholes option-pricing models, so it will be rapidly introduced.

10.2   THE BLACK OPTION-PRICING MODEL

A "caplet" is defined as a single call option on a forward interest rate $F(\tau, T)$, which starts
(fixes) at time τ and finishes at time T. If we assume that the option has a strike of $K\%$ and
is written on a principal P, then:

- at time τ, the fixing of F is observed to be $L\%$;
- if $L > K$, payout $= [L - K] * (T - \tau) * P$ conventionally paid at time T;
- if $L \leq K$, payout $=$ zero.

More generally the payout can be expressed as:

$$\max\{0, L - K\} * (T - \tau) * P$$

If the payout were to be made at time τ instead, adopting the FRA convention, then it
would have to be discounted back in the usual fashion, that is:

$$\max\{0, L - K\} * (T - \tau) * P/[1 + L * (T - \tau)]$$

Consider now a put option on a discount bond. Let:

$p(t, \tau, T)$	be the estimate at time t of the price at time τ of a discount bond that matures to pay 1 at time T

The payoff of S put options with strike p_K at maturity τ is defined as
$\max\{0, p_K - p(\tau, \tau, T)\} * S$ where the expressions are defined as:

$$p(\tau, \tau, T) = [1 + L * (T - \tau)]^{-1} \quad \text{and} \quad p_K = [1 + K * (T - \tau)]^{-1}$$

and substituting into the payout, we get

$$[\max\{0, L - K\} * (T - \tau) * P] * S * p_K/[1 + L * (T - \tau)]$$

Setting $S = 1/p_K$, we get an identical payoff to the caplet. We can therefore either represent
a caplet as a call option on a forward interest rate or a put option on a discount bond. This
latter result is especially useful as there are many closed-form solutions available for
forward discount bond prices and for options on discount bonds using "normal" (often
known as Vasicek) models.

The Black model for the caplet on $F(\tau, T)$ may be written as:

$$C = P * DF_T * \{F(\tau, T) * N(d_1) - K * N(d_2)\} * (T - \tau)$$

where σ is the volatility of the forward rate, $d_1 = \{\ln(F/K) + 0.5 * \sigma^2 \tau\}/\sigma\sqrt{\tau}$,
$d_2 = d_1 - \sigma\sqrt{\tau}$ and $N(x)$ the cumulative unit normal distribution.

Notice that the payout is discounted back from time T, following the convention that the
payout occurs at the end of the period, although the option matures at time τ. Therefore

the volatility, which would be quoted on the basis of some standard time period such as a year, is scaled by $\sqrt{\tau}$ and not by $\sqrt{T}$—see Section 10.3 for a more detailed discussion.

As an example, to price a caplet on a 3 mo. forward rate:

Today's date:	4 February 2008	
Principal amount:	$100m	
Forward rate:	Start date	6 August 09
	End date	6 November 09
Strike:	3.00%	
Volatility:	14.78% pa	

The dates for the forward rate use the normal daycount convention; if one was a non-business day, the date would move using the modified following day convention. The discount factors are:

6 August 09:	0.959112
6 November 09:	0.952586

which implies that $F = (0.959112/0.952586 - 1)/0.256 = 2.681\%$. Substituting into the formula, we get:

$\tau = 1.519$ (this uses a basis of ACT/360, which was used to annualise the volatility)

$d_1 = \{\ln(2.681\%/3.000\%) + 0.5 * 14.78\%^2 * 1.519\}/(14.78\% * 1.232) = -0.526$

$d_2 = -0.526 - 14.78\% * 1.232 = -0.708$

$\rightarrow N(d_1) = 0.299$ and $N(d_2) = 0.239$

$C = \$100m * 0.952586 * \{2.681\% * 0.299 - 3.000\% * 0.239\} * 0.256$

$= \$20,577$

Usually these options are quoted as a proportion of the principal amount, i.e. 2.06 bp. A cap is simply a series of independent caplets, usually based upon a strip of contiguous forward rates. Worksheet 10.2 has extended the caplet example to a 3-year cap, still with a strike of 3.000% against 3 mo. forward rates. There are only 11 caplets in this strip, as there is conventionally no option written on the first already-fixed forward rate. Columns [1] and [2] show the start and end dates of the forward rates, observing business day conventions.[1] The next three columns contain the strike, principal amount and volatility to be applied to each caplet. Finally the price of each caplet is calculated using the above formula; the intermediary calculations are shown in the columns at the end of the worksheet. The overall cost is 69 bp, or just under $700,000 on a constant principal of $100m.

---

[1] Remember Chapter 3, which discussed the reference rate approach. This has not been applied in most of the following examples, with the exception of implying forward volatilities, although in theory should be.

The Black formula is frequently criticised, but nevertheless is the de facto standard for first-generation options. Its use implies that the percentage returns on the forward rate are distributed normally with zero mean (or drift). One criticism is the apparent inconsistency that on the one hand the model treats the forward rate as stochastic, and yet uses an expected rate for discounting. It would seem more intuitive that high payouts, corresponding to high forward rates at maturity, should be discounted at a correspondingly high rate, whereas low payouts should be discounted at a lower rate. This is very much what happens in the tree approaches such as Black–Derman–Toy (BDT) as we shall see in Chapter 11. However, as Rebonato shows,[2] BDT implies a drift to the evolution of forward rates which exactly compensates for the different discounting processes, so that the results from Black and BDT are consistent with each other.

In theory, the payout of a caplet should be discounted back from time τ at a risk-free rate. In practice the market seldom (never?) does this, but uses Ibor-based discount factors that reduce the price of the option. One could argue that this is simple convenience, as such factors are readily available. It is probably also a pragmatic recognition that the other underlying model assumptions are not satisfied in practice and therefore option-pricing models are providing at best price "indications".

In the long run, interest rates exhibit mean reversion, i.e. if high then they are more likely to fall and conversely, if low then more likely to rise. This suggests that the scaling of volatility by $\sqrt{t}$ is likely to be an overestimate, especially for a long-dated option, and that the Black model therefore overprices options. Practitioners sometime suggest, with tongue firmly in cheek, that the impact of Ibor discounting is to adjust the price for mean reversion, but that's just wishful thinking.

10.3 INTEREST RATE VOLATILITY

The estimation of volatility is of course central to the pricing of options. The Black model is based upon the following evolution: that the return on a factor x, which is defined as the percentage change in that factor, over a period of time dt, is given by:

$$r_x = dx/x = \mu . dt + \sigma . \sqrt{dt} . \varepsilon \quad \text{where } \varepsilon \sim N(0,1)$$

Thus $\sigma . \sqrt{dt}$ is the standard deviation of r_x over the time period dt. In theory the returns should be defined using $r(t) = \ln(x_t/x_{t-1})$, i.e. continuously compounded returns. In practice they are often defined using simple returns, i.e. $r(t) = (x_t - x_{t-1})/x_{t-1}$. Numerically, for short time periods of time, the results are virtually identical. For example, a sample of 1-day returns on the USD 12 mo. cash rate gave a c–c volatility of 1.288% and a simple volatility of 1.291%.

The evolution implies that the returns are normally distributed. There is a large body of evidence that suggests that this is not correct. When markets are behaving fairly benignly, large movements do occur with greater frequency than expected from a normal distribution; some people have proposed fatter tailed distributions, such as a Student-t, as being more appropriate. When markets behave abnormally, then extreme moves such as $6, 7, 8, \ldots$ multiples of the standard deviation are observed.[3] This suggests that all

[2] R. Rebonato, *Interest Rate Options Models*, published by Wiley, 1996, p. 122.
[3] As recorded during the credit hiatus of 07/08.

exponentially tailed distributions are probably incorrect, and a proportionally tailed distribution such as a Pareto[4] would be more appropriate. Does this matter greatly? It depends; traders are (or should be) well aware of these deficiencies, and regard all option-pricing models as mere guides anyway. On the other hand, for a long-term end-user hoping that an option represents "good value", then such matters are extremely important. We will return to this debate shortly.

It is assumed that the returns are independently distributed, thus giving rise to the "square root" rule. This is equivalent to assuming that trends in x do not exist. Whilst this is generally true for liquid markets over short time horizons, it is frequently untrue for longer time horizons. A trend has effectively constant returns, i.e. its volatility is close to zero. Thus the square root rule will overestimate volatility in the presence of trends, and the Black model is likely to overprice long-term options in well-behaved markets.

Obviously the factor x_t has to be observed periodically. Most practitioners would use closing prices, so that a daily return would be based on close-to-close pricing. This is because closing prices are often recorded for risk management and P&L calculations independently of actual trading activities. However, closing prices are frequently subject to distortion as there may be very little market activity at that time of day, and therefore the prices are likely to be "indicative" and not represent actual transactions. Sometimes closing prices are recorded over a period such as an hour before the normal market closing time, and some average calculated. If there is an official fixing for the factor, such as for Libor rates, then this may be used instead. However, fixings are usually relatively early in the day, for example Libor fixes at 11 a.m., and therefore may not be representative of transactions throughout in the day.

A single observation per day is a crude indication of what may have happened during the day, and increasing use is being made of intraday price data. High-frequency data, driven by either time or event (i.e. tick movement or transaction) sampling, are becoming widely available. As a result, as expected, measured volatility appears to have increased. Some people use open-to-close prices as a surrogate, but a better measure is:

$$\sigma^2 = \frac{0.361}{n} \cdot \sum_{i=1}^{n} \{\ln(H_i/L_i)\}^2$$

where H_i and L_i are the high and low for day i. This is supposedly five to six times more accurate than using closing prices alone.[5] The highs and lows may be adjusted numerically to compensate for the fact that the *reported* high < *continuous* high, etc.

The definition of the "period of time" requires careful consideration. Naively one might argue that a 10-day period would run, for example, from Wednesday 18 June to Saturday 28 June 2008. However, this period includes two weekends. Are the returns from, say,

---

[4] The density function of a Pareto distribution is proportional to $x^{-\alpha}$, where α is a positive parameter. This implies that Prob{some random draw $y \geq x$} drops at the speed of α, and not exponentially which would of course be much faster. N. Taleb, Table 2, p. 264 of *The Black Swan*, published by Penguin in 2008, suggests an α of about 3 for financial markets.
[5] Derived by M. Parkinson, "The extreme value method for estimating the variance of the rate of return", *J. of Business*, **53**(1), 1980, pp. 61–5. For a more detailed description, see R. Tompkins, *Options Explained*[2], published by Macmillan, 1994, p. 133. If using high/low is more accurate than using merely closing prices, how about combining the two? See M. Garman *et al.*, "On the estimation of security price volatilities from historical data", *J. of Business*, **53**(1), 1980, pp. 67–78, this is based on Parkinson's working paper.

Saturday to Sunday statistically indistinguishable from the returns from Monday to Tuesday or Thursday to Friday? Early academic studies[6] found that the average return over a 3-day weekend, i.e. from Friday to Monday, is only about 10% higher than the average return between two consecutive business days. This suggests that market rates only move when the markets are active. Most practitioners therefore use business days to define the time period, so that 10 days from 18 June would be Wednesday 2 July. Now that some markets are truly global, trading in all time zones, such as USD/EUR spot rate or Eurodollar futures contract, the above discussion suggests that they should exhibit greater volatility than a domestic market open only 8 hours per day.

"Economic" days, i.e. days during which important economic figures are released, are likely to exhibit higher volatility than "normal" business days. Some practitioners modify their volatility formula to include the number of economic days in the sample period. The estimation of unconditional volatility from historic data is more of an art than a science, with individuals favouring many approaches: see for example Tompkins (ibid., Chapters 4 and 5) for a more in-depth discussion.

To price an option, the volatility of returns from today until the maturity of the option is required. The Black model assumes constant volatility over this period, unlike stochastic volatility and some of the numeric models. There are three ways in which this future volatility may be estimated:

(a) *to assume volatility is stationary, and to calculate historic volatility*

This is probably the most common approach. After calculating the returns, almost invariably over a 1-day time period, the standard deviation is estimated using the sampling expression:

$$\sigma^2 = \sum_{i=1}^{n}(r_i - \mu)^2/(n-1)$$

where μ is the average return over these observations.

The volatility for the option is then estimated by $\sigma \cdot \sqrt{T}$ where T is the number of business days from today until maturity. The choice of n is arbitrary but crucial. On the one hand, the standard error of σ is proportional to $\sqrt{n}$; therefore the larger number of observations selected, the smaller the error. But of course the assumption of stationarity is likely to be less true with increasing observations. A common rule-of-thumb is to match n with the maturity of the option, i.e. set n roughly equal to T.

One approach that is increasingly used, especially for short-dated options, say under 6 months' maturity, is to weight the returns on the basis that the more recent returns are likely to be more relevant than returns that occurred longer ago:

$$\sigma^2 = \sum_{i=1}^{n} w_i * (r_i - \mu)^2/(n-1)$$

where $\sum w_i = 1$.

If we assume that the returns are ordered such that r_i was the 1-day return observed i days ago, then the weights constructed $w_1 > w_2 > w_3 > \cdots$ An exponentially weighted scheme would set $w_i = \lambda^i / \sum_j \lambda^j$ where $\lambda < 1$; λ in the range of 0.90–0.95 is common. If

---

[6] E.F. Fama, "The behaviour of stock prices", *J. of Business*, **38**, January 1965, pp. 34–105; and K.R. French, "Stock returns and the weekend effect", *J of Financial Economics*, **8**, March 1980, pp. 55–69.

we assume an infinite series of returns, then the following recursive relationship may be derived:

$$(\sigma_{t+1})^2 = \lambda \cdot (\sigma_t)^2 + (1 - \lambda) \cdot (r_{t+1})^2$$

where the subscript refers to the time of the last available data, indicating that we are now treating volatility as conditional or time-variant. The estimate is adjusted as a new return is observed, and hence may be used for short-term forecasting.

(b) *to model volatility based upon historic information to provide a forecast*

We have already seen how the traditional method of calculating volatility may be modified to incorporate a weighting scheme, and this may be interpreted as a forecasting model. A simple weighted scheme is modelling the "responsiveness" of volatility to changes in the market returns. New returns are given greater weight, which will cause the volatility estimates themselves to be more volatile as shown in the graph:

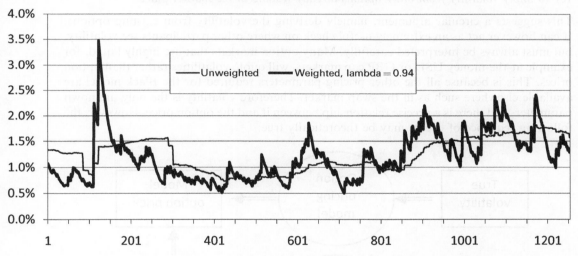

180-day volatility of 12mo. USD cash rate

ARCH (AutoRegressive Conditional Heteroskedastic) modelling takes this approach one stage further. A G(eneralised) ARCH(1,1) model is:

$$(\sigma_{t+1})^2 = v \cdot (1 - \alpha - \beta) + \alpha \cdot (\sigma_t)^2 + \beta \cdot (r_{t+1})^2$$

where v is the unconditional volatility estimated above, and where $\alpha > 0$, $1 > \beta > 0$, $\alpha + \beta \leq 1$. The parameters may be interpreted as:

- v is long-run volatility;
- α indicates the persistence of shocks, i.e. the larger the longer a shock lasts;
- β measures the reactivity of the market to shocks, i.e. the larger the faster.

Together, these two parameters model the rise and fall of volatility, unlike the single weighted scheme which treats the two the same. A typical result is:

	α	β
USD/GBP spot	0.931	0.052
JPY/USD spot	0.839	0.094

i.e. cable reacts slowly but persistently, $–¥ faster but drops off.

However, these methods are seldom applied to option pricing. Because of the need to estimate three parameters, a lot of historic data is required—say 500 days minimum. The resulting forecasts only appear to be better than either an unweighted or single-weighted estimates for about 20 days ahead, which is hardly significant in the lifetime of most options. ARCH models are of course useful in option trading, trying to position an option portfolio to anticipate the movement in volatility and in risk management.[7]

(c) *to imply volatility from other options already trading in the market place*

This suggests a circular argument, namely deriving the volatility from existing options. It can however act as an extremely useful check on where other participants see volatility, but must always be interpreted carefully. Many option markets that are highly liquid, for example at-the-money USD or GBP cap markets, will quote volatilities rather than option prices. This is because all the other pricing parameters required for the Black model are available elsewhere such as in the swap market. Therefore volatility is the only unknown parameter, and there is a precise relationship between it and the option price. However, the following sequence of events may be theoretically true:

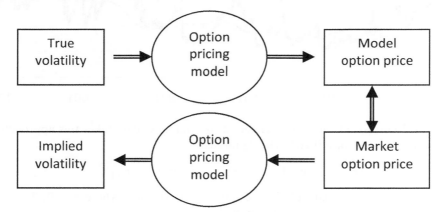

such that true volatility matches implied volatility. But of course this is only true if the price of the option in the market matches the model price, which in practice is highly unlikely. Whilst the Black model is universally used, its underlying assumptions and limitations are also well understood. Model prices are invariably adjusted to reflect a wide range

---

[7] There is an enormous volume of literature on GARCH modelling, and the above discussion does not do it justice. See for example T. Bollerslev *et al.* ("ARCH models" in *Handbook of Econometrics*, Vol. 4, edited by R.F. Engle *et al.*, North Holland, 1994) for an extensive review. GARCH modelling can be related to chaotic behaviour in the financial markets, which is an interesting development.

of factors, which in turn means that the volatility implied from the market price also incorporates these factors.

Table 10.1 shows the so-called "smile" surface for USD IR caps on 4 February 2008. The maturity of each cap is shown in the left-hand column. Continuing the example above, remember that the 3-year cap consists of 11 caplets. Because each caplet is independent, what constitutes ATM for an entire cap is not obvious. The usual convention is to set the strike of each caplet to be constant and equal to the fixed swap rate of the same maturity and frequency as the cap. Using current market data, a 3-year generic swap would have a breakeven quarterly fixed rate of 3.000%. Note that, strictly, the underlying swap should be a 2.75-year swap starting in 0.25 year's time. This has a breakeven rate of 2.987% (see Worksheet 10.2). The usual convention is to ignore this small element of forward starting. The market-implied volatility for the 3-year cap (i.e. 11 caplets) struck at 3.000% is 14.78%.

The top row of the table shows different cap strikes. Hence, for the 3-year cap struck at 2.5%, the implied volatility is 15.83%, whereas it is 15.59% for a strike of 3.5%. Looking along each row, it can be seen that the minimum volatility is for an ATM strike, and rises up for strikes on either side. The curve is not symmetric; ITM caps (i.e. with lower strikes) appear to have higher volatilities than OTM caps—sometimes referred to as a "sneer" effect!!

What causes the smile? There would appear to be two different arguments describing the source of factors at work. The first argument runs as follows:

- the Black model assumes that returns follow a normal distribution;
- in reality, large returns appear more frequently than theoretically justified;
- hence the "correct" distribution has "fatter tails" than the normal distribution;
- therefore the chance of an option having to make a large payout is greater than suggested by theory;
- hence the market option price should be increased over the model price;
- which in turn would lead to a higher implied volatility.

The fat-tailed effect will be greater for options that are farther away from the money, and therefore the price adjustment is likely to be greater.

The second argument says that there are a number of serious practical omissions from the model, such as:

- fixed costs of undertaking a transaction such as salaries, systems, rates and rents;
- variable costs of undertaking a transaction such as all the back-office processing;
- costs of risk management, especially the potential cost of imperfect hedging;
- capital charge on a transaction, and the required return on capital;
- the real cost of funding all these activities.

Both arguments have validity, and reality is probably a mixture of them both. This has not stopped some people, mainly academics, from assuming that the first argument is the sole source of price adjustment and backing out the implied distribution with its fat tails from smile data.[8]

---

[8] See, for example, M. Rubenstein, "Implied binomial trees", *J. of Finance*, **49**(3), 1994, pp. 771–818; and B Dupire, "Pricing with a smile", *Risk*, **7**, February 1994, pp. 18–20.

Table 10.1 Par cap smile curve—against 3 mo. USD Libor

Strike	ATM	1.50	1.75	2.00	2.25	2.50	3.00	3.50	4.00	5.00	6.00	7.00	8.00	10.00
1 yr	2.867	10.44	30.86	27.90	23.80	18.52	14.40	10.61	11.93	13.70	17.46	20.55	22.63	24.44	27.53
18 mo.	2.760	12.72	24.95	21.30	18.61	15.82	14.08	13.43	15.06	16.49	18.65	20.27	21.58	23.03	25.76
2 yr	2.766	13.53	23.34	19.32	17.56	15.68	14.49	14.16	15.49	16.69	18.70	20.30	21.63	23.17	26.06
3 yr	3.000	14.78	23.11	19.70	17.99	16.84	15.83	14.78	15.59	16.36	17.65	18.87	19.93	20.96	22.77
4 yr	3.235	15.27	21.67	20.49	18.84	17.73	16.77	15.61	15.53	16.06	17.14	18.15	19.05	19.80	21.48
5 yr	3.459	15.48	22.92	21.13	19.52	18.39	17.49	16.12	15.51	15.84	16.60	17.48	18.29	19.02	20.48
6 yr	3.663	15.52	22.15	20.81	19.89	18.71	17.82	16.37	15.69	15.65	16.17	16.88	17.58	18.28	19.64
7 yr	3.828	15.48	21.63	20.32	19.99	18.88	17.99	16.57	15.78	15.53	15.84	16.41	17.05	17.66	18.84
8 yr	3.964	15.38	21.12	21.34	20.10	19.01	18.13	16.70	15.82	15.39	15.55	16.00	16.54	17.10	18.12
9 yr	4.090	15.24	20.71	20.93	19.88	19.01	18.12	16.73	15.78	15.31	15.33	15.64	16.12	16.61	17.62
10 yr	4.197	15.11	20.43	20.64	19.66	19.06	18.15	16.73	15.71	15.26	15.05	15.27	15.74	16.25	17.16
12 yr	4.361	14.76	19.77	19.96	19.10	18.90	18.01	16.60	15.55	15.01	14.66	14.68	14.93	15.31	16.17
15 yr	4.536	14.25	18.94	19.12	19.26	18.45	17.67	16.34	15.35	14.71	14.11	14.01	14.19	14.49	15.14
20 yr	4.671	13.63	17.99	18.15	18.27	17.56	17.10	15.85	14.85	14.18	13.48	13.25	13.32	13.55	14.19
25 yr	4.719	13.13	17.31	17.48	17.60	16.90	16.52	15.33	14.41	13.76	12.99	12.75	12.81	13.03	13.67
30 yr	4.729	12.79	16.85	16.99	17.10	16.48	16.09	14.90	14.02	13.40	12.68	12.51	12.61	12.83	13.47

Source: ICAP plc.

The market price has to reflect all these factors. In addition, market prices are adjusted by perceived supply and demand for the options, forecast movements in market rates especially volatility, and not least a general desire whether or not to do a particular transaction. By the time all these adjustments have been (probably intuitively) incorporated in the pricing by the trader, it is hardly surprising that the market price may bear little resemblance to the model price.

Consider the actual ATM volatility curve itself, as shown below:

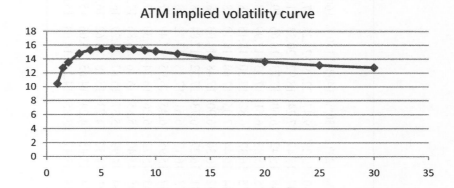

In practice, we would generally expect short-term interest rates to exhibit higher volatility than longer term rates. But nearly always, cap curves are humped around the 5-year point. Why? The usual explanation is supply and demand; the majority of bank customers buy caps with typical maturities between 3 and 7 years.

Understanding how the smile changes with maturity from the above-quoted table can be quite difficult as the ATM strike changes from row to row. Hence, ATM is not a single column but a diagonal. Define moneyness for a given option as (Forward rate/Strike); this means that, for example, if Strike < Forward rate, then the cap is ITM, and the moneyness>100%. The above table can be converted into a moneyness table (Table 10.2).

ATM is now a single column at 100% of moneyness, and the smiles can now be directly compared.[9] An alternative similar representation is to use delta as the dimension: ATM would correspond approximately to a delta of 50%, and then use other deltas on either side ranging from (say) 10% to 90%.

These two tables can also be used to demonstrate another concept. Consider again the 3-year cap: if the strike were 2.5%, then the implied volatility is 15.83%. The current underlying rate when this was being estimated was 3%. Suppose the underlying rate now shifts to 3.5%; what happens to the smile surface? A sticky smile approach suggests that the volatility remains at 15.83%. In contrast, a floating smile (also known as a sticky delta) approach would argue that the moneyness of this option has increased from 120% to 140%, and therefore the appropriate volatility would be 17.33%. My personal experience is to favour floating smiles, but many traders prefer sticky ones.

In summary so far, of the three alternative ways of estimating volatility for option pricing, forecasting is seldom used as the time period is too great. Ultimately historic data are used, but market-traded option prices frequently provide an additional check. Traders often calibrate their volatilities to the generic prices in the market; in this case, their models are effectively glorified interpolation devices.

---

[9] Note that this definition of moneyness reverses the table, so that ITM is on the right, and OTM on the left; for that reason, moneyness is sometimes defined as the strike/forward rate.

Table 10.2 Moneyness smile

	20%	30%	40%	50%	60%	70%	80%	90%	100%	110%	120%	130%	140%	150%	160%	170%	180%
1 yr	34.22	26.84	22.93	19.73	16.62	14.06	12.22	11.10	10.44	13.60	16.23	19.47	22.79	25.26	27.22	28.65	29.76
18 mo.	30.95	24.67	21.45	19.49	17.79	16.33	14.90	13.65	12.72	14.07	15.47	17.24	18.92	20.33	21.67	23.15	24.47
2 yr	31.59	24.93	21.52	19.55	17.92	16.57	15.38	14.36	13.53	14.48	15.42	16.60	17.73	18.66	19.66	21.30	22.75
3 yr	27.30	22.77	20.45	18.87	17.65	16.73	15.98	15.32	14.78	15.35	15.83	16.61	17.33	17.99	18.84	19.60	20.83
4 yr	26.66	22.14	19.87	18.57	17.53	16.73	16.11	15.63	15.27	15.75	16.32	16.82	17.50	18.15	18.74	19.48	20.18
5 yr	25.80	21.60	19.49	18.22	17.27	16.56	16.09	15.74	15.48	15.94	16.44	17.05	17.60	18.19	18.79	19.36	20.03
6 yr	25.29	21.14	19.07	17.81	16.95	16.34	15.95	15.69	15.52	15.92	16.30	16.90	17.48	18.03	18.57	19.16	19.72
7 yr	24.23	20.47	18.59	17.45	16.65	16.11	15.77	15.61	15.48	15.81	16.27	16.73	17.32	17.84	18.37	18.87	19.43
8 yr	23.13	19.76	18.07	17.06	16.33	15.85	15.54	15.45	15.38	15.73	16.17	16.61	17.18	17.72	18.21	18.72	19.22
9 yr	22.90	19.46	17.73	16.70	16.03	15.59	15.36	15.32	15.24	15.57	15.95	16.45	16.95	17.49	17.96	18.45	18.93
10 yr	22.16	18.98	17.38	16.43	15.74	15.27	15.10	15.12	15.11	15.43	15.72	16.26	16.74	17.30	17.80	18.26	18.76
12 yr	21.25	18.12	16.56	15.62	15.03	14.74	14.67	14.71	14.76	15.05	15.40	15.85	16.36	16.86	17.37	17.83	18.28
15 yr	19.26	16.80	15.58	14.84	14.36	14.10	14.04	14.11	14.25	14.64	14.99	15.37	15.87	16.29	16.78	17.22	17.62
20 yr	18.46	15.97	14.73	13.98	13.50	13.30	13.29	13.44	13.63	14.01	14.32	14.73	15.18	15.62	16.05	16.48	16.86
25 yr	18.02	15.50	14.25	13.49	13.00	12.79	12.77	12.93	13.13	13.54	13.85	14.24	14.65	15.06	15.45	15.86	16.23
30 yr	17.84	15.31	14.05	13.30	12.80	12.59	12.53	12.64	12.79	13.18	13.47	13.85	14.24	14.63	15.01	15.42	15.79

The existence of the smile causes a number of practical problems. For example, suppose a trader sells the 3-year cap struck at 2.5%, and then delta-hedges it with a 3-year cap struck at 3% (ATM). How well will this hedge work? If the underlying shifts, the speed of change of the two option values will differ as this speed also depends upon the volatility. This suggests that deriving consistent risk characteristics and hedging for an option portfolio with varying strikes is effectively impossible. As another example, consider again the above 3-year cap, but this time assume it also contains an embedded knock-out barrier at (say) 3.5%. What would be the correct volatility to use: 15.83% following the strike, 15.59% following the barrier or some combination?

A number of people, for example Dupire,[10] have introduced the concept of a local volatility (LV) surface $\sigma(K,T)$ where K is the strike of an option with maturity T. This may be calculated from:

$$\sigma^2(K,T) = 2 * \partial C(K,T)_T / \partial^2 C(K,T)_{KK}$$

where $C(K,T)$ is the price of a cap with strike K and maturity T; and
   $\partial C(K,T)_T$ is the first differential with respect to T, etc.

Whilst evidently the LV can be calculated for any given option, fitting a parametric function to enable smooth interpolation between the market quotes is fraught with numerical difficulties. A common alternative is to use a piecewise constant function. Unfortunately, LV models suffer from a very serious problem. As the underlying spot rate shifts, then we would expect the smile to be either sticky or floating. The LV model predicts that the smile will move in exactly the opposite direction, totally contrary to both intuition and market reality!

A further alternative is to assume that volatility is itself subject to a stochastic process. The simplest resulting model is the SABR model, developed by Hagan et al.,[11] and widely used in practice. This model is described in more detail in Section 10.13 (Appendix).

10.4 PAR AND FORWARD VOLATILITIES

The volatilities quoted above are "par" volatilities. This means, coming back to the 3-year ATM cap, that the same constant volatility of 14.78% is being used to calculate the prices of all 11 caplets. In practice, each caplet should be priced using the volatility for its own individual forward rate. This is called forward volatility (sometimes, rather confusingly, also called forward forward or spot volatility). Par volatilities represent an average of the forward volatilities over all the caplets in an entire cap, and are a convenient way of quoting volatility.

Given the above quotes, it is feasible to estimate implied forward volatilities, typically using a bootstrapping approach. Define V_T to be the par volatility for a generic cap of maturity T with some constant strike, and v_t to be the forward volatility of a single caplet maturing at time t. The price of this cap C_T could be estimated in one of two ways, using the par volatility for all caplets, or the different forward volatilities:

$$C_T = \sum_{t \le T} c_t(V_T) = \sum_{t \le T} c_t(v_t)$$

---

[10] B. Dupire, Risk, 1994.
[11] P. Hagan et al., "Managing smile risk", Wilmott Magazine, pp. 84–108, July 2002.

where c_t is the price of a single caplet of maturity t. Hence a recursive relationship can be defined

$$C_T = C_{T-1} + \sum_{T-1 < t \leq T} c_t(v_t) \qquad (10.1)$$

A crude but common assumption is to set v_t equal to a constant for $T - 1 < t \leq T$. Then we can solve sequentially for forward volatilities. Worksheet 10.6 performs this in three steps:

1. Calculate the 3-monthly forward rates off the current curve using the reference rate convention as described in Chapter 3.
2. For a given strike set in cell C8, price all the caps off the correct par volatilities.
3. The piecewise constant forward volatility curve is set in column [BA]. Based upon this curve, the individual caplets and hence the caps are priced. A built-in macro called Bootstrap_vol_curve changes the numbers in column [D] until the error terms in column [BJ] are all set to zero.

Obviously, discontinuous steps are undesirable, and an optimization approach may also be applied in an analogous way to implying forward rates out of a swap curve. Worksheet 10.7 is structured in exactly the same way as before, but this time minimizes the squared gradient of the forward volatility curve.

One further approach is to use the following formula:

$$(T_2 - T_1) * \sigma_{12}^2 = T_2 * \sigma_2^2 - T_1 * \sigma_1^2$$

where σ_k is the par volatility out to time T_k, and σ_{jk} the forward volatility between times T_j and T_k. Whilst obviously fairly simple, one difficulty with this approach is, because par volatilities are quoted on an annual (or longer) basis and we wish to estimate quarterly forward volatilities, we need to interpolate the par volatilities. Ideally, the interpolation method should be such that the resulting forward volatility curve is arbitrage-free. But precisely how to do this is unclear, and almost certainly not given by parametric interpolation; the curve shown below was based upon linear interpolation, and hence is not arbitrage-free.

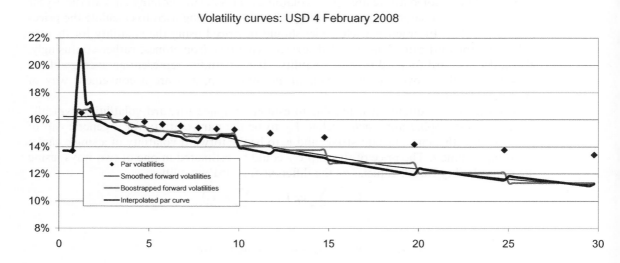

Volatility curves: USD 4 February 2008

These curves are often combined with statistical confidence bands. In practice it is found that volatilities do revert to a long-run level (as suggested by the ARCH model), which means that the confidence bands are wider at the short end than at the longer end. The bands are often called "volatility cones" due to their shape, and are used by traders to imply the likely movement of volatility through time.[12]

We have just derived forward volatilities from a single ATM par volatility curve. It is however, as we have discussed in Section 10.3, common practice to use volatility surfaces, i.e. a matrix of {strike vs. forward start date}, when pricing and valuing caps and floors. Forward surfaces have been produced in two worksheets: 10.9 was produced by boot-strapping each column, and 10.10 by using optimisation—this latter is shown in Table 10.3. This allows the smile effect to be incorporated. IR options on 3-month Libor are the most common, probably reflecting the fact that one can get exchange-traded options on 3-month deposit futures for hedging (see Chapter 2). Therefore the most liquid volatility surface would also be on 3-month Libor, and volatility surfaces for other tenors represented by an off-set surface from the 3-month one. A more complete approach therefore would be to model the entire two-dimensional surface. This surface is likely to contain gaps due to missing maturities and also missing volatilities for particular strikes. If the underlying forward interest rate curve is rising, a strike that is below but close to the money for a short maturity will be a long way from the money at a long maturity. As caps are usually only quoted relatively close to the money, there would be no long volatility quoted. This issue may seem academic, but actually has major practical ramifications. Suppose a trader sells a 10-year ATM cap. After 5 years, interest rates could have moved significantly so that the remaining caplets are nowhere close to ATM—yet they still need to be valued daily! Where do the risk controllers obtain the appropriate volatilities, as they are unlikely to be readily available in the current quotes?[13]

In the discussion below (and in Section 12.10 where the risk management of IR options is discussed), a single volatility curve has been used throughout for ease of exposition.

10.5   CAPS, FLOORS AND COLLARS

We have already discussed the pricing of caps using Black's model. Obviously the same model can be used to price a floor, which is a strip of put options on forward interest rates. Using the same notation as before:

- define a forward interest rate $F(\sigma, T)$, which starts at time τ and finishes at time T;
- assume that the option has a strike of $K\%$ and is written on a principal P;
- at time τ, the fixing of F is observed to be $L\%$;
- payout of the floorlet $= \max[0, K - L] * (T - \tau) * P$.

Black's model for the floorlet on $F(\tau, T)$ may be written as:

$$\mathrm{Fl} = P * \mathrm{DF}_T * \{K * N(-d_2) - F(\tau, T) * N(-d_1)\} * (T - \tau)$$

---

[12] See R. Tompkins, ibid., Chapter 5, or G. Burghardt *et al.*, "How to tell if options are cheap", *J. of Portfolio Management*, Winter 1990, pp. 72–8.
[13] This problem has provided the basis for a number of well-publicised losses by banks, as they have invariably been forced to rely on traders for the information. There are various "closed clubs" whereby banks anonymously share information.

Table 10.3   A smoothed forward volatility surface

Strike ⇒

Maturity	1.5	1.75	2	2.25	2.5	3	3.5	4	5	6	7	8	10
0.50	23.38%	22.88%	20.10%	16.54%	14.06%	11.52%	14.91%	16.22%	17.22%	18.57%	19.65%	20.74%	21.61%
0.75	23.37%	22.64%	20.11%	16.53%	14.06%	11.91%	14.94%	16.22%	17.22%	18.57%	19.64%	20.68%	21.58%
1.00	23.35%	22.22%	19.91%	16.42%	14.14%	12.57%	15.01%	16.22%	17.22%	18.56%	19.63%	20.56%	21.56%
1.25	23.33%	21.69%	18.83%	16.00%	14.33%	13.45%	15.11%	16.21%	17.22%	18.55%	19.61%	20.40%	21.48%
1.50	23.28%	21.17%	18.09%	15.84%	14.65%	14.19%	15.20%	16.21%	17.23%	18.53%	19.56%	20.22%	21.40%
1.75	23.24%	20.75%	17.77%	15.98%	15.13%	14.67%	15.28%	16.21%	17.24%	18.50%	19.48%	20.04%	21.25%
2.00	23.18%	20.48%	17.84%	16.40%	15.76%	15.09%	15.35%	16.22%	17.25%	18.47%	19.38%	19.87%	21.11%
2.25	23.08%	20.34%	18.22%	17.09%	16.53%	15.44%	15.42%	16.21%	17.26%	18.43%	19.27%	19.71%	20.96%
2.50	22.99%	20.30%	18.62%	17.72%	17.23%	15.74%	15.47%	16.20%	17.28%	18.40%	19.14%	19.58%	20.79%
2.75	22.88%	20.33%	18.98%	18.30%	17.85%	16.04%	15.49%	16.16%	17.30%	18.33%	19.03%	19.48%	20.66%
3.00	22.76%	20.42%	19.37%	18.83%	18.40%	16.32%	15.52%	16.10%	17.30%	18.23%	18.93%	19.40%	20.52%
3.25	22.65%	20.54%	19.72%	19.30%	18.87%	16.60%	15.52%	16.01%	17.25%	18.12%	18.85%	19.33%	20.42%
3.50	22.51%	20.65%	20.06%	19.71%	19.25%	16.81%	15.55%	15.92%	17.16%	17.98%	18.76%	19.26%	20.32%
3.75	22.37%	20.74%	20.36%	20.06%	19.57%	17.04%	15.57%	15.82%	17.03%	17.81%	18.64%	19.17%	20.26%
4.00	22.19%	20.78%	20.62%	20.33%	19.80%	17.22%	15.61%	15.73%	16.86%	17.60%	18.46%	19.07%	20.23%
4.25	22.02%	20.76%	20.82%	20.53%	19.95%	17.36%	15.66%	15.65%	16.65%	17.36%	18.24%	18.96%	20.19%
4.50	21.81%	20.68%	20.97%	20.64%	20.03%	17.47%	15.71%	15.57%	16.39%	17.12%	18.00%	18.81%	20.14%
4.75	21.59%	20.55%	21.05%	20.67%	20.01%	17.55%	15.76%	15.49%	16.15%	16.89%	17.76%	18.62%	20.02%
5.00	21.37%	20.39%	21.09%	20.61%	19.92%	17.58%	15.82%	15.42%	15.93%	16.68%	17.55%	18.38%	19.85%
5.25	21.13%	20.23%	21.08%	20.48%	19.75%	17.58%	15.90%	15.35%	15.76%	16.50%	17.31%	18.10%	19.53%
5.50	20.93%	20.09%	21.04%	20.34%	19.59%	17.58%	15.98%	15.28%	15.62%	16.31%	17.08%	17.83%	19.25%
5.75	20.72%	20.01%	20.98%	20.22%	19.45%	17.57%	16.04%	15.22%	15.49%	16.12%	16.86%	17.57%	18.94%
6.00	20.55%	20.02%	20.89%	20.10%	19.31%	17.55%	16.10%	15.16%	15.37%	15.94%	16.65%	17.32%	18.67%
6.25	20.39%	20.17%	20.78%	19.99%	19.18%	17.54%	16.13%	15.10%	15.25%	15.77%	16.44%	17.08%	18.37%
6.50	20.25%	20.45%	20.66%	19.89%	19.07%	17.52%	16.15%	15.06%	15.13%	15.61%	16.25%	16.84%	18.10%
6.75	20.12%	20.90%	20.53%	19.81%	18.97%	17.49%	16.13%	15.02%	15.04%	15.44%	16.06%	16.61%	17.85%
7.00	20.02%	21.49%	20.39%	19.74%	18.88%	17.45%	16.10%	14.99%	14.94%	15.28%	15.89%	16.37%	17.62%
7.25	19.93%	22.20%	20.23%	19.67%	18.79%	17.40%	16.06%	14.96%	14.80%	15.11%	15.72%	16.17%	17.41%
7.50	19.83%	22.62%	20.07%	19.60%	18.71%	17.35%	15.99%	14.94%	14.73%	14.95%	15.56%	15.97%	17.23%
7.75	19.75%	22.71%	19.85%	19.54%	18.63%	17.28%	15.91%	14.92%	14.64%	14.80%	15.41%	15.84%	17.08%
8.00	19.66%	22.41%	19.61%	19.47%	18.55%	17.22%	15.80%	14.92%	14.55%	14.64%	15.28%	15.76%	16.95%
8.25	19.57%	21.81%	19.34%	19.41%	18.47%	17.14%	15.69%	14.91%	14.45%	14.49%	15.15%	15.74%	16.85%
8.50	19.47%	21.18%	19.09%	19.35%	18.40%	17.05%	15.58%	14.89%	14.34%	14.34%	15.00%	15.67%	16.71%
8.75	19.39%	20.65%	18.87%	19.27%	18.33%	16.96%	15.48%	14.86%	14.22%	14.20%	14.81%	15.54%	16.51%
9.00	19.27%	20.17%	18.65%	19.18%	18.26%	16.87%	15.40%	14.82%	14.08%	14.06%	14.64%	15.41%	16.27%
9.25	19.16%	19.77%	18.46%	19.10%	18.18%	16.78%	15.33%	14.77%	13.94%	13.92%	14.43%	15.23%	15.96%
9.50	19.06%	19.42%	18.27%	19.02%	18.10%	16.69%	15.26%	14.71%	13.81%	13.79%	14.23%	14.98%	15.70%
9.75	18.93%	19.14%	18.10%	18.93%	18.02%	16.59%	15.19%	14.64%	13.70%	13.66%	14.03%	14.75%	15.44%

10.00	15.26%	14.45%	13.83%	13.54%	13.61%	14.56%	15.13%	16.49%	17.93%	18.84%	17.96%	18.90%	18.84%
10.25	15.08%	14.14%	13.64%	13.41%	13.55%	14.47%	15.05%	16.39%	17.85%	18.75%	17.86%	18.71%	18.76%
10.50	14.90%	13.89%	13.46%	13.30%	13.48%	14.39%	15.00%	16.29%	17.75%	18.65%	17.80%	18.54%	18.68%
10.75	14.75%	13.65%	13.29%	13.20%	13.42%	14.31%	14.95%	16.20%	17.66%	18.55%	17.79%	18.39%	18.61%
11.00	14.61%	13.47%	13.15%	13.10%	13.36%	14.23%	14.91%	16.11%	17.57%	18.45%	17.83%	18.26%	18.54%
11.25	14.42%	13.32%	13.04%	13.01%	13.29%	14.16%	14.88%	16.04%	17.48%	18.35%	17.93%	18.14%	18.45%
11.50	14.32%	13.20%	12.96%	12.94%	13.23%	14.09%	14.87%	15.97%	17.39%	18.25%	18.07%	18.03%	18.37%
11.75	14.19%	13.13%	12.90%	12.86%	13.16%	14.04%	14.87%	15.90%	17.30%	18.14%	18.28%	17.93%	18.28%
12.00	14.05%	13.09%	12.87%	12.79%	13.08%	13.99%	14.89%	15.85%	17.22%	18.02%	18.55%	17.84%	18.21%
12.25	13.95%	13.11%	12.86%	12.73%	13.00%	13.95%	14.89%	15.79%	17.14%	17.90%	18.88%	17.79%	18.15%
12.50	13.85%	13.11%	12.84%	12.68%	12.91%	13.89%	14.89%	15.75%	17.05%	17.80%	19.16%	17.71%	18.08%
12.75	13.75%	13.10%	12.81%	12.61%	12.83%	13.84%	14.87%	15.70%	16.97%	17.68%	19.38%	17.65%	18.04%
13.00	13.65%	13.04%	12.76%	12.54%	12.77%	13.80%	14.85%	15.66%	16.89%	17.56%	19.54%	17.59%	17.98%
13.25	13.56%	13.03%	12.71%	12.71%	12.68%	13.75%	14.83%	15.62%	16.82%	17.43%	19.64%	17.53%	17.91%
13.50	13.47%	12.98%	12.63%	12.41%	12.61%	13.69%	14.79%	15.57%	16.75%	17.29%	19.67%	17.48%	17.85%
13.75	13.39%	12.90%	12.56%	12.34%	12.55%	13.63%	14.75%	15.52%	16.68%	17.16%	19.63%	17.43%	17.78%
14.00	13.32%	12.84%	12.48%	12.27%	12.49%	13.58%	14.69%	15.46%	16.61%	17.03%	19.52%	17.39%	17.72%
14.25	13.24%	12.75%	12.39%	12.19%	12.43%	13.53%	14.62%	15.39%	16.54%	16.91%	19.36%	17.34%	17.66%
14.50	13.17%	12.63%	12.29%	12.12%	12.37%	13.48%	14.54%	15.32%	16.48%	16.80%	19.12%	17.29%	17.61%
14.75	13.11%	12.54%	12.19%	12.04%	12.31%	13.42%	14.46%	15.25%	16.41%	16.70%	18.85%	17.23%	17.56%
15.00	13.05%	12.40%	12.08%	11.97%	12.25%	13.37%	14.36%	15.17%	16.35%	16.60%	18.50%	17.18%	17.51%
15.25	12.99%	12.28%	11.97%	11.90%	12.19%	13.31%	14.26%	15.10%	16.29%	16.51%	18.15%	17.12%	17.46%
15.50	12.94%	12.16%	11.87%	11.84%	12.14%	13.26%	14.17%	15.02%	16.23%	16.43%	17.80%	17.07%	17.42%
15.75	12.88%	12.04%	11.78%	11.78%	12.10%	13.21%	14.08%	14.96%	16.18%	16.36%	17.52%	17.02%	17.37%
16.00	12.83%	11.95%	11.70%	11.72%	12.06%	13.15%	14.00%	14.90%	16.13%	16.28%	17.26%	16.97%	17.32%
16.25	12.79%	11.88%	11.63%	11.67%	12.03%	13.10%	13.92%	14.85%	16.09%	16.20%	17.06%	16.93%	17.26%
16.50	12.75%	11.82%	11.56%	11.62%	12.00%	13.04%	13.84%	14.81%	16.05%	16.13%	16.90%	16.90%	17.22%
16.75	12.71%	11.76%	11.51%	11.58%	11.97%	12.98%	13.77%	14.78%	16.01%	16.06%	16.78%	16.88%	17.16%
17.00	12.68%	11.72%	11.47%	11.54%	11.93%	12.93%	13.70%	14.76%	15.98%	15.99%	16.69%	16.87%	17.12%
17.25	12.65%	11.70%	11.45%	11.50%	11.90%	12.88%	13.63%	14.74%	15.95%	15.93%	16.64%	16.86%	17.08%
17.50	12.62%	11.68%	11.43%	11.46%	11.86%	12.81%	13.57%	14.73%	15.92%	15.88%	16.61%	16.85%	17.04%
17.75	12.60%	11.67%	11.42%	11.43%	11.81%	12.76%	13.52%	14.72%	15.88%	15.83%	16.59%	16.84%	17.00%
18.00	12.57%	11.66%	11.40%	11.40%	11.77%	12.71%	13.47%	14.70%	15.84%	15.79%	16.58%	16.83%	16.96%
18.25	12.55%	11.65%	11.38%	11.37%	11.73%	12.65%	13.42%	14.67%	15.80%	15.75%	16.56%	16.82%	16.92%
18.50	12.53%	11.63%	11.36%	11.34%	11.69%	12.61%	13.36%	14.62%	15.75%	15.71%	16.55%	16.80%	16.89%
18.75	12.51%	11.61%	11.33%	11.30%	11.65%	12.56%	13.31%	14.57%	15.70%	15.67%	16.52%	16.78%	16.84%
19.00	12.48%	11.59%	11.30%	11.27%	11.61%	12.52%	13.26%	14.49%	15.63%	15.63%	16.49%	16.74%	16.81%
19.25	12.45%	11.56%	11.27%	11.22%	11.57%	12.49%	13.23%	14.42%	15.58%	15.59%	16.46%	16.70%	16.77%
19.50	12.42%	11.52%	11.23%	11.18%	11.51%	12.45%	13.19%	14.33%	15.51%	15.55%	16.41%	16.65%	16.73%
19.75	12.39%	11.49%	11.19%	11.13%	11.46%	12.42%	13.16%	14.23%	15.44%	15.52%	16.36%	16.60%	16.70%
20.00	12.36%	11.44%	11.15%	11.08%	11.40%	12.39%	13.12%	14.12%	15.36%	15.48%	16.31%	16.54%	16.67%
20.25	12.32%	11.40%	11.11%	11.03%	11.34%	12.36%	13.08%	14.01%	15.28%	15.44%	16.25%	16.48%	16.64%
20.50	12.29%	11.36%	11.06%	10.97%	11.29%	12.34%	13.04%	13.90%	15.21%	15.41%	16.20%	16.42%	16.60%
20.75	12.26%	11.33%	11.02%	10.93%	11.23%	12.31%	13.00%	13.81%	15.13%	15.37%	16.15%	16.37%	16.57%

Table 10.3 (*cont.*)

Strike ⇒

Maturity	1.5	1.75	2	2.25	2.5	3	3.5	4	5	6	7	8	10
21.00	16.54%	16.32%	16.11%	15.33%	15.06%	13.72%	12.96%	12.27%	11.18%	10.88%	10.98%	11.29%	12.23%
21.25	16.51%	16.28%	16.07%	15.29%	14.99%	13.65%	12.93%	12.24%	11.14%	10.84%	10.95%	11.26%	12.20%
21.50	16.47%	16.24%	16.04%	15.25%	14.94%	13.59%	12.89%	12.20%	11.10%	10.80%	10.92%	11.24%	12.18%
21.75	16.43%	16.22%	16.01%	15.21%	14.89%	13.56%	12.85%	12.17%	11.06%	10.77%	10.90%	11.22%	12.16%
22.00	16.40%	16.20%	16.00%	15.18%	14.85%	13.53%	12.81%	12.12%	11.02%	10.75%	10.88%	11.20%	12.14%
22.25	16.37%	16.19%	15.99%	15.15%	14.81%	13.51%	12.77%	12.08%	10.99%	10.73%	10.87%	11.19%	12.13%
22.50	16.33%	16.18%	15.98%	15.13%	14.78%	13.51%	12.72%	12.04%	10.96%	10.71%	10.86%	11.19%	12.12%
22.75	16.30%	16.17%	15.97%	15.11%	14.75%	13.50%	12.68%	11.99%	10.93%	10.71%	10.86%	11.19%	12.12%
23.00	16.27%	16.16%	15.97%	15.09%	14.73%	13.49%	12.63%	11.95%	10.90%	10.71%	10.87%	11.20%	12.13%
23.25	16.24%	16.16%	15.96%	15.08%	14.71%	13.48%	12.59%	11.91%	10.88%	10.71%	10.88%	11.21%	12.14%
23.50	16.21%	16.14%	15.94%	15.07%	14.69%	13.47%	12.55%	11.86%	10.87%	10.72%	10.90%	11.22%	12.15%
23.75	16.18%	16.12%	15.92%	15.06%	14.67%	13.44%	12.51%	11.82%	10.85%	10.73%	10.93%	11.25%	12.17%
24.00	16.15%	16.09%	15.89%	15.05%	14.65%	13.41%	12.47%	11.78%	10.85%	10.75%	10.96%	11.28%	12.19%
24.25	16.11%	16.05%	15.85%	15.04%	14.62%	13.37%	12.43%	11.75%	10.84%	10.77%	11.00%	11.31%	12.22%
24.50	16.09%	16.00%	15.81%	15.03%	14.59%	13.31%	12.39%	11.71%	10.83%	10.80%	11.04%	11.35%	12.25%
24.75	16.06%	15.95%	15.73%	15.02%	14.56%	13.25%	12.35%	11.68%	10.82%	10.82%	11.08%	11.40%	12.28%
25.00	16.04%	15.90%	15.72%	15.01%	14.53%	13.19%	12.31%	11.64%	10.82%	10.85%	11.13%	11.45%	12.31%
25.25	16.03%	15.87%	15.67%	15.00%	14.50%	13.12%	12.27%	11.61%	10.81%	10.88%	11.18%	11.50%	12.35%
25.50	16.01%	15.81%	15.62%	15.00%	14.47%	13.06%	12.22%	11.58%	10.80%	10.90%	11.23%	11.55%	12.38%
25.75	16.00%	15.79%	15.58%	14.99%	14.44%	13.00%	12.19%	11.55%	10.80%	10.93%	11.27%	11.60%	12.41%
26.00	15.98%	15.75%	15.54%	14.98%	14.41%	12.95%	12.16%	11.53%	10.79%	10.95%	11.31%	11.64%	12.44%
26.25	15.97%	15.72%	15.51%	14.97%	14.38%	12.90%	12.13%	11.50%	10.79%	10.97%	11.35%	11.67%	12.46%
26.50	15.95%	15.69%	15.48%	14.96%	14.36%	12.87%	12.10%	11.48%	10.78%	10.99%	11.38%	11.70%	12.49%
26.75	15.94%	15.67%	15.46%	14.95%	14.34%	12.85%	12.07%	11.45%	10.78%	11.00%	11.40%	11.73%	12.51%
27.00	15.92%	15.66%	15.44%	14.94%	14.33%	12.83%	12.04%	11.43%	10.77%	11.02%	11.43%	11.74%	12.53%
27.25	15.91%	15.65%	15.43%	14.94%	14.32%	12.82%	12.01%	11.40%	10.76%	11.03%	11.44%	11.75%	12.54%
27.50	15.90%	15.65%	15.42%	14.93%	14.30%	12.82%	11.99%	11.38%	10.76%	11.03%	11.45%	11.76%	12.55%
27.75	15.89%	15.64%	15.42%	14.92%	14.30%	12.81%	11.96%	11.36%	10.75%	11.04%	11.46%	11.77%	12.56%
28.00	15.88%	15.64%	15.42%	14.92%	14.29%	12.81%	11.94%	11.34%	10.75%	11.04%	11.46%	11.77%	12.56%
28.25	15.87%	15.64%	15.42%	14.92%	14.29%	12.81%	11.93%	11.32%	10.75%	11.05%	11.47%	11.77%	12.57%
28.50	15.86%	15.64%	15.42%	14.92%	14.29%	12.81%	11.92%	11.30%	10.75%	11.05%	11.47%	11.77%	12.57%
28.75	15.85%	15.64%	15.42%	14.92%	14.29%	12.81%	11.91%	11.29%	10.75%	11.05%	11.47%	11.77%	12.57%
29.00	15.84%	15.64%	15.42%	14.92%	14.29%	12.81%	11.90%	11.27%	10.75%	11.05%	11.47%	11.77%	12.57%
29.25	15.83%	15.64%	15.42%	14.92%	14.29%	12.81%	11.90%	11.26%	10.75%	11.05%	11.47%	11.77%	12.57%
29.50	15.82%	15.64%	15.42%	14.92%	14.29%	12.81%	11.90%	11.26%	10.75%	11.05%	11.47%	11.77%	12.57%
29.75	15.81%	15.64%	15.42%	14.92%	14.29%	12.81%	11.90%	11.25%	10.75%	11.05%	11.47%	11.77%	12.57%
30.00	15.81%	15.64%	15.42%	14.92%	14.29%	12.81%	11.90%	11.25%	10.75%	11.05%	11.47%	11.77%	12.57%

As an example: to price a floorlet on a 3 mo. forward rate (i.e. the same period as above):

Today's date:	4 February 2008
Principal amount:	$100m
Forward rate:	Start date 6 August 09
	End date 6 November 09
Strike:	3.00%
Volatility:	14.78% pa

$$d_1 = \{\ln(2.681\%/3\%) + 0.5 * 14.78\% * 14.78\% * 1.519\}/14.78\% * 1.232 = -0.526$$

$$d_2 = -0.526 - 17\% * 1.232 = -0.7080$$

$$N(-d_1) = 0.700$$

$$N(-d_2) = 0.761$$

$$Fl = \$100m * 0.952586 * \{3\% * 0.761 - 2.681\% * 0.700\} * 0.256$$

$$= \$9,820 \quad \text{or } 9.82 \text{ bp}$$

An alternative approach would be to create a portfolio consisting of:

- short a caplet;
- long a floorlet;

on the same forward rate $F(\tau, T)$, with same strike K and principal amount, and using the same volatility. The payout is proportional to $\max[0, K - L] - \max[0, L - K] = [K - L]$ where L is the Libor fixing.

Now consider a one-period forward swaplet starting at τ and finishing at T:

- to receive fixed K;
- to pay floating.

The net settlement at the end of the period is again proportional to $[K - L]$. As this is identical to the portfolio payout, today's value of the swaplet and portfolio should also be equal. This gives:

$$\text{Price of floorlet} = \text{Value of swaplet} + \text{Price of caplet}$$

As the best estimate for the Libor fixing is the implied forward rate, the value of the swaplet is $[K - F] * (T - \tau) * DF_T$. Using the same example:

$$\text{Value of swaplet} = 10,000 * [3\% - 2.681\%] * 0.256 * 0.952586 = 7.764 \text{ bp}$$

$$\text{Value of caplet} = 2.06 \text{ bp (struck at 3\%)}$$

$$\text{Value of floorlet} = 7.76 + 2.06 = 9.82 \text{ bp} \quad \text{as before.}$$

Details of the calculations are shown in Worksheet 10.11. It is divided into two parts; the first calculates caplet prices and subsequently floorlet prices using the above put–call parity expression, whilst the second calculates floorlet prices followed by caplet prices. The columns are the same as before, with the introduction of column [15] which contains the new pricing.

A full relationship between caps, floors and forward swaps may be derived in an exactly analogous fashion. The value of a forward swap to receive a fixed rate K is given by:

$$\text{Value} = K * (Q_e - Q_s) - (\text{DF}_s - \text{DF}_e)$$

for a notional principal of 1. Thus, for the above example:

Start date:	6 May 2008	$\text{DF}_s = 0.992199$
End date:	7 February 2011	$\text{DF}_e = 0.912764$
		$Q_e - Q_s = 2.660$
Value of swap	=	$10{,}000 * \{3\% * 2.660 - (0.992199 - 0.912764)\} = 3.52\,\text{bp}$
Value of cap	=	$69.25\,\text{bp}$
Value of floor	=	$69.25 + 3.52 = 72.77\,\text{bp}$

The floor market is often less liquid than the cap and swap markets, and these relationships are widely used to act as an arbitrage check between the markets.

Many borrowers buy caps as protection against rising interest rates. The example cap above was struck at 3% at a cost of 69 bp, and the graph shows the constant strike compared with the forward rate curve. Is the cap providing good protection? At the short end, interest rates could rise by 50 bp before the appropriate caplets came into the money. So the protection is not very tight.

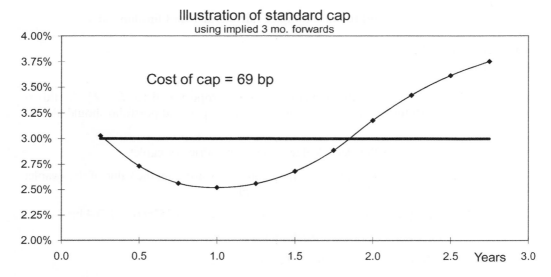

Illustration of standard cap
using implied 3 mo. forwards

Cost of cap = 69 bp

An alternative structure is a "curve cap", in which the strike is set to be a constant spread to the forward curve. Setting the strike spread to -8.75 bp, namely just below the forward curve, the cost of the curve cap:

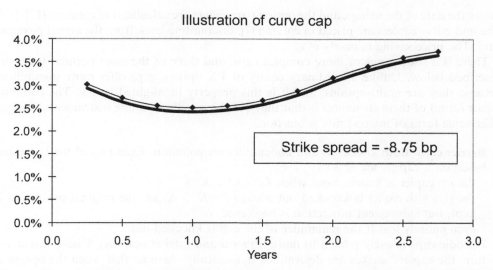

is exactly the same as the original cap (see Worksheet 10.12 for precise details). Each caplet is in the money but to the same absolute amount. Naturally, in this case, the smile effect has to be included in the pricing—if a constant par volatility of 14.8% was used, then the spread would only be −9.5 bp. One might argue that a traditional cap is for a borrower that cannot afford to pay above a certain level; a curve cap is for somebody that wants an insurance policy against rates rising but is content to pay if the actual fixings follow the forward curve. Another interesting extension to the vanilla cap is the "mid-curve" cap. Using the same notation as before, the payout of a caplet was defined as proportional to $\max[0, L - K]$ where L is the fixing of the forward rate $F(\tau, T)$. Modifying the notation for the forward rate to $F(t, \tau, T)$ where $t \leq \tau$ is the observation time, obviously $F(\tau, \tau, T)$ equals the actual fixing L, but when $t < \tau$, then $F(t, \tau, T)$ is an observation of a forward rate. Consider now a call option of maturity t on $F(t, \tau, T)$, i.e. where the payout is proportional to $\max[0, F(t, \tau, T) - K]$. Thus, comparing this option with a conventional caplet, the payout is based on a forward rate instead of a spot rate. The maturity of the mid-curve option is less, and therefore likely to be cheaper. However, it is also riskier because the forward rate at maturity may not be an accurate estimate of the spot rate at the fixing. Like many things, it's a trade-off.

Worksheet 10.13 shows the details. It prices both the conventional cap for 75 bp and a mid-curve cap. This latter has been defined as follows:

- total maturity of 3 year;
- conventional caplets in year 1;
- caplets in year 2 are based upon $F(1, \tau, T)$ where $\tau = 1$, 1.25, 1.5 and 1.75;
- caplets in year 3 are based upon $F(2, \tau, T)$ where $\tau = 2$, 2.25, 2.5 and 2.75;
- the payout for each option matches the conventional cap, i.e. at time T as before.

The time of payout needs to be defined; the usual choices are either as above or all made at the maturity of the options, as soon as the forward rates are fixed. From a bank's perspective, the latter is probably more acceptable as it would obviously reduce credit exposure; it is the same argument as for discounting a FRA. From an end-user's point of view, the former would match the timings of physical interest payments. Column [16] shows the date of the fixings, and the option parameters are calculated in columns [17]–[19]. The mid-curve caplets are priced in column [7], discounting back from the actual payment date. The price saving is nearly 6%.

There is a wide range of more complex caps, and three of the most popular types are described below. Unlike an ordinary equity or FX option, caps offer more possibilities because they are multi-options, and it is this property highlighted below. The common factor for all of these structures is that they are cheaper than vanilla instruments, and yet offer some form of interest rate protection.

1. Barrier caps. Both knock-ins and knock-outs are common. Examples of the latter are, based on a cap struck at K:
   ○ the ith caplet is knocked out when $L_i > K' > K$;
   ○ the $(i + 1)$th caplet is knocked out when $L_i > K' > K$, i.e. the original protection is kept, but subsequent protection is weakened; or
   ○ even entirely lost if the remainder of the cap is knocked out.
2. Periodic caps (closely related to multi-forward and ratchet options). Under this structure, the caplets' strikes are determined dynamically. Assume that when the option is entered into, the strike of the first caplet (K_1) is set to the current forward rate $F_1 + m$. If m is positive, which is most common, then the caplet is OTM and hence relatively cheap. The fixing of the floating rate is latterly observed (L_1) and the payout $= \max[0, L_1 - K_1]$. The strike of the second caplet (K_2) is simultaneously set to $L_1 + m$, again ensuring that it is OTM, and so on. The structure protects against spikes in the floating rate, but not against small movements.
3. Chooser caps. Consider a 3-year cap on 3 mo. Libor; this will consist of 11 caplets. Examples of a "5 chooser cap" would be:
   ○ you can choose which 5 out of the 11 original caplets to exercise, but only before or on the fixing date, i.e. no lookback;
   ○ you can choose to exercise a contiguous strip of 5 caplets;
   ○ the first 5 caplets that are ITM are automatically exercised.

Numerical models are really required to price these types of structures, although in practice variants of the Black model are frequently used.

When obtaining protection through the purchase of a cap, a common strategy to reduce the overall cost is to sell a floor at a lower strike. The impact of this is shown below:

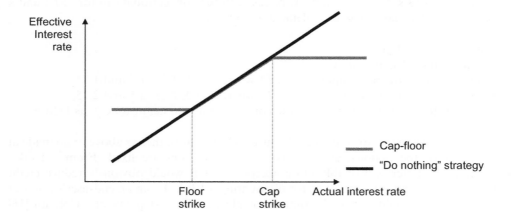

The strategy is often called a "collar" or cylinder" because the effective interest rate to be paid by a borrower is constrained to lie between the upper cap strike and the lower floor strike. The overall cost of the strategy depends upon the relative cost of the cap and floor, which in turn depends upon the positioning of the two strikes. Remember the basic sensitivity results:

- cost of cap *decreases* as the strike increases;
- cost of floor *increases* as the strike increases.

The usual approach to locating the strikes is first to set the cap strike, say at 3.5%. This gives a 3-year cap cost, as we have seen, of 34.8 bp on a par volatility of 15.59%. Second to decide upon the maximum overall cost that you wish to pay, say 20 bp. Therefore the floor must have a price of 14.8 bp which implies a strike of 2.425% on a par volatility of 16.13% (see Worksheet 10.14).

The borrower has bought the cap and sold the floor back to the bank. It would be unusual for the bank to buy the floor back on the same volatility; normally the bid (or ask) volatility would be used. If we assume a 1% spread, then the example would use 15.59% for the cap but only (15.98% − 1%) for the floor. As expected, the floor would be struck at a higher strike of 2.463% implying that the borrower would be paying a higher effective interest rate if the floating rate dropped.

Zero-cost collars are particularly popular as they involve no upfront payments at all. In this case, still using the 1% bid–offer spread, the floor would be struck at 2.723% on a volatility of 14.36%.

An alternative structure to collars is "participations", which are constructed by adjusting the amounts of the cap and floor. For example, assume the zero-cost collar above was based on a constant principal amount of \$100m. Instead of buying the floor struck at 2.723%, suppose it was struck at (say) 3%, hence increasing its value from 34.8 bp to 70 bp. The collar is no longer zero-cost. However, by only selling \$100m * (34.8 bp/70 bp) = \$50m, the overall structure is again zero-cost. The net effect is that there is full protection still against interest rates rising above 3.5%, the borrower would gain if interest rates fell between 3.5% and 3%, and would also gain on 50% of the borrowing if rates fall below 3%. Introducing the idea of participations (see Worksheet 10.15) increases the flexibility of these structures considerably, and there are many varieties:

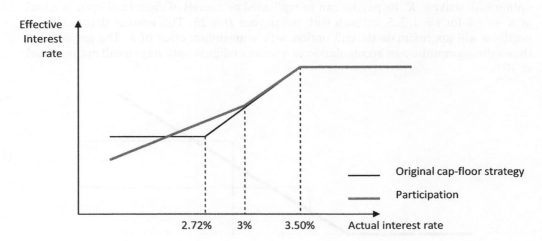

10.6 DIGITAL OPTIONS

Digital or binary caps are very fundamental structures, and are often embedded in more complex products. The payout from a digicaplet is simply $D * (T - \tau) * P$ if $L \geq K$ and zero otherwise, where D is some predetermined constant usually quoted as a percentage or in basis points, as shown below:

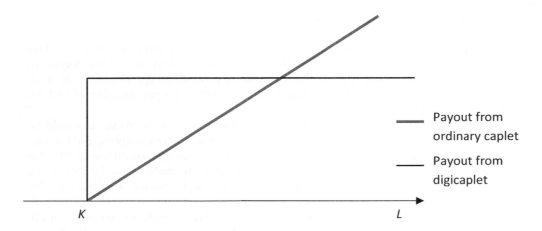

Payout from ordinary caplet

Payout from digicaplet

Using a Black model to price such an option is straightforward, that is (see Worksheet 10.16):

$$DC = DF_T * D * (T - \tau) * P * N(d_2)$$

This formula may be interpreted as "discounted constant payout" × "probability of being in the money at maturity". Digicaplets are usually cheaper than the equivalent ordinary caplet because the payout is limited; the exception arises when the option is close to ATM and has relatively low volatility.

Digital options may be regarded as fundamental building blocks, and in theory can be used to replicate ordinary options, or of course vice versa. They can also be used to price a European option with a complex payout strategy. For example, consider an ordinary call option with strike $= K$. Its payout can be replicated by a series of digital call options struck at $K + i * h$ for $i = 1, 3, 5, \ldots$ each with the payout $D = 2h$. This ensures that the digital portfolio will approximate the call option with a maximum error of h. The graph below shows the asymptotic cost accumulation of a series of digital options to a call option struck at 100:

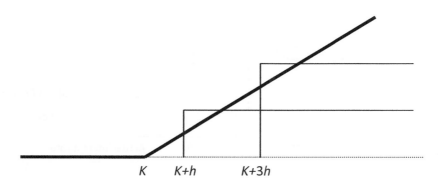

K $K+h$ $K+3h$

Hedging a single digital option can be difficult, due to the discontinuous nature of its payout, which is likely to be far less evident in a portfolio. Probably the most popular method for hedging (say) a sold digicap struck at K with payout D would be to buy N ordinary caps with strike $K - h$ and to sell N caps struck at $K + h$. The parameters would be determined by $D = 2Nh$: for example, if $K = 100$ and $D = 10$, then five caps would have to be bought and sold if $h = 1$:

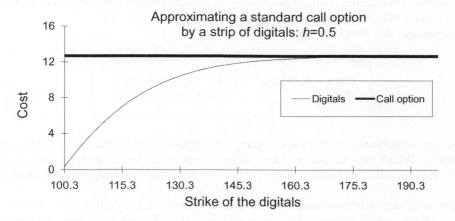

10.7 EMBEDDED STRUCTURES

Many structures are provided with embedded options. For example, many investors during the 1980s entered into pension arrangements with Equitable Life, a large UK insurance company. At maturity these pension schemes delivered annuities with guaranteed minimum levels; in essence the company had provided the investors with a floor. When these pensions were being sold, the floor was considerably OTM and was effectively ignored by the company. Unfortunately interest rates declined significantly during the 1990s and the floor became a long way ITM. The company had apparently paid no attention to the impact of declining rates until 1999; after a subsequent investigation, it was declared effectively insolvent!

It is obviously important to be able to price and to replicate such structures correctly. In this section we will discuss a number of structures, in particular bringing together swaps and options; in Chapter 11, we will consider more complex embedded structures. As the background, we will assume a company is raising $100m for 3 years at 3 mo. Libor flat. The company then wishes to enter into various structures to manage the interest rate risk.

For example, the company could buy a cap struck at 4% for 18 bp. As Worksheet 10.19 shows, spreading this cost over 3 years results in a margin of 6.2 bp; that is:

Libor + 6.2 bp	for Libor $\leq 4\%$
4.062%	for Libor $> 4\%$

This strategy is a common option on many retail mortgages, namely to buy a separate option over and above the mortgage.

Suppose however the company wishes to place a cap on the total interest rate payable of 4%, including the cost of the cap. In other words, Cap strike + Margin = 4%. The calculation is not so simple as the margin is obviously a function of the strike, and so an iterative method has to be used. The final cap is struck at 3.932% which costs 19.7 bp or 6.777 bp pa, and therefore the sum is equal to 4%.

One practical issue that must be taken into consideration: a conventional cap does not include the first fixing as discussed above, whereas almost invariably embedded constraints will apply across all fixings. In this case, the first fixing was 3.145%, i.e. below the cap strike, so the initial caplet is out of the money. In general there would be an additional cost of $DF_1 * \max\{F(\tau_1, T_1) - K, 0\} * (T_1 - \tau_1)$ to be included.

In summary, this structure would be:

Libor + 6.777 bp	for Libor $\leq$ 3.932%
4%	for Libor > 3.932%

This second structure is costing the company an additional 0.5 bp but limits the maximum rate to 4%. Which structure is preferred depends upon its view of interest rates over the next 3 years and the likely impact on the performance of the company (see Worksheet 10.20).

Swaps are frequently provided with embedded options on the floating side. In this case, the cost of the option is invariably integrated into the effective fixed rate. For example, consider a generic 3-year swap to receive the fixed rate annually and pay 3 mo. Libor; the current rate is 3.035% ANN. We wish to cap the Libor at 3.5%; the option price should be reflected in the fixed rate which of course should be lowered.

Looking at Worksheet 10.21, the cost of the cap is 34.4 bp. Spreading this out over 3 years:

$$34.4 \, \text{bp}/Q_3 = 132/2.87 = 12.00 \, \text{bp}$$

or this margin can be estimated by constructing the cashflows. Therefore the new rate is 3.035% − 12 bp = 2.915%.

Let's now turn the swap around the other way, and receive Libor subject to a floor at 3.5%. The same approach can be employed, but there is one additional complication. The first fixing of Libor was 3.145%, i.e. below the floor. The total cost of the floor is:

Cost of conventional floor @ 3.5%		= 170.87 bp
Cost of first fix	$(3.5\% - 3.145\%) * (6 \, \text{May–6 Feb})/360 * DF_{3\,\text{month}}$ =	8.81 bp

The adjustment to the fixed side is 179.68 bp/2.87 = 62.5 bp which of course in this case has to be added to the fixed rate as the floating rate receiver/fixed rate payer is benefiting from the option.

At the time of writing, due to the current credit crisis interest rates have come off. For a more complex example, assume that the company issues a reverse floating rate note to raise money; this strategy is attractive to investors who anticipate rates declining further. The coupon is set at 12% − 3.08 * 3 mo. Libor and is subject to a non-negativity constraint. The company has a funding target of 25 bp below Libor, and to achieve this it is prepared to consider inserting a cap on the coupon of the note:

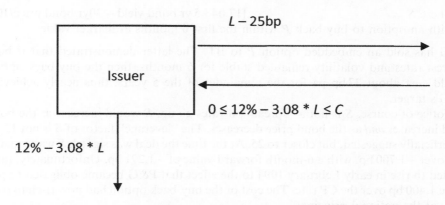

The objective therefore is to calculate the level of floor such that the swap has an overall value of zero, taking into account the embedded options. Looking at Worksheet 10.22, we can see that the swap, with zero sub-Libor margin and ignoring the options, has a current value of $-\$700,866$ from the point of view of the issuer. The fair breakeven margin is only 24 bp below Libor, so to achieve 25 bp below Libor is worth $26,039 to the issuer. The non-negativity constraint is equivalent to a cap being struck at $(12\%/3.08) = 3.896\%$; the value of this cap is $206,309 which benefits the issuer. Therefore the swap counterparty would demand compensation worth $26,039 + 206,309 = 232,348$. Placing a cap on the coupon struck at C is equivalent to the counterparty benefiting from a floor struck at $(12\% - C)/3.08$. As Worksheet 10.22 demonstrates, the breakeven value for C is 4.095%, giving a floor strike of 2.566% and an overall value of $232,348.

The key to pricing these structures is always to ask "who benefits?". Starting with the basic fair swap to receive $\{12\% - 3.08 * L\}$ and to pay $\{L - 24\,\text{bp}\}$ first add the cap. This benefits the issuer, and therefore the counterparty wishes to receive a higher cashflow. Then add the floor, this benefits the counterparty and hence the issuer will pay a lower cashflow.

There are a wide variety of embedded option structures. These became increasingly popular in the early 1990s, when interest rates were declining, and investors started to chase yield more and more. For example, the notorious swap executed between Procter & Gamble and Bankers Trust was an extreme example as discussed in the box below. More complex structures are discussed in Chapter 11.

Procter & Gamble Swap

The date is early November 1993. P&G wished to replace a maturing swap that achieved CP − 40 bp. Obviously, to repeat this rate would require assuming some risk, and they were prepared to gamble on USD interest rates remaining relatively constant over the next 6 months.

They entered into a 5-year swap with Bankers Trust:

- notional principal: $200m
- to receive: 5.30%
- to pay for first 6 months: daily average 30-day CP − 75 bp
- to pay for remaining 4.5 years: daily average 30-day CP − 75 bp + P
- where P was defined as: $\max\{0, S\}$ and

- where $S =$ [17.04 * 5 yr bond yield − 30yr bond price/100]
- with an option to buy back P within the first 6 months at market value.

P&G has sold an embedded option P to BT. The latter demonstrated that if both interest rates and volatility remained stable for 6 months, then the buy-back option would cost about 37 bp pa for the remainder of the 5 years, thus nearly achieving P&G's target.

Notice of course, S is not a "spread"; if rates go up, S would increase as the bond yield increases *and* as the bond price decreases. The "leverage" factor of S is not 17, as superficially suggested, but closer to 25. At the time the deal was signed, S was equal to just over −1,700 bp, with a 6-month forward value of −1,271 bp. Unfortunately, rates started to rise in early February 1994 to the effect that P&G became obligated to pay some 1,400 bp over the CP rate. The cost of the buy-back option had now risen to over 90% of the notional principal.

10.8 SWAPTIONS

A swaption is a single option on a forward swap. Some terminology:

Receiver's:	Forward swap to receive fixed, pay floating
Payer's:	Forward swap to pay fixed, receive floating

The notation generally used to characterize swaptions is {Length of option/Length of swap}. For example, 5/2 payer's is a 5-year option on a 2-year swap to pay fixed.

How does a swaption compare in terms of risk management control with a cap? Consider our company that is paying 3mo. Libor on its debt: it buys a payer's. If it exercises the single option, it will be receiving Libor quarterly and paying a fixed rate which is effectively an average of the implied forward rates. Obviously if Libor decreases after exercise then the company cannot benefit. As we may see below, it is typically cheaper but provides less protection.

Comparison between:	Cost
1 yr vanilla forward cap	27.3 bp
1/1 payer's swaption	24.4 bp

- out of 6 Feb 08
- on 3 mo. Libor from 6 Feb 09 to 8 Feb 10
- strike = 2.5%, vol off the forward vol surface
- the cap is most expensive, but has four exercise dates
- the swaption is a single option on the same exercise date
- average forward vol over the 1 year = 15%

European swaptions are usually priced using a Black model, just like caps and floors, which introduces some interesting issues. Consider a payer's swaption with strike K: let the value of the fixed and floating sides at maturity of the option be V_K and V_L, respectively. The payoff is $\max[0, V_L - V_K]$. As interest rates move during the lifetime of the option, both V_L and V_K change. Therefore the payoff is not in the usual form for a Black model, namely a stochastic underlying compared with a fixed strike, and spread option models such as Margrabe have been advocated by some practitioners[14]—see box below.

Margrabe spread option model:

$$\text{Payer's} = V_{0L} * N(d_1) - V_{0K} * N(d_2)$$

where V_{0L} is the PV of the floating side
   V_{0K} is the PV of the strike side
   $d_1 = [\ln(V_{0L}/V_{0K}) + \frac{1}{2} * \sigma^2 . t / (\sigma . \sqrt{t})$, etc.
   $\sigma^2 = (\sigma_L)^2 + (\sigma_K)^2 - 2 . \sigma_L . \sigma_K . \rho_{LK}$ and
σ_L and σ_K are the vols of the value of the floating and fixed sides, respectively, and
   ρ_{LK} the correlation between the two sides

However, we can manipulate the Black formula if we rewrite the future values as:

$$V_K = K * (Q_e - Q_s) / \text{DF}_s$$
$$V_L = (\text{DF}_s - \text{DF}_e) / \text{DF}_s$$

for a principal P equal to 1, and ensuring of course that the Q-factors are calculated using the correct frequency of cashflows. We know that the generic forward swap rate $F_{s,e}$ can be estimated using market rates:

$$F_{s,e} = (\text{DF}_s - \text{DF}_e) / (Q_e - Q_s)$$

Substituting into the payoff, we get:

$$\max[0, F_{s,e} - K] * (Q_e - Q_s) / \text{DF}_s$$

which gives a Black swaption-pricing model for a payer's:

$$\text{Payer's} = [F_{s,e} * N(d_1) - K * N(d_2)] * (Q_e - Q_s)$$

where d_1 and d_2 are defined in the usual way, and the volatility refers to the forward swap rate. The apparent assumption, as in the cap model, is that the estimation F is stochastic whereas the discounting process is not, but this is resolved as discussed above. Indeed, as a one-period swaption is a caplet, it would be surprising if the assumptions were not consistent.

Having said that, there is one inconsistency between the cap and swaption markets, namely:

- a cap model assumes forward interest rates are log-normally distributed;
- a swaption model assumes forward swap rates are log-normally distributed;
- a forward swap is a (approximately linear) function of forward interest rates.

---

[14] Tompkins, ibid., pp. 455–6.

The statements are together logically inconsistent; nevertheless the financial markets invariably price both caps and swaptions using Black models! This point will be discussed in more depth later in this section.

Worksheet 10.23 demonstrates the pricing of a range of payer's swaptions struck at 2.5%. The sheet is constructed to calculate 5-year sa forward swap rates every 3 months. Using the discount factors (column [1]) constructed from market data, first the appropriate Q-factors are calculated ([2]) and then the forward swap rates ([3]). For example:

		DF	Q	Forward
Start date:	08-Feb-10	0.945458	1.467199	4.33770%
End date:	06-Feb-15	0.759411	5.756264	

For a given volatility, d_1, $N(d_1)$ and $N(d_2)$ are calculated in columns [7]–[9]. The prices of the payer's are expressed in bp; the fair price for the 2/5 payer's is 788 bp as shown in column [4]. Notice that the price curve is rising with time; this is due both to increasing time value and also the rising forward swap curve which would of course be received.

The required volatility is that of the forward swap rate. Table 10.4 shows the ATM volatility surface for the euro on 6 February 2008; the length of the option is on the vertical axis, and the length of the underlying swap on the horizontal.

Given that far forward rates are generally less volatile than near rates, and that long rates are also less volatile than short rates, we would expect swaption volatility to decline with both increasing option maturity and increasing swap maturity, as demonstrated in the table. Smiles can also be observed in the swaptions market as well. Table 10.5 shows the moneyness smile for selected swaptions, based upon the ATM table (Table 10.4). Unlike cap volatilities, we need to interpolate swaption volatilities across a three-dimensional space.

Caps are options on forward interest rates, swaptions are options on forward swap rates. As a forward swap can be expressed as a function of forward interest rates, there should be at least a theoretical relationship between the two markets. As the cap market is usually considerably more liquid than the swaption market, it may make practical sense to imply swaption volatilities (albeit approximately) from the caplet vols. If $y = f(x_1, x_2, \ldots)$ where $f(\ )$ is a known function, and $\mathbf{x}$ is a stochastic vector, then

$$v_y \approx \sum_{i,j} \sum (\partial y / \partial x_i) \cdot (\partial y / \partial x_i) \cdot s_i \cdot s_j \cdot \rho_{i,j}$$

where v_y is the variance of y; s are the standard deviations; and $\rho_{i,j}$ is the correlation between x_i and x_j. Using the approximation: for a variable z, $v_z = E\{z\}^2 \cdot [\exp(\sigma_z^2 \cdot t) - 1] \approx E\{z\}^2 \cdot \sigma_z^2 \cdot t$, where σ_z is its volatility, swaption volatility can be estimated from the forward interest rate volatility.

We know that a forward swap rate $F_{s,e}$ may be expressed as:

$$F_{s,e} = (\text{DF}_s - \text{DF}_e)/(Q_e - Q_s) = \sum_{s+1}^{e} f_j * d_j * \text{DF}_j/(Q_e - Q_s) = \sum w_j * f_j$$

where, of course, w_j is itself a function of the forward rates f_j. The sensitivity with respect to

Table 10.4 ATM volatility surface for the Euro on 6 February 2008

Term	Tenor													
	1 yr	2 yr	3 yr	4 yr	5 yr	6 yr	7 yr	8 yr	9 yr	10 yr	15 yr	20 yr	25 yr	30 yr
1 mo.	13.9%	14.4%	14.7%	14.7%	14.7%	14.7%	14.4%	14.1%	14.1%	13.7%	13.1%	12.5%	12.0%	11.4%
2 mo.	13.8%	14.4%	14.8%	14.9%	15.0%	15.0%	14.6%	14.3%	14.3%	13.9%	13.3%	12.5%	12.0%	11.5%
3 mo.	14.1%	14.6%	15.0%	15.2%	15.1%	15.1%	14.8%	14.5%	14.5%	14.3%	13.7%	12.8%	12.3%	11.7%
6 mo.	14.8%	15.2%	15.2%	15.2%	15.1%	15.1%	14.8%	14.6%	14.6%	14.3%	13.8%	12.9%	12.4%	11.8%
9 mo.	15.4%	15.4%	15.4%	15.3%	15.1%	15.1%	14.8%	14.6%	14.6%	14.3%	13.8%	13.0%	12.5%	12.0%
1 yr	15.6%	15.6%	15.5%	15.3%	15.0%	15.0%	14.8%	14.6%	14.6%	14.3%	13.9%	13.1%	12.6%	12.1%
18 mo.	15.7%	15.6%	15.4%	15.3%	15.0%	15.0%	14.8%	14.5%	14.5%	14.2%	13.9%	13.1%	12.6%	12.2%
2 yr	16.0%	15.7%	15.5%	15.1%	15.0%	14.7%	14.5%	14.5%	14.3%	14.0%	13.8%	13.0%	12.6%	12.1%
3 yr	15.9%	15.7%	15.4%	15.2%	14.7%	14.5%	14.2%	13.9%	13.9%	13.7%	13.6%	12.9%	12.5%	12.0%
4 yr	15.7%	15.4%	15.0%	14.8%	14.4%	14.2%	13.8%	13.6%	13.4%	13.4%	13.4%	12.7%	12.2%	11.8%
5 yr	15.4%	15.1%	14.8%	14.4%	14.1%	13.8%	13.1%	12.9%	12.8%	12.8%	13.1%	12.4%	12.0%	11.6%
7 yr	14.4%	14.1%	13.9%	13.5%	13.2%	13.1%	12.2%	12.1%	12.0%	12.0%	12.5%	11.9%	11.5%	11.1%
10 yr	13.2%	12.9%	12.7%	12.5%	12.3%	12.2%	11.3%	11.3%	11.3%	11.2%	11.9%	11.3%	10.9%	10.4%
15 yr	11.9%	11.8%	11.7%	11.6%	11.4%	11.4%	10.7%	10.7%	10.7%	10.7%	11.2%	10.6%	10.3%	9.8%
20 yr	11.4%	11.2%	11.1%	11.0%	10.8%	10.8%	10.5%	10.5%	10.4%	10.4%	10.7%	10.2%	9.7%	9.4%
25 yr	11.0%	10.8%	10.7%	10.6%	10.4%	10.4%	10.3%	10.3%	10.4%	10.4%	10.4%	9.8%	9.5%	9.4%
30 yr	11.1%	10.8%	10.7%	10.5%	10.3%	10.3%	10.3%	10.3%	10.2%	10.2%	10.2%	9.6%	9.4%	9.3%

Table 10.5   Moneyness smile for selected swaptions

Term	Tenor	Strike price	ATM vol	−200	−100	−50	−25	0	25	50	100	200
3 mo.	2 yr	3.9951	14.60%	20.55%	16.64%	15.33%	14.88%	14.60%	14.48%	14.50%	14.88%	16.18%
3 mo.	5 yr	4.0201	15.10%	21.29%	17.22%	15.86%	15.39%	15.10%	14.97%	15.00%	15.38%	16.71%
3 mo.	10 yr	4.2658	13.70%	19.98%	15.76%	14.40%	13.96%	13.70%	13.62%	13.69%	14.14%	15.57%
3 mo.	20 yr.	4.3476	12.30%	19.22%	14.56%	13.06%	12.58%	12.30%	12.21%	12.29%	12.78%	14.29%
3 mo.	30 yr	4.3247	11.70%	19.17%	14.12%	12.52%	12.00%	11.70%	11.61%	11.69%	12.22%	13.81%
1 yr	2 yr	4.0507	15.60%	20.68%	17.32%	16.22%	15.85%	15.60%	15.47%	15.44%	15.65%	16.58%
1 yr	5 yr	4.0618	15.00%	20.40%	16.82%	15.66%	15.26%	15.00%	14.87%	14.85%	15.08%	16.08%
1 yr	10 yr	4.0604	13.90%	19.45%	15.71%	14.53%	14.14%	13.90%	13.80%	13.81%	14.12%	15.23%
1 yr	20 yr	4.2136	12.60%	18.73%	14.58%	13.29%	12.86%	12.60%	12.49%	12.51%	12.84%	14.01%
1 yr	30 yr	4.2795	12.10%	18.73%	14.23%	12.83%	12.38%	12.10%	11.98%	12.01%	12.37%	13.60%
5 yr	2 yr	4.1665	15.10%	19.87%	16.76%	15.75%	15.38%	15.10%	14.90%	14.79%	14.75%	15.16%
5 yr	5 yr	4.0162	14.10%	18.76%	15.68%	14.71%	14.36%	14.10%	13.92%	13.82%	13.81%	14.26%
5 yr	10 yr	4.2077	13.10%	18.13%	14.82%	13.76%	13.38%	13.10%	12.91%	12.80%	12.79%	13.27%
5 yr	20 yr	4.2779	12.00%	17.60%	13.90%	12.73%	12.31%	12.00%	11.80%	11.69%	11.71%	12.28%
5 yr	30 yr	4.3470	11.60%	17.62%	13.62%	12.37%	11.92%	11.60%	11.39%	11.29%	11.34%	11.98%
10 yr	2 yr	4.4552	12.90%	17.42%	14.44%	13.51%	13.17%	12.90%	12.71%	12.58%	12.48%	12.72%
10 yr	5 yr	4.4765	12.30%	17.00%	13.89%	12.92%	12.57%	12.30%	12.11%	11.98%	11.91%	12.19%
10 yr	10 yr	4.4759	11.90%	16.84%	13.56%	12.55%	12.18%	11.90%	11.70%	11.57%	11.49%	11.79%
10 yr	20 yr	4.5098	10.90%	16.26%	12.68%	11.59%	11.20%	10.90%	10.69%	10.57%	10.51%	10.87%
10 yr	30 yr	4.5098	10.40%	15.97%	12.23%	11.10%	10.70%	10.40%	10.20%	10.08%	10.04%	10.45%

a forward rate f_j for $s < j \le e$ is given by[15]:

$$\partial F_{s,e}/\partial f_j = [d_j/(1 + d_j \cdot f_j)] * \{DF_e + F_{s,e} \cdot (Q_e - Q_{j-1})\}/(Q_e - Q_s)$$

Details of the calculations are shown in Worksheet 10.26. The worksheet calculates the discount curve, sa Q-factors and a set of 5 yr sa forward swap rates. The calculations for a single swap, in this case a 5/10 swap, are highlighted in *italics*, and sensitivities to the 10 forward interest rates are calculated in column [2]. Assuming a volatility curve (column [1]), the standard deviation and hence volatility of the swap are given in column [3].

The volatility has been calculated with different correlation matrices between the forward rates. As expected, with perfect correlation, swaption volatility is, to all intents, the same as the flat forward rate volatility curve. As the correlation reduces, the swaption volatility reduces as well. Instead of continually re-calculating a full correlation matrix, a common assumption is to assume a "ridge" structure such as $\rho_{i,j} = \exp[-\lambda \cdot |i - j|]$ where i and j are the times to the fixings of f_i and f_j, respectively, and $\lambda > 0$ dictates the speed at which the correlation drops off.[16] The impact is shown in the graph below: a typical value for λ would be about 30%.

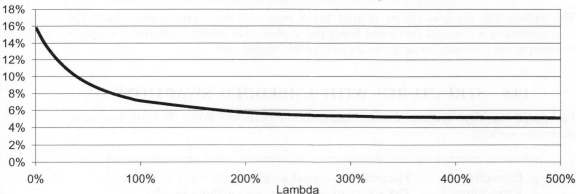

In practice, this approach is adequate to provide an indication of where the swaption volatility should be, but the swaption market has its own characteristics as distinct from the cap market. Relying on this relationship for pricing, and more for risk management, would introduce considerable basis risk.[17] This relationship is frequently used to imply correlation, and thus to calibrate IR simulations. This will be discussed in more detail in Chapter 11.

A receiver's swaption, namely to receive fixed and to pay floating, is equivalent to a floor and may be priced in a similar fashion either using a Black model directly:

$$\text{Receiver's} = [K * N(-d_2) - F_{s,e} * N(-d_1)] * (Q_e - Q_s)$$

or by using a call–put parity argument. Consider a portfolio:

$$+\text{Receiver's} - \text{Payer's} = \max[0, V_K - V_L] - \max[0, V_L - V_K] = V_K - V_L$$

---

[15] See R. Rebonato, *Modern Pricing of IR Derivatives*, 2002, eq. (CS10.3.4) for the same result. He also shows that, for flat forward curves, the complexity of the sensitivity expression is considerably reduced.

[16] This will be discussed in more detail in Chapter 11.

[17] As various banks have found to their cost.

i.e. equivalent to a forward swap to receive fixed, pay floating. Therefore

$$R = P + (K - F) * (Q_e - Q_s)$$

For example, the 2/5 receiver's swaption would be priced at:

$$788.68\,\text{bp} + 10{,}000 * (2.5\% - 4.3377\%) * (5.756 - 1.467) = 0.48\,\text{bp}$$

This result is of course replicated using the Black model, as shown in Worksheet 10.23.

The above discussion has implied that, when a swaption is exercised, a swap is delivered on the exercise date. It is feasible to get cash-settled swaptions, under which the cash value of the underlying swap is paid to the option purchaser. However, the valuation convention is slightly different. Normal swap valuation is done off a discount curve, which itself is constructed from the swap curve in some fashion. However, if the 2/5 swaption above was cash-settled, then at maturity the current 5-year rate S_5 is noted:

• the cashflows on the fixed side of the swap, including the notional principal amounts at the start and end, are constructed;
• these cashflows are discounted using S_5 only, treating it as if it were a bond yield; and
• the swap value calculated.

The reason for the convention is that there may well be disagreement about the construction of a discount curve and hence the implied cash amount, whereas the option counterparties are likely to agree on S_5 as a visible traded rate.

10.9 STRUCTURES WITH EMBEDDED SWAPTIONS

Embedded swaptions are less common than embedded caps and floors. Nevertheless, some structures such as:

Extendibles	The ability to extend a swap at the same fixed rate
Retractables	The ability to cancel the swap without penalty

without any lump-sum payments are readily available. For example, we wish to price an extendible swap (see Worksheet 10.27):

• 3-year sa swap;
• to pay fixed;
• extendible to 5 years at the option of the payer
  ○ current 3-year rate: 3.012%
  ○ 2-year forward swap rate: 4.235%

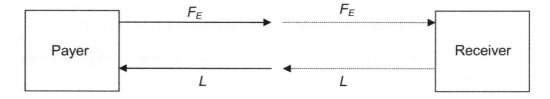

The payer of the fixed rate has effectively bought a 3/2 payer's swaption. The premium is included in the fixed rate $F_E = 3.012\% + m$, where m is a margin such that $\text{PV}(m)$ over the first 3 years is equal to the premium. Note that the premium is spread over only 3 years, as those payments are certain to be made, and not over 5 years. The rate has to be calculated iteratively, and a good starting point is the current 3-year rate:

Iteration	1	2	3	4	5	6	7	8	9
Strike (%)	3.012	3.784	3.434	3.578	3.515	3.542	3.530	3.536	3.533
Swaption (bp)	224	122	164	146	154	150	152	151.0	151.4
Margin (bp pa)	77.2	42.3	56.6	50.4	53.0	51.9	52.4	52.1	52.25

The fair rate for the payer's extendible is 3.534%, 52 bp above the generic swap rate.

A retractable would be priced in a similar fashion. For example, consider a 5-year swap, retractable to 3 years at the option of the payer:

Current 5-year rate: 3.474%

Again the quoted price F_R must equal $3.474\% + m_1$: this swap is also priced in the worksheet. The two rates, F_E and F_R, are of course identical (off the same volatility) because the two swaps have the same economic effect. There is therefore a potential arbitrage to be monitored.

One of the earliest uses for swaptions was to assist in the swapping of callable bonds. Consider a 5-year bond that has a single call date in 3 years' time. Remember that the issuer has the right to call, and is likely to exercise this right if rates decrease over the 3 years, and therefore has to pay a higher coupon to the investors. The issuer wishes to swap the bond into floating, as shown:

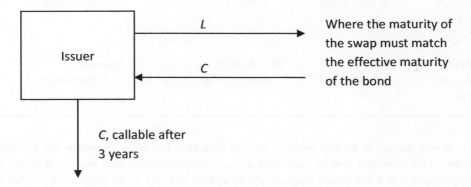

The naive approach is for the issuer to purchase a 3/2 swaption. This may be done in two ways:

(a) enter into a 3-year receiver's swap plus a 3/2 receiver's swaption;
(b) enter into a 5-year receiver's swap plus a 3/2 payer's swaption.

One problem with either structure is that the issuer has effectively to pay two option premia, one to the investor for the call, and one to the swaption counterparty for the option. Another problem is that, whilst either structure will achieve the issuer's objective, neither makes economic sense. Consider the two scenarios:

	Action on bond	Action on swaption (a)	Action on swaption (b)
Interest rates go up	No call —5-year bond	No exercise —3-year swap	Exercise —3-year swap
Interest rates go down	Call —3-year bond	Exercise —5-year swap	No exercise —5-year swap

Exercising the swaptions rationally results in a maturity mismatch under either scenario. It is more appropriate for the issuer to sell a swaption. For example:

(c) enter into a 3-year receiver's swap, and sell a 3/2 payer's swaption;
(d) enter into a 5-year receiver's swap, and sell a 3/2 receiver's swaption:

	Action on bond	Action on swaption (c)	Action on swaption (d)
Interest rates go up	No call —5-year bond	Exercise —5-year swap	No exercise —5-year swap
Interest rates go down	Call —3-year bond	No exercise —3-year swap	Exercise —3-year swap

The issuer is paying a higher coupon to the investor, but also receiving the swaption premium. The swaption will be exercised so that the maturities also match. Because the swaption market is a wholesale market, the swaption is likely to be priced fairer than the call option in the bond market,[18] and therefore the issuer may be able to achieve sub-Libor funding.

Worksheet 10.28 shows a simple example of swapping a 5-year bond paying 3.5% coupon annually and with a single call in 3 years at par, into a floating rate of 3 mo. Libor − 11.7 bp. Callable bonds usually have multiple call dates, very often coinciding with selected coupon dates. These will be modelled in Chapter 11.

---

[18] Indeed, for a long time, investors received very little compensation for embedded call options.

10.10   OPTIONS ON CREDIT DEFAULT SWAPS

As before, these are options on forward-starting CDSs. Usually a Black formula is used to price the options; for example, an option to buy a CDS on a premium of K:

$$[F_{s,e} * N(d_1) - K * N(d_2)] * \sum S_t * d_t * \mathrm{DF}_t$$

where the summation is taken over the forward swap. Notice that the only difference from the usual Black formula is the inclusion of survival probabilities. This formula is dependent upon one market assumption, namely if there is a credit event during the option period, then the swaption is cancelled without penalty.

In practice, the options are short-dated, with the vast majority less than 6 months. This is because the volatilities of CDS premia may be very high—see Table 10.6 using data drawn from 2000 to 2002—and therefore hedging the options is subject to significant risk.

Table 10.6   Estimated annual volatility for spreads on 5-year CDSs[19]

Name	Rating	Number of trades	Volatility pa
AT&T Corp.	A1 to A3	171	93.4%
DCX	A1 to A3	248	86.7%
Ford Motor Credit	A1 to A3	264	67.6%
GMAC	A2	174	69.2%
Sears Acceptance	A2 to A3	112	77.2%
Tyco	A3	120	130.3%
WorldCom	A3	123	106.0%

10.11   FX OPTIONS

Whilst this book is primarily about swaps and interest rate options, this is a brief section on FX options for completeness. Exotic options will not be described in any great detail as there are a large number of books available that describe both the theory and application of these options (see, for example, Haug[20]). The objective of this section is to cover briefly generic-option pricing, so that it may be used in the risk management chapters (i.e., Chapters 12 and 13).

Consider a simple call option on $-¥ with a strike K of 105 JPY per USD. As with a normal call, this gives:

- the right to buy or to receive the underlying numeraire currency, i.e. USD; and
- the right to sell or to pay JPY at the strike rate.

If the spot rate at expiry $S_T = ¥107$, then you can sell $1 and buy ¥107 in the spot market and make a riskless profit of ¥2 per $1.

---

[19] Extracted from Table 8 in *The Valuation of CDS Options* by J. Hull *et al.*, Working Paper, University of Toronto, January 2003.
[20] E. Haug, *The Complete Guide to Option Pricing Formulas*, McGraw-Hill, 1997.

Generic FX options are typically priced using the "Garman–Kohlhagen" (G–K) variant of the usual Black and Scholes model:

$$C = S_0 * df^f_T * N(d_1) - K * df^d_T * N(d_2)$$

where df^f_T is the discount factor on the foreign side, usually defined as $\exp\{-r_f * T\}$
   where r_f is the continuously compounded risk-free zero-coupon rate;
   df^d_T is the same on the domestic side;
   $d_1 = \{\ln(S_0/K) + (r_d - r_f + \frac{1}{2}\sigma^2) \cdot T\}/\sigma\sqrt{T}$;
   $d_2 = d_1 - \sigma\sqrt{T}$;
   T is the time to expiry (in years);
   σ is the annualised volatility of the spot rate;
   $N(x)$ is the cumulative unit normal.

This definition uses the usual (personally speaking, unhelpful) language of "foreign" and "domestic"; to translate, as the spot rate is quoted in terms of JPY per USD, JPY is the domestic currency, USD the foreign one.[21] The price of the option C will also be in the same units as the spot rate. Whilst the formula calls for risk-free rates for discounting, in practice, Libor discount factors are used.

This section will use USD/JPY examples, based out of the usual date of 4 February 2008. As with virtually all currencies, FX options are quoted with a 2-day settlement period, so the options should start on 6 February. As described above, yen uses same day discount factors, which therefore need to be adjusted for the settlement period. We wish to price a 6-month call option with the following data (the remainder are on Worksheet 10.29):

- strike: 105
- size: $100m
- annualised volatility: 10.35%
- current spot rate: 106.601

The steps are:

- given the discount factors from the current market data (see Market Date worksheet for details) out of the correct dates: columns [1] and [3];
- calculate the Act/365 continuously compounded zero-coupon rates: columns [2] and [4];
- estimate maturity (on a consistent act/365 basis)—see below;
- calculate d_1 and d_2, and hence price the call: 3.152¥ per 1$; or
- ¥315.2m for $100m (see Box 1 of Worksheet 10.30).

The volatility σ is usually calculated using business days τ only, whereas interest is calculated using calendar days T, so the daycounts may be slightly different; that is:

$$(r_¥ - r_\$) \cdot T + \frac{1}{2}\sigma^2 \cdot \tau, \quad \text{etc.}$$

which was why the c–c rates were calculated on an Act/365 basis.

In the early days of the market, FX options were traded on futures exchanges; the

---

[21] Following the convention that in many countries exchange rates are quoted in terms of units of the domestic currency per unit of foreign.

Philadelphia exchange was the first in 1982. But as the FX spot markets moved to electronic trading around the world, the options market became predominantly OTC.[22]

The price in the OTC market is usually quoted as a percentage of spot (i.e. C/S_0); that is:

$$3.152¥/106.601 = 2.956\% \text{ of principal of } \$100m$$

This method of quotation makes it independent of the size of transaction and of the currency of the premium.

The option to put (or sell) the USD and receive JPY may be similarly calculated using:

$$P = K * df_T^¥ * N(-d_2) - S_0 * df_T^\$ * N(-d_1)$$

It has a price of 2.780% of principal.

Whilst the G–K model is most popular, there is a "Black" equivalent using forward rates. The forward FX rate S_T may be estimated using S_0 and two sets of interest rates, as discussed above; that is:

$$S_T = S_0 . \exp\{r_\$. T\}/\exp\{r_¥ . T\} = S_0 . df_T^¥/df_T^\$$$

Substituting for S_0 in the above formula gives:

$$C = df_T^¥ * \{S_T * N(d_1) - K * N(d_1)\}$$

where $d_1 = \{\ln(S_T/K) + \frac{1}{2}\sigma^2 . T\}/\sigma\sqrt{T}$ (see Box 2 of Worksheet 10.30).

Because FX forward rates are traded, market quotes for S_T are available and it is feasible to substitute these directly into the formula. Unfortunately, the quoted rates may not be the same as the implied rates—see the table below—so option prices will be different! (They are not quite comparable as the implied rates are taken off the offer side of the curve.) So which should be used? The answer depends on the hedge:

- if spot FX trades are used to hedge, use the S_0 model;
- if FX forward trades are used to hedge, then use the S_T model.

Most people use the former because of the higher liquidity.

Maturity	Implied FX rates	Quoted mid FX rates
1 wk	106.538	
1 mo.	106.344	
3 mo.	105.829	105.99
6 mo.	105.191	105.46
12 mo.	104.039	104.55
USD–JPY forward rates		
(see Worksheet 10.29 for details)		

---

[22] In June 2001, the total open FX options on the Philadelphia exchange were 25,762. This is less than 5% of the total open contracts 10 years earlier.

The options model may also be described as a "carry" model, i.e. writing $r_b = r_d - r_f$ as the cost of carrying the hedge. This interest rate differential may be thought of as the expected rate of USD depreciation. Suppose a 1-year ATM spot (i.e. with strike equal to the current spot rate) call option is purchased; this option would decline in value as the USD theoretically depreciates over the year.

Call–put parity theorems obviously exist in FX options. For example:

1. Buy a call, sell a put on \$1 at a strike of 105
   ○   cost of strategy $= 3.152 - 2.964 = ¥0.187629$.
2. Enter into a forward contract to buy \$1, and sell ¥105 in 6 months' time
   ○   currently $S_6 = 105.188$, and therefore the contract is off-market with an anticipated future value of ¥0.188; or
   ○   present value $= 0.188 * 0.997807 = ¥0.187629$.

The call–put parity relationship is $C - P = (S_T - K) * df_T^{¥}$. When $K = S_T$, i.e. the options are ATM forward, then $C = P$ (see Box 3 of Worksheet 10.30).

The spot rate has been quoted as {¥ per \$}: these are so-called "European" terms. But suppose we wished to quote it in American terms, i.e. as {\$ per ¥}—do the same prices and relationships hold true?

Define:

- spot^ $= 1/106.601 = 0.009381$ \$/¥;
- strike^ $= 1/105 = 0.009524$ \$/¥.

We can calculate d_1 and d_2 in the usual way, but must reverse df_T^{d} and df_T^{f} because the numeraire domestic has been switched from USD to JPY. We can then price the call and put:

$$C^{\hat{}} = \$0.0002648 \quad \text{and} \quad P^{\hat{}} = \$0.0002816 \text{ per } ¥1$$

(see Box 4 of Worksheet 10.30).

Expressing these results as percentages, we get:

	% of strike	% of spot
Call^	2.780%	2.823%
Put^	2.956%	3.001%

which implies $C = P^{\hat{}} * K * S_0$, etc. So we can replicate the \$ numeraire results, and all the earlier relationships remain true.

The G–K model is the most widely used for European options, despite various attempts to introduce "better" theoretical models. Probably the most popular extensions are:

- Assuming the interest rates are also stochastic; for example Hilliard et al.[23] produced an

---

[23] J. Hilliard et al., "Currency option pricing with stochastic domestic and foreign interest rates", *JFQA*, **26**(2), 1991, pp. 139–51.

identical expression to the G–K model but with a variance term

$$v^2 = (\sigma_S)^2 \cdot T + \tfrac{1}{3} T^3 \cdot \{(\sigma_d)^2 + (\sigma_f)^2 - 2 \cdot \sigma_{df}\} + T^2 \cdot \{\sigma_{Sd} - \sigma_{Sf}\}$$

where subscripts S, d and f refer to the spot rate, and domestic and foreign interest rates, and where σ_x and σ_{xy} are volatility and covariance, respectively. Obviously this reduces to G–K for constant interest rates.

- Assuming the volatility is stochastic; for example Chesney et al.[24] produced a model with a mean-reverting stochastic process for the volatility. After fitting the various parameters of the stochastic process, this model did produce significantly different results from the G–K model. Unfortunately they also found that market prices were consistent with G–K prices assuming constant volatility, so may have created an arbitraging opportunity.
- Assuming that spot foreign exchange rates do not follow a Gaussian process but over the long-term are pulled by purchasing power parity, or one of the other broad macro assumptions. For example Cheung et al.[25] produced a modified G–K model but obviously with a number of additional parameters that require estimation.

American options can (in theory) be exercised at *any* time up to maturity, although in practice this is seldom the case simply because of finite business hours. They are usually priced with a numeric model or by approximations such as Barone-Adesi and Whaley or Bjerksund and Stensland.[26] For example, the 6-month option above:

	Call	Put
European	3.135	2.947
Barone-Adesi and Whaley	3.326	2.964
Bjerksund and Stensland	3.284	2.964

As expected the price is higher, especially for the call as it is ITM-forward.

10.12   HEDGING FX OPTIONS

Consider the 6-month USD–JPY call option described above. We have just sold the option and will as usual perform a delta-neutralising spot transaction. The delta for the option is:

$$\delta = df_T^\$ * N(d_1) = 0.51625$$

implying that if the spot rate shifted by 1 unit, the call price would increase by JPY0.516 per USD or by JPY51,624,598 in total. As we have sold the option, this will be a loss for us. We wish to enter into a reverse spot transaction that will off-set this change in value:

- buy $100m $* \delta = \$51,624,598$;
- sell ¥51,624,598 $* S_0 = $¥5,503,233,785.

If the spot rate shifts by 1 unit, the profit on this trade would be ¥51,624,598.

---

[24] M. Chesney et al., "Pricing European currency options: A comparison of the modified B&S model and a random variance model", *JFQA*, **24**(3), 1989, pp. 267–84.
[25] M. Cheung et al., *Pricing FX Options Incorporating Purchasing Power Parity*, Hong Kong University Press, 1992.
[26] Haug, ibid., pp. 22–9.

We now need to see what happens as the spot rate changes through time. Worksheet 10.31 is designed to perform random simulation of the spot, and the table (next page) is a short extract. It assumes only one change per day; therefore at the end of the first day the current P&L, defined by the net balance in ¥ plus the net balance in $ converted at the prevailing spot rate, is zero. The next day the spot rate shifts from JPY106.601 to JPY106.17 per USD. A number of things happen:

- The option may be bought back at the new price C_1 of ¥2.92688, thus representing a profit of $¥100m * (C_0 - C_1) = ¥22,465,968$.
- However, we estimated the new price should be $C_0 + \delta * (S_1 - S_0) = 2.92659$, so that we had expected a bigger profit. The difference of $-¥28,708$ is the negative gamma effect from which we of course lose.
- We assume that we borrowed the balance of the JPY required to undertake the spot trade, and deposited the USD proceeds
  - JPY interest payable $= -5,188,080,237 * \exp\{r_¥ * 1/365\} = ¥62,570$;
  - USD interest receivable $= 51,624,598 * \exp\{r_\$ * 1/365\} = \$4,408$;
  - converting the USD to JPY at S_1 gives a net balance of ¥405,368;
  - this is close to—strictly, should convert at S_0—the positive theta effect.
- On balance, therefore, the trade shows a profit of ¥376,660 as shown in the table on the facing page.

The hedge has to be re-balanced as the delta has shifted to 0.49461. The required delta hedge is to:

- buy $\$100m * \delta_1 = \$49,461,129$;
- sell $¥49,461,129 * S_1 = ¥5,251,053,833$.

However, we already have balances in our two money accounts from the previous day's hedge plus interest: therefore we need to reduce the USD balance by selling $2,167,877 and buying the equivalent amount of yen. Notice the resulting balances in the money accounts do not represent a perfect delta hedge now; this is mainly because the spot rate has not moved perfectly in line with the interest rate differential, but there are also some small theta effects.

Worksheet 10.31 then repeats this process each day until the option matures. On the last day, if the option expires OTM then delta should be very close to zero and the money accounts run down to zero as well. Conversely, if the option finishes ITM then the money accounts should be close to $-¥10.5bn$ and $+\$100m$, respectively.

The simulation is performed using the expression:

$$S_t = S_{t-1} * \exp\{(r_¥ - r_\$ - \tfrac{1}{2}\sigma^2).\Delta t + \sigma.\sqrt{\Delta t}.\varepsilon\}$$

where $\Delta t = 1/365$ years and $\varepsilon = N(0,1)$. The worksheet also permits the inclusion of a jump process $\kappa.(r_3 - 0.5)$—see column [B]—to demonstrate how delta-hedging can break down in these situations. The graph below shows the final balance of the net money accounts over 100 simulations:

Day	Day-count	Day-count	Spot rate (¥/$)	d_1	Call price (¥/$)	Mid delta	Call dealing (¥)	¥	$	Net balance (¥)	Net balance ($)	Close-out option (¥)	Current P&L
0	0.499		106.60	0.061	3.152	0.51625	315,153,548	(5,503,233,785)	51,624,598	(5,188,080,237)	51,624,598	(315,153,548)	0
1	0.496	0.003	106.17	0.006	2.927	0.49461		230,153,214	(2,167,877)	(4,957,989,593)	49,461,129	(292,687,581)	376,660
2	0.493	0.003	106.59	0.061	3.135	0.51632		(230,970,322)	2,166,992	(5,189,019,709)	51,632,344	(313,493,528)	754,657

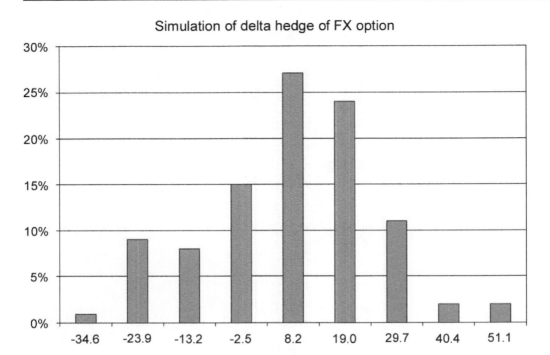

The average of the distribution is only ¥1.9m, very close to zero as expected. However, the distribution is not entirely symmetric, arising from the down-sided negative gamma and the up-sided theta. If gapping is permitted, then replication is far less effective, as the gamma dominates the theta—see graph below.

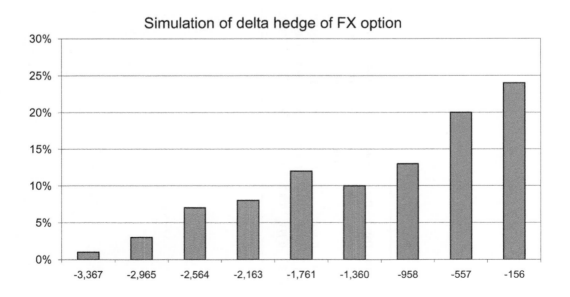

We have seen how a vanilla FX option may be delta-hedged with a succession of spot transactions. However, there are a number of practical problems:

- Delta-hedging is supposedly continuously re-balanced, but in practice always lagging one period behind. This doesn't matter if there is negligible gamma, i.e. the delta isn't changing very much, but for ATM short-dated options it becomes an increasing problem.
- Transaction costs have been ignored in this model, although it would be very simple to add them.
- Volatility of the spot rate is assumed to be constant over the lifetime of the option.
- The two interest risks are also assumed to be constant.
- The hedge has a cost of carry which may not be same as c–c "risk-free" rates as these are seldom (never?) available in practice.

Delta-hedging can also be used for American options, but there is one problem, as highlighted by the graph below. Early exercise when heavily in the money is an optimal strategy for the owner of an American option, hence the American delta converges to 1 much faster than the European option. This causes a discontinuity in the delta at the early exercise boundary, which results in a "gamma spike".

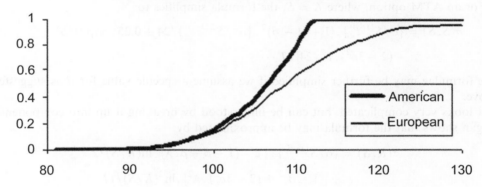

10.13   APPENDIX: THE SABR MODEL FOR STOCHASTIC VOLATILITY

The "stochastic $\alpha\beta\rho$" model, commonly known by the SABR acronym, was developed by Hagan *et al*. It assumes that forward rates F are stochastic:

$$dF_t = \alpha_t \cdot (F_t)^{\beta} \cdot dW_1$$

where the term α is itself stochastic:

$$d\alpha_t = v_t \cdot \alpha_t \cdot dW_2 \quad \text{and where} \quad dW_1 \cdot dW_2 = \rho \cdot dt$$

The terms:

> α is similar to volatility, but not quite the same;
> v may be interpreted as a measure of the volatility of volatility;
> ρ is the correlation between the forward rate and volatility;
> $0 \le \beta \le 1$ determines the speed of change of the forward rate. β may be estimated as described below, or it may be set in advance: $\beta = 0$ gives a normal model, $\beta = 1$ a log-normal model favoured by most traders around the world and $\beta = 0.5$ a stochastic Cox–Ingersoll–Ross model beloved by short-term US interest rate traders.

For an option of maturity T, with strike K and implied forward rate S, the following formula for a volatility surface $\{K, S\}$ is derived:

$$\sigma(K, S) = \alpha \cdot (z/x[z])/\{(S \cdot K)^{0.5(1-\beta)} \cdot (1 + (1 - \beta)^2 \ln^2(S/K)/24$$

$$+ (1 - \beta)^4 \ln^4(S/K)/1920 + \cdots)\}$$

$$* \{1 + [(1 - \beta)^2 \alpha^2/[24.(S \cdot K)^{(1-\beta)}] + \beta \alpha \rho v/[4 \cdot (S \cdot K)^{0.5(1-\beta)}]$$

$$+ (2 - 3 \cdot \rho^2) \cdot v^2/24] \cdot T + \cdots\}$$

where $x(z) = \ln\{[(1 - 2\rho z + z^2)^{0.5} + z - \rho]/1 - \rho\}$ and $z = v \cdot (S \cdot K)^{0.5(1-\beta)} \cdot \ln(S/K)/\alpha$.
For an ATM option, where $K = S$, the formula simplifies to:

$$\sigma(S, S) = \{\alpha/S^{(1-\beta)}\} \cdot [1 + (1 - \beta)^2 \cdot \{\alpha^2/S^{2.(1-\beta)}\}/24 + 0.25 \cdot \beta \alpha \rho v/(S)^{(1-\beta)}$$

$$+ (2 - 3\rho^2) \cdot v^2/24] \cdot T \cdots$$

The formulae may be further simplified if we assume a specific value for β as suggested above.

It looks very complicated, but can be understood by breaking it up into components. Hagan shows that the formula may be approximated by:

$$\sigma(K, S) = \{\alpha/S^{(1-\beta)}\} \cdot \{1 - (1 - \beta - \rho \cdot \lambda) \cdot \ln(K/S)/2$$

$$+ [(1 - \beta)^2 + (2 - 3\rho^2) \cdot \lambda^2] \cdot \ln^2(K/S)/12$$

where $\lambda = v \cdot S^{(1-\beta)}/\alpha$.

The first term $\{\alpha/S^{(1-\beta)}\}$ in the approximation is effectively the ATM volatility. This is determined almost entirely by β. The second term is the slope of the implied volatility with respect to K, known as the skew. This can be subdivided into two components: the $(1 - \beta)$ term is the downward-sloping beta skew, modified by the $\rho \cdot \lambda$ term representing the vanna skew arising from the correlation between the forward rate and the volatility. The third term is again the beta skew, but this time modified by the curvature of the volatility surface, known as volatility-gamma or "vol(-)ga".

Assume we possess a forward volatility surface, giving volatility for known strikes against option tenor (see Worksheet 10.33 for details). First we fix the value of β; in Worksheet 10.34 this is set to 1. From the ATM equation above, α may be determined analytically (by solving for the smallest positive root of a cubic) for given values of ρ and v, and for given and observable ATM volatility $\sigma(S, S)$. Finally, given market volatility across a range of strikes for a given option tenor, the ρ and v parameters can be estimated by some robust least-squares fitting algorithm such as Nelder–Mead.[27] By changing the input tenor, Worksheet 10.35 will display the SABR curve; for example, see the graph below:

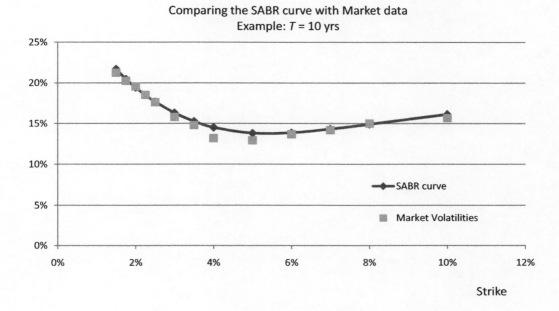

[27] See Spradlin, *The Nelder–Mead Method in Two Dimensions*, Embry–Riddle Aeronautical University, 2003. Available from *http://www.adeptscience.co.uk/maplearticles/f1198.html*

11

Swapping Structured Products

OBJECTIVE

The chapter concentrates on the modelling of more complex swaps. It starts with a description of some of the basic types, such as range accruals, sticky floaters, TARNs and callable structures. A binomial BDT interest rate model is constructed, and used to price various swaps such as Bermudan swaptions, callable CMSs and range accruals. Section 11.5 (Appendix) describes the construction of smile-based and trinomial, mean-reverting models and also two-factor models. The theory underpinning the Libor (or BGM) model is then developed, including calibration and estimation of implied correlation. It is then applied to products such as a sticky floater, a TARN and a callable snowball.

11.1 INTRODUCTION

Whenever it is perceived that market levels are at some extreme level, investors are often prepared to buy securities that pay high yields. For example, when interest rates were perceived to be both low and stable in the US in the early 1990s, or globally in the early part of this century, range accrual structures (as described later) were extremely popular. This was despite the fact that many investors lost large amounts of money as rates subsequently rose. Investors taking on increased risk to chase yield is a phenomenon that has been observed many times throughout history. What about issuers? No; they invariably swap the structures into some (usually floating) benchmark.

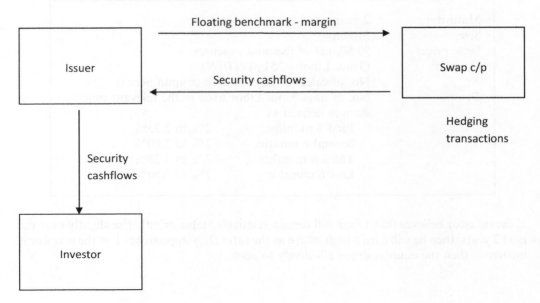

Therefore, what typically happens is the following:

1. The swap counterparty (usually a bank) will identify a group of potential investors, and create a structure that matches their desired risk-return profile.
2. At the same time, the counterparty will also structure the swap to achieve some target margin below the floating benchmark.
3. The counterparty will then approach a potential issuer (usually one with a good credit rating such as the World Bank, EBRD, EIB, KfW and so on), and suggest that if it issues the following structure, then it can achieve an overall funding rate.

What's in it for the various players?

*   the investor achieves a risk-return profile;
*   the issuer raises cheap funds;
*   the swap counterparty earns fees through the issuance and spreads through the hedging transactions, providing liquidity to the derivative markets.

In this chapter, some typical structures that have been issued will be discussed within an analysis framework. Each class of security will then be modelled, along with other complex swaps.

11.2 EXAMPLES OF SOME STRUCTURED SECURITIES

Probably the most popular structured products in the last few years have been range accruals. A very simple example was the following, issued by the World Bank in October 2004:

Maturity:	2 years
Size:	$100m
Issue price:	99.80, net of fees and expenses
Coupon:	$(3 \text{ mo. Libor} + 75 \text{ bp}) * (D/N)$
N:	No. of calendar days in each coupon period
D:	No. of days 3 mo. Libor fixed in the relevant range
	Ranges defined as:
	First 6 months: 2% to 2.75%
	Second 6 months: 2% to 3.00%
	Third 6 months: 2% to 3.25%
	Last 6 months: 2% to 3.50%

If the investor believes that Libor will remain relatively stable or only rise slightly over the next 2 years, then he will earn a high return as the ratio D/N approaches 1. If the investor is incorrect, then the coupon drops effectively to zero.

A more complex example was a spread steepener issued by the EIB in February 2005:

Nominal size:	€200m
Maturity:	February 2020
Coupon:	(10 yr CMS + 56 bp) $* (D/N)$ ANN 30/360
N:	No. of calendar days in period
D:	No. of days Slope = 10 yr CMS − 2 yr CMS fixes at or above accrual barrier
	If non-business day, then use last fixing
Accrual barrier:	0%

The investor has to take a view; this time whether the swap curve will remain positively sloped over the next 15 years. If she is correct, then she will earn a very handsome return bearing in mind the AAA rating of the issuer.

Any reference can be used within a range accrual as long as it has the potential to move, such as interest rates, share or commodity prices, and FX rates, and can be precisely observed regularly. A range has then to be defined; it may vary from period to period. Finally, the coupon (and occasionally redemption as well) is paid depending upon the D/N ratio. Another example was issued by BPI, the Portuguese bank, in February 2004:

Principal:	€50m	
Maturity:	5 years	
Redemption:	100	
Coupon:	5% $* (D/N)$ ANN	
N:	No. of calendar days in period	
D:	No. of fixings within range during period	
	If non-business day, then use last fixing	
Range:	0%–5%	
Reference:	In first year:	5 yr €uro swap rate
	In second year:	4 yr €uro swap rate
	In third year:	3 yr €uro swap rate
	In fourth year:	2 yr €uro swap rate
	In fifth year:	1 yr €uro swap rate
Calls:	On first, second, third and fourth coupon dates	

Notice in this case the underlying reference changes in each year, although the range remains constant. The security can also be called by BPI on selected coupon dates.

The simpler range accruals are fairly straightforward to analyse as they only depend upon the level of the reference on a given date. Consider the World Bank structure described above. For a given day, say 1 December 2005, if the Libor fixing lies within the range of 2–3.25%, then the coupon is increased by 1/66th as $N = 66$ for this coupon period. If the fixing lies outside the range, then there is no increase in coupon. The probability of the fixing lying within the range is given by (remember the formula for digital options in Section 10.6):

$$N(d_2 \mid K = 2\%) - N(d_2 \mid K = 3.25\%)$$

Using the market data on the issue date, the implied forward rate on this date was 3.0588%. Based on a volatility of 15%, $N(d_2 \mid K = 2\%) - N(d_2 \mid K = 3.25\%) = 99.61\% - 35.20\% = 64.41\%$. Repeating this for all business dates in this quarter gives an average probability of 63.54%. Therefore, the expected cashflow at the end of the period, based on an implied Libor fixing at the beginning of the period of 2.9477%, is:

$$\$100\text{m} * \{2.9477\% + 75\,\text{bp}) * 0.256 * 63.54\% = \$600,420$$

Therefore, the expected cashflows arising from the security can be valued, and hence the breakeven margin estimated of -45.2 bp using the usual formula (see, for example, Chapter 5 as well as the extract from Worksheet 11.1).

As we are only interested in the average probability over a coupon period, is it necessary to calculate the probability on a daily basis? Clearly the answer must be no; the probability could be sampled on a weekly, or even monthly, basis. Obviously this approximation loses accuracy if the implied forward curve was steep, but that is not the usual condition for issuing an accrual note anyway. The same approach is also used to construct a hedge.

When modelling accrual notes, it is important to take the smile effect into account, or to use a stochastic volatility model such as SABR. For the above example, as the bottom part of the range is increasing away from the money, the volatility is rising up the smile, whereas the upper remains close to ATM. For a par volatility of 18% for lower range, and only 14% for the upper, the breakeven margin increases to -48.6 bp.

In the World Bank note, the precise level of the fixing was irrelevant provided it lay in the range. GE issued a range note recently with the following payoff:

$$\sum \{3\,\text{mo. Libor fixings} + 75\,\text{bp} \}/N_t * \text{at the end of quarter } t$$

where the summation is taken over all Libor fixings that lie within a specified range. In this case, the level of the fixing is itself important. Modelling this structure requires not only digital options, but also normal caps and floors as well.

For the EIB spread accrual note described above, then the volatility of the reference slope is also dependent upon correlation between the 10 and 2-year CMS rates. This therefore introduces yet another parameter to be estimated. Modelling this note could be done analytically, but probably better by simulation, as discussed in Section 11.4.

This analytic approach cannot be used to model the BPI accrual note, as that also has an embedded call strip. On each call date, the issuer would have to make a decision: Is it better to call the note now, or better to wait until either the next call date or even redemption? This of course requires an estimate of the anticipated value of forward cashflows. Hence, we would describe any note with an embedded call as a forward-looking structure.

In contrast, consider the following two structures, both issued by the EIB in 2004:

Nominal size:	€100m
Maturity:	June 2010
Issue price (after fees and expenses):	99.625
Coupon:	6 mo. €uribor + 50 bp
Subject to constraint:	Coupon$(t) \leq$ Coupon$(t-1) + 20$ bp

and

Nominal size:	€165m
Maturity:	January 2014
Coupon:	First year: 4.75% ANN
	Thereafter: $3.75 * (10\,\text{yr CMS} - 2\,\text{yr CMS})$
Subject to the constraint	≥ 0

Mandatory early redemption on any coupon date if Total accrued coupon (including the current coupon) $\geq$ Knockout level. In this case, the Final coupon = Total accrued coupon (excluding current) − Knockout level, where the Knockout level = 20%. If there is no early redemption, the Final coupon = Knockout level − Total accrued coupon (excluding current).

The first structure is an example of a sticky floater, whereby the coupon can decline in line with a decrease in interest rates, but its rate of increase is capped. Notice that the cap is not linked to the last €uribor fixing, but to the previous coupon, which in turn may be linked to even earlier coupons. Hence the backward path of coupons is important in this case.

The second structure is an example of a Target Accrual Redemption Note (TARN). This note is guaranteed to pay a total coupon of 20%, but its lifetime is uncertain. If the 10–2 spread increases, then the note redeems early, and the investor has earned a high return on the initial investment. Conversely, if the note does not redeem early, then the investor receives a low 2% over the next 10 years. Modelling these again requires knowledge of earlier coupons, and is therefore also a backward structure.

Finally, consider the following structure issued by BPI in March 2004:

Maturity:	7 years
Redemption:	100
Coupon:	5.5% sa in first year
	Thereafter $\text{Coupon}(t) = \text{Coupon}(t-1) + K(t) - 6\,\text{mo. €uribor} \geq 0$
	where K starts at 2.5% and increments by 25 bp each period
Calls:	Every coupon date starting 5 March 2005

This structure is often called a snowball, as the coupons may increment up each period. It is a reverse-floating backward-looking structure, as the coupon in any period depends upon the path of earlier coupons. It is also a forward-looking structure due to the embedded call strip.

There are two main approaches that can be used to model these structures. Numerical models are usually applied to forward structures, whereas simulation is used to handle both backward and, with some difficulty, backward–forward structures. The next two sections will describe how these models work with various numerical examples.

11.3 NUMERICAL INTEREST RATE MODELS

These usually model short-term interest rates $r(t)$ according to the following stochastic process:

$$x(t + dt) - x(t) = dx = [\theta(t) - a(t) \cdot x(t)] \cdot dt + \sigma(t) \cdot dz$$

where x is a function of the rate; $\theta(t)$, $a(t)$ and $\sigma(t)$ are all time-varying parameters; and dz is assumed to be a unit-normal random variable. The two main approaches are:

$x(t) = r(t)$:	This gives rise to easy analytic expressions, but is generally difficult to calibrate with the existing markets, and can result in negative interest rates; typical examples are the Vasicek model and the Hull and White model.
$x(t) = \ln[r(t)]$:	The analysis is more difficult, but calibration is easier, and ensures that rates are always positive; typical examples are the various Black models such as the Black and Scholes model and the Black–Derman–Toy model as well as Libor-based simulation models.

This chapter will concentrate on the latter class of models as being more realistic, but the former class will be discussed in Section 11.5 (Appendix).

Re-write the above expression as:

$$\ln[r(t+dt)] = \ln[r(t)] + \mu(r,t) \,.\, dt + \sigma(t) \,.\, \sqrt{dt} \,.\, dz$$

where $\mu(r,t) = [\theta(t) - a(t) \,.\, \ln[r(t)]]$, and $\sigma(t)$ is now expressed on a pa basis. Assume a very simple binomial model, namely that given $r(t)$, there are only two possible outcomes:

$$\ln[r(t+dt)]^u = \ln[r(t)] + \mu \,.\, dt + \sigma \,.\, \sqrt{dt} \,.\, k$$

$$\ln[r(t+dt)]^d = \ln[r(t)] + \mu \,.\, dt - \sigma \,.\, \sqrt{dt} \,.\, k$$

where the time dimension has been omitted for ease of notation, and k is some constant multiplier. Define p as the probability of the up-rate occurring: hence the expected outcome is:

$$E\{\ln[r(t+dt)]\} = p * \{m + \sigma \,.\, \sqrt{dt} \,.\, k\} + (1 - p) * \{m - \sigma \,.\, \sqrt{dt} \,.\, k\}$$

where $m = \ln[r(t)] + \mu \,.\, dt$. But this expectation should equal m; solving gives $p = 0.5$ for all values of k.

The variance of $\ln[r(t+dt)]$ is given by:

$$p^2 * \{m + \sigma \,.\, \sqrt{dt} \,.\, k\}^2 + (1 - p)^2 * \{m - \sigma \,.\, \sqrt{dt} \,.\, k\}^2 - m^2$$

But this should equal $\sigma^2 \,.\, dt$; solving gives $k = 1$. These two results form the foundation of the Black–Derman–Toy (BDT) approach. Using these results gives:

$$\ln[r(t+dt)]^u - \ln[r(t+dt)]^d = 2 * \sigma \,.\, \sqrt{dt} \tag{11.1}$$

Assume we know an implied forward interest rate curve (of the correct tenor) r_t, probably taken off a swap curve (and hence a discount curve DF_t), and also an implied forward volatility curve σ_t, probably taken off the cap curve.

On the basis of a simple binomial model, adopt the notation that the rate $r_{t,k}$ fixes at the beginning of the time period $t = 0, 1, 2, \ldots$ where k identifies the sub-node within the tth period, $k = 0, 1, 2, \ldots, t$. It is assumed at this point that d_t is subject to some daycount convention (such as Act/360), and therefore may vary slightly from period to period. Thus, we can write:

$$\left.\begin{array}{c}\ln[r_{t,k}] = \ln[r_{t,k-1}] + 2 * \sigma_{t-1} \cdot \sqrt{d_t} \\[2mm] \text{or}\quad r_{t,k} = r_{t,k-1} * \exp\{2 * \sigma_{t-1} \cdot \sqrt{d_t}\} \\[2mm] \text{or}\quad r_{t,k} = r_{t,k-1} * \Delta_t^2 \end{array}\right\} \quad (11.2)$$

where the step length $\Delta_t = \exp\{\sigma_{t-1} \cdot \sqrt{d_t}\}$. Define the PV of a single cashflow of 1 at node (t,k)[1] as $X_{t,k}$ where:

$$X_{t,k} = 0.5 * \{X_{t-1,k-1} * \mathrm{DF}_{t-1,k-1} + X_{t-1,k} * \mathrm{DF}_{t-1,k}\} \quad \text{for } k = 0, \ldots, t \quad (11.3)$$

with the edge conditions $X_{t-1,-1} = X_{t-1,t} = 0$, and $X_{0,0} = 1$ and

$$\mathrm{DF}_{t,k} \text{ is a one-period discount factor} = 1/(1 + r_{t,k} * d_t) \quad (11.4)$$

On the basis of this definition, we know that

$$\sum_k X_{t,k} = \mathrm{DF}_t \quad (11.5)$$

Therefore, we can develop the following process for time period t:

1. Guess a value for $r_{t,0}$.
2. Calculate $r_{t,k}$ for $k = 1, 2, 3, \ldots, t$ from (11.2).
3. Calculate $\mathrm{DF}_{t,k}$ and $X_{t,k}$ from (11.4) and (11.3), respectively.
4. If eq. (11.5) is not satisfied, then adjust the initial guess.

A good starting point for $r_{j,0}$ recognises that the binomial tree should be approximately centred upon the current market forward rate curve. This suggests:

$$r_t \approx r_{t,0} * (\Delta_t)^t \quad (11.6)$$

Using this ensures convergence within a very few iterations.

As an example, we will build a tree and then use it to value an old swap which is linked to a structured security. This swap matures on 12 February 2013 with a fixed rate of 2.695% ANN 30/360. The floating side is quarterly minus 25 bp; the last Libor fixing at 2.15% was on 12 November 2007. The following DFs and forward volatilities have been estimated (from the normal swap and cap volatility curves, as usual), as shown in the table below. The forward rates are simply implied from the DFs.

Modelling dates	Accrual time Act/360	Libor DFs	Volatility term structure	Floating daycount Act/360 Qu	Forward rates
06-Feb-08	0.000	1	0%		3.21736%
12-Feb-08	0.017	0.999464	9.715%	0.256	3.13522%
12-May-08	0.267	0.991691	10.086%	0.250	3.01154%
12-Aug-08	0.522	0.984117	10.975%	0.256	2.71914%
12-Nov-08	0.778	0.977326	12.493%	0.256	2.55725%

See Spreadsheet "Ch 11.3 BDT Modelling a Swap".

---

[1] Known as an Arrow–Debreu price.

Step 1. The first rate in the tree is simply the first implied forward rate of 3.21736%. Note that this is not a 3-month rate, but corresponds to a short stub period of only 6 days, to get the rest of the tree aligned with the swap dates. Using this, $DF_{0,0} = 0.999464$, and $X_{1,0}$ and $X_{1,1}$ are both 0.499732.

Step 2. Using eq. (11.6) with a volatility of 9.715%, $r_{1,0}$ is initially estimated to be 3.09590%. Hence, we get $r_{1,1} = 3.17454\%$, $DF_{1,0}$ and $DF_{1,1}$ equal 0.9923197 and 0.9921261, respectively, and $X_{2,0}$, $X_{2,1}$ and $X_{2,2}$ equal 0.247947, 0.495846 and 0.247899, respectively. The sum of the Xs is 0.991691, which is the same as DF_2. Obviously, if this sum is not equal to the spot DF, the initial guess generated by eq. (11.6) would have to be modified.

Step 3. $r_{2,0}$ is estimated to be 2.715709% with a volatility of 10.086%, giving $r_{2,1}$ and $r_{2,2}$ of 3.00389% and 3.32266%, respectively. Continuing, $DF_{2,0}$, $DF_{2,1}$ and $DF_{2,2}$ equal 0.9931077, 0.9923819 and 0.9915803, respectively, and $X_{3,0}$, $X_{3,1}$, $X_{3,2}$ and $X_{3,3}$ equal 0.123119, 0.369153, 0.368940 and 0.122906. The sum of the Xs is again, to many decimal places, equal to DF_3.

This process is then continued. The initial starting point does increasingly result in an error, and then each stage has to be iteratively solved. Worksheet 11.3 contains a simple macro to do this iteratively. Worksheets 11.4 and 11.5 contain the tree of one-period DFs and the tree of X's, respectively:

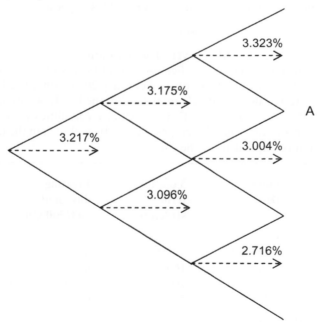

A small extract of the tree is shown above, and the full tree out for 5 years is shown on the facing page. The whole process has been automated in VBA (see Spreadsheet "BDT Builder")

0	1	2	3	4	5	6	7	8	9	10	11	12	13	14	15	16	17	18	19	20
3.22%	3.17%	3.32%	3.20%	3.27%	3.52%	3.90%	4.49%	5.24%	6.26%	7.30%	8.64%	10.09%	11.46%	12.55%	13.95%	14.80%	15.82%	16.78%	18.47%	20.30%
	3.10%	3.00%	2.86%	2.88%	3.07%	3.37%	3.86%	4.50%	5.36%	6.24%	7.33%	8.50%	9.62%	10.57%	11.75%	12.56%	13.49%	14.39%	15.85%	17.43%
		2.72%	2.56%	2.54%	2.67%	2.92%	3.31%	3.86%	4.59%	5.34%	6.22%	7.16%	8.08%	8.90%	9.90%	10.66%	11.51%	12.34%	13.60%	14.96%
			2.29%	2.24%	2.32%	2.52%	2.85%	3.31%	3.93%	4.57%	5.28%	6.03%	6.78%	7.49%	8.34%	9.04%	9.82%	10.58%	11.67%	12.84%
				1.97%	2.02%	2.18%	2.45%	2.84%	3.37%	3.90%	4.48%	5.08%	5.69%	6.31%	7.03%	7.67%	8.37%	9.08%	10.01%	11.02%
					1.76%	1.89%	2.10%	2.44%	2.88%	3.34%	3.80%	4.28%	4.78%	5.31%	5.92%	6.51%	7.14%	7.78%	8.59%	9.46%
						1.64%	1.80%	2.09%	2.47%	2.85%	3.22%	3.61%	4.01%	4.47%	4.99%	5.52%	6.09%	6.68%	7.37%	8.12%
							1.55%	1.80%	2.11%	2.44%	2.73%	3.04%	3.37%	3.77%	4.20%	4.68%	5.20%	5.73%	6.32%	6.97%
								1.54%	1.81%	2.09%	2.32%	2.56%	2.83%	3.17%	3.54%	3.97%	4.43%	4.91%	5.43%	5.99%
									1.55%	1.79%	1.97%	2.16%	2.38%	2.67%	2.98%	3.37%	3.78%	4.21%	4.66%	5.14%
										1.53%	1.67%	1.82%	2.00%	2.25%	2.51%	2.86%	3.22%	3.61%	4.00%	4.41%
											1.42%	1.53%	1.68%	1.89%	2.12%	2.43%	2.75%	3.10%	3.43%	3.79%
												1.29%	1.41%	1.59%	1.78%	2.06%	2.35%	2.66%	2.94%	3.25%
													1.18%	1.34%	1.50%	1.75%	2.00%	2.28%	2.52%	2.79%
														1.13%	1.27%	1.48%	1.71%	1.95%	2.17%	2.39%
															1.07%	1.26%	1.46%	1.68%	1.86%	2.06%
																1.07%	1.24%	1.44%	1.59%	1.76%
																	1.06%	1.23%	1.37%	1.51%
																		1.06%	1.17%	1.30%

The next task is to value the swap. First, we shall value it in the usual fashion off the swap curve using three approaches: the implied forward representation, the notional principal representation and taking the net cashflows from the IF approach and discounting them back one period at a time. Obviously, all three approaches produce the same value of 0.5625m as shown in Worksheet 11.3.

Turning to the tree, first we will use the NP representation. The final cashflow on the swap is $-100\text{m} * 2.695\% * d_{\text{Fix},N} - 100\text{m} + 100\text{m} * -25\,\text{bp} * d_{\text{Fl},N} = -102.7589\text{m}$ where $d_{\text{Fix},N}$ and $d_{\text{Fl},N}$ are the length of the last period on the fixed and floating sides, respectively. The cashflows may now be discounted back one period using the discounting tree. If $V_{k,t}$ is the value of the swap at node (k, t), then:

$$V_{k,t} = 0.5 * (V_{k,t+1} + V_{k-1,t+1}) * \text{DF}_{k-1,t} + 100\text{m} * -25\,\text{bp} * d_{\text{Fl},t}$$
$$- 100\text{m} * 2.695\% * d_{\text{Fix},t} \text{ (when due)}$$

where the fixed rate is only paid once a year. The penultimate cashflows, which correspond to the end of the period when the fixed Libor has to be paid, have to be modified. Instead of just receiving the margin, we now receive $100\text{m} * [1 + (2.15\% - 25\,\text{bp}) * d_{\text{Fl},1}]$. After this adjustment, the net value of the swap is 0.5625m, as before (see Worksheet 11.6 for the actual NP and IF cashflow trees).

Using the IF representation requires a little more care because Libor fixes at the beginning of a period, and pays at the end. Why does this cause problems? Consider the extract of the tree above. If we wish to enter a Libor cashflow at point A, which fixing should be used: 3.323% or 3.004%? The Libor cashflows have to be represented on a discounted basis (rather like a FRA cashflow)[2]:

$$\text{CF}_{k,t} = P * r_{k,t} * d_t/(1 + r_{k,t} * d_t)$$

Reverting to the tree, the cashflow at maturity is simply the final fixed payment. Then, the values are:

$$V_{k,t} = \{0.5 * (V_{k,t+1} + V_{k-1,t+1}) + 100\text{m} * (r_{k,t} - 25\,\text{bp}) * d_{\text{Fl},t}\} * \text{DF}_{k-1,t}$$
$$- 100\text{m} * 2.695\% * d_{\text{Fix},t} \text{ (when due)}$$

The final discounted value $V_{0,0}$ must of course use the Libor fixing, and not an implied rate.

Now make the problem more complex, and assume that the swap is callable by the bank on any fixed-coupon date. This means that, on a call date, the fixed and floating cashflows are made, and then the swap may be cancelled. This implies that the bank no longer has to make the coupon payments, but also no longer receives the Libor less the spread.

Using the IF representation, the expected value of the future cashflows at node (k, t) is as shown above. However, the Libor cashflow is fixed at time t but only paid at time $t + 1$. Thus, if the swap were called at time t, this Libor cashflow would not be paid. The bank would only want to call the swap if the future expected value was negative to it, so we can modify the folding-back rule as:

$$\max[0, \{0.5 * (V_{k,t+1} + V_{k-1,t+1}) + 100\text{m} * (r_{k,t} - 25\,\text{bp}) * d_{\text{Fl},t}\} * \text{DF}_{k-1,t}]$$

Modifying the tree gives the swap a new value of 0.7123m. The value of the embedded call strip is 0.1498m, in favour of the bank.

---

[2] I've often wondered whether this is why many structured securities use Libor in arrears. They would certainly be slightly easier to model.

Using the NP representation is slightly easier; the new folding-back rule is:

$$\max[-100, 0.5 * (V_{k,t+1} + V_{k-1,t+1}) * DF_{k-1,t}]$$

This gives the same value of 0.7123m (see Worksheet 11.7 for details).

We need to introduce some more terminology. The embedded call strip is effectively a Bermudan swaption, exercisable on a set of discrete dates. There are two fundamental types:

- fixed end, i.e. the underlying swap starts on the selected exercise date but has a constant maturity date;
- fixed length, i.e. the underlying swap starts on the selected exercise date and has a constant length of maturity.

For example, consider a 5/2 swaption with three exercise dates at the end of 3, 4 and 5 years:

Exercise date	Fixed end	Fixed length
3 years	4-year swap	2-year swap
4 years	3-year swap	2-year swap
5 years	2-year swap	2-year swap

Fixed end swaptions are needed to swap multiple call bonds, and to risk-manage a particular segment of the curve as it moves closer. Fixed length swaptions are used mainly when the time for an exposure to arise is unsure: for example, a company may want to enter into floating debt and swap it into fixed, but is unsure precisely when the debt will be called down.

American swaptions are less common than Bermudans, as they provide little additional practical benefit. One disadvantage is that early exercise on any date may lead to the underlying swap having undesirable broken dates, which would not be popular amongst the counterparties.

As the number of call dates increases, the call strip moves from European to American, and the price of the swap becomes asymptotic to the American price. For fixed end swaptions, the American price is reached with about 10 call dates—as may be seen in the graph below—and for fixed length swaptions, with only about four or five dates:

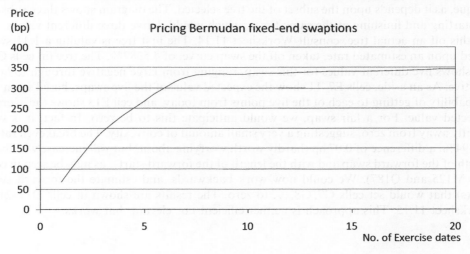

There is an old trader's trick to pricing Bermudan structures, namely price it to the first call, price it to the final maturity and take the higher of the two! It works remarkably well for monotonic curves.

The analytic pricing of CMS swaps, with convexity adjustment, was discussed in Chapter 7. These can also be priced off a tree. We will explore pricing a 5-year CMS, paying 3 mo. Libor and receiving the 10-year rate plus a margin on ANN Act/360 daycount. The models are somewhat complicated, and are summarised in Worksheet 11.8. First, we can calculate the margin analytically using no convexity adjustment in the usual fashion; this gives −128.27 bp (see Worksheets 11.10).

The rate tree is built in the usual fashion; however, because the frequency of the CMS is ANN, both a quarterly and an annual discounting tree are required (see Worksheet 11.12). Using the tree, the first step is to estimate the CMS fixings. For a forward-starting swap

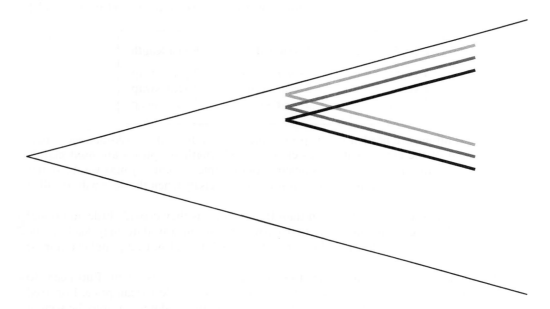

with a known fixed rate, then its forward value can be easily computed. This value is not unique, as it depends upon the subset of the tree selected. The diagram shows three subsets, all starting and finishing at the same times, which would derive three different values. To see this off an actual tree, consult Worksheet 11.14. The first tree is valuing a 1/11 swap based upon an estimated rate, taken off the swap curve, of 4.5387%. The tree (in cells G7–11) shows five different values for this swap, ranging from large negative through to large positive. As an aside, cells E7–11 show the expected value of the five swaps, based upon the probability of getting to each of the five points from today, and cell E13 shows the average expected value. For a fair swap, we would anticipate this to be zero. In fact, it is very slightly away from zero, suggesting a very small amount of convexity. The breakeven rate is 4.5394%, a difference of 0.07 bp (hardly worth worrying about, but will increase with both length of the forward swap and with the length of the forward start—as may be seen in cells I67, M125 and Q187). We could now work backwards, and estimate the forward swap rate(s) that would set cells G7, G8, . . . to zero. The results are shown in cells D17–21 in Worksheet 11.15. This approach is neither efficient nor elegant, but works.

An alternative, especially if working in VBA or some other programming language, would be to:

- estimate the Q from end to start for each of these five points;
- estimate the PV at each of the five points of a cashflow of 1 at the end of the swap;
- then the forward swap rate $= (1 - \text{PV})/Q$.

This is illustrated in Worksheets 11.16 and 11.17, respectively, and the results (for the 1/11 swap) are shown in cells C17–21 of Worksheet 11.15. The remaining CMS rates required have all been calculated using this approach.

The next step is to build the CMS pricing tree itself. Just like Libor, the CMS rate fixes at the beginning of the period, and pays at the end. This gives rise to the same difficulty as before, namely if we wish to model the cashflows directly, we do not uniquely know which CMS rate to use to model the cashflow. So we have to resort to the same idea as before, estimating the cashflows on a discount basis. But the CMS rates are ANN, so we first need to recast the discounting tree into annual steps—see cells M126:DZ246 in Worksheet 11.12. The pricing tree is created using the NP representation of Libor. The folding-back rule on a CMS fixing date is:

$$V_{k,t} = 0.5 * (V_{k,t+1} + V_{k-1,t+1}) * \text{DF}_{k-1,t} + 100\text{m} * (\text{CMS}_{k,t} + m) * d_{\text{CMS},t} * \text{DF}_{k,t}^{\text{ANN}}$$

where $d_{\text{CMS},t}$ is an annual daycount fraction, and $\text{DF}_{k,t}^{\text{ANN}}$ the annualised DFs. The breakeven margin of -132.6 bp gives the swap a net value of zero (see Worksheet 11.18).

The difference with the analytic price is just over 4 bp. But this ignored the convexity effect. Consistent estimates of swaption volatilities are required to make the analytic adjustment. Swaptions can be priced in two ways, off the tree or analytically. The payoff at maturity for a payer's swaption is:

$$\max\{0, V_{\text{Actual}} - V_{\text{Fixed}}\}$$

For an ATM swaption, we can take the 1/11 forward swap (priced off the curve at 4.5387%), value it off the tree back to the 1-year points (cells G7–11 as described above) and then apply the payoff function. This gives the value of the swaption at each point, which may then be folded back on the tree to calculate the expected present value of the swaption (see Worksheet 11.19).

But these European swaptions can also be priced using a Black model. Hence we can solve for the implied Black swaption volatilities. Entering this swaption volatility curve into the analytic convexity adjustment formula (see Worksheet 11.10) gives a breakeven margin of -133.5 bp; a difference of just under 1 bp from the tree price. As argued earlier, the analytic adjustment factor is thought to be too high, and this provides further (albeit small) justification to that statement.

We could now easily extend this model to introduce a call strip, say, for example, at par on each CMS coupon date. In this case, given that it is the issuer who has the right to call, the margin increases to -164 bp (see Worksheet 11.20).

In Section 11.2, range accruals were discussed. How can these be modelled on a tree, as callable accrual structures are popular? The answer is, with some limitations. For example: consider a simple 5-year accrual paying 3 mo. Libor $+50$ bp, but with the fixings of 3 mo. Libor subject to the following range:

Year	Lower	Upper
1	2.00%	3.50%
2	2.10%	4.00%
3	2.20%	4.50%
4	2.30%	5.00%
5	2.40%	5.50%

Using the same type of analytic model as described in Section 11.2, and using daily estimates, the note swaps into 3 mo. Libor − 27.6 bp (see Worksheet 11.22 for details). How can we approach this on a tree? Consider the small extract from the tree discussed above:

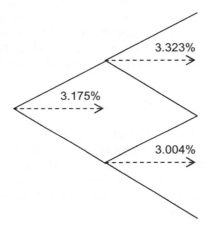

If interest rates rise, then we could assume that the fixings would smoothly change from 3.175% at the beginning of the period to 3.323% at the end. Thus, if we know the range, we could calculate the proportion of these fixings, call it P^{up} that lie in the range. Similarly, we could estimate P^{down} if rates dropped from 3.175% to 3.004%. But we know the probability of rates going up or down is 50%, hence the expected proportion $P = 0.5 * \{P^{up} + P^{down}\}$ which would of course be an estimate of the probability of fixings lying within the range. The above structure could then be modelled on the tree in the same way as before, by discounting the *expected* Libor cashflows. The graph below shows the tree probabilities compared with the analytic ones calculated using the Black digital model. The probabilities are very closely related, as is evident from the graph (see facing page). They are not identical because the tree was modelling on a binomial basis, whereas the analytic model was continuous; if the tree were more finely constructed, the two would converge. Folding back this 3-monthly tree and solving for the breakeven Libor margin gives −36 bp (see Worksheet 11.26).

There is another reason, other than the "large" tree step length, why the two margins are not the same. The analytic Libor rates were estimated off the swap curve, but are they the best estimates for the future value of Libor? If we estimate the expected value of 45/48 Libor from the tree, we get 4.66%, compared with an analytic value of 4.6088%. This is generally the case; the tree rates are higher than the analytic rates because we have assumed rates follow an asymmetric log-normal distribution with more up-side than down-side. In turn, the tree fixings are likely to be higher and, in this case, result in higher probabilities of being in the range; hence, both the graph and the resulting sub-Libor margin being higher. In my opinion, the tree approach is better as it does represent a more realistic (albeit stereotyped) evolution of the forward rates, but the analytic approach is both faster and more widely used.

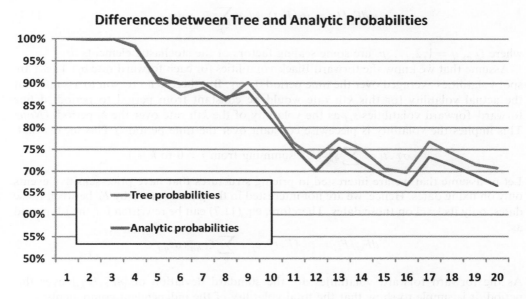

Finally, as before, we could now introduce a call strip. For example, suppose the issuer had the right to call back the security on any coupon date at par. The breakeven margin now increases significantly from -36 bp to -95 bp (see Worksheet 11.27 for details).

The above describes a simple range accrual, where the reference and the coupon are based on the same rate. Obviously many accruals are not like that, but the basic principles outlined above remain valid. Also, many other swaps containing forward-looking structures can be modelled in a similar fashion.

This section has discussed the construction and use of a particular numerical tree. There are a number of topics that have not been discussed, such as alternative formulations, including mean reversion, extending trees to trinomial and beyond, incorporating smile effects and so on. These are briefly discussed in Section 11.5 (Appendix).

11.4 SIMULATION MODELS

Tree structures are fairly fast to build, quick to run once built, allow the calculation of risk sensitivities, but are restrictive. There are many structures that cannot (at least not easily) be handled by trees, such as sticky floaters and TARNs that are path-dependent. We need therefore a more general approach which can be used to cope with these. Ideally, this approach may also provide a consistent pricing/risk framework for all structures, including more generic products. The Libor-based model—alternatively known as the BGM model after its founders Brace–Gatarek–Musiela or the Libor market model) has become the industry standard.

The model has been widely described in both books and articles,[3] and there is little point in trying to replicate them. A brief description, drawn mainly from Rebonato,[4] follows. Imagine a forward interest rate curve, consisting of a strip of forwards F_j, $j = 0, 1, \ldots, n$. These forwards would be fixed at time $t_0, t_1, t_2, \ldots$ Thus, the kth rate would be fixed at time t_k, and paid at t_{k+1} with tenor $\delta_k = t_{k+1} - t_k$. Consider this kth rate; assume it follows a lognormal process over a small time interval dt:

$$dF_k/F_k = \mu_k(F, t) \cdot dt + \sum_q \xi_{k,q} \cdot dz_q \qquad (11.7)$$

where $\xi_{k,q}$, $q = 1, 2, \ldots, p$, are some scaling factors of the stochastic elements dz_q.

Assume that we know the forward Black volatilities for each forward rate σ_k. These are spot volatilities averaged over the time period $0 - t_k$. But there is no reason to assume that the actual volatility for this kth rate would be constant from period to period: define forward–forward volatilities s_{kj} as the volatility of the kth rate over the δ_j period. (*Note*: This implies the volatility is piecewise constant over the time periods.) This means that:

$$\sigma_k^2 \cdot t_k = \sum s_{kj}^2 \cdot \delta_j \quad \text{summing from } j = 0 \text{ to } k - 1$$

Let us assume that we are interested in pricing structures that have price-sensitive events only on fixing dates. Hence, we are not interested in the path adopted by F_k between those dates, only its level on those dates. Therefore, eq. (11.7) can be rewritten for the jth period as:

$$dF_{kj}/F_{kj} = \mu_{kj}(F, t) \cdot \delta_j + \sum_q \xi_{k,q,j} \cdot dz_{q,j}$$

As the forward–forward volatilities are the standard deviation of $[dF_{kj}/F_{kj}]$ over this period, it is simple to show that the total volatility of the independent components:

$$\sum_q \xi_{k,q,j}^2 = s_{kj}^2 \cdot \delta_j$$

Defining $b_{k,q,j} = \xi_{k,q,j}/s_{kj}$ enables us to re-write the expression as:

$$dF_{kj}/F_{kj} = \mu_{kj}(F, t) \cdot \delta_j + s_{kj} \sum_q b_{k,q,j} \cdot dz_{q,j} \cdot \sqrt{\delta_j} \quad \text{where} \quad \sum_q b_{k,q,j}^2 = 1$$

If we denote the $n \times p$ matrix B_j with elements $\{b_{k,q,j}, k = 0, 1, 2, \ldots, n \text{ and } q = 1, 2, \ldots, p\}$, then it is fairly simple to show that $B_j \cdot B_j^{\text{Transpose}}$ has all the properties of a $n \times n$ correlation matrix, namely real, positive definite and symmetric. This implies that the volatility of a forward rate over a given time period depends upon both its volatility over that time period and also on the co-movement of the other forward rates over the period.

Determining the drift term $\mu_{kj}(F, t)$ is more difficult. As a theoretical aside, imagine that a security is being traded in a market. The price of the security is $f(t)$ at time t. If this market does not permit arbitrage, then, for any given numeraire security $g(t)$, there must exist a measure (or probability distribution) so that $f(0)/g(0) = E\{f(t)/g(t)\}$ for all securities. For example, set $g(t)$ to $DF(t, t_{k+1})$, namely the discount factor from time t to time t_{k+1}, and set $f(t) = [DF(t, t_k) - DF(t, t_{k+1})]/\delta_k$. Substituting, we get:

$$[DF(0, t_k) - DF(0, t_{k+1})]/\delta_k * DF(0, t_{k+1}) = E\{[DF(t, t_k) - DF(t, t_{k+1})]/\delta_k * DF(t, t_{k+1})\}$$

[3] For example, Part III in D. Brigo *et al.*, *Interest Rate Models: Theory and Practice*, Springer, 2006.
[4] R. Rebonato, *Modern Pricing of IR Derivatives*, Princeton University Press, 2002.

This is, of course, $F_k(0) = E\{F_k(t)\}$. In words, the expected value of a future forward interest rate is the current estimate of that forward rate only if the numeraire is $DF(t, t_{k+1})$, or alternatively if there is effectively zero drift. But if we applied the same numeraire to a different forward rate, say F_j, the result would not stand, and therefore there would be a drift term.

Rebonato, and many others, have shown that, to remove arbitrage from the market, one expression for the drift term of the kth rate over the jth period is:

$$\mu_{kj} = \sum_i R_{ij} \left\{ \sum_q \xi_{k,q,j} \cdot \xi_{i,q,j} \right\} = s_{kj} \cdot \sum_i s_{ij} \cdot R_{ij} \sum_q b_{k,q,j} \cdot b_{i,q,j}$$

where $R = \delta_j \cdot F_{ij}/[1 + \delta_j \cdot F_{ij}]$, and where the summation over i is taken from the fixing at time t_j to the fixing at time t_k.

There are other expressions, but this one is particularly useful in practice as it implies that the movement of the kth rate in the jth period depends upon the behaviour of all the rates that fix earlier, including their correlation with this rate, but not upon rates that fix later. This allows the drift terms to be sequentially evolved.

This drift term has an implied assumption. Strictly, the forward rates will evolve continuously through time, and therefore so will the drift term. However, if the time period is relatively short, say 3 months, we can use the estimates of the forward rates at the beginning of the jth period in the drift term to apply as an approximation over the entire period.

The model as described develops the evolution of forward interest rates, and uses Black caplet volatilities. Putting it all together:

$$F_{kj+1} = F_{kj} * \exp\left\{ [\mu_{kj} - \tfrac{1}{2}s_{kj}^2] \cdot \delta_j + s_{kj} \sum_q b_{k,q,j} \cdot dz_{q,j} \cdot \sqrt{\delta_j} \right\} \qquad (11.8)$$

It is also feasible to develop a forward swap rate model that uses swaption volatilities, and with a numeraire equal to a forward Q. This would be more appropriate for simulating forward swaps or CMS structures, but the drift term is more complex and the inputs less observable. In practice, the forward interest rate model is more commonly applied, especially when modelling mixtures of forward interest and swap rates.

Correlations between the forward rates are required inputs in this model. Whilst it might be feasible to use historic relationships, a parametric[5] form as discussed in Chapter 10 is far more common in practice. This would then enable the parameters to be estimated by calibrating the simulation to selected European swaptions, typically by minimising squared errors. This will be explored in more detail later in this section.

The next step is to estimate the B matrix from the correlation matrix. The number of parameters p may lie anywhere between 1 and n. If $p = 1$, then $\rho_{k,j} = b_k \cdot b_j$. But we know that $\rho_{k,k} = 1 = b_k^2 \rightarrow b_k = 1 \rightarrow$ all rates are perfectly correlated, and the forward curve will only exhibit parallel shifts. Alternatively, if $p = n$, then this is a full spanning model and B can be uniquely determined from the correlation matrix by a Cholesky decomposition. But we know that real forward curves tend to exhibit a limited range of movements, often characterised by parallel, rotation and curvature changes. An n-factor model may therefore introduce forward curve movements that are unlikely in the real world. For this reason,

---

[5] It might also be feasible to use a non-parametric approach, and fit a correlation matrix to swaptions using some form of bootstrapping. But this is likely to result in widely fluctuating and therefore unrealistic correlations.

setting $p = 3$ might be more appropriate. However, this means that B is determined numerically by minimising the errors between $B \cdot B^{\text{Transpose}}$ and the full correlation matrix. This approach is at the heart of principal components. For example, the correlation matrix below was created with a lambda of 50%.

	1	2	3	4	5	6	7	8
1	100%	88%	78%	69%	61%	54%	47%	42%
2	88%	100%	88%	78%	69%	61%	54%	47%
3	78%	88%	100%	88%	78%	69%	61%	54%
4	69%	78%	88%	100%	88%	78%	69%	61%
5	61%	69%	78%	88%	100%	88%	78%	69%
6	54%	61%	69%	78%	88%	100%	88%	78%
7	47%	54%	61%	69%	78%	88%	100%	88%
8	42%	47%	54%	61%	69%	78%	88%	100%

This was then decomposed into a number of B matrices using the angular algorithm described in Rebonato.[6] The full decomposed matrix is shown below:

1	0	0	0	0	0	0	0
0.882	0.470	0	0	0	0	0	0
0.779	0.415	0.470	0	0	0	0	0
0.687	0.366	0.415	0.470	0	0	0	0
0.607	0.323	0.366	0.415	0.470	0	0	0
0.535	0.285	0.323	0.366	0.415	0.470	0	0
0.472	0.252	0.285	0.323	0.366	0.415	0.470	0
0.417	0.222	0.252	0.285	0.323	0.366	0.415	0.470

Smaller matrices are shown for $p = 3$, 4 and 5, respectively, with least-squares errors of 18%, 7% and 3%.

0.127	0.421	0.898
0.268	0.312	0.912
0.509	0.079	0.857
0.741	−0.030	0.671
0.880	0.037	0.474
0.919	0.283	0.276
0.800	0.579	0.155
0.701	0.708	0.084

0.231	0.189	0.764	0.572
0.293	0.240	0.865	0.330
0.461	0.218	0.859	−0.040
0.695	0.108	0.701	−0.113
0.894	0.043	0.435	0.097
0.919	0.220	0.222	0.240
0.785	0.584	0.128	0.162
0.631	0.766	0.121	0.027

---

[6] Op. cit., Section 9.2.2. The models to do this are contained in the spreadsheet "Decomposing a Correlation Matrix".

0.419	0.093	0.538	0.188	0.701
0.426	0.093	0.674	0.428	0.415
0.458	0.141	0.812	0.322	0.080
0.614	0.156	0.772	−0.046	0.003
0.856	0.096	0.494	−0.118	0.020
0.947	0.179	0.217	0.152	−0.039
0.814	0.514	0.123	0.233	−0.059
0.615	0.771	0.165	0.019	0.010

There is still one more aspect to clarify before we can run a BGM simulation. Given a current market curve of forward rates, forward volatilities and some assumed B matrix, then we can apply eq. (11.8) to estimate $F_k(\delta_1)$ from $F_k(0)$ using a set of randomly sampled dzs. But what about the step from $F_k(\delta_1)$ to $F_k(\delta_2)$. What assumptions should we make about the future forward volatilities and correlations at time δ_1?

Introduce the concept of an instantaneous volatility $v(t, t_k)$; this is the volatility of the kth forward rate over a very short period of time starting at time t. We will assume that this takes the time-homogeneous form[7] of:

$$v(t, t_k) = [a + b(t_k - t)] * \exp\{-c \cdot (t_k - t)\} + d$$

where the parameters should satisfy certain constraints for realistic volatilities, such as $a + d$, c and $d > 0$. These volatilities are fundamental building blocks, from which we can construct periodic volatilities:

$$\sigma_k^2 \cdot t_k = \int v(t, t_k)^2 \cdot dt \quad \text{integrating from 0 to } t_k = V_k(t_k) - V_k(0)$$

and

$$s_{kj}^2 \cdot \delta_j = \int v(t, t_k)^2 \cdot dt \quad \text{integrating from } t_j \text{ to } t_{j+1} = V_k(t_{j+1}) - V_k(t_j)$$

It is simple albeit tedious to perform the integration analytically.[8] Hence, given a forward volatility curve, we can estimate the parameters $\{a, b, c, d\}$ by doing a least-squares minimisation. To ensure arbitrage exactness, define $K_k = \sigma_k^2 \cdot t_k / [V_k(t_k) - V_k(0)]$; this means that $[V_k(t_k) - V_k(0)] \cdot K_k$ exactly fits the market volatilities at time $t = 0$.

The table on the next page has been implied from the market-based Black forward volatilities (which in turn were implied from the quoted ATM cap prices), which are shown in the first column. The forward–forward volatilities evolve over quarterly periods, and of course drop off as the rates fix. See Worksheet 11.28 for further details; notice from the embedded graph that the volatilities faithfully replicate the humped nature of the original Black volatilities.

---

[7] See Rebonato, op. cit., Chapter 6 for an in-depth discussion of why this form is broadly acceptable.

[8] The indefinite integral of $v(t, t_k)^2$ is

$$(\tfrac{1}{4}c^3) \cdot (8ac^2 de^{-c\Delta} + 4c^3 d^2 t + 8bcde^{-c\Delta}[1 + c\Delta] + e^{-2c\Delta} \cdot \{2a^2 c^2 + 2abc[1 + 2c\Delta] + b^2[1 + 2c^2\Delta^2 + 2c\Delta]\})$$

where $\Delta = t_k - t$.

Forward–forward volatility curves from t_j to $t_{j+1} = t_j + $ Step $\Rightarrow$

$t_k =$	Black forward volatilities	$t_j =$ 0	0.25	0.5	0.75	1	1.25	1.5	1.75	2
0.25	9.7147%	9.7147%								
0.5	10.0856%	10.023%	10.147%							
0.75	10.9748%	10.841%	10.973%	11.109%						
1	12.4933%	12.267%	12.415%	12.566%	12.721%					
1.25	13.6952%	13.369%	13.527%	13.689%	13.856%	14.027%				
1.5	14.5518%	14.123%	14.287%	14.456%	14.629%	14.807%	14.990%			
1.75	15.0376%	14.511%	14.678%	14.848%	15.024%	15.204%	15.389%	15.579%		
2	15.1263%	14.516%	14.679%	14.847%	15.020%	15.197%	15.380%	15.567%	15.760%	
2.25	15.3588%	14.659%	14.821%	14.988%	15.159%	15.336%	15.517%	15.703%	15.894%	16.091%
2.5	15.7342%	14.937%	15.099%	15.266%	15.438%	15.615%	15.796%	15.983%	16.175%	16.372%
2.75	16.2600%	15.355%	15.519%	15.688%	15.862%	16.040%	16.224%	16.412%	16.606%	16.806%
3	16.9424%	15.918%	16.085%	16.256%	16.433%	16.615%	16.802%	16.994%	17.192%	17.395%
3.25	17.2880%	16.161%	16.328%	16.400%	16.675%	16.856%	17.043%	17.235%	17.432%	17.635%
3.5	17.2937%	16.088%	16.250%	16.417%	16.589%	16.767%	16.949%	17.136%	17.329%	17.528%
3.75	16.9550%	15.698%	15.853%	16.013%	16.178%	16.347%	16.522%	16.701%	16.886%	17.076%
4	16.2611%	14.986%	15.131%	15.280%	15.435%	15.593%	15.757%	15.925%	16.098%	16.265%
4.25	15.7285%	14.429%	14.566%	14.707%	14.853%	15.003%	15.157%	15.316%	15.480%	15.648%
4.5	15.3558%	14.026%	14.156%	14.290%	14.429%	14.571%	14.718%	14.870%	15.026%	15.186%

4.75	15.1452%	13.775%	13.900%	14.029%	14.162%	14.299%	14.440%	14.586%	14.736%	14.891%
5	15.1006%	13.678%	13.799%	13.924%	14.053%	14.187%	14.324%	14.466%	14.612%	14.762%
5.25	15.0536%	13.581%	13.698%	13.820%	13.945%	14.075%	14.208%	14.346%	14.488%	14.634%
5.5	15.0012%	13.481%	13.595%	13.713%	13.835%	13.960%	14.090%	14.223%	14.361%	14.503%
5.75	14.9465%	13.382%	13.492%	13.607%	13.724%	13.846%	13.972%	14.102%	14.235%	14.373%
6	14.8876%	13.281%	13.388%	13.499%	13.613%	13.731%	13.853%	13.978%	14.108%	14.242%
6.25	14.8269%	13.182%	13.285%	13.392%	13.502%	13.617%	13.735%	13.856%	13.982%	14.112%
6.5	14.7640%	13.082%	13.182%	13.285%	13.392%	13.503%	13.617%	13.735%	13.857%	13.982%
6.75	14.6978%	12.982%	13.079%	13.178%	13.282%	13.388%	13.499%	13.613%	13.731%	13.853%
7	14.6272%	12.881%	12.973%	13.070%	13.169%	13.273%	13.379%	13.490%	13.604%	13.722%
7.25	14.5639%	12.788%	12.877%	12.970%	13.066%	13.166%	13.269%	13.376%	13.486%	13.600%
7.5	14.5070%	12.702%	12.789%	12.878%	12.971%	13.068%	13.167%	13.270%	13.377%	13.487%
7.75	14.4565%	12.625%	12.708%	12.795%	12.884%	12.977%	13.073%	13.173%	13.276%	13.383%
8	14.4133%	12.556%	12.636%	12.719%	12.806%	12.896%	12.989%	13.085%	13.185%	13.288%
8.25	14.3762%	12.494%	12.571%	12.652%	12.735%	12.822%	12.911%	13.005%	13.101%	13.201%
8.5	14.3469%	12.441%	12.515%	12.593%	12.673%	12.757%	12.843%	12.933%	13.027%	13.123%
8.75	14.3224%	12.394%	12.466%	12.540%	12.618%	12.698%	12.782%	12.869%	12.959%	13.052%
9	14.3057%	12.356%	12.424%	12.496%	12.571%	12.649%	12.729%	12.813%	12.900%	12.991%
9.25	14.2933%	12.323%	12.389%	12.458%	12.530%	12.605%	12.683%	12.764%	12.848%	12.935%
9.5	14.2866%	12.296%	12.360%	12.426%	12.496%	12.568%	12.643%	12.721%	12.802%	12.887%
9.75	14.2866%	12.278%	12.339%	12.402%	12.469%	12.538%	12.611%	12.686%	12.765%	12.846%
10	14.2866%	12.260%	12.319%	12.380%	12.444%	12.511%	12.581%	12.653%	12.729%	12.808%

An alternative approach is to assume that s_{kj} is, as before, time-homogeneous, so that $s_{kj} = s_{k-j}$. Hence we can write:

$$\sigma_k^2 \cdot t_k = \sum s_{k-j}^2 \cdot \delta_j$$

Intuitively, $\sigma_k^2 \cdot t_k$ (as a statement of uncertainty) should be strictly increasing with time; in this case, the above expression can be exactly solved by simple bootstrapping. Unfortunately, in reality, the market volatilities $\sigma_k^2 \cdot t_k$ do not necessarily increase (see, for example, the data used to produce the table on the previous page), possibly due to supply and demand, and therefore this approach cannot be relied upon (see Worksheet 11.29 for an example).

In Chapter 10, the following parametric form for correlation was introduced:

$$\rho_{kj} = \exp\{-\lambda * |t_k - t_j|\}$$

where $\lambda > 0$ is a constant parameter. This assumes that forward rates that are equi-distant apart would have the same correlation, and rates that are far apart would have an effective zero-correlation. An extended formula would be:

$$\rho_{kj} = \rho_{\text{Long}} + (1 - \rho_{\text{Long}}) * \exp\{-\lambda * |t_k - t_j|\}$$

where ρ_{Long} is an asymptotic long correlation parameter. This implies that correlations can never drop down to zero. Notice that these expressions are independent of the current time t, which eases the computations considerably, but may also lead to correlations that do not follow market observations. However, given the paucity of possible calibration instruments, introducing more degrees of freedom by including a time dimension may lead to parameter instability.

In practice, forward rates at the long end of the curve are generally more highly correlated than rates at the short end; this is known as correlation convexity. There are formulae with more parameters that incorporate this, but they require considerably more computational effort, and run into the danger of overfitting.

We are now in a position to evolve a forward curve. Given:

- A current forward curve: F_{k_0} for $k = 1, 2, \ldots, n$.
- A current forward Black volatility curve: σ_k for $k = 1, 2, \ldots, n$;
  ○ the forward–forward volatility curves can be constructed from this.
- Correlation parameters: ρ_{Long} and λ;
  ○ the elements of matrix B can be computed

We will build a BGM simulation on a quarterly basis out for 20 years, and then calibrate it to some European swaption prices available from the marketplace. Spreadsheet "Example of BGM Sampling" shows all the details. The spreadsheet is divided as follows:

- "Market data" (Worksheet 11.30): this contains the two forward curves as input.
- "Forward-Forward Vols" (Worksheet 11.31): this generates forward–forward volatilities as described above.
- "Correlation Matrix" (Worksheet 11.32): this contains the generated correlation matrix for given values of ρ_{Long} and λ. A full-spanning B matrix is then calculated using a

Cholesky decomposition. Under this assumption (but not for other B matrices):

$$\sum_q b_{k,q,j} \cdot b_{i,q,j} = \rho_{ki}$$

which simplifies the drift term to

$$s_{kj} \cdot \sum_i s_{ij} \cdot R_{ij} \cdot \rho_{ki}$$

summed from $i = j, \ldots, k$

- "R(i,j)" (Worksheet 11.33): this calculates R_{ij} from each generated forward rate.
- "Sum s(i,j).R(i,j).((i,j)" (Worksheet 11.34): this calculates the intermediate summation as the name implies.
- "rv's" (Worksheet 11.35): this generates normally distributed random variates.
- "BGM Sampling" (Worksheet 11.36): this contains the heart of the algorithm, randomly generating the new forward curves every 3 months.

For any given forward rate, the model generates a path of quarterly observations from today (spot) until the fixing date. Whilst this may be very useful information for some structures, for most it is too much, as the only relevant piece of information is the estimated fixing. The path taken to get to this fixing is not relevant. But we were forced to model the forward rate path because of the need to re-estimate the drift term (which depends upon the generated forward rates) after relatively small time intervals.

Ideally however, we would like to make a single time step for the kth rate from $t = 0$ to $t = t_k$, but we do not know what drift term to use. However, Rebonato[9] suggests the following very long-step approach:

1. Generate a forward rate using:

$$F_{kk} = F_{k0} * \exp\left\{ \left[\mu_{k0} - \tfrac{1}{2}\sigma_k^2\right] \cdot t_k + \sigma_q \sum_q b_{k,q} \cdot dz_q \cdot \sqrt{t_k} \right\}$$

2. Calculate a new drift term μ_{kk} using F_{kk}, and hence an average drift

$$\mu_{kav} = 0.5\{\mu_{k0} + \mu_{kk}\}$$

3. Use this average term, and the same random variables as before, to compute a revised F_{kk}.

This is demonstrated in Spreadsheet 11.41, which consists of worksheets:

- "Market data" (Worksheet 11.37), "Forward-Forward Vols" (Worksheet 11.38) and "Correlation Matrix" (Worksheet 11.39) as before.
- "$\sigma(i).\rho(k,i)$": this calculates the intermediate summation as the name implies.
- "BGM long-step Sampling" (Worksheet 11.41): this represents the heart of the algorithm, and proceeds in the following steps:
  - columns [1] and [2] are the current forward rates and forward volatilities;
  - columns [3] and [4] calculate R_{k0} and the drift term at $t = 0$;

---

[9] He calls this very long-step, in comparison with the previous approach which is merely long-step, i.e. uses a quarterly time step, which itself is long in comparison with the instantaneous rates used in Heath–Jarrow–Morton. Op. cit., Chapter 4.

○ columns [5] and [6] generate correlated random variates;
○ column [7] calculates F_{kk} as above;
○ based upon this, columns [8], [9] and [10] calculate R_{kk}, the average R and hence the adjusted drift term, respectively;
○ finally, column [11] calculates the new forward rate curve using the long-step drift.

The correlation parameters ρ_{Long} and λ need to be calibrated. Worksheet 11.42 contains an example of calibration, i.e. fitting to some quoted European swaptions. The swaptions are the ATM ones created in Section 11.3; their prices are summarised in the following table:

Swaption	Strike	Black prices	Simulated prices
1/11	4.5387%	0.0201	0.0290
2/12	4.8599%	0.0299	0.0320
3/13	5.0945%	0.0366	0.0346
4/14	5.2778%	0.0409	0.0366

Using different values of ρ_{Long} and λ, the simulated prices were derived by minimising least-squares errors.

Consider the following "sticky" floater (this is a slight modification of the one issued by the EIB in 2004 described in Section 11.2):

Principal:	$100m
Maturity:	6 years
Issue price:	99.625
Coupon:	6 mo. Libor + 50 bp
Subject to:	$C_t \leq C_{t-1} + 20\,\text{bp}$

The stickiness constrains the increase in the coupon should rates rise, whilst any decline in rates is fully unchecked. The constraint cannot be represented by a simple spread option on $(C_t - C_{t-1})$ as C_{t-1} itself may well depend upon earlier coupons. Thus, simulation is the only practical approach. Spreadsheet 11.49 builds the BGM simulation as described above, but also introduces some other devices. First, Worksheet 11.48 in the spreadsheet swaps the unconstrained floater into 3 mo. Libor plus 56.6 bp using the usual asset-packaging approach as described in Chapter 5. Worksheet 11.49 then simulates both the constrained and unconstrained floaters simultaneously. Indeed it does the simulation twice, once using normal random variates and once using antithetic (i.e. the negative of the normal) variates. The resulting margin is then averaged in cells W29 and X29, respectively. This is likely to reduce overall fluctuations in the results considerably. The average breakeven margin is then calculated for both floaters. Finally, the corrected margin for the constrained floater is estimated by:

Simulated margin for constrained floater

$+$ (Simulated margin for unconstrained floater $-$ 56.6 bp)

This approach uses the error in pricing the unconstrained floater as a control. Whilst the unconstrained floater swapped into +56.6 bp, the presence of the constraint reduces the margin to −14 bp to the significant benefit of the issuer.

There is no particularly appropriate calibration for this structure; possibly caplets on 6 mo. Libor. This implies that the correlation structure is unlikely to have a significant effect.

The TARN described above could also be handled by simulation fairly easily. A simple control would be a note that paid $3.75 * (10 \, \text{yr CMS} - 2 \, \text{yr CMS})$. Of course, the maturity of the TARN is uncertain, but the control note could easily be modelled analytically for a range of possible maturities, and the correct maturity selected for each scenario of the TARN. An adjustment could then be made, not on average across all scenarios, but for each scenario. Spreadsheet 11.56 is divided into further worksheets:

- The first five worksheets, from "Market Data" (Worksheet 11.50) until "BGM very long-step sampling" (Worksheet 11.54) are the same as before.
- "Analytic Spread Floater" (Worksheet 11.55) calculates the breakeven margin for notes with a coupon of $3.75 * (10 \, \text{yr CMS} - 2 \, \text{yr CMS})$ for differing maturities.
- "Modelling a TARN" (Worksheet 11.56) contains the main model. This estimates the breakeven margin for the TARN for a range of scenarios under both normal and antithetic variates. It also calculates the breakeven margin for simulated spread floaters of differing maturities, and hence the correction factor for each scenario, based upon the appropriate lifetime of the TARN. The overall funding margin is estimated to be in the region of Libor − 10 to 15 bp (obviously this range could be refined by taking more than 500 scenarios).

Which structures would be most suitable to calibrate the simulation to this particular structure? The most appropriate would be fixed length European swaptions such as $N/2$ and $N/10$ where N would range from 1 year out to 10 years, such as $N = 2, 4, 6, 8, 10$.

Another fairly common structure is an index amortising swap. Amortising swaps were discussed in Chapter 4; in those, the amortising schedule was fixed. In index amortisers, the amortisation is driven by some function of a reference index. The function is usually a ratchet, namely that the principal of the swap may decrease, but can never increase again. For example, long-term fixed rate mortgages are common in the US; the rate charged contains the cost of an option permitting the mortgagor to repay the mortgage early without penalty. As interest rates drop, the speed of repayment accelerates, as mortgagors re-finance. Assume that the originating mortgage house had funded the lendings by issuing a floating rate note. It therefore has fixed rate receipts but a floating liability; this could be hedged by entering into an IRS to pay fixed, receive floating. But the prepayment option means that the receipts have an unknown amortising schedule. If, based on historic evidence and the current state of the economy, a likely prepayment schedule based on the movement of interest rates can be estimated, then this may be represented by an index amortising swap. Whilst these may be priced using an IRS plus a series of Bermudan down-and-in swaptions, the usual way is to simulate the movement of the rates, model the cashflows and calculate the average break-even fixed rate.

Of course, the actual prepayment schedule is unlikely to match the likely schedule estimated above. A balance guarantee (or guaranty) swap is similar to an index amortiser, but where the amortisation schedule exactly matches the actual schedule. These can be modelled by simulating index amortisers under a range of different (but likely) prepayment schedules, and taking some conservative outcome as the price.

The final structure to be considered in this section is a USD snowball similar to the one issued by BPI; this is summarised below:

Issue date:	6 February 2008
Maturity:	7 years
Redemption:	100
Coupon:	7% sa in first year
	Thereafter $\text{Coupon}(t) = \text{Coupon}(t-1) + K(t) - 6\,\text{mo. Libor} \geq 0$
	where K starts at 2% and increments by 25 bp each period
Calls:	Every coupon date starting 6 August 2009

A likely control structure would be a note paying $C(t) = R(t-1) + K(t) - R(t)$ where $R(x)$ is the Libor fixing for period x. The expected value of the coupon could be estimated from the expected value of $\{R(t-1) - R(t)\}$ from a Margrabe formula; this requires both volatilities and a spread correlation. More importantly, however, the call strip makes this an example of a backward–forward structure.

Handling call strips (or other forward-looking conditions) is difficult within simulations. A basic algorithm is as follows:

- let H_k be the value of some product at time t_k if the call has not yet been exercised;
- let G_k be the value of the product if the call is exercised at time t_k;
- hence, define the value of the product $V_k = \max\{H_k, G_k\}$;
- clearly, $H_{k-1} = E\{V_k * \text{DF}_k\}/\text{DF}_{k-1}$;
- this is a recursive structure; solve for H_0.

The main difficulty is to estimate H_k as this represents the expected value of the product if not called; to estimate this would require a large number of scenarios generated from time t_k. Under these conditions, the time for the simulation is effectively squared.

The problem may be simplified by recognising that an exercise region could be defined:

$$R_k = \{\omega \in \Omega \,|\, H_k(\omega) \leq G_k(\omega)\} \quad \text{for a given parameter } \omega$$

ω might represent the level of interest rates evolved through time, as we know that a callable bond will only be exercised when rates are low. Thus, for $\omega \in R_k$, the product can be assumed to be called, and not called outside this boundary. Various practical algorithms have been developed[10] using this idea; generally these algorithms produce upper and/or lower bounds on the valuation.

---

[10] For example, F. Longstaff *et al.*, "Valuing American options by simulation: A simple least-squares approach", *Review of Financial Studies*, Spring 2001, **14**(1), pp. 113–47; L. Andersen, "A simple approach to the pricing of Bermudan swaptions in the multi-factor LMM", available from SSRN, 1999; M. Pedersen, "Bermudan swaptions in the LMM", available from SSRN, 1999.

To illustrate one simple approximate approach, consider the swapping of a security into floating €uribor. From the point of view of the swap counterparty, the swap can be written as follows:

$$
\begin{array}{ll}
+P & -100 \\
-C_1 & +(\text{€}_1 + m) \\
-C_2 & +(\text{€}_2 + m) \\
-C_3 & +(\text{€}_3 + m) \\
\vdots & \\
-C_{T-1} & +(\text{€}_{T-1} + m) \\
-C_T - R & +(\text{€}_T + m) + 100
\end{array}
$$

It has been tacitly assumed that the frequencies of cashflows on the two sides are the same, but that is not relevant for the following discussion. Define $X(t)$ as the value of the swap at time t. This may be calculated in reverse:

$$
\begin{aligned}
X(T) &= -C_T - R + (\text{€}_T + m) + 100 \\
X(T-1) &= X(T) * \text{DF}_{T-1,T} - C_{T-1} + (\text{€}_{T-1} + m) \\
&\vdots \\
X(0) &= X(1) * \text{DF}_{0,1} + P - 100
\end{aligned}
$$

where $\text{DF}_{t-1,t}$ is the one-period discount factor $= \text{DF}_t/\text{DF}_{t-1}$. To fair-value the swap, solve for m so that $X(0) = 0$.

Assume that the swap counterparty has the right to call the swap at zero, i.e. is able to cancel the swap, at time t. He would still however have to pay and would receive the cashflows on that date. Hence, he would call if the future value to him $X(t+1) < 0$.

Therefore, the valuation equation could be modified to:

$$
X(t) = \max\{0, X(t+1)\} * \text{DF}_{t,t+1} - C_t + (\text{€}_t + m)
$$

The recursion could however still be solved for m so that $X(0) = 0$. Worksheet 11.34 "Modelling a callable snowball by simulation" on the accompanying CD demonstrates this approach. Worksheet 11.34 is broken down into two further worksheets:

- "Snowball" (Worksheet 11.35) models the structure without calls in the usual fashion.
- "Snowball with calls" (Worksheet 11.36) models the structure with calls; the sheet is set up to do eight iterations of a simple Newton–Raphson algorithm to solve for the breakeven margin.

As expected, the existence of the call strip inevitably improves the funding cost of the issuer. Reducing correlation, which allows individual rates to have more volatility, increases the value of the call strip significantly, as may be seen from the table below (purely for indication; the simulations were not done using the same random variates, and hence are not strictly comparable).

Changing correlation		
Beta	**Value of call strip**	**How often called**
50%	19.91	64.0%
75%	18.67	65.6%
100%	13.08	66.4%
150%	6.83	58.4%
250%	4.93	53.0%

11.5 APPENDIX: EXTENSIONS TO NUMERICAL TREES

The text of Chapter 11 concentrated on two main approaches, numerical methods exemplified by BDT and simulation methods based on the Libor model. Whilst the Libor model is becoming an industry standard, there are a number of other numerical models and approaches that are also widely used. The objective of this section is to discuss these briefly.

11.5.1 Incorporating a volatility smile[11]

Chapter 10 discussed volatility smiles arising in the interest rate options markets in some detail. Should these be incorporated into the numerical tree? Whilst the reasons for the smile may be debated, its existence and implication, namely that forward interest rates at some distance away from the current level appear to exhibit higher volatility, cannot be denied. Therefore, fitting the tree solely to the ATM forward volatility curve is not consistent with Black option pricing quoted in the market.

Assume, for a given time step t, we know a forward volatility curve $\sigma_{t-1}(K)$ where K is the strike axis, including $\sigma_{t-1,\text{ATM}}$. This last volatility is likely to be close to $\sigma_{t-1,t/2}$ if t is even, and $0.5 * [\sigma_{t-1,(t-1)/2} + \sigma_{t-1,(t+1)/2}]$ if t is odd. Define the ATM step length to be:

$$\Delta_t = \exp\{\sigma_{t-1,\text{ATM}} \cdot \sqrt{d_t}\}$$

For any column t, its midpoint $r_{t,t/2} \approx$ the forward rate r_t. For t odd, the actual rates are given by $r_{t,t/2\pm\frac{1}{2}+n}$ where $n = \pm0, \pm1, \ldots, \pm(t-1)/2$. Hence, the appropriately respective volatilities to use are at the points $K_n = \{t/2 + 2n \cdot \Delta_t\}$, interpolated off the volatility curve.[12] This involves an approximation: the use of Δ_t which is based only on ATM volatility, is used to estimate the interpolation along the K-axis. Hence we proceed as follows:

- guess $r_{t,t/2}$ from the known forward rate r_t;
- calculate the volatilities $\sigma_{t-1}(K_n)$ for $n = \pm0, \pm1, \ldots, \pm(t-1)/2$;

---

[11] See also J. James et al., Interest Rate Modelling, Chapter 19, published by Wiley 2000, for a discussion on the calibration of trees to smiles.
[12] Using perhaps a SABR model as described in Chapter 10.

- calculate $r_{t,t/2\pm\frac{1}{2}\pm k} = r_{t,t/2\pm\frac{1}{2}\pm(k-1)} \cdot \exp\{2 \cdot \sigma_{t-1}(K_n) \cdot \sqrt{d_t}\}$ where the step length now depends upon the volatility within the smile.

If t is even, then the rates are $r_{t,t/2+n}$ where $n = \pm 0, \pm 1, \ldots, \pm t/2$. In this case, $K_n = \{t/2 \pm (2n+1) \cdot \Delta_t\}$, etc.

We can now proceed in the same way, fitting $r_{t,t/2}$ to known market data. Spreadsheet 11.67 contains the relevant worksheets. Two rate trees are built, one with a smile based on the forward volatility surface below (see Worksheet 11.67), and one based purely on the ATM volatilities (see Worksheet 11.66). Notice that the smile is not symmetric, and that ATM is not necessarily the lowest volatility for a given maturity (see table on next page).

The diagram below shows the same column—the 2-year point—from the two rate trees:

Extract from tree: 2-year point		
	With smile	**Without smile**
0	8.1181%	7.5151%
1	6.6144%	6.3987%
2	5.4996%	5.4482%
3	4.6383%	4.6388%
4	3.9400%	3.9497%
5	3.3547%	3.3630%
6	2.8349%	2.8634%
7	2.3501%	2.4380%
8	1.2800%	2.0758%

As expected, the smile column has a wider spread of rates. But if we had selected another column, say the 5-year point, then the smile column would have lower rates because of the higher OTM volatility, but the high rates would be lower because of the lower ITM volatility. The two worksheets 11.66 and 11.67 price a $100m 5-year Bermudan floorlet, set with a fixed strike, and exercisable on any coupon date after the first year. If the strike is considerably OTM, so it is up in the wings of the smile, then the smile price at $13,035 is 14% higher than the non-smile price of $11,437. However, if the strike is close to ATM at 4%, then the two prices are only 2% apart at $190,365 and $186,095, respectively. This is because the averaging back on the tree is more around ATM, where the smile effects are considerably less.

11.5.2 Hull–White numerical trees

These are probably the other form of tree most commonly used for modelling interest rates. The commonest implementation uses the following generating process:

$$dr = [\theta(t) - \alpha(t) \cdot r(t)] \cdot dt + \varphi(t) \cdot dz$$

Years	−3.5%	−3.0%	−2.5%	−2.0%	−1.5%	−1.0%	−0.5%	ATM 0%	0.5%	1.0%	1.5%	2.0%	2.5%	3.0%
0.25	33.4%	33.4%	33.4%	33.0%	29.4%	23.5%	15.4%	10.44%	10.9%	12.3%	13.6%	15.1%	16.6%	18.0%
0.50	33.4%	33.4%	33.4%	32.9%	29.2%	23.1%	15.1%	10.44%	11.0%	12.3%	13.7%	15.2%	16.7%	18.1%
0.75	33.4%	33.4%	33.4%	32.6%	28.7%	22.2%	14.5%	10.44%	11.1%	12.5%	13.9%	15.4%	16.8%	18.2%
1.00	33.4%	33.4%	33.4%	32.2%	27.9%	20.8%	13.7%	10.44%	11.3%	12.7%	14.1%	15.6%	17.0%	18.4%
1.25	25.6%	25.6%	25.6%	20.0%	15.9%	15.0%	15.2%	15.31%	17.0%	18.2%	18.8%	19.1%	19.0%	18.8%
1.50	22.3%	22.3%	22.3%	13.8%	9.8%	13.3%	16.5%	17.33%	19.3%	20.5%	20.6%	20.4%	19.6%	18.7%
1.75	29.9%	29.9%	29.9%	22.6%	16.6%	17.0%	15.5%	15.33%	15.9%	16.3%	16.9%	17.4%	18.1%	18.8%
2.00	29.7%	29.7%	29.7%	18.5%	16.1%	16.5%	16.1%	16.08%	16.4%	16.6%	17.1%	17.5%	18.2%	18.9%
2.25	24.2%	24.2%	23.8%	19.0%	14.5%	17.1%	16.4%	16.13%	16.2%	16.5%	16.6%	16.7%	16.9%	17.1%
2.50	22.8%	22.8%	21.6%	16.0%	13.9%	17.4%	16.9%	16.71%	16.5%	16.5%	16.5%	16.5%	16.6%	16.8%
2.75	21.3%	21.3%	19.9%	13.6%	13.2%	17.8%	17.4%	17.28%	16.7%	16.6%	16.4%	16.3%	16.3%	16.3%
3.00	19.8%	19.8%	18.6%	12.4%	11.7%	18.2%	18.0%	17.86%	16.9%	16.6%	16.3%	16.0%	15.9%	15.9%
3.25	23.7%	23.7%	23.0%	19.2%	18.7%	17.3%	16.5%	16.30%	16.2%	16.3%	16.6%	16.9%	17.1%	17.2%
3.50	23.0%	23.0%	22.7%	18.5%	18.9%	17.5%	16.8%	16.54%	16.3%	16.2%	16.5%	16.8%	16.9%	17.1%
3.75	22.4%	22.4%	22.2%	17.9%	19.1%	17.7%	17.0%	16.77%	16.4%	16.2%	16.5%	16.8%	16.8%	16.9%
4.00	21.7%	21.7%	21.6%	17.3%	19.2%	17.9%	17.3%	17.00%	16.5%	16.2%	16.5%	16.7%	16.7%	16.7%
4.25	22.1%	22.1%	21.8%	20.0%	18.8%	17.6%	16.7%	16.14%	15.9%	15.8%	15.8%	15.8%	16.2%	16.6%
4.50	21.5%	21.5%	21.1%	19.9%	18.8%	17.6%	16.8%	16.24%	15.9%	15.7%	15.7%	15.7%	16.1%	16.4%
4.75	20.9%	20.9%	20.3%	19.8%	18.8%	17.7%	16.9%	16.34%	15.9%	15.7%	15.5%	15.5%	15.9%	16.3%
5.00	20.4%	20.4%	19.5%	19.8%	18.8%	17.7%	17.0%	16.45%	15.9%	15.6%	15.4%	15.4%	15.8%	16.1%

Unlike BDT, this is a normal model, permitting changes in the rates dr so that the rates may potentially go negative. Furthermore, the term $\varphi(t)$, whilst measuring uncertainty, is not a Black volatility, but is expressed as an absolute change in $r(t)$ measured in bp. The model permits mean reversion; namely, for positive values of $\theta(t)$ and $\alpha(t)$, the drift term may be negative for high values of $r(t)$, and positive for low values. This additional parameter requires a trinomial model, introducing an additional degree of freedom to that in a BDT model.

Model building starts from a simplified process:

$$dr = -\alpha(t).r(t).dt + \varphi(t).dz$$

Using a simple trinomial process as shown below:

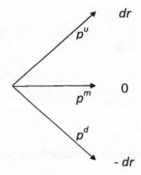

Dropping the (t) for clarity, we can write:

$$E\{dr\} = p^u.dr + p^m.0 + p^d.-dr$$

$$= -\alpha.r.dt$$

$$\text{Variance}\{dr\} = p^u.[dr^2 - (\alpha.r.dt)^2] + p^m.[-(\alpha.r.dt)^2] + p^d.[dr^2 - (\alpha.r.dt)^2]$$

$$= \varphi^2.dt$$

and $p^u + p^m + p^d = 1$

Solving for the probabilities, we get

$$p^u = [\varphi^2.dt + (\alpha.r.dt)^2 - \alpha.r.dt.dr]/2dr^2, \text{ etc.}$$

Unlike BDT, this is a lattice model which implies that the step lengths in the $\{r,t\}$ dimensions are predefined.[13] HW recommend the following relationship $dr^2 = 3\varphi^2.dt$. Furthermore, assume that the starting node is at the jth step in the r-dimension, where

---

[13] It is feasible to have uneven time steps to ensure that key dates t_1, t_2, t_3, etc. fall on nodes; for example, a cashflow date or a Bermudan exercise date. In this case, the central node is the one closest to $E\{r_{i+1}\} = r_i - \alpha_i.r_i.(t_{i+1} - t_i)$.

$j = 0, \pm 1, \pm 2, \ldots$, hence $r(t) = j \cdot dr$. Substituting and re-arranging gives:

$$p^u = \tfrac{1}{6} + [(\alpha \cdot j \cdot dt)^2 - (\alpha \cdot j \cdot dt)]/2$$

$$p^d = \tfrac{1}{6} + [(\alpha \cdot j \cdot dt)^2 + (\alpha \cdot j \cdot dt)]/2$$

$$p^m = \tfrac{2}{3} - (\alpha \cdot j \cdot dt)^2$$

Unfortunately, as j increases, it is possible for p^m to become negative; for positive α, the absolute value of j should not exceed $(0.816/\alpha \cdot dt)$. To overcome this, HW change the branching to (a) below for positive j, and to (b) for negative j:

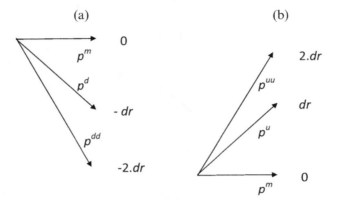

This implies the overall lattice structure resembles a pruned tree, as shown below:

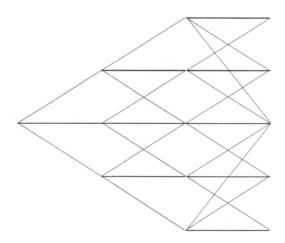

The new branching equations for (a) are:

$$p^m = \tfrac{7}{6} + [(\alpha \cdot j \cdot dt)^2 - 3 \cdot (\alpha \cdot j \cdot dt)]/2$$

$$p^d = -\tfrac{1}{3} - (\alpha \cdot j \cdot dt)^2 + 2 \cdot (\alpha \cdot j \cdot dt)$$

$$p^{dd} = \tfrac{1}{6} + [(\alpha \cdot j \cdot dt)^2 - (\alpha \cdot j \cdot dt)]/2$$

and for (b):

$$p^{uu} = \tfrac{1}{6} + [(\alpha . j . dt)^2 + (\alpha . j . dt)]/2$$

$$p^u = -\tfrac{1}{3} - (\alpha . j . dt)^2 - 2 . (\alpha . j . dt)$$

$$p^m = \tfrac{7}{6} + [(\alpha . j . dt)^2 + 3 . (\alpha . j . dt)]/2$$

These also need to be positive, which implies that the branching should not be switched until the absolute value of j exceeds $(0.184/\alpha . dt)$. In practice, it is probably most computationally efficient to switch as early as possible.

As an example, suppose we set $\alpha = 10\%$ and $\varphi = 88$ bp. If $dt = 0.25$ years, then $dr = 0.7623\%$. The normal trinomial branching probabilities are shown in the table below:

j	j*del r	pd	pm	pu
−8	−6.099%	0.0867	0.6267	0.2867
−7	−5.336%	0.0945	0.6360	0.2695
−6	−4.574%	0.1029	0.6442	0.2529
−5	−3.812%	0.1120	0.6510	0.2370
−4	−3.049%	0.1217	0.6567	0.2217
−3	−2.287%	0.1320	0.6610	0.2070
−2	−1.525%	0.1429	0.6642	0.1929
−1	−0.762%	0.1545	0.6660	0.1795
0	0.000%	0.1667	0.6667	0.1667
1	0.762%	0.1795	0.6660	0.1545
2	1.525%	0.1929	0.6642	0.1429
3	2.287%	0.2070	0.6610	0.1320
4	3.049%	0.2217	0.6567	0.1217
5	3.812%	0.2370	0.6510	0.1120
6	4.574%	0.2529	0.6442	0.1029
7	5.336%	0.2695	0.6360	0.0945
8	6.099%	0.2867	0.6267	0.0867

The skewed branching could commence at $j = \pm 8$ (the smallest integer above $0.184/\alpha . dt$), and in that case, the first probabilities would be:

p^{dd}	p^d	p^m	p^u	p^{uu}
		0.8867	0.0267	0.0867
0.0867	0.0267	0.8867		

The second step is to fit the lattice to market data. This can be done first by introducing the drift term $\theta(t)$ so that the rate evolution fits to the current forward curve. For various reasons which will be obvious later, the tree evolves forward continuously compounded zero-coupon rates, and not forward simple rates as in BDT. Second, φ may be made time-dependent, thus ultimately fitting it to a volatility curve.

We can proceed in a very similar fashion to the BDT algorithm. Assume we are at node $\{m, j\}$; this means there have been m time steps of length dt, and j rate steps of size dr. We know the discount factor DF_m off the current curve; this is the same for all j nodes at time m. We can write, as before—see eq. (11.5):

$$DF_m = \sum_j X_{m,j} \qquad (11.9)$$

The recursive relationship for $X_{m,j}$ is a generalisation of eq. (11.3), because now there are more than two possible predecessor nodes:

$$X_{m,j} = \sum_k x_{m-1,k} \cdot p_{m-1,k,j} \cdot DF_{m-1,k} \qquad (11.10)$$

where k is the set of predecessor nodes, $p_{m-1,k,j}$ is the probability of moving from node $\{m-1, k\}$ to node $\{m, j\}$, and $DF_{m-1,k}$ is the one-period discount factor from node $\{m-1, k\}$ to period m. This discount factor is currently set (in the first step) to $\exp\{-k \cdot dr \cdot dt\}$.

Based on the current set of rates developed in the first step (see table on previous page), it is highly unlikely that eq. (11.9) is true. Introduce θ_{m-1} so that:

$$DF(\theta)_{m-1,k} = \exp\{-[\theta_{m-1} + k \cdot dr] \cdot dt\} = \exp\{-\theta_{m-1} \cdot dt\} \cdot DF(0)_{m-1,k}$$

and

$$X(\theta)_{m,j} = X(0)_{m,j} \cdot \exp\{-\theta_{m-1} \cdot dt\}$$

We can now solve eq. (11.9) for θ_{m-1}:

$$\theta_{m-1} = \ln\left\{ \sum_j X(0)_{m,j}/DF_m \right\} \Big/ dt$$

This enables the lattice to be built without any step-by-step iteration, which makes it considerably faster than BDT. If simple forward rates were used instead of c–c zero rates, then the same approach could be applied, but θ could only be estimated iteratively.

Spreadsheet 11.69 contains the relevant worksheets. Worksheet 11.69 builds a HW tree using the market data out of 4 February 2008. This is done in two steps as described above, first building the tree centred upon $r = 0\%$, and then fitted to the current zero curve. A volatility curve is also introduced; this was a forward Black curve $\sigma(t)$ which was then converted approximately into bp volatility by the formula $\varphi(t) \approx \sigma(t) * r(t)$. In turn, this changes the interest rate step length due to the relationship $dr(t)^2 = 3\varphi(t)^2 \cdot dt$. The final tree is only built out to $j = \pm 8$ for an α of 10% as described above.

The resultant tree is then used to price a 5-year Bermudan caplet, struck at 3% (see Worksheet 11.70). Obviously the zero rate on the tree at maturity has to be converted into a simple forward rate by $r_t = [\exp\{-z_t \cdot dt\} - 1]/dt$. The final payoff is calculated as $\max\{0, r_t - \text{Strike}\} * d_t * DF_t$. The expected results are calculated using the probabilities, and then folded back to the earlier period using the appropriate rate for discounting. As this is a Bermudan option, then, at each period, the folded back value is compared with the value of exercising earlier, and the maximum taken. The price of the Bermudan caplet is

37.285 bp. The price of a European version would be very similar, at 37.057 bp. The very small differences in the prices is due to the relative low number of times it is optimal to exercise early (see the early exercise tree in cells {K57:AA76} in Worksheet 11.70). This can be compared with the prices off a BDT tree of 35.689 bp and 35.606 bp, respectively (see Worksheet 11.80 contained in Spreadsheet 11.80 for details), and the Black price of 35.649 bp for the European version.

But the HW tree was built assuming a known mean reversion parameter $a(t)$ and bp volatilities $\varphi(t)$. These input parameters are unobservable, so $a(t)$ was set to a constant 10% and the volatilities estimated from the Black forward volatility curve using an approximation. In practice the HW tree needs to be calibrated, namely the input parameters estimated, to market observations. For example, we could take the Black volatility curve, calculate the Black European caplet prices for a range of maturities and then use those prices to imply the HW parameters. But the two parameters are not independent, but interact in opposite directions, so separating the effects of the two vectors from market data would be very difficult. In practice, therefore, it is common to set $a(t)$ to a time-independent constant a, and then solve for $\varphi(t)$ and a.

For example, assume we have three ATM European swaptions as shown below:

2/4 receivers struck at 4.164%:	Price = 92.57 bp
2/6 receivers struck at 4.431%:	Price = 151.14 bp
4/4 receivers struck at 4.825%:	Price = 143.01 bp

The fixed side of each forward swap is assumed (to make the example simple) to be quarterly Act/360. The prices were estimated off a BDT tree (see Worksheet 11.81 for details). We assume five HW parameters: a, $\varphi(0\text{--}2)$, $\varphi(2\text{--}4)$, $\varphi(4\text{--}6)$ and $\varphi(6\text{--}8)$. (*Note*: This creates a piecewise constant volatility curve.) Optimal values for these parameters are estimated by minimising max{individual squared errors} (an alternative would be minimising the sum of squared errors):

$\varphi(0\text{--}2)$	0.534%
$\varphi(2\text{--}4)$	0.393%
$\varphi(4\text{--}6)$	0.239%
$\varphi(6\text{--}8)$	0.781%
a	14.67%

These give a maximum pricing error across the three swaptions of ±0.3 bp. Full details are shown in the following worksheets:

- "Time-dependent H&W (2)" (Worksheet 11.71).
- "Pricing Euro swaption 2x4" (Worksheet 11.72).
- "Pricing Euro swaption 2x6" (Worksheet 11.73).
- "Pricing Euro swaption 4x4" (Worksheet 11.74).

11.5.3 Extensions to BDT and HW models

A wide range of alternative tree and lattice models have been proposed in the literature.[14] However, the two models above are by far the most common ones in practical use. The HW model described above was a normal model, namely changes in rates follow a normal distribution. It is possible for rates therefore to go negative; the author has used a HW model to price a zero-strike interest rate floor, and got a positive value! It is feasible to modify the algorithm to become log-normal by using $r_t = \exp\{x_t\}$ where x_t follows the normal process. By modifying the initial expectation and variance equations, Black market data may be used to build the model. We now have a trinomial, mean-reverting log-normal process. This version is often referred to as a Black–Karasinski model,[15] as it may also be regarded as an extension to the binomial BDT model. Another way of implementing this model is to use BDT, but with varying time steps as the additional parameter. Of course, the resulting models cannot be solved analytically, but only iteratively as BDT.

Another problem with the HW model is that the mean reversion parameter can end up negative, resulting in mean diversion. This usually arises when calibrating to a humped Black volatility curve—as often found in practice and described in Chapter 10—as the short end has rising volatility. Constraining this parameter to be positive results in a downward-sloping volatility curve with no hump, thus being unable to fit to the market data. HW tried to overcome this problem by introducing a two-factor model. All the numerical models discussed so far in this chapter are one-factor models, evolving a short interest rate through time, and hoping it will fit to the market data. Implicitly, we are assuming that the observed rates forming the interest rate curve will evolve through time by parallel shifts, i.e. the rates will exhibit perfect correlations. For many structures, this is a perfectly adequate assumption, but for others such as steepener products this is unrealistic.

Two-factor models are usually expressed in two different ways:

- $r_t = \alpha \cdot x_t + \beta \cdot y_t$ where x_t and y_t are subject to their own random processes:

$$dx_t = \mu^x(x,t) \cdot dt + \phi^x(x,t) \cdot dz_x(t)$$
$$dy_t = \mu^y(y,t) \cdot dt + \phi^y(y,t) \cdot dz_y(t)$$

where $dz_x(t) \cdot dz_y(t) = \rho \, dt$;
- the short rate has the usual generating process:

$$dr_t = \mu^r(r,t) \cdot dt + \phi^r(r,t) \cdot dz_r(t)$$

but the drift or stochastic term is also subject to its own generating process, again with a correlation between them. For example, HW introduced their two-factor model[16] as:

$$dr = [\theta(t) + x - \alpha(t) \cdot r(t)] \cdot dt + \varphi(t) \cdot dz_1$$
$$dx = -b \cdot x \cdot dt + \sigma \cdot dz_2 \quad \text{with } dz_1 \cdot dz_2 = \rho \cdot dt$$

The two ways are however economically equivalent.

[14] See, for example, the discussion in James et al., ibid., Chapter 14.
[15] F. Black et al., "Bond and option pricing when short rates are lognormal", *Financial Analysts Journal*, **47**, pp. 52-59, 1991. See Section 3.5 in Brigo, *ibid.*, for a detailed discussion on the construction of the BK tree.
[16] J. Hull et al., "Numerical procedures for implementing term structure models II: Two-factor models'", *Journal of Derivatives*, pp. 37–48, Winter, 1994.

HW construct a two-dimensional (r, x) tree which is trinomial in both dimensions. If the correlation is assumed to be zero for the moment, then it is feasible to write down expectations and variances for r and x at time $t + dt$ given knowledge of $r(t)$ and $x(t)$. For example, if the current node at time t is (i, j), which means location at the point $(i \cdot dr, j \cdot dx)$, then:

$$E_{i,j}^r = E\{r(t + dt) \mid r(t) = i \cdot dr, x(t) = j \cdot dx\}$$

$$V_{i,j}^r = \text{Variance}\{r(t + dt) \mid r(t) = i \cdot dr, x(t) = j \cdot dx\}, \text{etc.}$$

Assume the possible nodes at time $t + dt$ reachable from (i, j) are:

$$\{k + 1, h + 1\}, \{k + 1, h\}, \{k + 1, h - 1\}, \{k, h + 1\}, \{k, h\},$$
$$\{k, h - 1\}, \{k - 1, h + 1\}, \{k - 1, h\}, \{k - 1, h - 1\}$$

where k and h are selected so that

$$k \cdot dr \approx E_{i,j}^r \quad \text{and} \quad h \cdot dx \approx E_{i,j}^x$$

As it is assumed there are nine reachable nodes, this implies there are nine probabilities π^{uu}, π^{um}, etc. at each step. Because of the assumption of independence, these probabilities are simply the product of the marginal probabilities, e.g. $\pi^{uu} = p_r^u \cdot p_x^u$, etc. Define Π_0 as the 3×3 matrix of these "zero-correlation" probabilities.

The final step is to perturb the entries in Π_0 so that the correlation (strictly, conditional covariance) ρ between $r(t + dt)$ and $x(t + dt)$ may be approximated. We can write the following expression:

$$dr_{i+1} \cdot dx_{j+1}\{-\pi^{ud^*} + \pi^{uu^*} + \pi^{dd^*} - \pi^{du^*}\}/V_i^r \cdot V_j^x$$

where $\pi^{ud^*} = \pi^{ud} + \varepsilon^{ud}$, etc. As $dr(t)^2 = 3\varphi(t)^2 \cdot dt$ where $\varphi(t) = V_i^r$, this simplifies as $dt \to 0$ to:

$$-\varepsilon^{ud} + \varepsilon^{uu} + \varepsilon^{dd} - \varepsilon^{du} = \rho/3$$

The marginal probabilities must still be maintained, which means that the sum of the shifts in each row and column must be zero. Under these conditions, the shifts can be explicitly computed:

$$\Pi_\rho = \Pi_0 + (\rho/36) * \begin{pmatrix} -1 & -4 & 5 \\ -4 & 8 & -4 \\ 5 & -4 & -1 \end{pmatrix} \quad \text{for } \rho > 0$$

and

$$\Pi_\rho = \Pi_0 - (\rho/36) * \begin{pmatrix} 5 & -4 & -1 \\ -4 & 8 & -4 \\ -1 & -4 & 5 \end{pmatrix} \quad \text{for } \rho < 0$$

Unfortunately, this approach can result in negative entries in Π_ρ, so that the correlation on that node may have to be modified.

It is also feasible to develop two-factor binomial models; for example, see Brigo[17] for a normal model, and Peterson[18] for a two-factor Black–Karasinski log-normal model.

---

[17] Brigo *et al.*, ibid., Section 4.2.6.
[18] S. Peterson *et al.*, *A Two-factor Lognormal Model of the Term Structure and Valuation of American-style Options on Bonds*, working paper published in 1999. This is downloadable from *en.scientificcommons.org/sandra_peterson*

12
Traditional Market Risk Management

OBJECTIVE

Traditional risk management, often called "desktop" risk management, for derivatives has developed significantly over the past 20 years. This chapter discusses two main types of interest rate risk management. First, gridpoint risk management, which assumes that all the rates in a term structure behave independently. It describes different interest representations, i.e. market, forward and zero-coupon rates, and shows how different risk reports, sensitivities and equivalences, may be constructed for each of these.

Second, it looks at yield curve risk management, which assumes that rates move according to some pattern. This is discussed only in the context of market rates following after an analysis of curve movements in Section 12.12 (Appendix). Simple delta and delta–gamma hedging against parallel shifts are introduced, followed by the concepts of other shifts such as rotations. Swap futures are introduced as a potential hedging instrument instead of bonds. Theta risk, i.e. the risk of losses simply through the passage of time, is then briefly discussed.

The risk management of CCS portfolios is not discussed as the sensitivities can be broken up into two IR risks and a spot FX risk. Typically these risks are then transferred into the relevant IR and FX portfolios for the reporting and management of risk.

Finally the risk management of IR option portfolios and of inflation swaps are briefly considered. For IR options, their Greeks are explored, concentrating particularly on long-term options where the Greeks are less intuitive, and also how they change through time. The section also shows how to construct robust hedges using different mathematical programming formulations. For inflation swaps, a delta inflation hedge equivalent is constructed based upon the market data and swaps discussed in Chapter 7, and its effectiveness examined by simulation.

12.1 INTRODUCTION

The focus of risk management within banks has shifted over the past 30 years. When transactions were on-balance sheet and actually involved principal flows, the main concern was credit risk, i.e. will I get my money back? Market risk was deemed to be far less important and was often confined to interest rate risk arising from the funding of the bank, namely in the ALM area. Here techniques such as gap analysis, namely identifying future periods of time during which the bank would be net lender or net borrower, were popular. With the explosive growth in off-balance sheet activities during the 1980s which only involved notional principals, market risk increased in significance. Gap techniques became discredited at the same time because of their inability to handle complex structures and particularly options. So a whole new edifice of risk techniques have been developed during the 1980s and 1990s to manage the market risk of structured portfolios. This chapter will concentrate on the methods developed in the 1980s and which are still very widely used. They have however been superseded by newer techniques which are the topics of Chapter 13.

At the inception of any transaction, both sides are deemed to be valued equally. For a swap, the fundamental concept in pricing is that the value of the cashflows to be received equals the value of the cashflows to be paid. For an option, its (theoretical) price is the expected discounted value of future payoffs. But as time passes, market rates move and one party gains in value to the detriment of the other party. The objectives of this chapter are to:

- analyse how changing interest and exchange rates effect the valuation of swap portfolios;
- construct hedging or equivalent portfolios.

Before we start, it is probably worth reviewing just what we mean by risk in this context. For a company, risk is often synonymous with uncertainty. Hence a floating cashflow is a risky cashflow, which is why companies frequently want to swap from floating to fixed. It is not taking a view on the future direction of rates, but removing the uncertainty. Banks on the other hand very often fund themselves at floating rates, so from their perspective a floating cashflow that is received and passed on constitutes no market risk. Recall that this was the intuitive argument underpinning the zero valuation of the floating side, including the notional principal amounts, of a generic swap. Banks, on the other hand, invariably mark their trading books to market, so for them risk is any event that will cause a change in the present value. If we crudely characterise the valuation process as:

$$PV = \sum_t CF_t * DF_t$$

then there are two sources of risk, namely changes in future cashflows and changes in discounting. These are frequently referred to as delta-0 and delta-1 risk, respectively.

In this chapter, we will investigate how derivatives respond to various types of changes in rates, and how we might manage those exposures. We will initially concentrate on interest rate swaps, and then briefly cross-currency swaps. Finally we will consider various strategies to hedge option portfolios.

First, consider the single IR swap shown in the box below:

Today's date:	4 February 2008
Swap details:	
Principal:	USD10m
Start date:	15-Nov-05
Fixed rate:	3.725% ANN to receive
Floating:	3 mo. Libor to pay
Last fixing date:	15-Nov-07
Last fixing:	3.2500%

This swap may be represented as a stream of cashflows, as shown below. The first cashflow on the floating side is of course known, but the remaining Libor values are currently unfixed. Replacing these Libors with the notional principals allows us to represent the swap as a single cashflow ladder (see Worksheet 12.2):

	Pay side cashflow (USDm)	Receive side cashflow (USDm)	Net cash ladder
6-Feb-08			
15-Feb-08	-0.0831		-10.0831
15-May-08	$-L$		
15-Aug-08	$-L$		
17-Nov-08	$-L$	0.3808	0.3808
16-Feb-09	$-L$		
15-May-09	$-L$		
17-Aug-09	$-L$		
16-Nov-09	$-L$	0.3766	0.3766
15-Feb-10	$-L$		
17-May-10	$-L$		
16-Aug-10	$-L$		
15-Nov-10	$-L$	0.3766	10.3766

We could of course have represented the swap using implied forwards instead, and the overall risk management results would be identical. But there is a good practical reason for using the notional principal representation. As interest rates move around on the 4th February, the above cashflows do not change. Indeed the only time they change is when one rolls off and there is a new fixing, i.e. every 3 months. In contrast, the implied method would have the cashflows changing whenever the rates change, which simply means a lot more work for no particular reward. However, this principal representation will only provide total risk, and will not break the risk up into delta-0 and delta-1.

We can obviously represent a range of other linear instruments such as FRAs, fixed or floating loans and deposits, bonds and FRNs, in a similar fashion. Futures present a small problem as they margin daily. We know that the tick value of a single eurodollar contract is $25 per bp, paid each day. If this were to be paid at the end of the forward rate T, then it would be worth $25/DF_T$. Therefore a $1m futures contract may be regarded as equivalent to $(1/DF_T)$ million of a FRA. For short-dated futures, the adjustment is relatively small and frequently ignored, but it may be very significant for longer dated transaction as we saw in Chapter 2 hedging a money market swap with a futures strip. Similar adjustments should be made to incorporate bond futures.

It would be extremely convenient if options, especially interest rate options such as caps, floors and swaptions, could be represented in a similar fashion. The Black price for a cap is:

$$C = P * \mathrm{DF}_T * [T - t] * \{F't, T) * N(d_1) - K * N(d_2)\}$$

using the same notation as in Chapter 10. If we substitute for the forward rate $F(t, T)$ using the usual formula and rearrange:

$$C = \{P * N(d_1)\} * \mathrm{DF}_t - \{P * [N(d_1) + N(d_2) * (T - t) * K]\} * \mathrm{DF}_T$$

It is now in the desired form of two (variable) cashflows at time t and T, and may be entered into a cash ladder. If we also assume that $N(d_1) = N(d_2) = N(d)$, which is patently not correct but approximately true, then the expression re-arranges to:

$$C = N(d) * \{+P * \mathrm{DF}_1 - P * [1 + (T - t) * K] * \mathrm{DF}_T\}$$

The cashflows themselves in { } are exactly the same as from a simple FRA, as shown in the diagram below.

Therefore $C = N(d) * \{\text{PV of the FRA}\}$ where $N(d)$ is (approximately) the probability of exercise. If for example the option is heavily OTM, then $N(d)$ is close to zero, the option carries little interest rate risk and would not appear in the cash ladder.

Thus, for first-order interest rate risk management purposes, we can represent virtually all instruments in the same framework, namely as a stream of fixed or varying cashflows discounted back.

For illustrative purposes, we will use a small USD swap portfolio represented in this fashion throughout the chapter (see Worksheet 12.3). A small set of market data have been selected, comprising cash rates at the short end, and then swap rates. Interest rate futures could have been easily included as well. Note that it was assumed that the 6, 8 and 9-year swap rates were assumed missing (i.e. less liquid), and hence had to estimated by interpolation. A discount curve was implied from these data, and the portfolio valued as shown in Worksheet 12.4: it is currently worth $-\$8,600,134$. Note again, of course, that this requires some further interpolation to get DFs on the correct cashflow dates.

12.2 INTEREST RATE RISK MANAGEMENT

Before we can proceed with looking at some interest rate risk management techniques with this portfolio, we have two decisions to make. First, what form of interest rates shall we use? There are three common choices: market rates, forward rates and zero-coupon rates. Each has advantages and disadvantages:

Market rates:	Observable but not comparable because of differing tenors.
Forwards rates:	Not observable except at the short end from the futures market, but may be constructed to be of the same tenor.
Zero-coupon rates:	Neither observable nor comparable, but most finance theorists use them as they (especially continuously compounded zeros) are easy to manipulate mathematically.

Zeros were most popular when the theory of these newer risk techniques was being developed, and a few of the older risk systems still use them. However, it is much more common to use the market rate, probably because of the rise of the independent risk manager who wishes to ensure that all inputs are capable of being checked at arm's length. We shall in fact analyse the portfolio using all three forms.

Second, interest rates possess a term structure. What do we assume about this structure, and how it behaves? We can imagine a continuum:

Completely independent, zero correlation	Imperfect correlation	Completely dependent, perfect correlation
Gridpoint	Value-at-Risk	Curve

ranging from zero-correlation with all rates moving independently along the curve through to perfect correlation when the curve moves in some form of pattern. This latter does not necessarily imply perfect positive correlation, i.e. all rates must move in a parallel shift, but would include movements such as rotations, where rates on one side of the pivot would be perfectly negatively correlated with the rates on the other side. We will first of all look at gridpoint hedging, then at curve hedging, and the next chapter considers imperfect hedging under the general Value-at-Risk topic.

12.3 GRIDPOINT RISK MANAGEMENT—MARKET RATES

If a market rate shifts, then the DFs will change, and the value is likely to change as well. We can easily produce a market rate sensitivity report by taking each market rate in turn, shifting it by a predefined amount and recording the resulting change in value:

Market rate sensitivity report	
Market rates	**Change in value ($)**
3 mo. cash	−1,461.51
6 mo. cash	158.35
12 mo. cash	−20.82
2 yr swap	−2,038.12
3 yr swap	−13,964.86
4 yr swap	−23,341.32
5 yr swap	−23,920.42
7 yr swap	57,281.30
10 yr swap	10,544.93
(based upon a 1 bp increase in each rate)	

Such a report is often referred to as a PVBP (present value of a basis point) or a PV01 report (see Worksheet 12.5 for details). These sensitivities may either be calculated by perturbation or analytically.

Most modern systems use perturbation, namely start with the first rate, change it by a predefined amount (usually 1 bp), re-calculate the DFs, re-value the portfolio, and record the change in the value. Move the rate back to its original level, and move onto the next rate. This is often referred to as "blipping" or "bumping" a curve. Analytic methods represent the value of a swap (portfolio) as a function of the original market rates, and then differentiate this function with respect to each rate in turn. Obviously analytic methods are very fast once they have been implemented. But they are also considerably more difficult to set up, especially because of the inevitable presence of interpolation, and to maintain if there are any changes in the curve construction methodology.[1] To speed up a perturbation method, modern systems make extensive use of caching, namely the storing of intermediary results, and ultimately would simply throw more computing power into the fray.

We can see that if the long end of the curve moved up, the portfolio gains in value; a move up in the medium term however would result in a loss. Summing the sensitivities gives $3,237.53. Strictly speaking, this is not quite correct as it ignores second-order effects but it is frequently done, and provides a good estimate of the change in value if the entire curve underwent a parallel movement of 1 bp—we will check the accuracy of this value in Secction 12.7.

12.4 EQUIVALENT PORTFOLIOS

The sensitivity report is expressed in terms of money for a predefined movement. However, an alternative way of expressing these exposures is by creating an equivalence report. This takes a set of generic instruments, one per gridpoint, and constructs a portfolio that has exactly the same sensitivity as the original portfolio. This has two advantages, first it enables the trader to identify what transactions need to be done to reduce the exposures, and second equivalence reports are additive across systems. We will come back to this second point at the end of Sections 12.5 and 12.6.

Consider a 5-year generic swap: the current rate is 3.505% and it obviously has a zero-value as shown below.

Example of a 5-year generic swap			
Generic rate	3.505%		
		DFs	**Cashflows**
6-Feb-08		1	−100
6-Feb-09	1.017	0.971397	3.5634
8-Feb-10	1.019	0.945458	3.5732
7-Feb-11	1.011	0.912764	3.5439
6-Feb-12	1.011	0.876830	3.5439
6-Feb-13	1.017	0.838308	103.5634
		PV = 0.0000	

---

[1] As an example of an analytic method, see P. Miron and P. Swannell, "Pricing and hedging swaps", *Euromoney*, 1991. Very often the older systems employ "mapping" techniques which allocate the actual cashflows onto the maturity gridpoints whilst maintaining various desired properties—see Chapter 8 of Miron and Swannell—and also Section 12.6 below.

Suppose the 3-year swap rate increases by 1 bp; the curve is re-bootstrapped, and the swap re-valued. The DFs from the 3-year point onwards change, but the value of the 5-year swap remains zero! This often seems counterintuitive at first glance but makes perfect sense: as the 5-year rate has not changed, a 5-year generic swap must retain its zero-value irrespective of what else the swap curve is doing. Notice also something else; when the 3-year rate rises, the 3-year DF reduces as expected, but the subsequent DFs rise! Again, often unexpected until you examine the bootstrapping formula; then it becomes very obvious; their results are all demonstrated in Worksheet 12.6.

Example of a 5-year generic swap—changing the 3-year swap rate

Generic rate   3.505%

		Rates (%)	DFs	Cash-flows	Shift in rates	New rates (%)	New DFs	Change in DFs
6-Feb-08			1	100			1	
6-Feb-09	1.017	2.89625	0.971397	3.5634		2.89625	0.971397	
8-Feb-10	1.019	2.795	0.945458	3.5732		2.795	0.945458	
7-Feb-11	1.011	3.035	0.912764	3.5439	1	3.045	0.912485	−0.0002788
6-Feb-11	1.011	3.275	0.876830	3.5439		3.275	0.876839	0.0000089
6-Feb-13	1.017	3.505	0.838308	103.5634		3.505	0.838317	0.0000092
			PV = 0.0000				**0.0000**	

The generic swap is in fact only sensitive to changes in its own rate—they are said to be "orthogonal". For a 1 bp increase in the 5-year rate, a $100m receiver's swap loses $46,127 in value. From above, the portfolio lost $23,920 when the 5-year rate increased by 1 bp. Therefore this portfolio sensitivity must be equivalent to $23,920/(46,127/100) = 51.86$m of the 5-year swap to receive fixed.

Example of a 5-year generic swap—changing the 5-year swap rate

Generic rate   7.135%

		Rates (%)	DFs	Cash-flows	Shift in rates	New rates (%)	New DFs
6-Feb-08			1	−100			1
6-Feb-09	1.017	2.89625	0.971397	3.5634		2.89625	0.971397
8-Feb-10	1.019	2.795	0.945458	3.5732		2.795	0.945458
7-Feb-11	1.011	3.035	0.912764	3.5439		3.035	0.912764
6-Feb-12	1.011	3.275	0.876830	3.5439		3.275	0.876830
6-Feb-13	1.017	3.505	0.838308	103.5634	1	3.515	0.837862
			PV = 0.0000				**(46,127.34)**

It is therefore straightforward to construct an equivalence portfolio of the nine market instruments that would have the same first-order sensitivity as the original swap portfolio.[2]

Constructing an equivalent portfolio

	Portfolio	Generic instruments	Equivalence m USD
3 mo. cash	−1,461.51	−2,480.44	58.92 to receive
6 mo. cash	158.35	−4,977.36	3.18 to pay
12 mo. cash	−20.82	−9,874.89	0.21 to receive
2 yr swap	−2,038.12	−19,512.35	10.45 to receive
3 yr swap	−13,964.86	−28,740.52	48.59 to receive
4 yr swap	−23,341.32	−37,605.39	62.07 to receive
5 yr swap	−23,920.42	−46,127.34	51.86 to receive
7 yr swap	57,281.30	−61,929.38	92.49 to pay
10 yr swap	10,544.93	−82,764.17	12.74 to pay

To repeat, the advantage of equivalence reports is that they imply not just the size of the sensitivity, but also how a trader may react to manage the sensitivity.

12.5 GRIDPOINT RISK MANAGEMENT—FORWARD RATES

We will now repeat the analysis, but this time using 3-monthly forward rates as the underlying factors. The first step is to build the forward curve: see column [1] of Box 1 in Worksheet 12.7. If a shift on a forward rate is imposed in column [2], then the new forward curve and new DFs are calculated in columns [3] and [4].

We can now calculate the sensitivity of the portfolio and each of the generic instruments to shifts in each of the forward rates, as shown below. Unlike the market rates, the generic instruments are sensitive to all forward rates within their maturity range. This is because a blip in a forward rate $F(t, T)$ is (approximately) equivalent to a parallel shift in all market rates with maturity equal to or greater than t. The results are shown in Box 4 of the worksheet.

This gives sensitivities with respect to each forward rate. However, there are of course a large number of forward rates—40 over a 10-year period. So it is very common to combine the sensitivities into time buckets. The buckets are (fairly arbitrarily) chosen to be the differences in the tenors of each neighbouring pair of market rates. Estimation of the total sensitivity in each bucket was done quite crudely by simply summing the sensitivities with respect to the forward rates in each bucket. This is not theoretically correct as one should generate the actual forward rates of the differing tenors, but the error will be very small. The effect of defining the buckets in this fashion means that the matrix of generic sensitivities is square and upper-triangular, as shown below.

---

[2] See columns AK to AO of Worksheet 12.6, which demonstrates the calculation of the sensitivity of each market instrument.

Table 12.3   Bucketed forward rate sensitivities

Bucket	Port-folio	3 mo. cash	6 mo. cash	12 mo. cash	2 yr swap	3 yr swap	4 yr swap	5 yr swap	7 yr swap	10 yr swap
3 mo.	−3,101	−2,480	−2,480	−2,480	−2,480	−2,480	−2,480	−2,480	−2,480	−2,480
3 mo.	−1,677		−2,536	−2,536	−2,536	−2,536	−2,536	−2,536	−2,536	−2,536
6 mo.	−3,518			−5,077	−5,077	−5,077	−5,077	−5,077	−5,077	−5,077
1 yr	−6,842				−9,846	−9,822	−9,798	−9,775	−9,737	−9,699
1 yr	−5,664					−9,429	−9,382	−9,337	−9,262	−9,188
1 yr	−1,105						−9,068	−9,001	−8,892	−8,783
1 yr	4,371							−8,728	−8,584	−8,440
2 yr	16,826								−16,123	−15,741
3 yr	3,575									−21,182

The sensitivity report for the portfolio, given on the left-hand-side of the table, is quite different from the market rate sensitivity report. But this is only to be expected as the imposed shifts in the rates are completely different. Shifting a single forward rate moves all the DFs after its fixing date, which is approximately equivalent to a parallel shift in the market curve after this date. Compare that with shifting a single market rate, which would appear as a spike on the market curve. Sensitivity reports using different representations of interest rates cannot really be compared, even intuitively. However, the total change in value, calculated by adding the sensitivities as before, is $2,864.75 which is very similar to the number for market rates. This suggests that a parallel shift in market rates is approximately equivalent to a parallel shift in forward rates.

We can calculate another equivalent portfolio. However, its calculation is not as straightforward as before because the generic instruments are not orthogonal, and we have to use a technique known as "reverse bootstrapping" or "pyramiding". Starting with the generic instrument of longest maturity, we would require:

$$3,575/(-21,182/100) = -16.88\text{m of a 10-year swap to pay fixed}$$

as the equivalence over the final bucket. (*Note*: The negative sign on the principal has been retained.) Working back, both the 7 and 10-year swaps have sensitivities over the 5 to 7-year bucket, hence we have to adjust the sensitivity of the portfolio to account for the amount of the 7-year swap already done:

$$\text{Net sensitivity} = 16,826 - [(-16.88) * (-15,741/100)] = 14,169.62$$

and then calculate the residual equivalence:

$$14,169.62/(-16,123/100) = -87.88\text{m of a 7-year swap to pay fixed}$$

The process is then repeated, working backwards.

Alternatively, if **A** is the (square) matrix of generic sensitivities, and S_P the vector of portfolio sensitivities, then the equivalence portfolio is given simply by $100 . \mathbf{A}^{-1} . S_P$. This approach can also be used if the selected buckets do not give rise to an upper-triangular structure.

Using forward rate sensitivity to construct an equivalent portfolio

Equivalence (USDm)

3 mo. cash	58.92 to receive
6 mo. cash	3.19 to pay
12 mo. cash	0.23 to receive
2 yr swap	10.15 to receive
3 yr swap	48.58 to receive
4 yr swap	62.43 to receive
5 yr swap	52.67 to receive
7 yr swap	87.88 to pay
10 yr swap	16.88 to pay

Whilst the sensitivity reports were very different, the equivalence reports, as one would expect, are much more similar. They are not identical because they are calculated under structures of different shifts. In extremis, equivalence reports can be combined from different portfolios to produce an overall risk report.

12.6 GRIDPOINT RISK MANAGEMENT—ZERO-COUPON RATES

Finally, and briefly, we will analyse the portfolio using zero-coupon rates. We will use continuously compounded rates as this form is extremely popular; i.e. $DF_t = \exp\{-z_t, t\}$. As alluded to above, this form of zeros is probably used because the function is easy to differentiate, and therefore makes analytic calculations simpler.

In exactly the same way as before, we calculate the zero-coupon rates, shift them, re-calculate the discount curve and re-value both the portfolio and the generic instruments (see Boxes 1 and 2 of Worksheet 12.8). One point to be careful about: we are using 6, 8 and 9-year zero rates because, if we did not, we could not exactly replicate the original discount curve and hence we would find that the portfolio would have a slightly different value before any rate shift (see Box 1 of Worksheet 12.8).

As one would expect, zero-coupon sensitivities are much closer to market rate sensitivities than those of forward rates. This is because the first two are both comparable spot rates, and very different from forward rates.

As before, the rates are not orthogonal, so we have to use reverse bootstrapping. However, we have to decide what to do about the sensitivities from the 6, 8 and 9-year zero rates, because the matrix of sensitivities in Box 2 of Worksheet 12.8 is not square. For example, we could simply add together the 6-year and 7-year sensitivities as we did before. In the case of forward rates this made practical sense as the result would have been (approximately) the sensitivity due to a single 2-year forward rate from 5 to 7 years. But, in this case, it is probably better to use a mapping technique. There are a wide variety of such methods, but the one described below is probably the most popular.

Generalising the problem, we have a sensitivity S_T due to a rate of maturity T which we wish to allocate onto the gridpoints t and t' where $t \leq T < t'$ in such a way that we wish to preserve some desirable properties. From the definition of DF_T above, we can write $PV_T = CF_T * \exp\{-z_T . T\}$ for some cashflow CF_T. The sensitivity S_T of this value with respect to z_T is simply $PV_T \cdot T$. Let us assume we wish to estimate S_t and $S_{t'}$ so that both the total value and total sensitivity is preserved; that is:

$$S_t + S_{t'} = S_T \quad \text{and} \quad PV_t + PV_{t'} = PV_T$$

Substituting $PV_T = S_T/T$, etc. we can solve for S_t and $S_{t'}$; that is:

$$S_t = S_T * [(t' - T)/T]/[(t' - t)/t] \quad \text{and} \quad S_{t'} = S_T * [(T - t)/T]/[(t' - t)/t']$$

Thus, we can allocate the 6-year sensitivity of the portfolio to the 5 and 7- year gridpoints, as shown in the box below. We now have sensitivities for our nine market instruments as shown in Box 2. These sensitivities are similar to market rate, which is hardly surprising as they are both spot rates. The equivalent portfolio can now be calculated using reverse bootstrapping again.

Mapping the 6-year sensitivity				
	Time	Weights	Portfolio sensitivity	Mapped sensitivity
5 yr point	5.075	0.417		2,833.81
6 yr point	6.089		6,799.90	
7 yr point	7.103	0.583		3,966.09
	Sum 1			

See Box 2 of Worksheet 12.8:

Table 12.6   Using zero-coupon rate sensitivity to construct an equivalent portfolio

	Equivalence (USDm)
3 mo. cash	58.92 to receive
6 mo. cash	3.18 to pay
12 mo. cash	0.22 to receive
2 yr swap	10.45 to receive
3 yr swap	48.59 to receive
4 yr swap	62.07 to receive
5 yr swap	52.85 to receive
7 yr swap	88.67 to pay
10yr swap	16.22 to pay

In summary, the equivalence portfolios are all very similar, despite the fact that the sensitivity reports are very different. They will not be identical because the movements imposed on each of the three curves are not the same when translated into a common framework. But the similarity is reassuring; a portfolio should be effectively hedged in a similar fashion irrespective of how the sensitivity is calculated (see Worksheet 12.9).

12.7   YIELD CURVE RISK MANAGEMENT

Gridpoint risk management assumed that all interest rates were uncorrelated. The other extreme is to assume that the curve moves according to some structure. However, before we make this assumption, it is probably worthwhile to look at some historical evidence. The graph below shows the correlation between changes in the 5-year rate with the other points along a USD swap curve, represented in the three different ways:

- the correlation between the changes in the 5-year market rate and changes in other market rates is consistently high, except for the cash market;
- the correlation between the 5-year zero-coupon rate and the other zero rates is still very high, albeit not quite as high as for market rates;
- the correlation between 12-month forward rates is extremely low, except between the 5/6 and 6/7 rates.

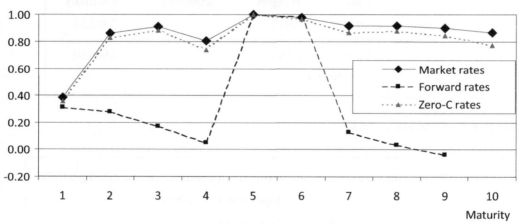

The results might be intuitively expected as both market and zero-rate are spot rates, and hence possess considerably overlap, unlike forward rates. Indeed forward rate correlation matrices typically possess a sharp "ridge" structure, i.e. high correlation along the principal diagonal but dropping off rapidly—almost negatively exponentially—on either side.[3]

Similar results have been observed over other periods of time and with a range of different currencies. Section 12.12 (Appendix) describes some further analysis, including the use of principal components. The implication of this analysis is that yield curve risk management is most sensibly restricted to market rates and possibly zero rates, but should not be applied to forward rates. We will only consider market rates in this context.

Let us first assume that the market curve undergoes a parallel shift; i.e. if the curve is represented by the rate r, then it changes by Δr. If the current value of the portfolio is V, then its new value after the rate shift is given approximately by Taylor's theorem

---

[3] Remember the discussion on correlations for use in the Libor model in Chapter 11.

(expansion, series, ...):

$$V(r + \Delta r) \approx V(r) + \Delta r * (\partial V / \partial r) + \tfrac{1}{2} * \Delta r^2 * (\partial^2 V / \partial r^2) + \cdots$$

where $(\partial V / \partial r)$ is the delta sensitivity of the portfolio; and
$(\partial^2 V / \partial r^2)$ is the gamma (in the swap context, often called convexity of curvature) of the portfolio.

If Δr is measured in basis points, then $(\partial V / \partial r)$ is the PVBP of the portfolio estimated by shifting the entire curve up by a basis point: from Worksheet 12.10, PVBP = \$3,228.89.[4] Strictly, this measures the delta at $(r + \tfrac{1}{2} \text{bp})$, so to calculate it more precisely, we should estimate the average by:

Delta-up:	3,228.89 (as before)
Delta-down:	3,251.90 (calculated by 1 bp shift downwards)
Average delta:	3,240.39

We can use the same results to estimate the gamma. This is defined as the change in the delta for a shift in the rate: i.e. (Delta-up − Delta-down) = −23.01 per bp as the distance between the mid-points of delta-up and delta-down is only 1 bp.

As an example, suppose the entire curve shifts by −100 bp; the actual change in value is −\$444,376. Using the first-order approximation:

$$(-100) * 3,240.39 = -\$324,039, \text{ an error of some } 27\%$$

Using the second-order terms as well

$$-324,039 + \tfrac{1}{2} * (-100)^2 * -23.01 = -\$439,114, \text{ an error of only } 1.18\%$$

Taylor's theorem lies at the heart of all risk management as it permits estimation of the change in the value of an instrument/portfolio for given changes in its underlying parameters. Suppose, for example, we wish to hedge this portfolio with two bonds B_1 and B_2. We create a super portfolio SP = $\{V + n_1 * B_1 + n_2 * B_2\}$ where n_1 and n_2 are the amounts of the bond we wish to buy or sell. We can write:

$$\Delta SP \approx \Delta r * \{(\partial V / \partial r) + n_1 * (\partial B_1 / \partial r) + n_2 * (\partial B_2 / \partial r)\}$$
$$+ \tfrac{1}{2}(\Delta r)^2 * \{(\partial^2 V / \partial r^2) + n_1 * (\partial^2 B_1 / \partial r^2) + n_2 * (\partial^2 B_2 / \partial r^2)\}$$

Define an effective hedge so that $\Delta SP = 0$ for any movement in r. Ignoring for the moment the gamma terms, the only way we can set $\Delta SP = 0$ for any Δr is by setting:

$$\{(\partial V / \partial r) + n_1 * (\partial B_1 / \partial r) + n_2 * (\partial B_2 / \partial r)\} = 0$$

If we arbitrarily set $n_2 = 0$, then

$$n_1 = -(\partial V / \partial r) / (\partial B_1 / \partial r)$$

gives the amount of B_1 required to delta-hedge the portfolio. We have of course used precisely this expression earlier to estimate the equivalences.

---

[4] Compare this number with \$3,237.53 calculated earlier by shifting each of the market rates in turn, and then summing the sensitivities. The error involved in the latter is negligible.

Turning to the actual portfolio, we are going to hedge this with a T-bond as follows:

Maturity:	15-January-2013
Coupon:	2.875% sa
Dirty price:	100.4609 Act/Act

In practice, such a bond would be valued off the bond curve. We want it to hedge a swap portfolio, and hence we have introduced some basis risk, namely that the swap spread may change. This is quite common; hedging seldom eliminates risk, but as in this case it merely substitutes basis risk for absolute level risk. We then need to make a judgement about which form of risk is smaller. So, for risk management purposes, we are going to assume that the spread remains constant. In that case it matters very little whether the bond is valued off the bond curve or the swap (equals bond plus spread) curve as we are only interested in the change in value: for convenience, therefore, we will value everything off the swap curve. We calculate the average deltas for the portfolio and the bond, and hence the hedge ratio as above (see Worksheet 12.11).

	Delta ($)
Portfolio:	3,240.39
Bond:	−44,454.52 per 100m nominal
Hedge ratio:	7.29m to buy

The effectiveness of this delta hedge may be measured by creating

$$SP = \{V + 7.29\text{m} * B_1\}$$

and measuring its change in value as r changes. For example, Worksheet 12.11 shows that if the curve shifts up by 100 bp, SP loses $101,005 in value. For large changes up or down, the negative gamma from the portfolio appears to dominate, and losses would be made.

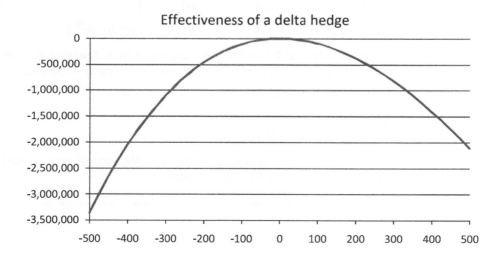

To remove this effect as well, returning back to the SP, we need to set both delta and gamma terms to zero; that is:

$$(\partial V/\partial r) + n_1 * (\partial B_1/\partial r) + n_2 * (\partial B_2/\partial r) = 0$$

$$(\partial^2 V/\partial r^2) + n_1 * (\partial^2 B_1/\partial r^2) + n_2 * (\partial^2 B_2/\partial r^2) = 0$$

To do this, we need a second T-bond:

Bond 2

Maturity:	15-November-2017
Coupon:	4.25% sa
Dirty price:	104.9531

and to calculate the various sensitivity parameters:

	Portfolio	Bond 1	Bond 2
Average delta	3,240	−44,455	−80,389
Gamma	−23.01	25.58	80.40

See Worksheet 12.12. Notice that the SP gamma from the delta hedge alone is:

$$-23.01 + 7.29\text{m} * (25.58/100) = -\$21.15 \text{ per bp}$$

i.e. the delta hedge hardly reduces the negative gamma of the portfolio. Solving the delta–gamma equations gives $n_1 = -104.75$m and $n_2 = 61.96$m. We are long the longest bond, as this will provide most gamma to offset the portfolio, and short the short bond as this creates the delta hedge. The actual ΔSP against the 100 bp shift is now only −\$1,135 compared with −\$101,005 for the delta hedge alone.

The overall improvement in effectiveness is shown below for ±500 bp shifts. The residual is no longer always negative, but changes sign, implying that the third-order term[5] in the Taylor's expansion is negative.

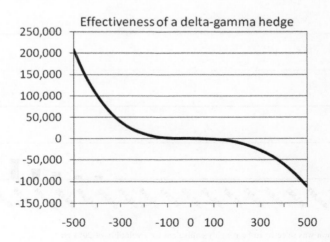

[5] Sometimes called the "omega" or last word in risk management!!

There is no reason why this type of analysis has to be restricted to parallel shifts. As discussed in Section 12.12 (Appendix), about 10% of the market curve movement can be attributed to rotational shifts. Define a rotational delta as the change in the value of the portfolio as the market curve rotates around the 5-year point according to the formula:

$$\Delta r_t = s * (t - 5) \text{ bp} \quad \text{where we arbitrarily set } s = 1$$

The parallel deltas and gammas, plus the rotational deltas have been calculated for the portfolio plus three bonds, and then hedge ratios estimated (see Worksheet 12.13).

	Bond 1	Bond 2	Bond 3	Portfolio
Average delta	−44,455	−80,389	−160,388	3,240
Gamma	25.58	80.40	373.03	−23.01
Average rotation	1,194	−384,554	−3,865,444	231,010
Hedge (USDm)	−118.64	72.10	−1.23	

All simultaneous {parallel + rotational} shifts can be described in terms of a parallel shift plus a rotation around the standardised pivot. Suppose the curve shifts up by 100 bp and simultaneously rotates by −3 bp around the pivot. The portfolio on its own loses −$444,656 in value, but the SP only changes by −$7,699.

To test the overall hedge effectiveness, movement in the curve was simulated by (see Worksheet 12.14):

$$\Delta r_t = s * (t - P) \text{ bp}$$

where P is drawn from a uniform distribution between $[0, 10]$ and s from $N(0, 1.4\%/\sqrt{250})$.[6] The resulting hedge effectiveness is shown by the distribution below; the error is relatively small although demonstrates a negative rotational gamma.

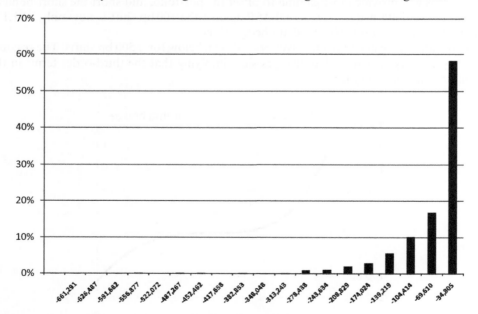

12.8 BOND AND SWAP FUTURES

Hedging a swap portfolio with bonds appears to work extremely well. However, the bonds are usually government bonds because of the need for liquidity, and therefore this style of hedging necessitates the assumption that the bond–swap spread remains constant. Unfortunately in practice, this spread can be quite volatile and, as we shall see in Chapter 13, the optimal hedge effectiveness can be quite low. Furthermore, using cash bonds for hedging would involve significant cashflows upfront, to buy or sell the bonds, which would have funding and balance sheet implications.

There are some alternatives. One alternative would be to hedge with bonds that were much more in line with the swap curve, but unfortunately such bonds are seldom available with adequate liquidity. Perhaps the only category that has been a serious contender is the Pfandbriefe[7] bonds issued in Germany, which have traditionally had a very close correlation to the swap curve.

A second alternative would be to use bond futures, namely contracts on the future delivery of governmental bonds. Whilst these would still be subject to basis risk, they would not involve the large upfront cashflows. Both the US and the Eurozone has a range of bond futures as shown in the table below:

Maturity of bond	US	Eurozone
2 years	2-year note	Schatz
5 years	5-year note	Bobl
10 years	10-year note	Bund
30 years	30-year long bond	Buxl

All the contracts have good liquidity, with the exception of the Buxl, for the next two to three futures maturity dates.

As an example, consider the US 10-year note. The underlying is a US government note with a face value of $100,000, and a maturity between 6.5 and 10 years on the first day of a delivery month. The invoice price is the futures Settlement price * Conversion factor + Accrued interest. The conversion factor is estimated so that the delivered note gives a 6% yield-to-maturity. Delivery months are March, June, September and December, and the last trading date is the 7th business day before the last business date of each delivery month. The contracts are margined in the usual fashion.

Despite their apparent attractiveness, bond futures are seldom used as hedging instruments. There are a number of reasons for this:

- the restrictive range of maturities;
- the underlying is not a real bond;
- the uncertainty caused by the delivery option.

A third alternative is swap futures, where the underlying is a forward swap, valued off the relevant swap curve. The swap is standardised, namely with a notional size of 100,000, and

---

[7] Highly liquid mortgage-backed bonds, typically issued in large sizes and with a good range of maturities.

with a semi-annual fixed rate of 6% against 3 mo. floating. A range of maturities are offered:

- 5, 10 and 30 year on USD are traded at CBOT;
- 2, 5 and 10 year on both USD and euro are traded at Euronext (LIFFE) in London.

The delivery months are, as before, March, June, September and December, with the third Wednesday being the delivery date. The products are cash-settled, not actually delivered, and there are the usual margining processes.

Unfortunately, despite the fact that these contracts have been around for some 10 years, and possess much less basis risk than bonds or bond futures, the volumes are extremely low on both exchanges. This is in direct contrast to the initial hopes, especially in Europe as the swap market is considerably more homogeneous than the Eurozone governmental bond market.

12.9 THETA RISK

So far we have considered the possible losses that might be made if the market moves against the portfolio, and how these losses may be reduced by hedging. But just suppose that, as time passes, the market moves solely in accordance to the implied forward rates. What would be the impact on the value of the portfolio, and of course the hedge?

There are a number of ways that are used to assess this impact. Probably the theoretically correct approach is as follows. Assume that we have a current forward rate curve $F_0 = \{F_{0/\tau}, F_{\tau/2}, F_{2/3}, \ldots\}$. As time passes from $t = 0$ to $t = \tau$ the first forward rate $F_{0/\tau}$ falls away, and the new curve is $F_\tau = \{F_{\tau/2}, F_{2/3}, \ldots\}$. Notice that it is still the same forward rates as before, as they are still our best estimate of the curve, but all starting one period earlier.

If we have a fixed cashflow at time $T > \tau$, then its initial value is $V_0 = \mathrm{CF}_T * \mathrm{DF}_{0,T}$, and after the passage of time $V_\tau = \mathrm{CF}_T * \mathrm{DF}_{\tau,T}$. The new discount factor $\mathrm{DF}_{\tau,T}$ is simply given by $\mathrm{DF}_{0,T}/\mathrm{DF}_{0,\tau}$, hence $V_\tau = V_0/\mathrm{DF}_{0,\tau}$. Therefore the theta of the cashflow is $V_\tau - V_0 = V_0 * (1/\mathrm{DF}_{0,\tau} - 1)$ over that period of time. Extending this to an entire portfolio is trivial. A 7-day period is frequently used for estimating theta, but it should vary depending upon the liquidity of the market.

If the cashflow time T lies between 0 and τ, then the cashflow would have to be either deposited (if positive) or borrowed (if negative) from time T until $t = \tau$. The discounting process implies that all interest accrues at Libor flat, therefore if the depositing or borrowing rate is away from Libor, this would incur an additional reward or penalty.

The above approach effectively holds the forward curve constant, and moves the observer one period up the curve. An alternative popular, but in my view incorrect, approach is to hold the observer constant and move the curve as shown below:

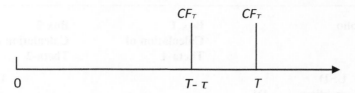

In this case, the new value $V_\tau = \text{CF}_T * \text{DF}_{0,T-\tau} = \text{CF}_T * \text{DF}_{0,T}/\text{DF}_{T-\tau,T} = V_0/\text{DF}_{T-\tau,T}$. Extending this to an entire portfolio is less straightforward, as the adjustment term is specific to the timing of each cashflow, but still easy. This approach is analogous to the theta for options. The box on the next page shows the calculation of a 7-day theta for the two approaches (see Worksheet 12.15).

Because of the negative monotonicity of the discount function, $\text{DF}_{0,\tau} > \text{DF}_{T-\tau,T}$ and therefore the theta from the second approach will always be absolutely greater than the theta from the first approach. The size of the difference increases with the steepness of the forward curve

A third approach is to use an accrual concept as in the bond market. Suppose that this cashflow CF_T has been calculated by $P * d * r$ where d is the appropriate length of the interest period. If d_{01} is the length of time from $t = 0$ to $t = 1$, then $V_1 = V_0 + \text{CF}_T * d_{01}/d$. But this method:

- ignores discounting;
- tacitly assumes that the period d started some time before $t = 0$;
- is difficult to apply to a portfolio of cashflows as it really concentrates only on the most immediate cashflow;

and is therefore not really appropriate for derivative portfolios.

Related to theta is of course the "cost-of-carry", which is the ongoing cost of funding a portfolio. It arises because swap portfolios have to make payments, which presumably would have to be borrowed at some cost, and to receive payments, which are subsequently invested. Any differences between the implied cost of funds on the swap, and the actual cost of borrowing/investing, would be reflected in the cost-of-carry. This was briefly discussed in Section 2.5, in the context of forward valuing. This cost of carry is also affected by hedging. If a portfolio is hedging by buying or selling a bond, what is the cost of raising the money to buy the bond or what is the return on the sale proceeds? Theta concentrates on the changes in value of future cashflows; cost-of-carry concentrates on the costs inherent in actual realised cashflows. Together, they represent an overall picture of the daily running costs of a swap portfolio under the assumption that interest rates remain unchanged. From a management perspective, it is vital that the two are always reported together.

12.10 RISK MANAGEMENT OF IR OPTION PORTFOLIOS

The risk management of swap portfolios has been discussed in some detail in the previous sections of this chapter. Many of the techniques such as delta and delta–gamma hedging are equally applicable to options as well, but there are also some additional complications such as volatility risk. In this section, we will describe some of the practical problems involved in the hedging of IR option portfolios, and introduce some additional techniques.

Swap portfolio			Box 1 Calculation of Theta-1		Box 2 Calculation of Theta-2		
	USD cashflow (USDm)	DFs				USD cashflow (USDm)	DFs
6-Feb-08		1	13-Feb-08	0.999393	6-Feb-08		
15-Feb-08	−50.4153	0.999220			8-Feb-08	−50.4153	0.999827
25-Feb-08	−126.0427	0.998353			18-Feb-08	−126.0427	0.998960
13-Mar-08	−75.7109	0.996880			6-Mar-08	−75.7109	0.997486
17-Mar-08	75.7015	0.996533			10-Mar-08	75.7015	0.997140
23-Apr-08	100.8152	0.993326			16-Apr-08	100.8152	0.993932
26-May-08	2.5875	0.990543			19-May-08	2.5875	0.991123
23-Jul-08	−3.9650	0.985741			16-Jul-08	−3.9650	0.986321
17-Sep-08	−2.6116	0.981572			10-Sep-08	−2.6116	0.982074
17-Nov-08	1.9039	0.977201			10-Nov-08	1.9039	0.977703
15-Dec-08	2.5875	0.975195			8-Dec-08	2.5875	0.975696
25-May-09	2.5594	0.963764			18-May-09	2.5594	0.964258
23-Jul-09	−3.9542	0.959594			16-Jul-09	−3.9542	0.960088
17-Sep-09	−2.6044	0.955635			10-Sep-09	−2.6044	0.956130
16-Nov-09	1.8832	0.951395			9-Nov-09	1.8832	0.951889
14-Dec-09	2.5594	0.949416			7-Dec-09	2.5594	0.949910
24-May-10	2.5594	0.936027			17-May-10	2.5594	0.936655
23-Jul-10	−3.9542	0.930638			16-Jul-10	−3.9542	0.931266
17-Sep-10	−2.6044	0.925608			10-Sep-10	−2.6044	0.926237
15-Nov-10	51.8832	0.920309			8-Nov-10	51.8832	0.920937
13-Dec-10	2.5594	0.917794			6-Dec-10	2.5594	0.918422
24-May-11	2.5664	0.902300			17-May-11	2.5664	0.902991
25-Jul-11	−3.9758	0.896179			18-Jul-11	−3.9758	0.896870
19-Sep-11	−2.6187	0.890651			12-Sep-11	−2.6187	0.891342
13-Dec-11	77.5664	0.882260			6-Dec-11	77.5664	0.882951
24-May-12	2.5734	0.865463			17-May-12	2.5734	0.866200
23-Jul-12	−3.9433	0.859148			16-Jul-12	−3.9433	0.859885
17-Sep-12	−2.5973	0.853254			10-Sep-12	−2.5973	0.853990
24-May-13	127.5664	0.826957			17-May-13	127.5664	0.827700
23-Jul-13	−3.9542	0.820592			16-Jul-13	−3.9542	0.821335
17-Sep-13	−77.6044	0.814651			10-Sep-13	−77.6044	0.815394
23-Jul-14	-3.9542	0.781187			16-Jul-14	−3.9542	0.781958
23-Jul-15	−103.9542	0.742347			16-Jul-15	−103.9542	0.743061
	PV = −8,577,255					PV = −8,586,248	
			Theta = −5,207.47		Theta = −8,992.91		

Consider a single caplet—its price is given by:

$$C = P * \mathrm{DF}_T * \{F(\tau, T) * N(d_1) - K * N(d_2)\} * (T - \tau)$$

The classic formulae for the "Greeks" may be easily calculated. For example, we can estimate the option delta by differentiating with respect to $F(\tau, T)$ which gives:

$$\delta_0 = P * \mathrm{DF}_T * N(d_1) * (T - \tau)$$

Below the delta has been estimated for two options, one short and one long, over a range of strikes from -50% to $+50\%$ of the prevailing forward rate using the current market data out of 4 February 2008, as shown in the graph below (see Worksheet 12.18):

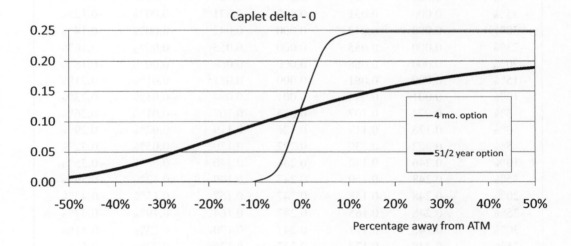

Note that the delta does not range from 0 (for OTM options) through to 1 (for ITM options) as in the classical B&S formula because of discounting and the tenor terms, although they appear to be fairly symmetric around ATM. The delta graph for the short-dated option is that typically found in most books on options. However many IR options are long-dated, and the behaviour of their deltas is perhaps less intuitive. For example, the impact of the discount term is much greater in the long option, so that delta reaches a lower maximum.

Actually, one should be more careful because, under the usual caplet convention of fixing at the start of the forward period and paying at the end, the discount factor DF_T is also a function of $F(\tau, T)$. Writing $\mathrm{DF}_T = \mathrm{DF}_\tau / [1 + F(\tau, T) * (T - \tau)]$ and differentiating we get:

$$\partial \mathrm{DF}_T / \partial F(\tau, T) = Q_F * \mathrm{DF}_T \quad \text{where } Q_F = -(T - \tau) / [1 + F(\tau, T) * (T - \tau)]$$

Therefore $\delta_1 = Q_F * C$, and total delta is given by:

$$\delta = P * \mathrm{DF}_T * N(d_1) * (T - \tau) + Q_F * C$$

This additional term, earlier called delta-1, has a very small effect, reducing the delta typically by less than 1% except for heavily ITM very long-dated options, as shown in the table below, and is generally ignorable (and will be in the ensuing discussion).

Table 12.7	Delta-0 and total delta for a range of options					
ATM	Delta-0		Delta-0 + 1		Percentage difference	
	S-T option	L-T option	S-T option	L-T option	S-T option	L-T option
−50%	0.000	0.008	0.000	0.008	0.00%	−0.07%
−45%	0.000	0.014	0.000	0.014	0.00%	−0.09%
−40%	0.000	0.021	0.000	0.021	0.00%	−0.10%
−35%	0.000	0.031	0.000	0.031	0.00%	−0.12%
−30%	0.000	0.042	0.000	0.042	0.00%	−0.14%
−25%	0.000	0.055	0.000	0.055	0.00%	−0.16%
−20%	0.000	0.068	0.000	0.068	0.00%	−0.18%
−15%	0.000	0.081	0.000	0.081	−0.01%	−0.21%
−10%	0.001	0.094	0.001	0.094	−0.01%	−0.23%
−5%	0.024	0.107	0.024	0.107	−0.01%	−0.26%
0%	0.126	0.119	0.126	0.119	−0.02%	−0.29%
5%	0.222	0.130	0.222	0.130	−0.05%	−0.32%
10%	0.246	0.140	0.246	0.140	−0.08%	−0.35%
15%	0.248	0.150	0.247	0.149	−0.12%	−0.39%
20%	0.248	0.158	0.247	0.157	−0.15%	−0.43%
25%	0.248	0.165	0.247	0.164	−0.19%	−0.47%
30%	0.248	0.171	0.247	0.170	−0.23%	−0.51%
35%	0.248	0.177	0.247	0.176	−0.27%	−0.55%
40%	0.248	0.182	0.247	0.181	−0.31%	−0.59%
45%	0.248	0.186	0.247	0.185	−0.35%	−0.63%
50%	0.248	0.189	0.247	0.188	−0.39%	−0.68%

In practice, it is often useful with long-dated options to understand how delta and other parameters will change through time. This enables the trader to anticipate how the hedge will have to be re-balanced if rates do not shift, but simply time passes. The following diagram shows the impact of time on three options; each started out with a maturity of just over 6.5 years, and the strike was set to be ATM, 75% of ATM and 125% of ATM, respectively. As time passes, we assume that the implied forward rate does not shift but its volatility changes according to the forward volatility curve and the discount factor rolls off. As we can see, at short maturities the deltas are as expected heading to 50%, 100% and 0%, respectively. However, when the options have long maturities, the deltas are much more similar. The long-dated heavily OTM option does not have a zero delta, because there is ample time for the option to move into the money, and therefore requires almost as much delta hedging as the other options (see Worksheet 12.19).

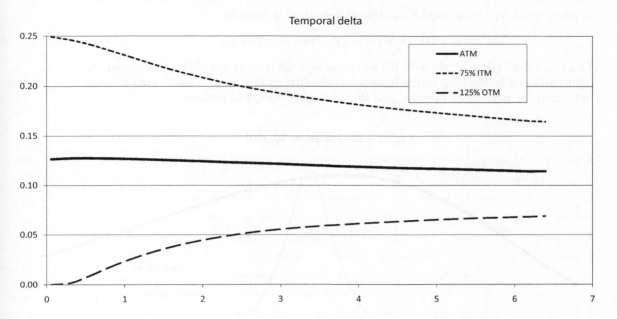

The caplet gamma is given by:

$$\gamma_0 = \mathrm{DF}_T * N'(d_1) * (T - \tau)/F(\tau, T)/(\sigma . \sqrt{\tau}) \quad \text{where } N'(x) = \exp\{-\tfrac{1}{2}x^2\}/\sqrt{2\pi}$$

This ignores the impact on discounting as being negligible. The result as the options move from OTM to ITM is shown in the graph below; the left-hand axis refers to the short option, the right-hand one to the long option. Gamma increases quite significantly over a short range as the maturity shortens, reflecting of course the increasing steepness in the delta curve. It is also virtually symmetric around ATM, whereas for long-dated options gamma is higher for OTM options. This suggests that dynamic delta hedging of long options is likely to be relatively successful.

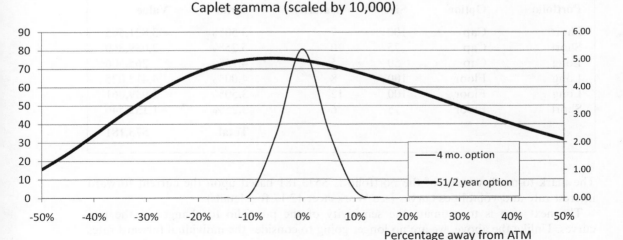

Vega, or sensitivity with respect to forward volatility, is given by:

$$v = \mathrm{DF}_T * N'(d_1) * (T - \tau) * F(\tau, T) * \sqrt{\tau}$$

This is graphed below, again with the left-hand axis referring to the short option, and the right-hand one to the long one. Changes in volatility, as one might expect, are far more significant for long-dated options, and slightly higher for OTM options.

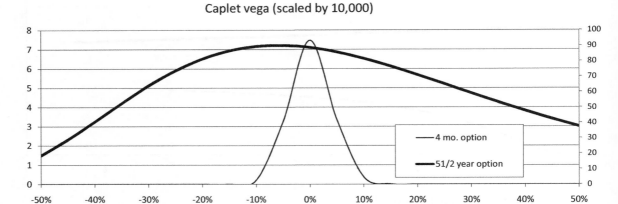

Caplet vega (scaled by 10,000)

The above discussion has concentrated on the behaviour of a single caplet. This of course is not terribly useful in practice, and we really should concentrate on the behaviour of multi-option portfolios. We will therefore use the following small-option portfolio:

Settlement date	4-Feb-08				
Portfolio	**Option**	**Size**	**Maturity**	**Strike**	**Value**
Short	Cap	100	7	3.50%	−3,821,505
Short	Cap	75	10	5.25%	−2,089,360
Long	Cap	50	5	4.75%	265,506
Long	Floor	100	8	4.00%	4,412,025
Long	Floor	100	12	3.50%	2,939,061
Short	Floor	75	6	3.25%	−1,132,546
				Total	**573,181**

The mark-to-market value of the portfolio is \$573,181 based upon the current forward interest rate and volatilities curves (see Worksheet 12.17 for details).

The next step is to estimate the sensitivity of the portfolio to changes in the two curves. Unlike the above, we are no longer going to consider the individual forward rates underlying each option, but will work with the two market curves themselves. Each forward interest rate and volatility was treated as independent; hence sensitivity vectors are created as shown in the table below. The gamma vector is simply defined as $(PVBP^+ - PVBP^-)$, and the Vega estimated by perturbing each forward volatility by 1 bp upwards.[8]

Table 12.8 Sensitivities of option portfolio to gridpoint changes in 3 mo. forward rates and 3 mo. forward volatilities

	PVBP	Gamma	Vega
1	−12,484	−683.78	−2.00
2	−34,893	−1,249.46	−6.89
3	−32,942	−502.53	−6.05
4	−32,152	−364.68	−5.05
5	−31,909	−493.14	−9.30
6	−32,956	−416.96	−10.74
7	−32,514	−357.30	−10.40
8	−33,169	−362.78	−10.34
9	−31,675	1.21	3.69
10	−32,595	169.74	6.60
11	−32,288	233.66	15.74
12	−30,343	275.83	20.83
13	−28,489	271.31	23.47
14	−29,640	274.75	19.60
15	−28,004	267.52	28.18
16	−27,373	254.98	24.36
17	−26,900	232.53	23.98
18	−26,410	219.70	22.74
19	−26,236	200.90	22.21
20	−31,472	−91.93	−20.42
21	−30,214	−87.34	−22.24
22	−31,073	−75.53	−26.80
23	−31,549	−51.16	−12.61
24	−32,357	1.88	4.05
25	−31,081	−1.03	−2.05
26	−31,858	−0.96	−3.19
27	−18,066	97.12	34.40
28	−14,163	99.92	46.06
29	−11,784	50.75	18.21
30	−10,046	−11.17	−17.85
31	−10,053	−16.20	−18.98
32	−10,278	−24.56	−21.23
33	−9,643	−19.64	−23.61
34	−10,284	−23.00	−23.75
35	−9,945	−23.03	−24.74

[8] A detailed explanation of how the production of these sensitivities may be automated is provided in Worksheet 12.16.

Table 12.8 (*cont.*)

36	−9,928	−21.71	−26.13
37	−9,911	−22.31	−28.87
38	−4,411	59.72	25.96
39	−1,716	74.18	51.13
40	−1,749	72.03	51.69
41	−1,987	82.61	57.07
42	−2,043	86.73	55.28
43	−1,980	83.40	56.93
44	−1,891	78.92	56.43
45	−1,730	71.21	55.46
46	−1,303	64.55	40.06
47	0	0.00	0.00
48	0	0.00	0.00
49	0	0.00	0.00
50	0	0.00	0.00

It would be feasible to dynamically delta-hedge against shifts in the forward and volatility curves by creating equivalences and re-balancing, very much as described earlier. However, we will use the opportunity to hedge the portfolio more robustly, and introduce some further techniques as follows.

We are going to use a mixture of generic swaps and caps[9] as shown below (the equivalent sensitivity vectors are calculated in Worksheet 12.21):

Generic hedging instruments (nominal principal $1m)

	Swap 1	Swap 2	Swap 3	
Maturity (years)	3	7	12	
Current rate	3.035%	3.885%	4.265%	ANN Act/360

	Cap 1	Cap 2	Cap 3	
Maturity	3	5	10	
ATM strike	2.988%	3.477%	4.229%	against 3mo. Libor

The strikes were calculated to be ATM forward quarterly swaps.

There are not enough instruments for gridpoint hedging, even if one wanted to, and full-yield curve hedging seems to introduce too much basis risk. Therefore we will maturity-band the sensitivity vectors into 0–3 years, 3–7 years and 7+ years as shown below.

[9] Exchange-traded instruments such as deposit futures and short options could also be used in these methods using stack and strip concepts (see Worksheet 12.20).

	Option portfolio	Swap 1	Swap 2	Swap 3	Cap 1	Cap 2	Cap 3
IR delta							
Band 1: 0–3 years	−369,918	−2,934	−2,909	−2,898	1,248	574	79
Band 2: 3–7 years	−444,888	0	−3,360	−3,297	0	1,345	1,931
Band 3: 7+ years	−110,682	0	0	−2,118	0	0	1,575
IR gamma							
Band 1: 0–3 years	−3,750	1	1	1	180	92	39
Band 2: 3–7 years	1,613	0	2	2	0	41	83
Band 3: 7+ years	562	0	0	1	0	0	28
IR vega							
Band 1: 0–3 years	−14	0	0	0	3	3	2
Band 2: 3–7 years	162	0	0	0	0	4	12
Band 3: 7+ years	283	0	0	0	0	0	10

Suppose we create a Super Portfolio

$$\mathrm{SP} = \left\{ \mathrm{OP} + \sum_i n_{S_i} * S_i + \sum_i n_{C_i} * C_i \right\}$$

from the option portfolio plus amounts of the hedging instruments. The resulting sensitivities of the SP in each band k are given by:

$$\text{Delta:} \quad \delta_{\mathrm{SP},k} = \delta_{\mathrm{OP},k} + \sum_i n_{S_i} * \delta_{S_i,k} + \sum_i n_{C_i} * \delta_{C_i,k} \quad \text{for } k = 1, 2, 3$$

$$\text{Gamma:} \quad \gamma_{\mathrm{SP},k} = \gamma_{\mathrm{OP},k} + \sum_i n_{S_i} * \gamma_{S_i,k} + \sum_i n_{C_i} * \gamma_{C_i,k}$$

$$\text{Vega:} \quad \upsilon_{\mathrm{SP},k} = \upsilon_{\mathrm{OP},k} + \sum_i n_{S_i} * \upsilon_{S_i,k} + \sum_i n_{C_i} * \upsilon_{C_i,k}$$

For hedging purposes we would like to select the ns such that $x_{\mathrm{SP},k} = 0$ for all k and where $x = \{\delta, \gamma, \upsilon\}$. However, we have nine equations but only six hedging instruments, so it is unlikely we can achieve this. We will adopt a robust approach using linear programming.[10] Let us create the following expressions:

$$S_x * x_{\mathrm{SP},k} + u_{x,k} - v_{x,k} = 0 \quad \text{for all } k \text{ and } x$$

where $u_{x,k}$ and $v_{x,k}$ are non-negative variables. Hence the sum $\{u_{x,k} + v_{x,k}\}$ measures the absolute distance of $x_{\mathrm{SP},k}$ from zero. S_x is simply a scaling constant to ensure that the magnitudes of the sensitivities are similar—see below. The objective therefore is to

---

[10] Strictly speaking, "goal" programming.

minimise the penalty function

$$\sum_{x,k}\{w_{u,x,k} * u_{x,k} + w_{v,x,k} * v_{x,k}\}$$

where $w_{u,x,k}$ and $w_{v,x,k}$ are optional (usually) positive weights that may be used to emphasise the importance of making sure that certain of the sensitivities are reduced to zero; for example, we might argue that it is essential that SP is delta-neutral, hence $w_{u,\delta,k}$ and $w_{v,\delta,k}$ could be an order of magnitude greater than the other weights. Positive gamma may well be acceptable; in this case, $w_{u,\gamma,k}$ would be positive, but $w_{v,\gamma,k}$ zero or even negative (see Plain Goal Programming box in Worksheet 12.22).

The worksheet is built in effectively the following steps:

1. Guess the hedging amounts n_{S_i} and n_{C_i}.
2. Calculate the net sensitivities $x_{SP,k}$ of the SP.
3. Calculate the u and v-variables using the goal expressions $S_x * x_{SP,k} + u_{x,k} - v_{x,k} = 0$. (*Note*: As both u and v have to be ≥ 0 one will be equal to zero and the other to $-S_x * x_{SP,k}$.)
4. Calculate the value of the penalty function using the u–v weights.

Then, using Solver, change the hedging amounts to minimise the penalty function.

For the ws to play their role of controlling the relative importance of the various goals, the us and vs must be of similar magnitudes—hence the scaling Ss. Worksheet 12.22 has used $S_x = (1/\mu_{OP,x})$ where $\mu_{OP,x}$ is the absolute average sensitivity of the option portfolio with respect to x over all the buckets.

The minimum value of the penalty function is 2.06; because it is positive, not all the net sensitivities of the SP are zero, as may be seen in the box below:

Net sensitivities			
	Delta	**Gamma**	**Vega**
Band 1: 0–3 years	0.00	0.00	35.20
Band 2: 3–7 years	0.00	0.00	−40.31
Band 3: 7+ years	0.00	0.00	111.69

Whilst the delta and gamma net sensitivities are zero, vega is not because:

(a) the penalty weights on gamma were twice greater than on vega; if the weights were switched, then the net vega sensitivities would become zero;
(b) the hedging swaps will ensure a feasible delta hedge because they only possess delta.

The resulting hedge is shown in the hedging portfolio table overleaf.

An alternative formulation is to adopt a minimax approach,[11] i.e. minimise λ defined as $\max\{w_{u,x,k} * u_{x,k} + w_{v,x,k} * v_{x,k}\}$.[12] Unlike the first formulation, which will try to achieve some of the goals whilst leaving others unsatisfied, this one attempts to satisfice each goal equally (see "Robust Programming box" from Worksheet 12.22).

This illustrative worksheet has been formulated in a slightly more complex fashion, combining the two approaches. The penalty function is:

$$\sum_k \{w_{u,\delta,k} * u_{\delta,k} + w_{v,\delta,k} * v_{\delta,k}\} + \lambda$$

where $\lambda - \{w_{u,x,k} * u_{x,k} + w_{v,x,k} * v_{x,k}\} \geq 0$ for all $x = \{\gamma, v\}$ and all k.

This ensures that the net delta sensitivity is zero if possible, and that any remaining infeasibility is spread over both the gamma and vega sensitivities, as shown in the box below.

	Delta	Gamma	Vega
Band 1: 0–3 years	0.00	00.00	39.54
Band 2: 3–7 years	0.00	00.00	−55.08
Band 3: 7+ years	0.00	−126.17	69.04

The resulting hedges are shown in the box below:

Hedging portfolios	Hedge GP	Hedge RP
Swap 1	25.75	24.88
Swap 2	−77.75	−73.57
Swap 3	−65.19	−68.41
Cap 1	24.61	21.07
Cap 2	1.77	10.51
Cap 3	−17.41	−21.74
(expressed in $m of NPA)		

The structure of the two hedges is very similar, as may be expected. On balance, the portfolio was a net seller of caps and buyer of floors; hence, intuitively, the hedge should consist of net long caps plus swap payers (as indicated by the negative NPA).

The effectiveness of these hedges was then tested by imposing parallel shifts on both the forward rate and forward volatility curves simultaneously in steps of 50 bp upto ±250 bp. The full results of the 121 different scenarios are shown in the worksheet. If we define $\Delta V_{Y,r,\sigma}$ as the change in value of portfolio $Y = \{OP, GP \text{ hedge, } RP \text{ hedge}\}$ under scenario

---

[11] Sometimes known as "robust" programming.
[12] Which may be represented within a linear framework as $\lambda - \{w_{u,x,k} * u_{x,k} + w_{v,x,k} * v_{x,k}\} \geq 0$ for all x and k.

$\{r, \sigma\}$, then a measure of the total change in value over all scenarios is

$$\Delta V_Y = \left\{ \sum_{r,\sigma} (\Delta V_{Y,r,\sigma})^2 \right\}^{1/2}$$

The effectiveness of the hedge may be measured by $[1 - \Delta V_Y / \Delta V_{OP}]$: this measure exceeds 98% for both GP and RP hedges. Both formulations therefore would appear to provide good hedging over a wide range of parallel shifts.

An alternative is to use scenario analysis. Suppose a number of scenarios $p = 1, 2, \ldots, N$ are created; each scenario consists of a defined (not necessarily parallel) shift in the forward rate and/or forward volatility curves. Calculate the change in the value of the option portfolio ΔOP_p and the changes in value of the hedging instruments $\{\Delta S_{i,p}$ and $\Delta C_{i,p}\}$ under each scenario, and hence the change in the value of SP:

$$\Delta SP_p = \left\{ \Delta OP_p + \sum_i n_{S_i} * \Delta S_{i,p} + \sum_i n_{C_i} * \Delta C_{i,p} \right\} \quad \text{for each } p = 1, \ldots, N$$

As before, the ideal hedge would set $\Delta SP_p = 0$ under each p but this is unlikely to be feasible due to the limitations of the hedging instruments. But, using the same ideas as above, we could create the following equation:

$$\Delta SP_p + u_p - v_p = 0$$

and then either minimise $\sum_p \{w_{u,p} * u_p + w_{v,p} * v_p\}$ or create another lambda-style robust expression.[13] The advantage of this type of approach is that it can be manipulated to deal with a wide range of gapping or jump scenarios, whilst the "Greek" approach is less suited to handle these as the Greeks are local measures.

More exotic options, especially those that involve a discontinuity in the payoff such as digitals and barriers, are considerably more difficult to risk-manage. For example, the "Greek" characteristics of a digital caplet are quite different from those of an ordinary caplet. As the price of a digital cannot exceed the payout, delta increases as the option moves from OTM to ATM but then drops back towards zero for ITM. This means that gamma is initially positive but then switches to be negative. From above, vega is always positive for a normal caplet because increased volatility increases the changes of a larger payout. If a digital option is OTM, then vega is also positive as expected because this has increased the probability of the option moving into the money. However, for an ATM or ITM option, vega is typically negative because low volatility will keep the option ITM whereas high volatility increases the probability that the option will go OTM. As an ATM option approaches maturity, these switches in sign become increasingly extreme which can result in costly and yet ineffective hedging.

Thus the simple sensitivities for exotics are themselves relatively unstable, and delta hedging alone is seldom adequate, especially near the discontinuities. If a whole portfolio is to be risk-managed, then the discontinuities arising from a single option may have little overall effect, and delta hedging may be appropriate. For the risk management of a small number of options with discontinuities, more robust hedging should be used possibly using

---

[13] The author first used techniques such as these to hedge IR option portfolios in the late 1980s. At that time Discount Corporation of New York Futures (later subsumed into Dean Witter) used to provide its clients with a service calculating robust exchange-traded hedges for their IR option books based upon similar techniques.

the methods described above, and possibly in combination with the concept of "static" hedging, which has been developed for this situation.[14]

12.11 HEDGING OF INFLATION SWAPS

This section is included to complement the section on inflation swap pricing, and to demonstrate a further use of the equivalence concepts.

There are three sources of market risk in an inflation swap:

1. Movement in the inflation rates, which may be hedged with index-linked bonds or generic swaps.
2. Movement in gilt discount rates, may be hedged with conventional gilts.
3. Movement in Libor rates, used for discounting and possibly estimation, and may be hedged in the usual fashion in the swap book.

Inflation risk is unique. We can use very similar techniques to those described above to create, for example, a portfolio of generic zero-coupon swaps that will delta-hedge the inflation risk in a swap portfolio (full details are contained in Worksheet 8.42).

For example, suppose we have a portfolio consisting of three of the swaps described in Chapter 10, namely the YoY swap (ignoring changes in the convexity effect), the fixed–floating inflation swap and the inflated fixed–Libor swap. The swaps extend out to 2034. We plan to calculate to delta-hedge the portfolio using four selected generic zero-swaps with maturities 5, 10, 20 and 30 years, respectively. The first step is to calculate the delta sensitivities of the portfolio and the hedging swaps due to shifts in the market zero-coupon inflation curve—the results are shown in the table below.

Maturity	New value of portfolio	Change in value of zero-coupon swaps (GBP for 1m nominal)			
		5	10	20	30
1	−610.25	0.00	0.00	0.00	0.00
2	−1,065.91	0.00	0.00	0.00	0.00
3	−1,574.87	0.00	0.00	0.00	0.00
4	−2,042.91	0.00	0.00	0.00	0.00
5	−1,954.74	−439.62	0.00	0.00	0.00
6	81,246.41	0.00	0.00	0.00	0.00
7	75,360.96	0.00	0.00	0.00	0.00
8	−11,968.32	0.00	0.00	0.00	0.00
9	−13,296.25	0.00	0.00	0.00	0.00
10	−22,350.29	0.00	−812.19	0.00	0.00

---

[14] See, for example, E. Derman *et al.*, "Forever hedged", and P. Carr *et al.*, "Static simplicity", both in *Risk*, 7, 1994, pp. 39–45 and pp. 45–9, respectively.

Maturity (cont.)	New value of portfolio	Change in value of zero-coupon swaps (GBP for 1m nominal)			
		5	10	20	30
12	−43,317.86	0.00	0.00	0.00	0.00
15	−85,445.46	0.00	0.00	0.00	0.00
20	−148,597.97	0.00	0.00	−1,503.84	0.00
25	−102,739.12	0.00	0.00	0.00	0.00
30	−3,204.30	0.00	0.00	0.00	−2,193.42
40	0.00	0.00	0.00	0.00	0.00
50	0.00	0.00	0.00	0.00	0.00

As expected, zero-coupon swaps are orthogonal in terms of their sensitivities (in a similar fashion as generic IRS are to changes in their market rates). The next step is to bucket the sensitivities: four buckets are intuitively obvious, as shown below.

	Maturities	Portfolio	Swap 5	Swap 10	Swap 20	Swap 30
Band 1	0–5	−7,248.68	−439.62	0.00	0.00	0.00
Band 2	5–10	108,992.51	0.00	−812.19	0.00	0.00
Band 3	10–20	−277,361.29	0.00	0.00	−1,503.84	0.00
Band 4	20–30	−105,943.41	0.00	0.00	0.00	−2,193.42

The next step is to calculate the delta hedge (the negative sign implies paying fixed inflation):

	Hedge	
Swap 5	−16.49m GBP	To pay fixed
Swap 10	134.20m GBP	To receive fixed
Swap 20	−184.44m GBP	To pay fixed
Swap 30	−48.30m GBP	To pay fixed

The effectiveness of the hedge can be demonstrated against a ±1% parallel shift in the growth curve as shown in the graph below; this shows the net difference between changes in the portfolio and hedge. There is, of course, significant basis risk in this hedge if the growth curve does not behave in a parallel fashion:

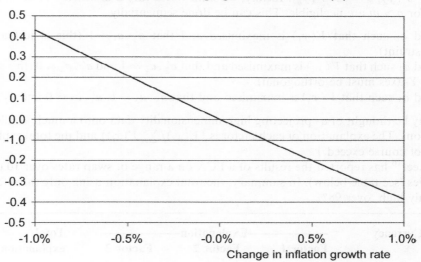

Effectiveness of hedging an inflation swap portfolio

12.12 APPENDIX: ANALYSIS OF SWAP CURVES

The movement of interest rate curves through time has been intensively studied by many market practitioners; if one can develop a "good" model, then it is likely that safe profitable opportunities can be identified. There is also an extensive academic literature[15] and it is not the purpose of this appendix to replicate it. The objective is to briefly discuss an approach that has been gaining acceptance within the risk management community over the past decade.

Assume we have available a set of interest rate curve data $X = \{x_{it}, i = 1, \ldots, n$ maturities, $t = 1, \ldots, T$ time}where x_{it} represents the arithmetic change in rate i from time $t - 1$ to time t. We want to understand how the curve evolves through time. One way of doing this is to track each one of the ith gridpoints individually, as we did in gridpoint risk management. But this ignores any correlation structure along the curve, and is therefore likely to be inefficient.

An alternative is to use the techniques of principal component analysis. Think of a curve at time t as a vector of rate changes x_t, i.e. as a single point in an n-dimensional space. PCA transforms these data into $Y = \mathbf{A} . X$ where Y is also dimension $\{n \times T\}$ and hence $\mathbf{A}$ is a square $\{n \times n\}$ matrix. Initially, think of this as simply a rotation of the original X axes into a set of orthogonal (i.e. at right angles) Y-axes.

We can therefore write $y_j = a'_j . X$ where y_j and a'_j are the jth rows of Y and $\mathbf{A}$, respectively. The variance of y_j is $V(y_j) = a'_j . V(X) . a_j$ where $V(X)$ is X's full covariance matrix. The total variance in the original data is given by $\sum_i V(x_i)$, i.e. the sum of the variances corresponding to each gridpoint. The above transformation cannot change the total variance, i.e. we know that $\sum_i V(x_i) = \sum_j V(y_j)$.

[15] See, for example, N. Anderson *et al.*, "New estimates of the UK real and nominal curves", *Bank of England Quarterly Bulletin*, November 1999, pp. 384–92 or N. Anderson *et al.*, *Estimating and Interpreting the Yield Curve*, published by Wiley, 1997 as relatively modern introductions to both the academic and practitioner literature.

What we want to do is select the vectors $a_1', a_2', \ldots, a_n'$ so that $V(y_1) > V(y_2) > \cdots > V(y_n)$. Ideally, we want to identify a dimension $m \ll n$ such that $V(y_p)$ for $p > m$ are negligible. This can be done sequentially:

1. Find a_1 such that $V(y_1)$ is maximised and that $a_1' \cdot a_1 = 1$ (this is just a scaling constraint).
2. Find a_2 such that $V(y_2)$ is maximised and that $a_2' \cdot a_2 = 1$ and $a_1' \cdot a_2 = 0$ (this says that the Y-axes must be orthogonal).
3. Find a_3 such that $V(y_3)$ is maximised and that $a_3' \cdot a_3 = 1$, $a_1' \cdot a_3 = 0$ and $a_2' \cdot a_3 = 0$.

This may be thought of as projecting high-dimensionality data onto a much smaller set of dimensions. The explanation of each factor is $\{V(y_j)/\sum_i V(x_i)\}$ and the total explanation cannot of course exceed 1.

Niffikeer[16] has reported the results of a PCA on a range of swap rates over 10 different currencies (see table below). In summary, the total explanation using only three factors is uniformly high, over 98%.

Currency	Explanation			Total explanation
	Factor 1	Factor 2	Factor 3	
USD	95.0%	3.6%	0.7%	99.3%
GBP	91.0%	6.9%	1.0%	98.9%
DEM	90.8%	7.2%	1.1%	99.1%
CHF	93.1%	4.5%	1.0%	98.6%
ITL	94.0%	4.6%	0.8%	99.4%
JPY	91.7%	6.1%	1.2%	99.0%
NLG	90.9%	6.7%	1.2%	98.8%
BEF	88.6%	8.5%	1.5%	98.6%
FRF	91.6%	6.8%	0.9%	99.3%
ESP	90.1%	6.4%	1.4%	98.6%

But there is a problem with such results, namely how can they be used in practice? The difficulty is that the a vectors will have no precise interpretation. The vectors for the USD data are shown below:

Maturity	Vector 1	Vector 2	Vector 3
2 yr	0.94210	0.30335	0.11583
3 yr	0.96519	0.24357	0.04931
4 yr	0.97917	0.14803	−0.05694
5 yr	0.98689	0.06814	−0.10037
6 yr	0.99519	−0.01824	−0.08994
7 yr	0.98536	−0.11355	−0.07781
8 yr	0.98606	−0.15837	0.01315
9 yr	0.97682	−0.20651	0.05592
10 yr	0.95590	−0.25644	0.12827

---

[16] C. Niffikeer et al., A synthetic factor approach to the estimation of VaR of a portfolio of IRS", *J. of Banking & Finance*, **24**, 2000, pp. 1903–32.

These vectors are usually "interpreted" as representing a parallel shift, a rotation and a change in curvature, respectively. However, they are not exactly these curve movements.

Niffikeer proceeds to fit synthetic orthogonal factors, i.e. ones that are precisely defined in advance. A simple example would be to break the curve into three buckets and represent the movements as:

	Bucket 1	Bucket 2	Bucket 3
Parallel	+1	+1	+1
Rotational	+1	0	−1
Curvature	+1	−2	+1

The synthetic parallel factor is fitted to the data first, then the rotational factor to the residuals and finally the curvature factor. Obviously the level of explanation with these synthetic factors cannot be as high as from the PCA, but the reduction is only about 1% on average across all currencies.

This analysis provides a strong rationale for curve risk management, although the explanation for forward rate curve is very much lower. Hedging against parallel shifts alone is likely to remove some 90% of fluctuation in valuation. PCA is also becoming widely used in curve modelling and VaR (see Chapters 11 and 13) to reduce substantially the number of risk factors. However, like all statistical techniques, the analysis is of course very dependent upon historic data being a good representation of the future. An over-reliance on such findings to hedge against unstable market movements is extremely unwise, as many practitioners have found to their cost.

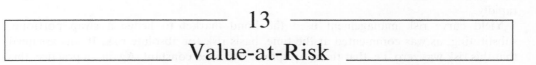

13
Value-at-Risk

OBJECTIVE

This chapter discusses the more recent risk management techniques that have been developed over the past decade, recognising that markets are not perfect and that hedges sometimes have to be constructed from less-than-perfect instruments. Value-at-Risk approaches have become standard in many banks, despite various criticisms over the years, and this chapter will explore some of the practical issues that arise from their implementation.

The chapter starts with a very simple transaction, and demonstrates how one-factor VaR may be calculated in using both historic simulation and a delta (or parametric) approximation. The example is then extended to a two-factor model and eventually to a more general multi-factor model. The last section here also looks at the relationship between delta hedging, minimum VaR hedging and hedge effectiveness.

Some background work is then discussed, such as the selection of risk factors, alternative ways of implementing VaR in practice and, in particular, practical problems of estimating volatility and correlation.

A small sold FX option portfolio is then introduced as a further example of a position having negative gamma. Its VaR is calculated using both the above methods, plus Monte Carlo simulation, comparing the various results. There are however various difficulties implementing the simulation methods, and ways of improving and speeding them up are discussed, such as extreme value theory in Section 13.15 (Appendix), weighted historic simulation and sampling strategies.

The chapter finishes with four final topics. First, as trading spreads is becoming more common especially within Europe, the calculation of spread VaR from market data is demonstrated. The calculation of equity VaR with and without the use of indices is then discussed. Finally, possible strategies to shock testing and the implementation of stress testing in an imperfect world are described.

13.1 INTRODUCTION

The techniques described in Chapter 12 are often called traditional or "desktop" risk management. The latter name refers to the fact that individual trading desks usually only enter into a limited range of risks, and the more traditional risk measurement methods are perfectly adequate in this situation. However, we made some quite extreme correlation assumptions about interest rate movements, namely that either the curve exhibited zero or perfect correlation. Obviously, in practice the truth lies somewhere in between. But these assumptions are frequently acceptable provided that the movement in interest rates is relatively small. Related to this statement, although not identical, is that the risk management time horizon is relatively short, i.e. the position can be traded or hedged rapidly.

Yield curve risk management used the bond market to hedge a swap portfolio, substituting, as was commented at the time, basis risk for absolute risk. It was assumed that this risk was zero, i.e. that the swap spread remained constant. Again, in practice, this is not true.

In the mid-1980s, concern at the levels of unregulated risks banks were entering into as a result of the exponentially expanding off-balance sheet derivatives markets led bank regulators to introduce the fundamental concept of obliging banks to allocate a certain amount of capital against some overall measures of risk. The regulations started by defining the amount of capital required to support a measured amount of credit exposure. By the early 1990s, attention had moved on to market risk exposure, especially in trading activities.

The important point is that both banks and their regulators realised that these capital-based approaches required measurement techniques that spanned across a range of different activities, and not just a single trading desk. After conducting a number of simulations, a very crude "static framework" methodology was suggested by the regulators, first for credit risk and then for market risk. This basically meant that a bank would enter very high-level summaries of their activities into a black box, and the output was the amount of regulatory capital required to sustain those activities. Intuitively, banks felt that if they could develop more precise methods of defining their risks, and persuade the regulators of this increased precision, then the levels of required capital would be reduced to their obvious benefit. The measurement of market risk was generally deemed to be an order of magnitude (at least!!) easier than modelling credit risk. By 1995 the regulators permitted "internal", i.e. individual bank-developed, market risk measurement models which would then be used to derive the capital required. Permission was granted under strict approval conditions. The new Basel Accord, published in 2004, and subsequently revised, permits a limited range of internal models for credit risk, as well as a wider range of market risk models (under the broad heading of Incremental Risk Charge[1]).

The most popular, although by no means the only, internal model is Value-at-Risk (VaR). This family of approaches has become standard not only for modelling bank-wide market risk, but also for credit and increasingly operational risk as well. This chapter will describe and contrast the major methods for calculating market risk VaR, and will finish with a brief discussion on credit-related topics. Because VaR is designed to measure market risks arising from a wide range of activities, more complex portfolios will be used as examples than in previous chapters.

Is VaR a completely novel approach, or is it a natural development out of the desktop approaches previously described? This is a question that will be discussed during this chapter.

13.2 A VERY SIMPLE EXAMPLE

It is 8 am on 4 February 2008. A bank dealer has just received a call from a customer to borrow USD100m for 12 months. He quoted 2.90% which was accepted, and he

---

[1] See Basel Committee for Banking Supervision, *Guidelines for Computing Capital for Incremental Risk in the Trading Book*, 2009. This also requires capital to be allocated against, amongst other risk types, spread risk and basis risk.

confirms:

$100m to be paid by the bank on 6 February 2008

$100m plus interest $= \$100\text{m} * (1 + 2.90\% * (6 \text{ Feb } 2009 - 6 \text{ Feb } 2008)/360)$

$= \$102,948,333$ to be received from the customer on

6 February 2008

A bank would routinely value each transaction to the current market rates. The current 12 mo. rate is 2.89625%, hence the mark-to-market value of the money to be received in 1 year's time would be calculated as:

$$\$102,948,333/(1 + 2.89625\% * 1.017) = 100,003,703$$

An overall profit of $3,703 for a couple of minutes work. (Bid–offer spreads have been ignored in this discussion for ease of explanation.) See Worksheet 13.2 for initial details.

The bank now has a market risk. If interest rates rise, it would lose value. The dealer can easily estimate the impact of moving rates by calculating the sensitivity of the transaction. For example, the PVBP is estimated by increasing the rate by 1 bp and revaluing, we get:

$$\$102,948,333/(1 + 2.90625\% * 1.017) = 99,993,828$$

i.e. a loss in value of −$9,875, as shown in column [2] of Worksheet 13.2.

So much for traditional measures, but it does not address an important management question, namely "how much value might the trader lose over one day?" The trader had some historic records of the 12 month cash rate from the past 2 years (or, to be more precise, the last 500 business days). The graph below shows the daily percentage changes[2] in the rate. These changes were calculated using $\Delta_t = \ln(r_t/r_{t-1})$; an alternative would have been to use simple changes given by $(r_t - r_{t-1})/r_{t-1}$—the worksheet can be shifted between the two definitions. For a 1-day time horizon, the difference is negligible. Most of the changes were fairly small and randomly up or down, but there had been some large moves recently, implying a move into a regime of high volatility. The largest up-move was 8.8%, which, if repeated, would have resulted in a loss in excess of $250,000 over the day (see diagram at the top of the next page).

We wish to calculate the potential loss due to adverse movements in this 12 month rate over this trading day. Let us assume that the past is an accurate representation of the future, and also that all the historic changes over the past 2 years are equally likely to occur in the future. (These assumptions are discussed in more detail in Section 13.6.) Therefore, we can estimate new rates $R_t = r_0 * \exp(\Delta_t))$ for $t = 1, 2, \ldots, 500$, where r_0 is the current level 2.89625%. Hence we can calculate the loss or gain in value for each new rate.

---

[2] It is common to analyse rate movements on a "return" or percentage basis, i.e. what was the percentage movement from one day to the next, instead of an absolute basis measured by simply taking the difference in rates. The reason for this is that a 50 bp absolute shift when rates are 2% is far less likely than the same shift when rates are 10%. Percentage shifts on the other hand are by and large independent of the current level of rates, and therefore consistently comparable. There are also some pragmatic theoretical reasons, such as the widely used assumption of returns being normally distributed in option pricing.

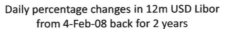

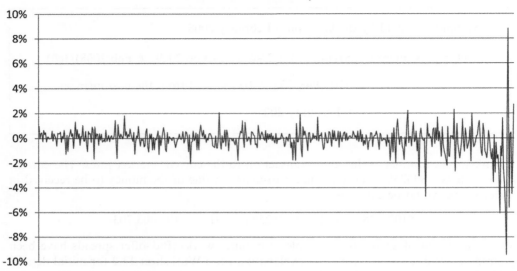

Over all the new rates, we find that the average change in value is $3,072, implying that rates have fallen slightly over the 2 years. However, the best and worst change is $258,066 and −$262,864, respectively, with a standard deviation of $31,356, indicating a wide range of daily changes are possible. However, such days are very infrequent, as can be seen from the histogram on the facing page.

The histogram was created by dividing the {maximum − minimum} range up into a number of buckets, in this case 10, and then counting the percentage of observations lying in each bucket. The histogram shows the mid-point of each bucket on the x-axis.

We can now estimate the daily VaR, using either the raw changes in value themselves or the histogram. For example, one approximation for 95% VaR is to find the $(1 − 95\%) * 500 = 25$th worst result, namely −$33,299. An alternative, if using Excel, is to use the "PERCENTILE(array of results, 1−95%)" command which gives −$32,509. A third alternative is to calculate the accumulative frequency, and then interpolate the appropriate tail; this gives −$35,433 when using 20 buckets. As expected, the three results are similar, but not identical. Some further results are shown in the table below:

Confidence level	Small	Percentile	Interpolated frequency
99%	−59,690	−58,104	−59,904
95%	−33,299	−32,509	−35,443
90%	−19,922	−19,698	−26,608

In words, we could interpret the VaR result as:

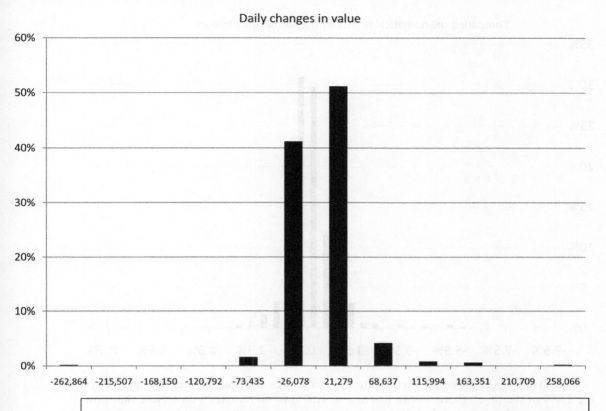

Daily changes in value

"There is a 5% chance that the trader could lose $33,299 or worse over a 1-day time horizon as the result of adverse market movements."

Alternatively, we could say that there is a 95% chance that the losses will not exceed $33,299, and indeed there is some potential upside. The VaR statement must contain three elements:

1. The size of potential loss.
2. The probability of this loss or worse.
3. The time horizon.

It is incomplete if it is missing any of them.

This approach is called historic simulation, and is very widely used by banks, especially when calculating their regulatory VaR numbers. The above discussion is extremely simple, and it will be extended in Section 13.8.

We can also approach this problem in a different way, by concentrating on the change in the rates. A new histogram has been created, this time bucketing the changes in the rates into 50 bp bins (see next page). Consider one bucket, for example the one centred on 1.75%. Increases in the range from 1.5% to 2.0% occurred eight times in the past 500 days or 1.6% of the time. Applying this average movement to the current level of rate, i.e. from 2.89625% to 2.89625% ∗ exp(1.75%) = 2.94738%, would result in a loss of $50,472.16 (see column [3] of Worksheet 13.3 for confirmation).

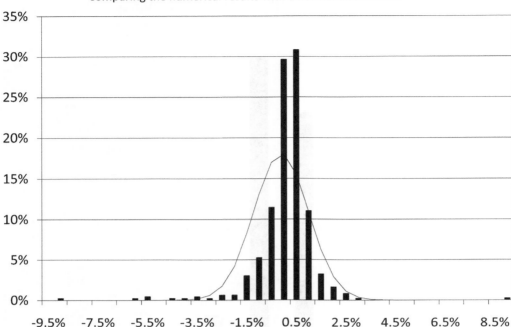

Of course a bigger movement in the rate may occur. For example, we find that on 14 days (or 2.8% of the time), there was an increase of 1.50% *or larger* over 1 day. Note that now we do not use the centre of the bucket, but the lower edge to indicate the size of movement, because we are interested in a particular increase *or worse*. This movement would result in a loss of $43,210.80 (as confirmed in column [4]).

Based on the same assumption as before, namely that these events are a good indication of the future, another VaR statement would be:

> *"There is a 2.8% chance that the trader could lose $43,211 or worse over a 1-day time horizon as a result of adverse market movements."*

In calculating the VaR above, we used a "full valuation" approach, i.e. we shifted the rate by 1.75% and then re-valued the trade. An alternative is to use a PVBP approximation as discussed in Chapter 12:

$$\Delta \text{Value} \approx \text{PVBP} * \text{Shift in rates (in bp)}$$

For example, the 1.50% movement in rates was equivalent to:

$$\Delta r = 2.89625\% * \exp(1.50\%) - 2.89625\% = 0.0004377 \text{ or } 4.38 \text{ bp}$$

Therefore:

$$\Delta \text{Value} \approx \$9,875.26 * 4.38 \text{ bp} = 43,225.21$$

The difference between the exact amount of $43,211 and the first-order approximation of $43,225 is predominantly due to second-order (gamma) effects.

This approach may be simplified further by using the approximation:

$$2.89625\% * \exp(1.50\%) - 2.89625\% \approx 2.89625\% * 1.50\% = 4.34 \text{ bp}$$

This gives a very similar result (see column [5] of Worksheet 13.2):

$$\Delta \text{Value} = \$9,875.26 * 4.34 \text{ bp} = \$42,901.83$$

Based on historic return data, we find:

$$\text{Daily mean } (\mu) = -0.113\%$$

$$\text{Daily standard deviation } (\sigma) = 1.105\%$$

The mean is often called the "drift" or "trend", whilst the standard deviation is of course simply the daily volatility of the rate. The percentage movement in the rate of 1.50% may be re-written in terms of multiples of the volatility, i.e. $1.50\% = 1.358 * \sigma$. The number 1.358 is called the "multiplier" (we will use the symbol k to represent it). Using the above approximation, and drawing all this together, the PVBP VaR (also known as "parametric" or delta VaR) may be estimated as:

$$\text{VaR} = 10,000 * \text{PVBP} * r * k * \sigma = 10,000 * 9,875 * 2.89625\% * 1.358 * 1.105\% = \$42,902$$

Notice that strictly speaking this is negative as the PVBP is negative for an increase in rate. But conventionally VaRs are always quoted as a positive number even though they refer to a potential loss. This result has been replicated more formally, as shown in the box below:

Proof of one-factor delta VaR

To formalise what we have done so far, assume that there is a change Δr in the rate r. The change in value is approximately given by Taylor's theorem:

$$\Delta \text{Value} \approx \partial \text{Value}/\partial r * \Delta r = \partial \text{Value}/\partial r * r * (\Delta r / r)$$

where $(\Delta r / r)$ is a return. As $[\partial \text{Value}/\partial r * r]$ is currently known:

$$\text{st dev}\{\Delta \text{Value}\} \approx \partial \text{Value}/\partial r * r * \text{st dev}(\Delta r / r) = \partial \text{Value}/\partial r * r * \sigma$$

Therefore, if we characterise VaR by k multiples of st dev$\{\Delta \text{Value}\}$, we can write:

$$\text{VaR} = \partial \text{Value}/\partial r * r * k * \sigma$$

The value of the transaction may be written as:

$$\text{Value} = \$102,948,333/(1 + r.d) - 100,000,000$$

where r is the rate and d the daycount fraction (365/360). Differentiating, we get:

$$\partial \text{Value}/\partial r = -\$102,948,333 * d/(1 + r.d)^2 = -\$98,762,353.76$$

Note that this analytic delta is approximately $10,000 * \text{PVBP}$. The Delta VaR is therefore:

$$\text{Delta VaR} = -\$98,762,353.76 * 2.89625\% * 1.358 * 1.105\% = \$42,906$$

i.e. very similar to the previous estimate.

Interest rates have trended slightly downwards over this period, which will improve the profitability of the deal if continued. However, short-term trends are notoriously unstable, and it is common practice to ignore them, as we have above, when calculating VaR over short-time horizons. It is straightforward to modify the above formula to include a trend term if the time horizon were longer. The trend is of course reflected in the 2.8% probability, as it is inherent in the historic data used to derive the histogram.

Notice that this expression for VaR includes the traditional sensitivity measure. But that measure assumes a predefined movement in the rate, whereas VaR has additionally attempted to make a statistical statement about the likely size of movement. It is important to recognise that VaR extends the PVBP analysis, and does not necessarily supplant it.

We estimated there was a 2.8% probability of suffering this loss or worse. Obviously, as the multiplier is increased, the VaR also increases but the probability decreases. The relationship between the size of the multiplier and the probability is defined by the numerical histogram, and we have made no other distributional assumptions.

A widely used assumption is that the returns follow a Normal distribution. Is this realistic? The graph on p. 314 superimposes a Normal distribution on the actual returns. Not only does the numerical distribution have longer tails than the Normal distribution, but it is also more peaked as well (i.e. it is leptokurtic).

For a Normal distribution, the relationship between the multiplier and the probability is defined theoretically as follows:

Multiplier	Probability
1	15.9%
1.28	10.0%
1.645	5.0%
2	2.3%
2.326	1.0%
3	0.1%

Most practitioners start with the probability—5% and 1% are the most popular—which then defines the multiplier. For example, to calculate the 95% VaR:

$$\text{VaR} = 10,000 * \$9,875 * 2.89625\% * 1.645 * 1.105\% = \$51,968 \text{ per day}$$

This number is very different from the 95% VaR estimated using historic simulation, or indeed the VaR estimated directly from the rate histogram of $33,070. Why is that? Whilst the numerical distribution has longer tails than the normal, the tails at the 95% point are actually much fatter, so that the 95% multiplier for the normal is considerably greater than the multiplier of 1.055 for the numerical distribution (see Worksheet 13.4 for details).

In practice, it has often been observed that the probability of large movements is considerably underestimated by a normal distribution: i.e., the numerical distributions have fatter tails. For example, many markets suffered enormous and successive movements during 2008, equivalent to multipliers of 6 and above. Under the assumption of normality, the probability of such movements occurring is infinitesimal. If we felt that the normal was inappropriate, then we could work with the numeric distribution itself, as above, or with a different theoretical distribution which may fit the data better. Student-t is a common choice, but it does have an additional parameter which has to be fitted.

Personally, I think the reader should recognise that VaR depends upon what has happened in the past, and that large market movements are very uncommon (albeit not as uncommon as implied by the normal distribution, but still very rare). VaR estimates therefore work well when the past is a good predictor of the future; the distributional assumption is unlikely to have a major effect on the estimate. However, VaR grossly underestimates what happens when markets behave abnormally; that is why stress testing (see Section 14) is a necessary supplement to measures such as sensitivities and VaR. But I think it is wrong to reject VaR. It is surely far better to rely upon, not just one, but a range of measures that work under different circumstances.

The above calculations have all been based on a holding time horizon of 1 day, because the historic observations used to estimate volatility were daily. If we wish to increase the time horizon to, say, 10 days (which is the regulatory requirement), an estimate of 10-day volatility is required. This could be done by estimating the returns from day_i to day_{i+10}, day_{i+11} to day_{i+20}, etc. To collect a meaningful amount of data so that the confidence level in the volatility estimate is high would require going back some considerable time (such as 5,000 days or 20 years). Markets are likely to be very different then. An alternative approach would be to calculate the returns based on the periods from day_i to day_{i+10}, day_{i+1} to day_{i+11}, etc. This introduces significant auto-correlation, reducing the volatility, as the sampling periods obviously overlap, but is often the practice. However, the most widely used approach (inherent in most closed-form option-pricing formulae) is simply to scale up the 1-day volatility using the square-root rule,[3] namely:

$$\text{10-day volatility} = \sqrt{10} * \text{1-day volatility}$$

As discussed in the footnote, this relies upon assumptions of independence which are unlikely to be fully justified in practice. If a market is trending, its volatility is reducing, so the VaR produced by this rule is likely to be an overestimate of the actual VaR. But of course, a trending market violates the earlier assumption of no trends, so that should be taken into account when estimating the potential loss of value.

13.3 A VERY SIMPLE EXAMPLE EXTENDED

The above example calculated the VaR for a simple USD transaction. Let us assume that we are now a South African bank, implying that all transactions have to be valued in ZAR. This introduces the additional complication of movement in the exchange rate. The spot rate on 4 February 2008 was 7.444 ZAR per USD with a daily volatility of 0.910%, measured over the past two years.

Estimating the risk of the transaction in ZAR requires a decision to be made about the initial cash outflow. Is the $100m valued at today's spot rate, or at some spot rate in the

---

[3] If the daily return is defined as $x_i = \ln(r_i/r_{i-1})$, then the return over a period from $i - 1$ to $i + N$ is $\ln(r_{i+N}/r_{i-1}) = \sum x_k$, summed from $k = i$ to $i + N$. On the assumptions that the actual return for each day is independent of the returns on the other days, i.e. no trends, and that the volatility is the same for each day, then the result follows.

future? The two valuation equations may be written respectively as:

$$\text{Value} = \$102{,}948{,}333/(1 + r\,.\,d) * S - \$100{,}000{,}00 * S_0$$

$$\text{Value} = \{\$102{,}948{,}333/(1 + r\,.\,d) - \$100{,}000{,}00\} * S$$

where S is a potentially variable exchange rate. The net valuation of the transaction is ZAR27,569 no matter how the deal is represented, but the FX risk is very different, as shown in the table below:

Sensitivities (per bp)	Using S_0	Using S
IR risk	−73,511	−73,511
FX risk	10,000	0.3703

Obviously, in the second case, the FX risks associated with the two cashflows largely cancel. As it is common market practice to use a 2-day settlement period for FX, then the FX rate for the initial outflow should be locked in at the time of the transaction (and therefore carry no FX risk), leaving the FX risk on the future cashflow fully exposed. Hence, in the example below, we will use the S_0 representation.

Using the parametric approach, the 95% VaR for each of the two risk factors, r and S, may be calculated separately as above:

1. $\text{PVBP}_r = -\text{ZAR}73{,}511$ (this is the USD PVBP $* S$) per 1 USD bp
     $\text{PVBP}_S = \$10{,}000$ per 1 bp shift in S.

(This PVBP is defined as $\Delta\text{Value}/\Delta S$ which has dimensions of $\text{ZAR}/\,[\text{ZAR}/\text{USD}] = \text{USD}$.)

2. $\text{VaR}_r = -10{,}000 * 73{,}511 * 2.89625\% * 1.645 * 1.105\% = -\text{ZAR}386{,}851$
     $\text{VaR}_S = 10{,}000 * 10{,}000 * 7.444 * 1.645 * 0.910\% \qquad = \text{ZAR}11{,}147{,}976.$

VaR_S is much higher than VaR_r, despite the spot volatility being lower than the rate volatility. This is because PVBP works in terms of absolute movements, whereas VaR works in terms of percentage movements. A 1% move in 7.444 is a much greater absolute movement than a 1% shift in the rate. Note that the negative sign on VaR_r has been retained, although obviously for reporting purposes it would be ignored (see Worksheet 13.5 for details).

VaR was introduced as a risk measurement technique that can span across a range of different activities, in contrast to the simpler PVBP approaches. Note that the units of PVBPs are different and therefore not combinable, whereas the units of VaRs are consistently money (in this case, ZAR).

However, we need to develop a method of combining together individual VaRs in some appropriate fashion into a single risk measure. The standard deviation of the overall value of the transaction may be approximated using the following result.

Before we do the calculation, what do we expect intuitively? If the interest rate increases, the trade loses value, whilst if the spot rate increases the trade gains in value. If USD interest rates increase then we would expect the dollar to strengthen in the short term, i.e. S to increase. Therefore we anticipate a positive correlation between changes in r and S, and

Proof of the two-factor Delta VaR

Suppose there is a simultaneous shift Δr and ΔS in both r and S, respectively. As a first-order approximation, the change in value is:

$$\Delta\text{Value} \approx \partial\text{Value}/\partial r * \Delta r + \partial\text{Value}/\partial S * \Delta S$$

$$= \partial\text{Value}/\partial r * r * (\Delta r/r) + \partial\text{Value}/\partial S * S * (\Delta S/S)$$

where the terms in ( ) are returns.

The standard deviation of ΔValue may be easily calculated as follows:

1. $\text{Var(iance)}(\Delta\text{Value}) = E\{\Delta\text{Value}^2\} - E\{\Delta\text{Value}\}^2$.

2. But $E\{\Delta\text{Value}\} = \partial\text{Value}/\partial r * E\{\Delta r\} + \partial\text{Value}/\partial S * E\{\Delta S\} = 0$ as we have assumed that all trends are zero, or ignorable:

3. $E\{\Delta\text{Value}^2\} = [\partial\text{Value}/\partial r * r]^2 * E\{(\Delta r/r)^2\}$

$$+ [\partial\text{Value}/\partial S * S]^2 * E\{(\Delta S/S)^2\}$$

$$+ 2 * [\partial\text{Value}/\partial r * r] * [\partial\text{Value}/\partial S * S] * E\{(\Delta r/r)(\Delta S/S)\}$$

4. $\text{Var}(\Delta\text{Value}) = [\partial\text{Value}/\partial r * r * \sigma_r]^2$

$$+ [\partial\text{Value}/\partial S * S * \sigma_S]^2$$

$$+ 2 * [\partial\text{Value}/\partial r * r * \sigma_r] * [[\partial\text{Value}/\partial S * S * \sigma_S] * \rho_{r,S}$$

where $\rho_{r,S}$ is the correlation between the returns.

As before, if Delta VaR is a multiple of the standard deviation of ΔValue, we can easily write:

$$\{\text{VaR}_{\text{Total}}\}^2 = \{\text{VaR}_r\}^2 + \{\text{VaR}_S\}^2 + 2 * \{\text{VaR}_r * \text{VaR}_{\text{FX}} * \rho_{r,S}\}$$

More generally, if C represents the 2×2 correlation matrix $\begin{bmatrix} 1 & \rho_{r,S} \\ \rho_{r,S} & 1 \end{bmatrix}$ then the

above expression may be written as $\boldsymbol{VaR'.C.VaR}$ where $\boldsymbol{VaR}$ is the vector of individual VaRs. This expression gives rise to yet another name for Delta VaR, namely VCV.

that this correlation should reduce the overall risk. Let us assume $\rho_{r,S} = 0.5$:

$$\{\text{VaR}_{\text{Total}}\}_2 = \{-386{,}851\}^2 + \{11{,}147{,}976\}^2 + 2 * \{-386{,}851\} * \{11{,}147{,}976\} * 0.5$$

i.e. $\text{VaR}_{\text{Total}} = \text{ZAR } 10{,}959{,}672$ per day

The total VaR has indeed been reduced from VaR_S but notice that the sign of VaR_r must be retained in the calculations. The graph at the top of the next page shows the impact of changing correlation:

Some special cases:

a. Zero correlation: $\{\text{VaR}_{\text{Total}}\}^2 = \{\text{VaR}_r\}^2 + \{\text{VaR}_S\}^2$.

b. Positive perfect correlation: $\text{VaR}_{\text{Total}} = \text{VaR}_r + \text{VaR}_S$.

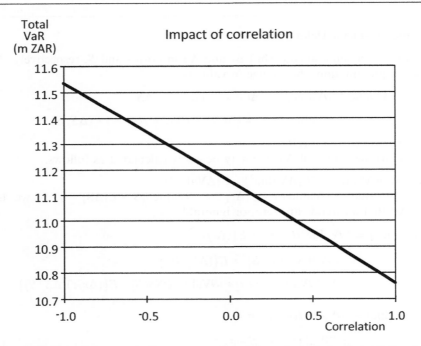

Many banks believe that correlations are too unstable to include in their VaR calculations, and often combine individual VaRs using one of the above expressions. It is important to appreciate that, like it or not, a correlation assumption is being tacitly made.

Historic simulation may also be applied to this situation, using historical interest and FX rates for the past 500 days. In a similar way to before, we can take the percentage changes that occurred on a given day in the past, apply them to the current levels of the two risk factors to estimate new values, calculate the new value of the transaction in ZAR and hence the change in value. The histogram on the facing page shows the final result.

VaRs may also be calculated in the various ways as described above; see the table below:

Confidence level	Small	Percentile	Interpolated frequency
99%	-15,159,896	-15,021,318	-14,830,419
95%	-10,909,714	-10,781,364	-11,187,903
90%	-8,168,600	-8,092,117	-8,037,204

In this case, there is no need to calculate the correlation explicitly, but it is implicit within the historic data.

Changing the time horizon introduces a further complication. For the delta method, scaling the volatility or scaling the individual VaRs is the same, as the formula is linear. But that is not necessarily true in historic simulation. Should the scaling be applied to the final VaR number, or to the historic changes themselves. The impact will be different as VaR is not a linear function of the changes. Worksheet 13.6 calculates VaR both ways. For example, applying the scaling to the changes gives a 10-day 95% VaR of ZAR33.56m, whereas to VaR itself gives 34.09m. Was the ordering of these results expected; yes, because the deal has an overall positive convexity in terms of the two risk factors. I think the first approach is more correct, as it applies larger changes as implied whilst retaining the implicit correlation structure, but the second approach, applying scaling to the resulting VaR is probably much more common.

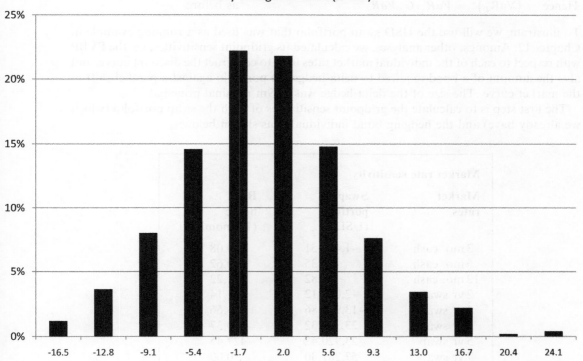

In summary, what can we conclude? Traditional risk management revolves around sensitivity analysis, namely the potential to lose money for a pre-defined movement in one or more risk factors. Delta VaR combines sensitivity with volatility, which is a measure of the likely size of movement over a given time horizon, to produce a risk measure that is defined in monetary terms. It then goes further, to associate a multiplier of the volatility with a probability by assuming some underlying (analytic or numeric) distribution. Finally, because the dimension of the risk measures is consistent across all risk factors, they may be approximately combined together using correlation. So VaR started off with a traditional approach, but rapidly extended risk measurement into new directions.

13.4 MULTI-FACTOR DELTA VaR

The above result may be easily generalised to encompass N factors. If the value of a portfolio P depends upon the current levels of the risk factors x_i, $i = 1, \ldots, N$, then as the factors change:

$$\Delta\text{Value} \approx \sum_i \delta_i * \Delta x_i = \sum_i \delta_i * x_i * \{\Delta x_i / x_i\} \quad \text{where } \delta_i = \partial\text{Value}/\partial x_i$$

$$\text{and} \quad \text{var}(\Delta\text{Value}) = \sum_{ij} [\delta_i * x_i * \sigma_i] * \rho_{i,j} * [\delta_j * x_j * \sigma_j]$$

$$\text{Hence} \quad \{\text{VaR}_P\}^2 = VaR' . C . VaR \qquad\qquad \text{as before}$$

To illustrate, we will use the USD swap portfolio that was used as a running example in Chapter 12. Amongst other analyses, we calculated its gridpoint sensitivities, i.e. the PVBP with respect to each of the individual market rates used to construct the discount curve, and also the amount of a bond required to delta-hedge the portfolio against a parallel shift in the market curve. The size of the delta hedge was 7.29m nominal principal.

The first step is to calculate the gridpoint sensitivities of both the swap portfolio (which we already have) and the hedging bond individually, as shown below:

Market rate sensitivity		
Market rates	**Swap portfolio (USD)**	**Bond hedge (1m nominal)**
3 mo. cash	−1,461.51	−0.08
6 mo. cash	158.35	−0.62
12 mo. cash	−20.82	1.22
2 yr swap	−2,038.12	1.14
3 yr swap	−13,964.86	1.66
4 yr swap	−23,341.32	−20.37
5 yr swap	−23,920.42	−427.45
7 yr swap	57,281.30	0.00
10 yr swap	10,544.93	0.00

The results are shown in columns [1] and [2] of Worksheets 13.8 and also in Worksheet 13.9.

The second stage, given the volatilities and correlations of the individual market rates calculated using historic data—as shown in Worksheet 13.7—is to calculate individual VaRs using the usual delta formula. The results are shown in column [5] of Worksheet 13.9 for the swap portfolio and column [6] for 1m nominal of the bond. The 95% Delta VaRs are then calculated for each, using the correlation matrix, to be $104,817 and $3,115, respectively.

The impact of a hedge may be calculated by first constructing new individual VaR values as follows:

$$\text{VaR}(i)_{\text{Portfolio \& Hedge}} = \text{VaR}(i)_{\text{Portfolio}} + \text{Hedge ratio} * \text{VaR}(i)_{\text{1m nominal hedge}}$$

for the ith market rate—see column [7] which is using the delta hedge ratio of 7.29m of the bond. The total VaR has been reduced from $104,817 to $99,548, i.e. only just over 5%.

Delta hedging the portfolio has not in fact reduced overall VaR very significantly. We could see if the VaR hedge could be improved. The total VaR is given by:

$$\{VaR_{Total}\}^2 = \{VaR_{Portfolio} + n_H \cdot VaR_{Bond}\}' \cdot C \cdot \{VaR_{Portfolio} + n_H \cdot VaR_{Bond}\}$$

for some hedge ratio n_H. If we differentiate with respect to n_H, and set the result to zero, we get the minimum VaR hedge ratio:

$$n_H^* = -\{VaR'_{Portfolio} \cdot C \cdot VaR_{Bond}\}/\{VaR'_{Bond} \cdot C \cdot VaR_{Bond}\}$$

Column [8] of Worksheet 13.9 calculates the VaR for this hedge ratio, which results in a VaR reduction of 5.8%.

The optimal hedge cannot reduce the total VaR to zero, as we can see in the graph below. The expected reduction in VaR may be calculated by substituting back; that is:

$$VaR_{Total} = VaR_{Portfolio} * \sqrt{\{1 - \rho_{average}^2\}}$$

where $VaR_{Portfolio}$ is the VaR of the unhedged portfolio and $\rho_{average}$ is defined by $\pm\{VaR'_{Portfolio} \cdot C \cdot VaR_{Bond}\}/\{VaR_{Portfolio} \cdot VaR_{Bond}\}$. Worksheet 13.9 calculates the average correlation to be 33.5%, which means that the total VaR can only be reduced to $(1 - 0.335^2)^{1/2} = 94.2\%$ of the unhedged portfolio. Perfect hedging can only be achieved in the exceptional circumstance that $\rho_{average} = 1$, i.e. with a perfect correlation matrix, as shown in column [9].

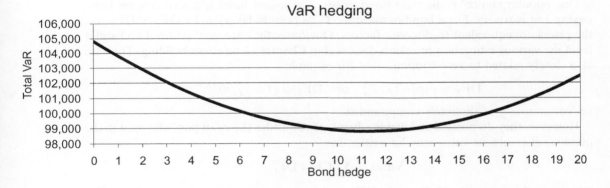

Before finishing this section, it may be worth noting as an aside that a closely related style of hedging, usually called "minimum variance hedging", has been widely used in many physical futures markets for a long time. For example, you wish to hedge the price of Norwegian crude oil. There is no directly relevant futures contract, but there are Brent oil futures. By collecting price histories of Norwegian crude and Brent futures, the correlation may be measured and the anticipated effectiveness of the hedge assessed.

One of the techniques employed in these markets, which could also be used in the VaR hedging above, is the concept of "big step" correlation. Consider a historic price series; divide it into two series of small movements and large movements by defining some filter. Then take a second series and sub-divide that into two; obviously in this case we do not apply the filter again, but simply ensure that the movements on the corresponding dates are included. Because movements in market prices are due to the interaction of many factors, the correlation between the two series of small movements is very often extremely low. However, a big movement may have been caused by a single large exogenous event likely to affect both series; the result is that the correlation between the series of large movements is usually very much higher. One approach therefore to the creation of a hedge is to base it solely on big-step correlations, on the grounds that this would provide protection against large movements and accept that the hedge will be ineffective against small movements. The level of the filter is probably best determined by simulation.[4]

13.5 CHOICE OF RISK FACTORS AND CASHFLOW MAPPING

The value of a portfolio is likely to depend upon a variety of different underlying risk factors. There tends to be little debate about some factors. For example, if the valuation requires the conversion from a number of different currencies, then the various spot rates would be used as factors. If the portfolio had an equity or commodity proportion, then unless it was very heavily weighted towards a very small number of stocks or commodities, indices are usually used as surrogates—see Section 13.12 for further details.

A more conscious choice has to be made for interest rates. The examples above have all used market rates. It would however have been perfectly feasible to use forward or zero-coupon rates as alternative frameworks. Obviously the volatilities and correlations would have to be calculated for these rates. Because these rates are not directly observable but are themselves constructed from market data, there may be differences in the derived data which would in turn lead to differences in estimated VaRs.

One popular choice[5] is discount bond prices. A discount bond is a zero-coupon bond paying 1 at maturity. For a bond of maturity T, its price today $p_T = 1 * \mathrm{DF}_T = \mathrm{DF}_T$, i.e. the prices are equivalent to discount factors. Obviously they are very artificial and suffer from the various estimation problems discussed in Chapter 13 on curve building. They are also closely related to zero-coupon rates; for example:

$$\mathrm{DF}_T = \exp\{-z_T . T\} \quad \text{or} \quad \mathrm{DF}_T = (1 + z_T/n)^{-n.T}$$

i.e. continuously or discretely compounded.

However, they do possess one major advantage. Consider the swap portfolio used in the previous example; its value may be written as:

$$\text{Value} = \sum \mathrm{CF}_t * \mathrm{DF}_t$$

Obviously this expression is linear in DFs, and hence has zero second-order effects. The delta method for calculating VaR should therefore provide identical results to any full valuation approach. Differentiating with respect to one of the DFs, say DF_s, the derivative is equal to CF_s. This method is often discussed in terms of "cashflows", without the explicit recognition that the cashflow is simply the discount bond price derivative, and as such follows the earlier VaR derivation. The formula we had above for individual VaRs may be simplified:

$$\mathrm{VaR}_s = \partial V_s/\partial p_s * p_s * k * \sigma_s = \mathrm{CF}_s * p_s * k * \sigma_s = \mathrm{PV}_s * k * \sigma_s$$

---

[4] The author used this technique to hedge a portfolio of A$ eurobonds being traded in London with the A$ bond futures contract traded in Sydney. Obviously the markets are related, but only loosely. He took the price histories of some typical old eurobonds, regressed them against the bond futures, estimated optimal filters and developed decision rules for creating a hedge against the actual trading book.

[5] Encouraged by RiskMetrics and the publications of JP Morgan.

i.e. the present value of each cashflow multiplied by the volatility of the appropriate bond price.

Because many traditional risk management systems work in terms of zero-coupon rates, simple transformations can be applied to convert them into zero-coupon price terms. For example, rate volatility may be converted into price volatility by using the widely used approximation[6]:

$$\sigma_p = \sigma_y * (y/p) * \partial p/\partial y$$

Consider the artificial zero-coupon yield curve below:

Maturity	Yield	Yield volatility	Modified duration	Price volatility
3 year	8%	2.78%	2.778	0.62%
4 year	9%	2.53%	3.670	0.84%
5 year	10%	2.42%	4.545	1.10%
7 year	12%	2.25%	6.250	1.69%

This uses the formulae $p_T = (1 + y_T)^{-T}$ and modified duration $= -(1/p) * \partial p/\partial y = T/(1 + y)$. Notice that the results are probably intuitive, namely that interest rates typically exhibit declining volatilities as maturity increases, whereas bond prices always have increasing volatilities with maturity.

The earlier swap portfolio example had cashflows occurring on a variety of dates. However, we only have knowledge, i.e. volatilities and correlations, about specific rates, often called "gridpoints". The portfolio was valued by using the following process:

1. A given set of market rates had to be completed, i.e. missing ones estimated, by some type of interpolation.
2. The discount curve calculated by bootstrapping the completed market curve.
3. The discount factors on the cashflow dates estimated again by some type of interpolation, and finally the cashflows are discounted to produce the value.

Estimation of the VaR followed the same process. Delta sensitivity was calculated by shifting a market rate, and recording the change in the value at the end of the process. The interpolation methods used for VaR calculations are those used for the original valuation process; there is internal consistency. The process has mapped the portfolio sensitivities onto the gridpoints.

---

[6] Often written as $\sigma_p = \sigma_y * y * \text{MD}$ which stands for modified duration. This is derived from two approximations:
1. If $p = f(y)$, then $s_p \approx \partial f/\partial y . s_y$ where s is the standard deviation.
2. $v_p = (\mu_p)^2 * [\exp(\sigma_p)^2 . t^1] \approx (\mu_p)^2 * (\sigma_p)^2 . t$ where v is variance and μ_p the expected value of p, and where p is distributed log-normally.

We could of course adopt exactly the same process when using discount bond prices. Worksheet 13.10 shows the following example:

- Box 1 contains some gridpoint data in terms of discount bond prices at years 1 and 2 (these are taken directly off the previous swap portfolio example) plus price volatilities and a price correlation based upon historic data.
- Box 2 contains a single fixed cashflow approximately midway between the gridpoints.

Generalising, we have a cashflow at time T, and two gridpoints t_i and t_{i+1} which bracket T. First, we need to value this cashflow. Let us estimate $DF_T = I_T(DF_i, DF_{i+1})$ where I is some interpolation function. Worksheet 13.10 uses continuously compounded interpolation, i.e. zero-coupon yields are calculated in column [1] of Box 3, linearly interpolated in column [2] of Box 4, and finally converted back into a bond price in column [3] of Box 4. The cashflow in Box 2 has a value of -2.48811 (USDm). Linear interpolation weights are shown separately in column [1] of Box 4 for future purposes.

If $V_T = CF_T * DF_T$, then we can estimate the two sensitivities $\partial V_T / \partial DF_i = CF_T * \partial I_T / \partial DF_i$ and $\partial V_T / \partial DF_{i+1} = CF_T * \partial I_T / \partial DF_{i+1}$ either by perturbation or analytically as shown in columns [2] and [3], respectively, in Box 5 of Worksheet 13.10. Given the price volatility data, individual VaRs may be calculated (using analytic sensitivities, but it hardly matters which), and hence the total VaR of $2,817 using the correlation coefficient. This very much repeats the VaR method described above.

An alternative approach is to allocate the cashflow CF_T onto the two gridpoints. We have already seen one way of doing this (see Section 12.6) by defining the resulting cashflows as CF_i and CF_{i+1} which are subject to the following constraints:

- preserve cashflow: $CF_T = CF_i + CF_{i+1}$
- preserve value: $V_T = CF_i * DF_i + CF_{i+1} * DF_{i+1}$

and solve for CF_i and CF_{i+1} as shown in Box 6 of Worksheet 13.10. Individual VaRs may then be calculated using the above expression, and finally the total VaR. The result is not the same as the previous total VaR, because the allocation is not consistent with the valuation structure, in that sensitivity is not maintained. However, it is not grossly different, as may be seen by changing the correlation.

Another popular approach is first to estimate the VaR of the cashflow by interpolation, and then do the allocation whilst preserving this VaR. For example, the price volatilities in Box 1 are converted into yield volatilities (see column [2] of Box 2 of Worksheet 13.10), linearly interpolated and converted back to price volatilities (see row "linearly interpolated"; columns [1] and [2] of Box 7). The VaR is now easily calculated to be $V_T * \sigma_T * k = \$3,173$. We now wish to calculate the allocated cashflows so that:

- preserve value: $V_T = V_i + V_{i+1}$
- preserve VaR: $VaR_T = VaR(CF_i, CF_{i+1})$

As before, we have two equations, and can therefore solve for the two CFs as shown in

Box 8 of Worksheet 13.10.[7] The resulting VaR matches, of course, the VaR estimated by interpolating the volatilities.

But this VaR is not the same as the VaR of \$2,817 calculated originally. Furthermore, if the correlation shifts, we find that the original VaR changes but this new one does not! This is because the correlation was not used in the latter's calculation. The problem lies in the following:

1. y_i and y_{i+1} were interpolated to get y_T.
2. Yield volatilities σ_i and σ_{i+1} were interpolated to get σ_T.

But σ_T is a property of y_T, and therefore we should be able to construct an expression for it directly without interpolation. Define:

$$y_T = \omega_T \cdot y_i + (1 - \omega_T) \cdot y_{i+1}$$

where ω_T and $(1 - \omega_T)$ are the interpolation weights given in Box 4 of Worksheet 13.10. Then:

$$v(y_T) = (\omega_T)^2 \cdot v(y_i) + (1 - \omega_T)^2 \cdot v(y_{i+1}) + 2\omega_T \cdot (1 - \omega_T) \cdot s(y_i) \cdot s(y_{i+1}) \cdot \rho_{i,i+1}$$

where $v(.)$ and $s(.)$ are variance and standard deviation, respectively. The approximation relating v and σ (see footnote 6) may then be used to estimate σ_T. The end-results are shown in row "calculated", column [1] of Box 7 of Worksheet 13.10:

- the new σ_T is estimated to be 1.508% compared with the linearly interpolated value of 1.699%;
- the total VaR is now identical to the original value.

Furthermore, as the correlation shifts, σ_T changes accordingly and the VaRs calculated using the original sensitivity approach and this latest approach remain identical.

To summarise, the cashflow approach has some attractions in that it permits a portfolio to be repesented solely by cashflows accumulated at gridpoints. It is therefore simple to add new transactions into the portfolio, as these easily modify the cashflows. However, there are some difficulties, and simple interpolation is not sufficient to implement this method. The sensitivity approach uses allocation methods that must already exist within, and are consistent with, valuation methods, easily allows a range of different interest rate risk factors and require little additional work to implement. This latter approach will be used throughout the remainder of this chapter.

---

[7] That is, the VaR equation may be written as:

$$(V_T * \sigma_T)^2 = (\sigma_i * V_i)^2 + (\sigma_{i+1} * V_{i+1})^2 + 2 * \sigma_i * V_i * \sigma_{i+1} * V_{i+1} * \rho_{i,i+1}$$

Substituting for V_{i+1} and re-arranging, we get:

$$[\sigma_i^2 + \sigma_{i+1}^2 - 2\sigma_i\sigma_{i+1}\rho_{i,i+1}]x_i^2 + [2\sigma_i\sigma_{i+1}\rho_{i,i+1} - 2\sigma_{i+1}^2]x_i + [\sigma_{i+1}^2 - \sigma_T^2] = 0$$

where $x_i = V_i/V_T$. This may be easily solved as $ax^2 + bx + c = 0$. The root is chosen so that, if possible, the signs of CF_i and CF_{i+1} match that of CF_T.

13.6 ESTIMATION OF VOLATILITY AND CORRELATIONS

This was discussed at some length in Chapter 10; everything that was ascribed to volatility also applies to correlation. For relatively short time horizons, say under 1 month, weighted or GARCH estimation schemes are more popular than unweighted, unconditional estimation. Implied volatilities are seldom if ever used. This is for consistency. VaR is specifically designed to measure the risk over a range of different activities, possibly taking place in different geographical locations, and in different time zones. A large number of risk factors may be used to capture this risk. It is highly unlikely that there will be liquid options traded on all the risk factors. So whilst it may be feasible to obtain implied volatilities on some factors, it would not be possible to get them on all factors, and therefore it would be necessary to mix historic and implied volatilities—hardly a good idea!

Calculating the estimates is fraught with practical difficulties. A time series of consistent, cleansed data is required for each risk factor. Non-business days will leave gaps in this time series, and many data providers plug the gaps by simply repeating the previous business day's value. The problem is exacerbated when trying to estimate the correlation between two risk factors from different countries as the non-business days are unlikely to match. One alternative is simply to omit all data referring to a day which is a non-business day in some country, but that may require the rejection of substantial amounts of data. This is hardly adequate for the calculation of accurate estimates, and complex statistical algorithms have been constructed to bridge the gaps more appropriately.[8]

A similar issue is asynchronous data, i.e. data that are available at different points in time. For example, using closing prices in Tokyo and in New York means about a 14-hour gap. But the markets will not have remained constant, so the estimated correlations are likely to be biased downwards. Again algorithms have to be developed to make adjustments.

These issues do not simply result in slight mis-estimates. A correlation matrix is by definition positive semi-definite[9]: if it were not, then it would be possible to find ourselves having to take the square root of a negative number when calculating the parametric VaR. If all the correlations are calculated consistently, then there are no problems. But the data issues described above, unless tackled carefully, can result in an infeasible correlation matrix.[10]

Consider a typical international bank operating in, say, 20 currencies. If we assume two yield curves per currency (bond and swap), each represented by 10 datapoints (the regulatory minimum is 6 per curve), then this suggests:

$$IR: \quad 20 * 2 * 10 = 400$$

$$FX: \qquad\qquad = 19$$

i.e. 419 volatilities and 87,571 correlations! A lot of data to be gathered, cleansed and estimated, even if it is only once a quarter. Luckily there are practical ways around this. Most transactions that the bank does are likely to be single currency, and the main risk for many of them is a change in the absolute level of the curve. As we have seen in the Appendix to Chapter 12, market rates are quite highly correlated. If these are the risk

---

[8] See, for example, the EM algorithm developed by JP Morgan, *Risk Metrics Technical Document*, Fourth Edition, 1996, Chapter 8.
[9] That is, the value $x' . C . x \geq 0$ for any vector x.
[10] See also the discussion in Chapter 3 of P. Best, *Implementing VaR*, published by Wiley, 1998.

factors, then only two or at the most three points would be required to capture the curve movement adequately for risk management purposes. Unless the bank is doing a lot of spread trades, correlation between the two curves in each currency is not very important, and could be reduced to the correlation between two indicative points, one on each curve. Furthermore, unless the bank is doing a lot of cross-currency trades, such as hedging JPY bonds with USD instruments, then the cross-correlations can also be reduced to that between two indicative points. This would reduce the IR gridpoints down to about 120, but more importantly the correlations required to just over 1,500.[11] So it is feasible to reduce the data requirements quite significantly without seriously jeopardising the effectiveness of risk management.

The estimation of volatility and correlation are crucial to the estimation of VaR, and the above discussion only outlines some of the issues. See, for example, Best (footnote 10) for a much more detailed discussion.

13.7   A RUNNING EXAMPLE

The swap portfolio was used above to illustrate how to estimate the VaR of a portfolio, and to compare it with a delta hedge. However, we wish to discuss other VaR issues, and the swap portfolio lacks the various required properties. Hence the portfolio below will be used as a running example throughout the rest of this chapter.

$–€ FX option portfolio (all options sold out of 4 February 2008)				
1	9-month USD	call	on USD10m	at strike 1.469
2	15-month USD	put	on USD20m	at strike 1.460
3	3-month USD	call	on USD25m	at strike 1.478
4	21-month USD	put	on USD15m	at strike 1.450
5	7-month USD	call	on USD20m	at strike 1.472
6	18-month USD	put	on USD15m	at strike 1.455

The current market data are shown below: they have been reduced so that each curve only consists of three points. There are therefore only seven risk factors, six interest rates plus the spot rate. This is hardly realistic, but adequate for illustrative purposes. In particular, the example does not include changes in the volatility of the spot rate as a risk factor in itself, as required by the current capital regulations. This in turn would lead to additional data estimation requirements for the volatility of the volatility, as well as its correlation with the other factors.

---

[11] a.   Three points per curve= $40 * 3 = 120$ intra-curve correlations.
   b.   Single point inter-curve correlation= $0.5 * 40 * 39 = 780$.
   c.   FX correlations= $0.5 * 19 * 18 = 171$.
   d.   FX/IR correlations= (max)$0.5 * 40 * 19 = 380$.

Current market levels	Interest rates		
		USD	EUR
$–€ spot rate: 1.4832	6 mo. cash	3.098%	4.364%
	12 mo. cash	2.896%	4.344%
Volatility of spot FX: 6.6% pa	2 yr swap	2.795%	3.991%

The first stage is to value the portfolio as shown in Worksheet 13.12. The discount curves are built, and then zero-coupon curves interpolated.[12] The appropriate zero-coupon rates for each option are calculated in columns [7] and [8]. Finally the option prices, quoted in terms of euros, are calculated by means of a macro and shown in column [10]. The value of the total portfolio is −€3,052,543; negative as all options have been sold and the premia taken upfront.

The second stage is to calculate the portfolio sensitivities. Changes in the risk factors (in bp) may be entered into the shift area. The resulting PVBPs are given in the box on Worksheet 13.13. The daily volatility and correlation data for the calculation of the VaR are calculated from historic data (see Worksheet 13.11), and summarised below:

	USD rates			EUR rates			
	6 mo.	12 mo.	2 yr	6 mo.	12 mo.	2 yr	FX
Volatility (pd)	0.8494%	1.1047%	1.3200%	0.3789%	0.5243%	0.7669%	0.4138%
6 mo.	100%	91.55%	57.03%	45.85%	43.53%	−0.64%	−5.51%
12 mo.	91.55%	100%	61.54%	48.54%	53.46%	−4.23%	−4.99%
2 yr	57.03%	61.54%	100%	30.56%	29.57%	−1.51%	−12.91%
6 mo.	45.85%	48.54%	30.56%	100%	86.57%	7.78%	6.56%
12 mo.	43.53%	53.46%	29.57%	86.57%	100%	6.20%	8.63%
2 yr	−0.64%	−4.23%	−1.51%	7.78%	6.20%	100%	−6.51%
FX	−5.51%	−4.99%	−12.91%	6.56%	8.63%	−6.51%	100%

We wish to estimate the 1-day 99% VaR. Individual VaRs are calculated in column [4] of Worksheet 13.13 using the normal formula $VaR_x = 10,000 * PVBP_x * x * k * \sigma_x$ and finally the total VaR. The worksheet shows that the portfolio has a Delta VaR of €265,301.

13.8 SIMULATION METHODS

In Section 13.2 we briefly discussed two approaches; the delta approach which we have subsequently expanded, and historic simulation. This latter approach involved shifting risk factors by amounts that had occurred historically, and then re-valuing the transaction. This valuation approach is a simple example of a simulation method. There are two simulation approaches widely used, namely historic and Monte Carlo. The former takes changes in risk factors that have *actually* happened in the past, applies them to the current level of

---

[12] The zeroth point is determined by backward extrapolation.

factors and re-values. The latter randomly generates the changes in risk factors according to some volatility/correlation structure which itself is typically based upon historic behaviour. In this section we will measure the VaR of the FX option portfolio using these two approaches.

For historic simulation, 500 days (approximately 2 years of business days) of 1-day logarithmic percentage changes have been collected. Each change is applied to the current market rate, i.e. $r_{new} = r_{current} * \exp[\%r_{change}]$, to create new factors, as shown below:

	USD			EUR			€/S
	6 mo.	12 mo.	2 yr	6 mo.	12 mo.	2 yr	
Current rates	3.09750%	2.89625%	2.79500%	4.3640%	4.3440%	3.9905%	1.48320
First change vector	0.0000%	0.0000%	0.1974%	−0.1102%	−0.5195%	−0.4022%	0.0252%
Resulting new curve	3.09750%	2.89625%	2.80052%	4.35919%	4.32149%	3.97448%	1.483574

Given the new curve, Worksheet 13.14 calculates the new value of the FX option portfolio, and hence its change in value. This is repeated for all 500 days, and then the 1-day 99% VaR is estimated. As discussed above, there are various ways in which this may be done; Worksheet 13.14 uses the "PERCENTILE" command to give €353,031. This result is significantly higher than the Delta VaR, due to the negative gamma in the portfolio, as all the options have been sold. This means, of course, that as the market moves, the change in value is always worse than implied by the delta approach.

In principle, historic simulation is relatively simple to implement; all that is required is a historic dataset to generate the change vectors which are then applied in turn to the current levels of the risk factors. Some extensions will be discussed in Section 13.9.

Monte Carlo (MC) simulation, on the other hand, generates the change vectors randomly using the statistical properties of the risk factors. The BGM simulation model, as described in considerable detail in Chapter 11, modelled forward rates. The same approach could be adopted here. Alternatively, as we are not so concerned about valuing a transaction, but are interested in the changes in value, we might model the market rates themselves, using historical data for calibration. This approach may not be consistent with the current market, but would be simple to implement for risk management purposes.

If $X_i(t)$ represents the value of the ith risk factor at time t, then we could assume a generation process such as:

$$dX_i(t) = X_i(t + dt) - X_i(t) = \mu_i\{t, X_i(t)\} \cdot dt + \sum_k \sigma_{it}\{t, X_i(t)\} \cdot dz_k(t)$$

i.e. the change in the ith risk factor at time t over an infinitesimally short period of time dt is due to a trend term (which itself may depend upon both time and the current level) plus a number of inter-correlated stochastic movements where usually $dz_i \sim N\{0,1\}$ and $E\{dz_i, dz_j\} = \rho_{ij}$. As a special case:

$$dX_i(t)/X_i(t) = \mu_i \cdot dt + \sigma_i \cdot dz_i(t)$$

with a constant drift and single constant volatility describes the usual log-normal process for Black and Scholes options. It can be easily shown that[13]:

$$X_i(T) = X_i(0) * \exp\{(\mu_i - \tfrac{1}{2}\sigma_i^2) . T + \sigma_i . \sqrt{T} . dz_i\}$$

This means that the continuously compounded return over the period T is $\sim N\{(\mu_i - \tfrac{1}{2}\sigma_i^2) . T, \sigma_i . \sqrt{T}\}$. Notice that this formula implies that time horizon scaling is applied to the changes in each risk factor, and not to the overall VaR.

The above approach has been used to estimate the VaR of the FX option portfolio. First, the correlation matrix has been estimated using historic data, and then decomposed; see below as well as the correlation and decomposed matrices from Worksheet 13.11.

Worksheet 13.15 then uses a Table function to generate 500 random scenarios, and to construct the histogram as before. It operates in the following steps:

1. Generate a random vector of seven normal distributed variables, each drawn from a distribution with zero mean and appropriate standard deviation (volatility).
2. Apply the decomposed correlation matrix to generate the correlated random vector.
3. Calculate the new levels of each risk factor using the above formula using the appropriate time horizon.
4. Re-value the option portfolio (as in historic simulation).
5. Repeat this process as often as required—the worksheet does 500 samples.

Worksheet 13.15 simultaneously uses antithetic sampling, i.e. the negative of the random vector generated in #1 above, to generate another 500 results. The VaR number is then calculated from the overall 1,000 observations:

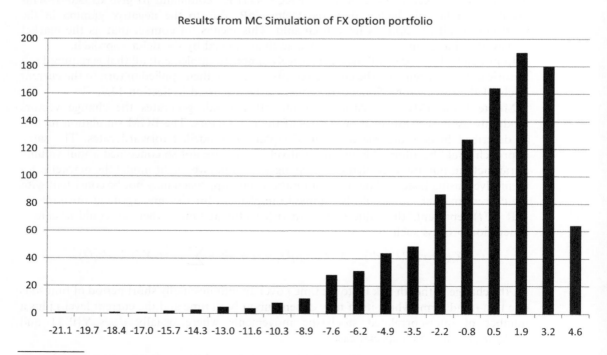

Results from MC Simulation of FX option portfolio

---
[13] By defining $Y = \ln(X)$, applying Ito's lemma and integrating from 0 to T. See, for example, Hull, ibid., pp. 230–1.

The resulting histogram, which is similar to that generated by historic simulation, is shown above. The 1-day 99% VaR estimate is €307,832 (but will obviously change for each simulation); this is significantly different from either the Delta VaR or the HS VaR. When implementing the MC VaR, we are assuming that the underlying risk factors are being sampled from a multivariate normal distribution—which is unlikely to be correct. The results are summarised in the table below:

VaR method	Ignores convexity	Assumes normality of risk factors	Assumes normality of result distribution	1-day 99% VaR	10-day 99% VaR
Delta	Yes	Yes	Yes	265,301	838,955
HS	No	No	No	353,031	1,448,619
MC	No	Yes	No	307,832	1,229,906

In comparison with the delta method, simulation approaches are deemed to be more accurate but inherently slower because they require a full re-valuation of the portfolio for each scenario. If the normality assumption can be justified, then MC will ultimately produce more accurate results than HS, simply by dint of running more scenarios.

If the time horizon is increased to 10 days, then the divergence between the delta and the simulation methods becomes increasingly obvious as convexity becomes more important.

13.9 SHORTCOMINGS AND EXTENSIONS TO SIMULATION METHODS

Historic simulation is very simple to apply in practice, although there are often data integrity issues to be resolved during the collection of data from disparate sources and time zones, as discussed above. There are some other difficulties as well.

For example, the figure below shows the progressive calculation of the 99% VaR as the number of scenarios increases up to 500:

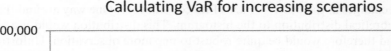

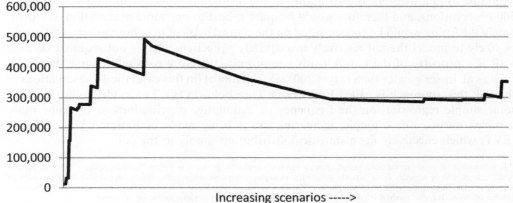

Calculating VaR for increasing scenarios

Increasing scenarios ----->

The early part of the chart is extremely characteristic, with large upward jumps followed by slow declines. This is easily explained. Suppose 100 simulations have been done so far; the 99% VaR estimate will be determined at most by the two largest losses so far recorded. The impact of the 101st simulation now has to be included:

Either	a.	the new change in value shows a loss greater than the current VaR estimate; the new VaR estimate is therefore increased, and possibly substantially
Or	b.	the new change in value shows a gain or a loss less than the current VaR estimate; the new VaR estimate is reduced but typically by a small amount, as there are already 99 observations on the right-hand side of the distribution.

Thus VaR estimates from a small number of scenarios are often described as unreliable or "choppy". To overcome this, a large number of scenarios are required until the estimate smoothes out, as shown by the latter part of the chart.

This introduces a second issue, namely that of "relevance"; just how relevant are changes that occurred some 2 years ago in estimating the VaR going forward from today? It is often argued that, especially for short-term VaR, what has happened most recently is of most relevance. This issue is sometimes referred to as "stationarity", i.e. do the historic data possess significant trends?

Unfortunately the immediate solutions to these two shortcomings are in conflict. One can increase the reliability of the VaR estimate by increasing the number of scenarios, but that in turn reduces the relevance. Notice that this problem does not arise with MC simulation, as the number of randomly generated *relevant* scenarios can be increased without limit.[14]

The reason for the unreliability of VaR estimates is, for example, we only use 5 scenarios out of 500 to estimate 99% VaR. Any change in one of those 5 may change the VaR dramatically, whilst changes in the other 495 are of no consequence. One way around this would be to fit a theoretical distribution to the histogram. This distribution would use all 500 observations, and therefore would be quite robust to one more observation. Unfortunately the fitting would be concentrated on the central mass of the observations, and would be likely to model the tail relatively inaccurately—precisely what is not required because VaR is a property of the tail. A ready compromise therefore is to select some threshold, such as all losses greater than (say) €200,000, and model (in this case) the 34 observations in the tail; this approach is called Peaks Over Threshold (POT). The model could be either some simple regression on the frequency or cumulative distributions or by some more complex means. For example, increasing use is being made of Extreme Value Theory (EVT) which effectively fits a statistical distribution simply to the tail.

---

[14] It is possible to combine random sampling with historic simulation in what is called "bootstrapping". Normal historic simulation effectively samples from historic data without replacement and where observations are drawn in their order of occurrence. The bootstrap method is to sample from the data with replacement, i.e. it is possible to use the same change vector a number of times. But this method is critically dependent on the assumption of stationarity, i.e. no trends.

In the discussion that follows, the histogram will be flipped over, so that we are analysing its positive right-hand tail—this follows the usual convention in statistics. A common assumption is that the tail follows a negative exponential distribution:

$$g(y) = (1/\beta) \cdot \exp\{-y/\beta\} \quad \text{for } y \geq 0$$

where $y = $ Change in value $-$ Threshold.

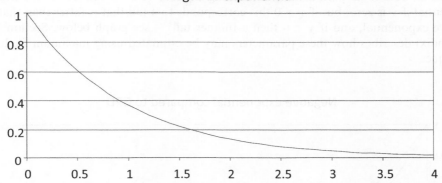

Negative exponential

Section 13.15 (Appendix) shows how to estimate an optimal β from a set of tail observations, and also how to calculate the VaR using the formula:

$$\text{VaR}_P = t - \beta * \ln\{(N/n_t) \cdot (1 - P)\}$$

where n_t is the number of observations above some threshold t; N is total number of observations; and P is the VaR probability (typically 95% or 99%). The results are very similar to the earlier historic simulation, suggesting that the simulation had stabilised by 500 observations—as we can see from the above graph.

VaR using a negative exponential model		
	$\beta = $€86,677	
VaR confidence level	95%	99%
VaR–Neg Exp	226,652	366,153
Expected loss	313,329	452,830

See Worksheet 13.16. Now we have a model of the tail, we can explore other properties. An extremely useful one is the "mean excess function" defined as:

$$e_y(v) = E\{y - v \mid y > v\}$$

In words, it is the expected value of a loss, given that the loss will exceed a certain level. For example, if we set $v = \text{VaR}$, we find for a negative exponential model that:

$$e_y(\text{VaR}) = \text{VaR} + \beta$$

i.e. how much on average might you lose, given that the VaR level has been exceeded? This is probably a much more interesting statistic than the VaR number itself.

Unfortunately, whilst negative exponential distribution is very simple, it only possesses one parameter which is really for location. In practice, this is seldom sufficient, especially as the output from a simulation may have fat tails which decline more slowly than a negative exponential. A distribution frequently used in practice is the Generalised Pareto, whose density function is expressed as follows:

$$g(y) = (1/\beta) * [1 + \chi * y/\beta]^{-(1+1/\chi)} \quad \text{for } y \geq 0$$

This has an additional parameter χ controlling the tail. The GP reduces to the negative exponential if χ is zero, but if $\chi > 0$ this corresponds to a tail that is fatter than that of a negative exponential, and if $\chi < 0$ then a thinner tail[15]—see graph below. Section 13.15 (Appendix) describes how these parameters may be estimated using maximum likelihood techniques.

Negative exponential compared to GPD

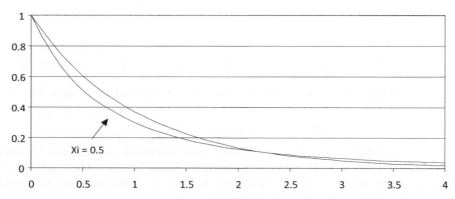

Worksheet 13.17 calculates χ whilst holding β equal to the negative exponential value:

VaR using a Generalised Pareto model		
	$\beta = €86,677$	$\chi = 0.070$
VaR confidence level	95%	99%
VaR–GP	226,941	377,817
Expected loss	322,170	484,402

Notice that χ is positive, suggesting that historic simulation actually generated a fatter tail than the negative exponential. The new VaR estimates are therefore higher.

Modelling may be approached in a different fashion, which provides some additional insights. Take the 500 observations and divide them into (say) 20 blocks, each containing 25 contiguous observations. Record the largest percentage loss Z_i suffered within each block i; these are shown on the far right-hand side of Worksheet 13.14.

---

[15] In this case the region of y is restricted to ensure that $[1 + \chi * y/\beta] > 0$.

Section 13.15 (Appendix) discusses the Generalised Extreme Value distribution that the Zs might, at least in theory, be drawn from. This distribution is given by:

$$H(x) = \exp\{-[1 + \alpha . x]^{-1/\alpha}\}$$

where $x = (Z - m)/s$; m and s are location and dispersion parameters; and α models the tail. The GEV is given different names depending on the value of α; if $\alpha > 0$ then this is called a Fréchet distribution and has fat tails.

Worksheet 13.18 takes the extreme block losses in column [1], re-orders them in column [2] and calculates estimators for α in column [4] as described in Section 13.15 (Appendix). Values for m and s are then estimated by maximising a likelihood function in column [7]. A number of the estimators for α were used, and the one that gave the highest overall likelihood selected.

The results from the worksheet are shown in the box below:

Percentiles	VaR	VaR (%)	VaR ($)
99%		26.123%	797,409
95%		18.026%	550,247
27.74%	95%	6.830%	208,500
77.78%	99%	11.826%	361,008

As discussed in Section 13.15 (Appendix), a percentile from a GEV distribution describes a property of an extreme. For example, based on the results above, there is a 5% chance that the worst loss out of a block of 25 observations will exceed 18.026% of the current value, i.e. €550,247. To estimate the level such that there is a 5% probability that any observation will exceed it, this corresponds to $95\%^{25} = 27.74\%$ percentile. Thus one can see that the VaR numbers provided by this method are again very similar to those estimated by historic simulation.

However, this form of modelling has another very interesting use, namely in the estimation of worst-case scenarios. For example, the interpretation of the 99% percentile could be "there is a 1% probability that the worst loss on any day in a month (say, 25 business days) will exceed €797,409".

The reason for discussing these two EVT approaches is that they extend historic simulation in two ways:

- because they make use of more observations than simply the few in the far end of the tail, the VaRs are less choppy and hence more reliable;
- modelling the tail enables statistical statements about the tail that could not have been addressed using more conventional analysis, and in particular about the likely size of loss given that the loss has exceeded the VaR level.

Both methods however assume stationarity, i.e. analysis does not depend upon the temporal ordering of observations. The graph below shows the extreme losses from each block ordered back through time.

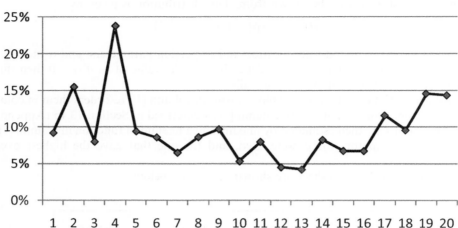

Crudely classifying market conditions into high, medium and low volatility, subjectively it would appear that the market is now moving into a period of higher volatility after low volatility for most of the past 2 years. Nearly 2 years ago, there were a couple of exceptional days, when the losses spiked up, but nothing more. If the reader examines the detailed HS calculations, he (or she) will see that all the other big losses occurred in the very recent past.

Risk managers are often divided on the following question: should the rising volatility have a greater impact on the VaR estimate, or should the VaR be equally weighted across the entire 2 years? Some prefer to use recent market behaviour as the best predictor for future behaviour, and others would rather look back across the entire range of information available. Either methodology is permitted under the Basel Accord.

If we wanted to modify historic simulations to be more weighted to recent market behaviour, then a simple way would be to scale each of the changes as follows:

- let V_N and C_N be the current volatility vector and correlation matrix, and V_H and C_H the historic volatility vector and correlation matrix, respectively;
- let Δr_H be a historic change vector;
- estimate $\Delta r_N = (V_N/V_H) * \Delta r_H$ for adjusting for shifts in volatilities;
- $\Delta r_N = C_N^{1/2} . C_H^{-1/2} . \Delta r_H$ where the square root matrices are given by a Cholesky decomposition for shifts in correlations.

A more sophisticated approach[16] modifies historic simulation so that a weight, related to the length of the historic period, is attached to each observation. Observations corresponding to recent changes in risk factors carry higher weights than observations from more distant periods. For example (see Worksheet 13.19):

- Let $i = 0, 1, 2, 3, \ldots, K$ represent the time of historic information (where 0 is the most recent) (column [1]).

---

[16] See J. Boudoukh *et al.*, "The best of both worlds", *Risk*, **11**(5), 1998, pp. 64–7.

- Let ΔP_i be the percentage change in value of the portfolio due to the ith set of returns (column [2]).
- Define weights $w_i = [(1 - \lambda)/(1 - \lambda^K)] \cdot \lambda^{i-1}$ where $\sum_i w_i = 1$ and where λ is some positive number < 1. The worksheet shows the weights in column [3] using $\lambda = 95\%$ and $K = 500$.
- Place ΔP_i in ascending order, together with the associated weights (columns [4] and [5]).
- Accumulate the weights; see column [6].
- To obtain $q\%$ VaR, locate $(1 - q\%)$ in the accumulated weights column and read off the associated ΔP_q. This may require interpolation to find the exact point. Finally, calculate $\text{VaR}_q = \text{Current value} * \Delta P_q$.

The following results are calculated in Worksheet 13.20:

VaR	Interpolated return	Absolute VaR
99%	−14.71%	448,921
95%	−9.63%	294,056

As expected, the VaRs are considerably higher than those calculated using unweighted HS.

The accuracy for most parameter estimation from a Monte Carlo simulation is proportional to $1/\sqrt{n}$ where n is the number of scenarios. A typical number in practice, especially for pricing, is $n = 10{,}000$ which will give an error of 1%. Most simulations however are run with a stopping rule, which will stop the simulation if the parameter being estimated is not changing by more than a defined amount per set of scenarios. This accuracy is on average, and it is feasible for the simulation to have to run for many more scenarios before stopping.

Given that each scenario requires a number of random variables, Monte Carlo is both computationally intense and also critically dependent upon the quality of the random number generator. Strictly speaking, these numbers are only pseudo-random, i.e. they have been generated by an algorithm using deterministic rules with no random components. These rules take an initial value (called a "seed") and generate a series of numbers which should pass the standard tests for randomness. Eventually the generated number will be equal to the seed, so that the generator will now cycle, producing the same series. The cycle length must be much greater than the number of random numbers required for the simulation; if not, the apparent accuracy is spurious.

Worksheet 13.15 simulated changes in the risk factors using the expression:

$$X_i(T) = X_i(0) * \exp\{(\mu_i - \tfrac{1}{2}\sigma_i^2) \cdot T + \sigma_i \cdot \sqrt{T} \cdot dz_i\} \quad \text{for } i = 1, \ldots, 7$$

where dz_i is a random number drawn from $N(0, \mathbf{C})$. Most random number generators generate numbers drawn from a uniform distribution $U[0, 1]$. This means that all the numbers lie between 0 and 1, and each value has an equal chance of being generated. The random number is then transformed from uniform to normal by inverting the normal cumulative function Φ as shown below:

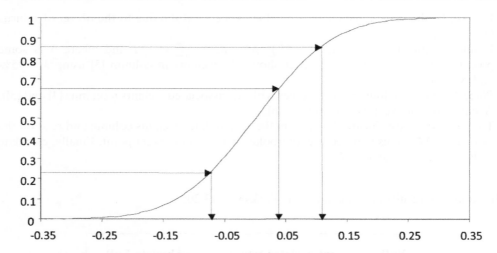

The reason why so many samples have to be taken is to ensure that the random samples cover the whole of the 0–1 line, and do not cluster. But this idea gives rise to quasi-random sampling, i.e. if you want to ensure that there is good coverage along the line, why not:

- divide the line up into a number of segments (say, N);
- use the midpoint of the first segment as the uniform random number;
- and transform that to a normal sample;
- the next time a random number is required to be drawn from the same distribution, use the midpoint of the second segment;

and so on? No random sampling at all! The error for an approach such as this is proportional to $1/n$. Unfortunately it will not work in practice because the simulation cannot stop until all segments have been sampled, i.e. there is no stopping rule. Hence the number of simulations that have to be run is N^K where K is the number of risk factors.

However, there are techniques which pick the segments quasi-randomly, and can therefore reduce the number of samples required significantly, with an error of the order $\ln(n)^{K-1}/n$. Unfortunately the methods do tend to break down with high K—sometimes called the "curse of dimensionality". Stein's algorithm is one that has proved to be remarkably robust, and appears to work well even for high K.[17] There are a range of other variance reduction techniques that we have already seen in this book, such as antithetic sampling and control variates.

13.10 DELTA–GAMMA AND OTHER METHODS

In summary, delta approaches are fast but likely to be inaccurate in the presence of significant second-order (and higher) effects; simulation methods however are much more accurate but slow. Are there any compromises that might produce fast accurate results?

---

[17] A good broad introduction to sampling is Chapter 3 in P. Glasserman, *Monte Carlo Methods in Financial Engineering*, Springer, 2000. See also M. Stein, "Large scale properties of simulations using Latin hypercube sampling", *Technometrics*, **29**(2), 1987, pp. 143–51.

One approach is to introduce the second term explicitly into the VaR calculations. This may be done either by extending the delta approach or by simulation.

For a particular portfolio, the change in value for a single risk factor x is approximately given by Taylor's theorem:

$$\Delta \text{Value} \approx (\partial PV/\partial x) \cdot \Delta x + \tfrac{1}{2} \cdot (\partial^2 PV/\partial x^2) \cdot (\Delta x)^2$$

For an option, especially if it is not too close to maturity, the approximation is quite good. The pair of graphs show the effectiveness of the approximation for an ATM option with 1 year and 0.25 years to maturity, respectively. The changes in the underlying have to be quite large before the approximation becomes ineffective.

0.25 year ATM call option

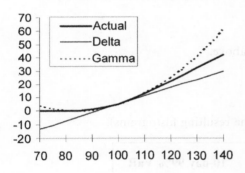

1 year ATM call option

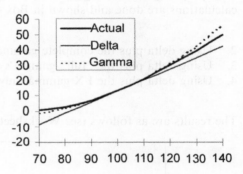

Write the above equation as:

$$\Delta \text{Value} \approx (\partial PV/\partial x) \cdot x \cdot (\Delta x/x) + \tfrac{1}{2} \cdot (\partial^2 PV/\partial x^2) \cdot x^2 \cdot (\Delta x/x)^2$$

If it is assumed that $(\Delta x/x)$ is distributed normally, then $(\Delta x/x)^2$ is chi-squared, and unfortunately ΔValue has a distribution which cannot be analytically defined. The standard deviation of the distribution can be estimated relatively easily, but the relationship between the multiplier and probability can only be numerically calculated. Most methods use approximations to estimate the final distribution, although it is possible to derive an exact expression.[18]

An alternative approach is to modify the simulation methods. For multiple risk factors, the above equation may be written as:

$$\Delta \text{Value} \approx \delta \cdot \Delta x + \tfrac{1}{2} \cdot \Delta x' \cdot \Gamma \cdot \Delta x$$

where Δx is the vector of changes in the risk factors, and δ and Γ the delta vector and gamma matrix for the portfolio. Notice that this expression has no knowledge of individual transactions within the portfolio. If a particular change Δx is observed, ΔValue can be calculated extremely quickly (see Box 1 of Worksheet 13.21).

The delta vector in Worksheet 13.20 had already been calculated when we estimated the VCV VaR. The gamma matrix elements were estimated by:

a. For the ith risk factor
    o $\gamma_{ii} = \delta_i^+ - \delta_j^-$ (as in Chapter 12).

---

[18] See, for example, J. Cardenas *et al.*, "VaR: One step beyond", *Risk*, **10**(10), 1997, pp. 72–5.

b.   For a pair of different risk factors i and j
   ○   assume that $\Delta x_i = \Delta x_j = 1$ bp and that all other Δxs are zero;
   ○   therefore, $\Delta\text{Value} \approx \delta_i + \delta_j + \frac{1}{2}\cdot(\gamma_{ij} + \gamma_{ji}) = \delta_i + \delta_j + \gamma_{ij}$ as $\gamma = \gamma_{ji}$;
   ○   i.e. $\gamma_{ij} = \Delta\text{Value} - (\delta_i + \delta_j)$.

The full delta–gamma data are shown in Worksheet 13.21. In practice, many risk management systems could not calculate a complete gamma matrix with all the cross-pairs, but only a full gamma matrix which consists of the leading diagonal with no crosses. There may even be systems that can only calculate gamma with respect to the underlying alone (as commonly defined in option textbooks). The results below were also calculated for these situations.

   Worksheet 13.21 uses historic simulation data, and calculates the absolute change in basis points by $10{,}000 * r_{\text{current}} * [\exp\{\%r_{\text{change}} * \sqrt{T}\} - 1]$ as shown in Box 3. Four sets of calculations are done and shown in Box 4:

2.   Using delta plus the complete gamma matrix as above.
3.   Using delta plus the "full" gamma's matrix.
4.   Using delta plus the FX gamma only.

The results are as follows (see Worksheet 13.21 for the resulting histograms):

	10-day 99% VaR
Delta approximation	959,388
Delta–gamma approximation	−1,243,388
Delta–full gamma approximation	−1,243,378
Delta–FX gamma approximation	−1,242,914

As expected, the delta approximation closely replicates the delta method whilst the three gamma methods produce VaRs similar to the full simulation. Indeed there is little different between the three, which suggests that in many situations a full gamma approach is likely to be adequate. Obviously, individual options do not have to be re-valued, and therefore this simulation is very much quicker than a full simulation, especially when applied to a much larger portfolio:

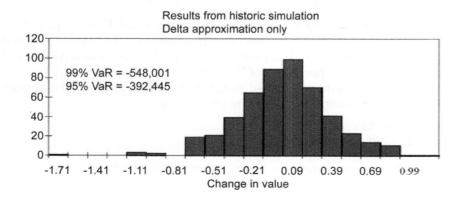

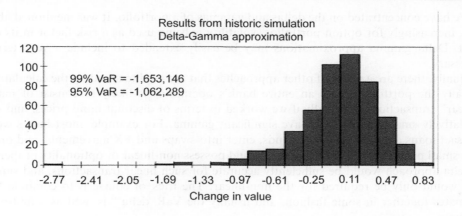

Results from historic simulation
Delta-Gamma approximation

99% VaR = -1,653,146
95% VaR = -1,062,289

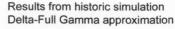

Results from historic simulation
Delta-Full Gamma approximation

99% VaR = -1,636,911
95% VaR = -1,031,911

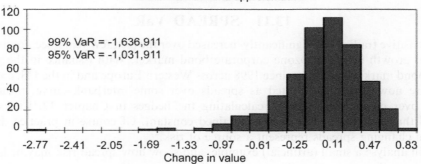

Results from historic simulation
Delta-FX Gamma approximation

99% VaR = -1,636,270
95% VaR = -1,031,270

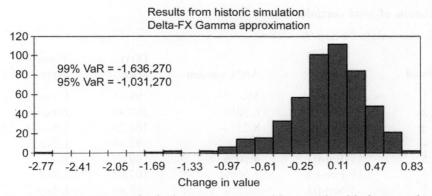

In summary delta–gamma methods do appear to provide considerably increased accuracy over delta methods, and yet are much faster than full simulations. However, they will only work when the third-order effects are relatively small. One approach that has been applied to overcome these effects is to use "gridpoint" approximations, i.e. instead of using a single delta and gamma for all changes, to use different deltas and gammas at different gridpoints.[19] However, for portfolios that contain significant third-order effects due to high gearing or discontinuous payouts, there is little substitute for full simulation.

[19] See, for example, M. Pritsker, "Evaluating VaR methodologies", Chapter 27 in *Understanding and Applying VaR*, published by Risk, 1997.

We have concentrated on the deltas and gammas of a portfolio. It was mentioned above that, increasingly for option portfolios, volatility is being used as a risk factor in its own right. Delta–gamma approximations may be easily extended to include a vega term if necessary.

Finally, there are a range of other approaches that are used to speed up the calculations. Usually the portfolio across an entire bank's operations is likely to consist of mainly "linear" transactions, especially if we worked in terms of discount bond prices, and only a relatively small residual will have significant gamma. For example, most banks would transact loans and deposits, buy bonds, enter into swaps and FX agreements, and only a very small proportion of their business would possess non-linear or optionality properties. A delta approach would be sufficiently accurate for such linear transactions, and simulation would only be required for the non-linear. The trick of course is to combine VaR estimates together in some fashion, and usually the VaR–delta[20] is used as a first-order estimate.

13.11   SPREAD VaR

Credit-sensitive trading has significantly increased over the past few years: see, for example, the rapid growth in the eurozone corporate bond market. With issuance in the governmental bond markets declining since 1998 across Western Europe and in the US, corporate bonds are now frequently quoted as spreads over some interbank curve, rather than spreads over governments. When calculating the hedges in Chapter 12, we explicitly assumed that the bond–swap spread remained constant. Of course in practice this isn't true, and changing spreads represent a source of risk.[21]

We will analyse a small (artificial) example, and show how spread risk may be isolated.

Details of bond portfolio

Today's date 24-Sep-99

Bond	Maturity	ANN coupon	Dirty price	Valuation curve
1	29-Mar-04	5%	98.61	Libor 1
2	12-Jun-02	6.50%	100.49	Libor 2
3	10-Dec-01	8.25%	104.23	Libor 3
4	13-Sep-02	7%	93.48	Libor 3
5	17-Jun-03	4.50%	99.68	Bond
6	19-Feb-01	5.50%	102.98	Libor 1
7	5-Sep-03	6.75%	98.49	Libor 2
8	8-Jul-02	4.75%	100.60	Bond
9	25-May-04	9.50%	99.38	Libor 3
10	10-Nov-03	7%	104.90	Libor 2

---

[20] See M. Garman, "Improving on VaR", *Risk*, **9**(5), 1996, pp. 61–3.
[21] Following the financial crisis in 2007 and onwards, it became increasingly evident that the regulatory treatment of credit spread risk was inadequate. In July 2009, the Basel Committee issued a new paper *Guidelines for Computing Capital for Incremental Risk in the Trading Book*. This requires banks to estimate, amongst other risks, the 1-year 99.9% credit spread risk.

There are 10 bonds in the portfolio, valued off four different curves. The bond curve is the base curve, and the Libor curves are increasing spreads over it. The current levels of each curve are known, together with volatility and correlation histories:

Current curves				
	Bond	**Libor 1**	**Libor 2**	**Libor 3**
1 yr	4.688%	5.438%	6.438%	8.438%
3 yr	4.731%	5.581%	6.781%	9.181%
5 yr	4.855%	5.805%	7.205%	10.205%

The total 1-day, 95% VaR of the portfolio may be easily calculated in the usual way as follows:

- calculate the sensitivities of each bond with respect to its valuation curve;
- sum the sensitivities for each curve to get the total sensitivity with respect to each curve;
- apply the Delta VaR approach in the usual way, using the data in Box 1 of Worksheet 13.25, which gives a total VaR = \$59.168m.

But where did this VaR come from? Define V_i as the vector of individual VaRs from the ith curve, and C_{ii} as the corresponding 3×3 correlation sub-matrix. We can calculate the VaR due to each one of the individual curves moving; for example, the VaR due to the Libor 3 curve moving is $\{V_3 . C_{33} . V_3\}^{1/2} = \$32.486m$. We can also calculate the contribution due to the interaction between the curves by using $\{2 * V_i . C_{ij} . V_j\}$: note that this number is not necessarily non-negative as C_{ij} is not a proper positive semi-definite correlation matrix, and therefore a square root cannot be taken. The results are shown in Box 2. The total contribution of the four curves may be calculated in a variety of ways; in the box, all the interaction VaR was allocated to the curve with the lower credit.

The problem with this type of analysis is that we can say nothing about the source of the movement: was it due to the bond curve or to one of the spreads? The difficulty is that the Libor curve implicitly includes the bond and spread curves. In order to be able to break the VaR down into its fundamental components, we need to transform the world from {Bond − Libor} into {Bond − Spread} where the spreads are additive over the bond curve. In this world the effects may be easily separated. Unlike before, the bond valued off the Libor 3 curve will now have sensitivities to the bond curve as well as the three spread curves.

The spread properties must first be calculated:

- a current spread S is simply the difference between two curves X and Y;
- spread volatilities can be calculated using $\mathrm{var}(S) = \mathrm{var}(X) - 2 * \mathrm{cov}(X, Y) + \mathrm{var}(Y)$;
- the correlations can be calculated from $\mathrm{cov}(X, S) = \mathrm{cov}(X, X) - \mathrm{cov}(X, Y)$, etc.

Worksheet 13.22 shows the precise details, and the resulting {Bond − Spread} data (see Boxes 1 and 2).

First, the total VaR can be re-calculated (see Box 3 of Worksheet 13.25). This is of course exactly the same as before: no risk has been generated or removed. However, individual

VaRs are quite different; for example, the bond curve VaR is now much higher because, when that curve moves, it affects all the bonds. If we look at the components as shown in Box 4, we see that some of the interaction effects are negative suggesting that there is a negative correlation between some of the components, unlike in the {Bond − Libor} world. The percentage contributions are quite different as well, suggesting much greater potential losses if the bond curve moves adversely (see Boxes 3 and 4 of Worksheet 13.25).

But the major advantage to this approach is in a better understanding of the true risks being run. For example, suppose we have a portfolio which is long Libor 3 bonds and short government bonds. We could manipulate the amount of the government bonds so that the net VaR off the bond curve is very low. However, this hedge will have no effect if any of the spreads shifted, so our VaR report should still show relatively high VaR for the spread risk.

13.12   EQUITY VaR

Finally, a brief look at calculating VaR when there are equities (or indeed commodities) in the portfolio. Equities may be handled quite simply by treating each one as a separate risk factor. For example, consider the following simple USD portfolio:

	Holding	Current price	Current value (USD)
Stock 1	100,000	10	1,000,000
Stock 2	500,000	4	2,000,000
Index	1,000,000	5	5,000,000
Equity forward			−953,193
Total (USD)			7,046,807
Total (EUR)			4,751,083
3 mo. USD Libor		3.145%	
USD–EUR spot rate		1.4832	

It consists of two stocks, a holding of the index and an equity forward contract to pay $12 per share on 500,000 shares of stock 1 in 3 months' time. Assuming (quite simplistically) zero growth in the share price, the value of the forward is $500{,}000 * [10 - 12 * \mathrm{DF}_3]$. We wish to calculate the 1-day 95% VaR in euros. We have therefore five risk factors: the two stock prices, the index price, 3 mo. Libor and the spot rate. Given appropriate volatilities and correlations, it is straightforward to calculate VaR = €305,849 (see Worksheet 13.27).

However, using individual stocks may increase the data requirements significantly. Consider, for example, a single portfolio replicating the S&P 500: the number of cross-correlations is in excess of 100,000! For a bank in which equity constitutes a significant proportion of activity, the accuracy provided by modelling individual stocks may well warrant the time and cost of collecting and cleansing the data. But for many organisations, the effort is simply not worthwhile.

Beta analysis of the equity market is very common, where beta is defined in:

$$r_s = \alpha_s + \beta_s . r_I + \varepsilon_s$$

where r_s and r_I are the return on a share s and on the index I, respectively;
 α_s is excess return on share (in theory, this should be zero);
 β_s is the coefficient linking share performance to the index; and
 ε_s is an error term, assumed to be uncorrelated with either the market or the other stocks.

We can therefore write[22]:

$$\text{var}(r_s) = \beta_s^2 * \text{var}(r_I) + \text{var}(\varepsilon_s) \rightarrow \sigma_s^2 = \beta_s^2 \sigma_I^2 + \sigma_{\varepsilon s}^2$$

If we assume that the idiosyncratic risk $\sigma_{\varepsilon s}^2$ represents a proportion x_s of the total risk, so that $\sigma_{\varepsilon s}^2 = x_s * \sigma_s^2$, it's easy to show that β_s should be approximately equal to $(\sigma_s / \sigma_I) * \sqrt{(1 - x_s)}$. Building on this, we would expect the correlations $\rho_{s,I} = \sqrt{(1 - x_s)}$ and $\rho_{1,2} = \sqrt{(1 - x_1)} * \sqrt{(1 - x_2)}$. We can therefore replace the individual stocks in the above example by the index; that is:

$$\text{VaR(equity)} = \{\delta_I * I + \delta_1 * S_1 * \beta_1 + \delta_2 * S_2 * \beta_2\} * \sigma_I * 1.645$$

where δ_I is sensitivity with respect to the index, etc. Continuing the example, we have now reduced the portfolio down to effectively three factors (see Worksheet 13.28).

Factors	Beta	VaR individual stocks	VaR using beta analysis
Stock 1	51.1%	84,166	
Stock 2	95.6%	56,111	
Stock index		122,743	244,969
3 mo. Libor		489	489
FX		−122,736	−122,736
Total VaR		305,849	284,780

Depending upon a single factor to represent each stock is of course a gross approximation, but it is a trade-off between accuracy and data availability. It is feasible to extend the above analysis into using more factors[23] to represent the behaviour of the individual stocks, but such methods are not so widely accepted.

13.13 SHOCK TESTING OF VaR

VaR, and indeed traditional risk measurement, measures risk under "normal" market conditions. All the methods described ultimately use historic information, whether it is

---

[22] This may be easily generalised for a portfolio: if $\mathbf{r}_P = \mathbf{w}' \cdot \mathbf{r}$ then

$$\text{var}(\mathbf{r}_P) = \mathbf{w}' \cdot C_v \cdot \mathbf{w} = (\mathbf{w}' \cdot \beta \cdot \beta' \cdot \mathbf{w}) * \text{var}(\mathbf{r}_I) + \mathbf{w}' \cdot D_\varepsilon \cdot \mathbf{w}$$

where D_ε is a diagonal matrix of $\text{var}(\varepsilon_s)$.
[23] See, for example, R. Roll *et al.*, "The Arbitrage Pricing Theory approach to strategic portfolio planning", *Financial Analysts J.*, May/June 1984, pp. 14–26, or M.A. Berry *et al.*, "Sorting out risks using known APT factors", *Financial Analysts J.*, March/April 1988, pp. 29-42.

directly through simulation or indirectly through the calculation of volatilities and correlations, and therefore are tacitly suggesting that the future will resemble the past. If the past period had low market volatility, then obviously the VaR estimates of the future would reflect that. There is a definite user and regulatory requirement for additional "stress" testing, i.e. re-valuation under extreme movements of market factors. The requirement for this has become more evident rather than less over the past few years.[24]

In practice, a distinction needs to be made between a stress test and a shock test. Stress testing usually involves the construction of severe but plausible scenarios that would affect the entire organisation. Within a scenario, not only may markets behave abnormally, but credit and liquidity risks are likely to increase significantly, prudent valuations may be difficult to achieve, model assumptions may break down, hedging strategies may fail and so on. These scenarios are often based upon real historic events such as the Asian crisis of 1997, the Russian crisis of 1998, and of course the worldwide recession of 2007–9.

A shock test is somewhat narrower in its scope, and usually confined to significant movements in the financial markets, without any subsequent other effects. They are widely applied by market risk managers, often on a daily basis, to explore the acceptability of these large movements and to investigate the effectiveness of hedging strategies. For example, in Section 12.10 the robustness of a hedge was tested by using 121 IR/volatility shock scenarios.

Unfortunately, in many banks, the term "stress testing" is applied to shock tests, leading to general confusion. A discussion of proper stress testing, and how it is applied, is to a large extent outside the scope of this book, although Section 13.14 will briefly discuss it. The current section will briefly describe some of the issues involved in shock testing, and how they may be overcome.

A classic approach to shock testing is to change the current level of market factors. For example, shifting each factor by some (positive or negative) multiple of its volatility, i.e. $f^{new} = f^{old} * \exp\{+m.\sigma\} \approx f^{old} * (1 + m.\sigma)$ where σ is the time horizon-adjusted volatility. An alternative is to make an absolute shift in the factor level, but this may result in negative factors. The selected portfolio could then be re-valued using the shifted factors, and the change in value reported.

The above, whilst sounding simple, presents difficulties in the context of imperfect risk management, namely in the presence of an explicit (or even implicit) correlation matrix. The pattern of shifts must be consistent with the structure of the correlations. Various approaches have been tried in practice. For example, one approach is to sub-divide the market risk factors into two sets. The first small set consists of "important" mainly independent factors which may be shifted as above. The second, much larger, set consists of factors that will change as a result of correlated relationships. For example, two factors in Set 1 could be the 5 yr swap rates in two different currencies on the basis that their correlation is likely to be fairly low; then all the other swap rates would be put into Set 2 as they are likely to be highly correlated with one of these two 5 yr rates. Their shifts would then be driven by the shifts in the 5 yr rates.

For example, let F_1 and F_2 be the two sets. Assume that the covariance matrix C can be

---

[24] The Basel Committee published a number of relevant consultative papers in January 2009 emphasising this requirement; for example, *Principles for Sound Stress Testing Practices and Supervision*, January 2009 (see also footnote 21).

partitioned into sub-matrices:

$$\{\mathbf{C}_{11} \text{ corresponding to } F_1, n \times n$$
$$\mathbf{C}_{22} \text{ corresponding to } F_2, m \times m$$
$$\mathbf{C}_{12} = \mathbf{C}_{21} \text{ the cross-matrices, } n \times m \text{ and } m \times n\}$$

So we could:

- generate the set of percentage changes R_1 for set F_1;
- calculate the changes for F_2 by $R_2 = \mathbf{C}_{21} . \mathbf{C}_{11}^{-1} . R_1$.

If we are prepared to make some distributional assumptions, then these could be taken further. Let us assume that percentage changes in the risk factors are all drawn from a multivariate Gaussian (or a Gaussian copula). Then, random scenarios would be the following:

- generate the set of scenarios R_1 for set F_1;
- calculate the new mean vector of Set 2, $\boldsymbol{\mu}_{2,\text{new}} = \boldsymbol{\mu}_{2,\text{old}} + \mathbf{C}_{21} . \mathbf{C}_{11}^{-1} . (\mathbf{R}_1 - \boldsymbol{\mu}_1)$;
- calculate the new conditional correlation sub-matrix $\mathbf{C}_{22,\text{new}} = \mathbf{C}_{22} - \mathbf{C}_{21} . \mathbf{C}_{11}^{-1} . \mathbf{C}_{12}$;
- randomly sample the set of scenarios R_2.

Changing the levels of the factors is the main form of shock testing, primarily because these are events that can happen very rapidly. But it is also useful to shock the volatilities and correlations in a consistent fashion. As they are time-based averages, they react more slowly than levels, but can have significant effects. Shifting volatility is also equivalent to changing the time horizon, which is itself a surrogate for liquidity.

It is probably sensible to use the same sub-division as above. Shift the volatilities in Set 1, and then interpolate/extrapolate in some fashion to estimate the shift in the volatilities in Set 2. Shifting the factors or the volatilities by large amounts is likely to increase risk measures but probably gain few other insights. The impact of shocking the correlation matrix on the other hand is far less intuitive, and may reveal a range of unexpected events. Unfortunately this form of shock testing is also the most complicated because we have to ensure that the resulting, shocked matrix is still a well-specified correlation matrix, i.e. it must satisfy certain properties including remaining positive semi-definite under all circumstances.

For example, suppose that we partition the correlation matrix Ω as $\{\Omega_{aa}, \Omega_{ab}, \Omega_{ba}, \Omega_{bb}\}$ where the sub-matrix Ω_{aa} is to be shocked:

- Let Ω_{aa}^s be the new shocked matrix; for the moment, assume that it is itself well-specified.
- It is perfectly feasible however to find that $\Omega^s = \{\Omega_{aa}^s, \Omega_{ab}, \Omega_{ba}, \Omega_{bb}\}$ is not well-specified.
- Thus either Ω_{aa}^s or the cross-matrices $\Omega_{ab} = \Omega_{ba}$ will have to be adjusted until Ω^s is well-specified.
- Kupiec[25] has suggested a simple (albeit potentially computer-intensive) algorithm when Ω^s is not well-specified

---

[25] P.H. Kupiec, "Stress testing in a VaR framework", *J. of Derivatives*, **6**(1), 1998, pp. 7–24.

○ define $\Omega^{sc} = (1 - c) . \Omega^s + c . \Omega$ for $0 \leq c \leq 1$;
○ where Ω^{s0} is not well-specified, whilst Ω^{s1} is well-specified;
○ there is likely to exist a positive value of c so that Ω^{sc} is well-specified.

How should Ω_{aa} be shocked? Selecting the actual correlation shifts is less straightforward. Percentage shifts can only apply, and these must be bounded to ensure that the correlations lie between ± 1 is true at all times. It may be better to consider shift strategies such as shifting all correlations closer to zero or to ± 1, or even setting the correlations equal to the extremes. If Ω^s_{aa} is not a well-specified matrix, then one approach might be to find a sub-matrix of it that was well-specified, and use the above algorithm. An alternative would be to use, for example, the hypersphere decomposition algorithm designed by Rebonato and Jackel.[26]

13.14   STRESS TESTING OF VaR

One definition of a stress test is the determination of potential loss if a severe but plausible scenario occurred. This is not the only definition that is used, as we will discuss shortly. The performance of stress tests during 2007–9 came in for a lot of criticism, and the Basel Committee issued a number of documents in early 2009 proposing changes to the regulatory framework. One change in particular was the introduction of stressed VaR.

There are two forms of stress test widely used. Event stress testing, as described above, starts with a scenario, and then analyses the implication of the scenario. The scenario may be based upon a real historical event, such as the stock market crashes in 1987, 1989, 1997 or 2008, or upon a hypothetical event such as terrorists gaining control over a nuclear weapon. The other form is a portfolio approach (sometimes called reverse stress testing); this starts with a portfolio and then risk managers try to construct plausible scenarios that would have a major impact on the portfolio. Usually, event tests are firm-wide, whilst portfolio tests are specific to a business or sub-business line.

In 2009, the implementation of stress testing within financial firms was widely criticised[27] for the following reasons:

• testing was performed by the risk function, with little prior or subsequent involvement by the business lines or the senior management;
• testing was often applied to different parts of the institution, with little attempt to develop a firm-wide view, and to different risk types (such as market risk, funding liquidity risk or credit risk) in isolation without considering any interaction;
• testing was too often mechanical and routine, with little attention being paid to the results;
• the scenarios, whilst often historic, were frequently based upon relatively recent benign events, and not the major events in the further past;
• the stress tests were often not very flexible, incapable of responding rapidly to changes in the economic environment or financial markets.

---

[26] R. Rebonato & P. Jackel, *The Most General Methodology to Create a Valid Correlation Matrix for Risk Management and Option Pricing Purposes*, QUARC research paper, NatWest Bank, October 1999.
[27] See, for example, *Observations on Risk Management Practices during the Recent Market Turbulence*, published by Senior Supervisors Group, March 2008 (available from FSA or Federal Reserve websites).

As a result of these failings, the Basel Committee demanded far-reaching changes to the practice of stress testing:

- far greater involvement of senior management during both the construction of stress tests and in understanding the potential impact;
- far more use of firm-wide tests, covering all major risk factors simultaneously and not in isolation;
- use of more aggressive scenarios based upon 25 years of history.

One change that is very relevant to this book was the introduction of "stressed" VaR.[28] This required banks to identify at least one historic 12-month period of severe stress that would be relevant to the current portfolio; for example, the events of 2007/8 would certainly be deemed sufficiently severe for Western banks. Banks must then calculate the 10-day 99% VaR based upon the assumption that the events that occurred within that period would occur again upon the current portfolio. The new capital charge is effectively the sum of normal VaR and stressed VaR.

13.15   APPENDIX: EXTREME VALUE THEORY

Suppose there is a set of observations z_i, $i = 1, \ldots, n_t$, from a simulation such that $z_i \geq$ a defined threshold t.[29] Define $y_i = z_i - t \geq 0$.

13.15.1   Peaks over threshold: negative exponential

The negative exponential distribution has a density function:

$$g(y) = (1/\beta) \cdot \exp\{-y/\beta\} \quad \text{for } y \geq 0$$

This can be interpreted: $g(y)$ is the likelihood of y actually being observed as a single sample drawn from a negative exponential distribution with parameter β. The likelihood function is similarly defined as:

$$\text{LF}\{y_1, y_2, y_3, \ldots, y_n \mid \beta\} = g(y_1) \cdot g(y_2) \cdot g(y_3) \cdots g(y_n)$$

The process of maximum likelihood estimation is to find the value of β that maximises LF, i.e. the most likely distribution for the observed samples. The usual method is to find β such that:

$$\partial \text{LF}/\partial \beta = 0$$

Very often it is easier to work with ln(LF) as:

$$\partial \ln(\text{LF})/\partial \beta = [\partial \text{LF}/\partial \beta]/\text{LF}$$

and therefore any value of β that sets $\partial \text{LF}/\partial \beta$ to zero will also set $\partial \ln(\text{LF})/\partial \beta$. As:

$$\ln[g(y)] = -\ln(\beta) - (y/\beta)$$

---

[28] See revision to paragraph 718(xxvi)(i) on p. 18 in *Revisions to the Basel II Market Risk Framework*, published by Basel Committee on Banking Supervision, July 2009.
[29] Note that we are dealing with the positive, right-hand tail of observations.

the (logarithmic) likelihood function is:

$$\ln(\text{LF}) = -n_t \cdot \ln \beta - (1/\beta) \cdot \sum_i y_i$$

Differentiating with respect to β and setting to zero, we get the optimal value of $\beta = (1/n_t) \cdot \sum_i y_i$ We could now calculate a VaR off the negative exponential by using the cumulative probability distribution:

$$G(u) = \text{prob}\{0 \le y \le u\} = 1 - \exp\{-u/\beta\} \quad \text{for some } u \ge 0$$

i.e. $u_q = -\beta \cdot \ln(q)$ where q is the probability of exceeding $u_q = 1 - G(u_q)$. But we need to convert this result back into the z-world. We can re-write $\text{prob}\{0 \le y \le u\}$ as $\text{prob}\{t \le z \le u + t\}$ given that $z \ge t$, by simply substituting for y. If we represent the cumulative z-distribution as F, this probability may also be written as:

$$\{F(u+t) - F(t)\}/\text{prob}(z \ge t) = \{F(u+t) - F(t)\}/\{1 - F(t)\}$$

Therefore:

$$F(u+t) = F(t) + G(u) * \{1 - F(t)\}$$

$F(t)$ is simply the probability that an observation will not be in the tail. Our best estimate for this is $\{1 - n_t/N\}$ where N is the total number of observations in the simulation. Substituting, we get:

$$F(z_q) = 1 - (n_t/N) * \exp\{-(z_q - t)/\beta\}$$

or

$$z_q = t - \beta * \ln\{(N/n_t) \cdot (1 - F(z_q))\} = t - \beta * \ln\{(N/n_t) \cdot q\}$$

13.15.2 Peaks over threshold: Generalised Pareto[30]

The Generalised Pareto distribution has a cumulative density function as follows:

$$G(y) = 1 - [1 + \chi * y/\beta]^{-1/\chi}$$

where χ is a "tail" parameter. If $\chi = 0$ then the GP reduces to a negative exponential. If $\chi > 0$ the GP has a fatter tail than the negative exponential, if $\chi < 0$ then a thinner tail. So it simply allows a second parameter to fit the observations more accurately. The density function is:

$$g(y) = (1/\beta) * [1 + \chi * y/\beta]^{-(1+1/\chi)}$$

The (logarithmic) likelihood function is:

$$\text{LF} = -n_t \cdot \ln \beta - (1 + 1/\chi) \cdot \sum_i \ln(1 + \tau \cdot y_i)$$

where $\tau = \chi/\beta$. By setting the two differentials, $\partial \text{LF}/\partial \beta$ and $\partial \text{LF}/\partial \chi$, to zero, we get:

$$\beta = \left\{ \sum_i u_i \right\} \Big/ \left\{ n_t - \tau \cdot \sum_i u_i \right\} = f_1(\tau) \quad \text{where } u_i = y_i/(1 + \tau \cdot y_i) \qquad (13.1)$$

$$\chi = (1/n_t) \sum_i \ln(1 + \tau \cdot y_i) = f_2(\tau) \qquad (13.2)$$

which may be solved iteratively. However, the solution is not well-behaved, and a

---

[30] See *EVT for Risk Management*, working paper by A.J. McNeil, ETH Zentrum, May 1999.

pragmatic two-step alternative that works well in practice is to estimate β using the negative exponential formula, and then improve the tail fit by calculating χ by maximising LF.

Once χ and β have been estimated, the $q\%$ VaR estimate may be calculated from:

$$\text{VaR}_q = t + (\beta/\chi) * \{[(n_t/N) * (1 - q)]^{-\chi} - 1\}$$

using the same argument as above.

Other estimates may also be calculated. The mean excess function for estimating expected losses, given a particular level L has been exceeded, is given by ES_L defined as:

$$ES_L = L + E\{y - L \,|\, y > L\} = \{L + \beta - \chi \cdot t\}/\{1 - \chi\}$$

This formula applies when $\chi = 0$, i.e. for a negative exponential. Of particular interest is the expected loss when the VaR is exceeded; that is:

$$ES_q = \{\text{VaR}_q + \beta - \chi \cdot t\}/\{1 - \chi\}$$

13.15.3 Block maxima

This is based upon the statistics of extremes, also known as order statistics. Consider a distribution, say a normal one. Assume that you take k random samples from that distribution z_i, $i = 1, \ldots, k$, and assume that they have been placed in order so that $Z_1 = z_{[1]} \geq z_{[2]} \geq \cdots$. We then repeat the whole process, generating the largest sample Z_2 for the second set, and so on. We end up with a set of observations of maxima Z_j where j is the sample set. Order statistics is the study of these maxima, and in particular what can be said that is independent of the original underlying distribution.

It has been found that these maxima asymptotically follow a Generalised Extreme Value distribution[31]:

$$H(x) = \exp\{-[1 + \alpha \cdot x]^{-1/\alpha}\}$$

where $x = (Z - m)/s$ is a normalised variable, and α is a "shape" parameter. If:

$\alpha > 0$ the distribution is called a "Fréchet" where $1 + \alpha \cdot \min\{y_i\} > 0$

$\alpha < 0$ the distribution is called a "Weibull"

$\alpha = 0$ the distribution is called a "Gumbel" simplifying to $H(y) = \exp\{-e^{-y}\}$

and its density function is:

$$h(x) = \exp(-[1 + \alpha \cdot x]^{-1/\alpha}) * [1 + \alpha \cdot x]^{-(1+1/\alpha)} * (1/s)$$

Trying to estimate a likelihood function for all three parameters simultaneously is complicated by non-linearities, and a common approach is to adopt a semi-parametric method, i.e. estimate α somewhat crudely first, and then fit m and s by regression or maximum likelihood methods. For example, given the set of extreme losses Z_i, $i = 1, \ldots, n$, from the n blocks, re-order them so that $Z_{[j]} \geq Z_{[j+1]}$. A Hill estimator for α is given by $\{\text{average}[\ln Z_{[1]} \cdots \ln Z_{[p]}] - \ln Z_{[p]}\}$ for some threshold p.[32] There is little guidance for the setting of p, but we can use increasing values until α stabilises.

---

[31] See, for example, Chapter 14 in I. Stuart *et al.*, *Kendall's Advanced Theory of Statistics*, published by Griffin, Fifth Edition, 1987. For their application in risk management, see the articles by K. Dowd on EVT in *Financial Engineering News*, issues 11 to 13, 1999 plus references.
[32] This is probably the most popular approach—see B. Hill, "A simple general approach to inference about the tail of a distribution", *Annals of Statistics*, **35**, 1975, pp. 1163–73.

The fitted distribution can provide information about the extremes of a set of data. For example, suppose we estimate $\text{Prob}\{Z \geq L\}$ for some cut-off L. Now Z is the extreme value drawn from a set of samples, i.e. $\{Z \geq z_1, Z \geq z_2, \ldots, Z \geq z_k\}$ where z_i is the ith observation in the set. If we assume that the observations are independent, then $\text{Prob}\{z \geq L\} = \text{Prob}\{Z \geq L\}^k$.

Index

Printed and bound by CPI Group (UK) Ltd, Croydon, CR0 4YY

23/04/2025

14660971-0005